W9-AED-697

Uncertain Chances

UNCERTAIN CHANCES

Science, Skepticism, and Belief in Nineteenth-Century American Literature

Maurice S. Lee

OXFORD
UNIVERSITY PRESS

OXFORD
UNIVERSITY PRESS

Oxford University Press, Inc., publishes works that further
Oxford University's objective of excellence
in research, scholarship, and education.

Oxford New York
Auckland   Cape Town   Dar es Salaam   Hong Kong   Karachi
Kuala Lumpur   Madrid   Melbourne   Mexico City   Nairobi
New Delhi   Shanghai   Taipei   Toronto

With offices in
Argentina   Austria   Brazil   Chile   Czech Republic   France   Greece
Guatemala   Hungary   Italy   Japan   Poland   Portugal   Singapore
South Korea   Switzerland   Thailand   Turkey   Ukraine   Vietnam

Copyright © 2012 by Oxford University Press, Inc.

Published by Oxford University Press, Inc.
198 Madison Avenue, New York, New York 10016

www.oup.com

Oxford is a registered trademark of Oxford University Press

Library of Congress Cataloging-in-Publication Data
Lee, Maurice S.
Uncertain chances : science, skepticism, and belief in nineteenth-century American literature / Maurice S. Lee.
     p.   cm.
Includes bibliographical references and index.
ISBN 978-0-19-979757-8 (hardcover : alk. paper) 1. American literature—19th century—History and criticism.
2. Chance in literature. 3. Probability in literature. 4. Skepticism in literature. 5. Belief and doubt in literature.
6. Pragmatism in literature. 7. United States—Intellectual life—19th century. 8. Literature and science—United
States—History—19th century. 9. Christianity and literature—United States—History—19th century. I. Title.
PS217.C46L44   2011
810.9'384—dc22   2011002599

For Matteo, who loves to climb and jump,
For Nico, who drew dragons on the back of the manuscript,
and
For Marisa, who holds us together.

CONTENTS

ACKNOWLEDGMENTS

Chance is the subject of this book, and this book has been subject to many happy chances, not the least of which is the wealth of opportunities to work on and test out its claims. A shortened version of this book's chapter on Poe appeared in *American Literature*; many thanks to Priscilla Wald, Emily Dings, and the essay's anonymous readers for improving the piece. A portion of the Dickinson chapter was published in *Raritan* under the generous guidance of Jackson Lears and Stephanie Volmer, and a section of the Douglass chapter appears in *Frederick Douglass and Herman Melville: Essays in Relation*, edited by Robert S. Levine and Samuel Otter, both of who were immensely helpful with the essay itself and the progress of my thinking in general.

A fellowship from the National Endowment for the Humanities, together with support from the Boston University Humanities Foundation, first allowed me to take up this book in earnest, and a Charles A. Ryskamp fellowship from the American Council of Learned Societies gave me more precious time. I would not have enjoyed such opportunities without the support of Michael Colacurcio, Katherine O'Connor, Sam Otter, Eric Sundquist, Pauline Yu, and my wonderful colleagues in the English Department at Boston University, especially William Carroll, Susan Mizruchi, and James Winn. Two colloquia at Boston University provided interdisciplinary forums to share some of the ideas in this book: thanks to everyone at Tertulia for support and good cheer, and thanks to my convivial Humanities Foundation Research Fellows—Charles Griswold, Peter Hawkins, Walter Hopp, Jennifer Knust, Laura Korobkin, Jeffrey Mehlman, Thomas Peattie, and Rosanna Warren. Other readers who brought their expertise, wisdom, and constructive skepticism to various chapters include Jennifer Baker, Gregg Crane, John Ernest, Paul Huhr, Gene Jarrett, Cristanne Miller, Tom Otten, Scott Peeples, Jason Puskar, William Rossi, John Stauffer, Kevin Van Anglen, and Eric Wertheimer. Special thanks to Rob Chodat and Susan Mizruchi for extended critiques and conversations. At Oxford University Press, Brendan O'Neill, Marc Schneider, and Rick Stinson were excellent shepherds and advisers, and John Barnard helped extensively with the preparation of the manuscript. Though it comes later than I would have wished it, I especially want to acknowledge the influence of the late Barbara Packer, a wonderful teacher and scholar who, among other things, first taught me *Walden* and asked during my oral exam why Ishmael decides to go whaling.

Much love goes out to friends who care enough about me to care about my work, especially Danno, Rob, Vince and Jen, and Kelly and Eloise, who have been subjected to the ideas in this book for years. As always, much love to Grandma, Mom and Vince, and Andrew, Yuko, Jamie, and Mari, as well as to the extended Milanese family and their partners. Most of all, this book is for my wife and kids, my luckiest chances of all.

Uncertain Chances

Introduction

M aybe modernity began in Ellington, Connecticut on July 30, 1804. A minister working on the roof of the town's meetinghouse slipped, fell sixty-eight feet, and survived, in part because he crashed through a plank suspended in the framing and, lower down, landed on a workbench that further broke his fall. He had a nail driven into his skull and crippled a leg for life, and when reflecting on the incident in his memoirs, he praised the "special interposition of a kind Providence." A doubter with a taste for theodicy might wonder why God would allow such an accident in the first place, but for a Calvinist minister (named Diodate Brockway, no less) the invocation of heaven's design was a deeply felt and powerfully conventional response, even as such providential explanation came under increasing duress. Like the minister himself, the *Middlesex Gazette* discerned in the extraordinary fall from the meetinghouse a "preserving providence, superior to any human calculations," and yet an urge to analyze Brockway's salvation—or was it dumb luck?—remained: "Calculating upon the doctrine of chances, his out of any proposed number, appears to be the only favorable one. If we view the hand of Providence, it seems that he was to fall, but yet to be preserved."[1] Much depends upon the word *If.* Perhaps the unnamed author of the article knew of Abraham De Moivre's *Doctrine of Chances* (1717), a pioneering work of probability theory purchased by Thomas Jefferson and Benjamin Franklin and advertised in the early American press. Or maybe the author had heard of the doctrine of chances through its occasional treatment in the period's scientific literature, philosophical works, sermons, and newspaper articles. Whatever the case, the *Middlesex Gazette*'s wavering between providence and probability registers the beginnings of an uneven shift from faith in Christian teleology and confidence in rational certitude toward a more modern, more skeptical worldview in which chance, long dismissed as a nominal concept marking the limits of human knowledge, came to be regarded as an actual force subject to degrees of human control.

To read nineteenth-century American literature with an eye toward chance is to broach some unfamiliar questions that turn out to have broad interpretive use. What exactly does Poe mean in his detective fiction when he refers to the "Calculus of Probabilities"? If *Moby-Dick* (1851) is about free will versus fate, why does Ishmael identify three principal agents—"chance, free will, and necessity"?[2] Can Thoreau in his literary and naturalist work simultaneously abandon himself to chance and search for unchanging higher laws? How does Douglass turn his era's probabilistic methods against a burgeoning statistical racism? Can Dickinson in her poetry describe how chance feels when it escapes consciousness, theology, and language? And what might chance mean for other American authors from Edwards, Franklin, and Jefferson, to Hawthorne, Emerson, and James McCune Smith, to Elizabeth Stuart Phelps and Du Bois? Such questions bear on a longstanding interest of literary criticism: How do writers, historically understood, approach problems of skepticism and faith? For scholars who study nineteenth-century America, responses typically involve the decline or displacement of religious authority, the rise of scientific positivism, the advent of post-metaphysical philosophy, and the disenchanting trauma of the Civil War. As a concept that comes to mediate uncertainty and belief, chance relates to all of these major developments, though it also deserves attention in its own right as a vitally destabilizing aspect of modernity's unfinished emergence.

The premise of this book is that nineteenth-century American literature took part in a broad intellectual and cultural shift in which chance became increasingly treated as a challenge to be managed but never mastered. In their dealings with chance, literary figures engage a surprising array of debates—in theology, philosophy, logic, and mathematics, in the natural and social sciences, and in everyday practices such as weather forecasting, insurance, investment, and gaming. Poe, Melville, Douglass, Thoreau, Dickinson, and others join in their era's general rethinking of chance, though their contributions to the discussion are distinctive, not only because they imaginatively pursue moral, political, and psychological lines of inquiry not usually associated with the subject but also because as writers they are uniquely attuned to the aesthetic implications of probability and chance.

By reading their work in relation to the rise of chance and the spread of the probabilistic revolution, this book shows how chance is thematically, formally, and meta-critically significant for American writers during a period when changing attitudes toward chance reconfigure the relationships between science, religion, and literature (especially romanticism). Attention to chance reshapes literary-critical practices, now and in the nineteenth century, for chance entails specific approaches to uncertainty quite different from the radical skepticism usually associated with the romantics and their post-structural heirs, who can dwell on epistemological quandaries of subjectivity and semiotics to a point where indeterminacy threatens to corrode sufficient claims to truth and action. Emphasizing chance also departs from Wittgensteinian engagements with skepticism most forcefully advanced in nineteenth-century American literary studies by the provocations of Stanley Cavell. The following chapters share with Cavell, Charles Altieri, and others a desire to move beyond Cartesian problematics through literature, but they do so with more commitment to classical skepticism, empiricism, and the philosophy of science than to the shared inheritances of language coming after Kant. Which is to say that the epistemological limits marked by probabilism and chance do not necessarily impel textual interpretation toward the linguistic turns of deconstruction or ordinary language philosophy. As Emerson suggests in "Montaigne, or the Skeptic" (1850) when associating skepticism with causal uncertainty, nineteenth-century authors encountering chance move with varying degrees of confidence, anxiety, and wonder from representation toward agency, from ideation toward experience, and from Cartesian and linguistic conundrums toward more practical—and pragmatist—positions. They may even suggest ways of living and writing under conditions of doubt.

First, some historical contextualization. Most philosophers, mathematicians, physicists, neuroscientists, and biologists treat chance and probability ahistorically, though how humans understand the possibilities of chance is, of course, temporally and culturally shaped. The rise of chance in modern Western thought is less a march than a drift, less an orderly progression of great ideas and events and more a set of loosely related developments based on the idea that the power of chance can be to some extent governed, and even harnessed. As intellectual historians over the last few decades have shown, chance became increasingly visible across the nineteenth century, though critical treatments of the subject began much earlier. Classical philosophers and early modern skeptics saw chance as something more than a privative concept, while Fermat, Huygens, and Pascal in the seventeenth century lay the mathematical groundwork for the probability theorems of the Bernoullis, De Moivre, and Thomas Bayes. As knowledge became defined by its predictive capacity more than its apodictic certainty—and as Baconian empiricism and the "modern fact" led to quantitative conceptualizations of reality—the influence of probabilistic thinking in the seventeenth and eighteenth centuries spread beyond mathematics to natural history, theology, jurisprudence, and emerging social sciences such as political economy and statistical sociology. Prior to 1800, the probabilistic revolution took place primarily in European intellectual circles and specific industries such as annuities and shipping, though rapidly evolving attitudes toward chance soon became transatlantic phenomena.[3]

A robust body of scholarship in the history of science has traced what Ian Hacking has called the "the taming of chance" through a wide range of disciplines in the nineteenth century. Laplace's 1814 summa of probability theory, *Philosophical Essay on Probabilities*, inspired mathematicians such as Siméon Denis Poisson, Charles Babbage, Augustus De Morgan, George Boole, and John Venn. These thinkers tended to work on abstract problems involving dice, cards, coins, and bags full of marbles, though of more importance to this book, they showed how rational laws can be inferred from masses of data and seemingly random variations. The basic idea, sometimes termed "frequentism," is startlingly obvious today: chancy (or more specifically, stochastic) events regress to a mean when considered in large numbers, even if as a problematic feature of induction margins of error and statistical outliers remain. Probability thus constitutes a limitation of knowledge in general and of inferential reasoning in particular, for if quantitative thinking helps predict outcomes en masse, chance always retains some unsettling sway (a point the twenty-first century has painfully if temporarily relearned with the failures of its risk-management methods).[4]

Progress in nineteenth-century probability theory instigated and ran parallel with advances in a number of other fields—political economy (from Malthus on), quantitative sociology (especially in the work of Adolphe Quetelet), logic (John Herschel and John Stuart Mill), and game theory (Antoine-Augustin Cournot). In the mid-century, James Maxwell along with Ludwig Boltzmann qualified Newtonian mechanics by theorizing the stochastic motion of gas molecules, while Darwin cast doubt on the argument from design by taking the accidents of variation and the chances of natural selection as main mechanisms of the natural world. Later in the century, Francis Galton applied statistical methods to a variety of subjects, most infamously heredity and race; and when Charles Peirce marveled in 1893 that the middle decades of the nineteenth century constituted the most productive fifty years in the history of science, he singled out "[t]he idea that chance begets order" as the era's fundamental insight. With startling speed, the new sciences of chance pushed a paradigm shift that remains in force today.[5]

For Peirce and others, the rise of probabilism and chance extended beyond the natural and social sciences. Herbert Spencer applied the probabilistic logic of statistics and natural selection to ethics, religion, and political philosophy (as did Mill). Henry Buckle, renowned in the nineteenth century, pursued history as a probabilistic enterprise, as did the less assured Henry Adams. The pragmatists shook metaphysical foundations by admitting chance into their philosophy, while some literary writers had already entertained the radical possibilities of chance, which appeared to take on explanatory force in every aspect of life, even religion. By the middle of the nineteenth century, an 1814 statement from Laplace did not seem so outlandish. "[T]he most important questions of life," he wrote, "are indeed for the most part only problems of probability," a claim Peirce sharpened in 1878: "All human affairs rest upon probabilities."[6] As thoroughly as Diodate Brockway's providence, chance can become a totalizing concept, and yet for all their emphatic language and pan-disciplinary ambitions, nineteenth-century theorists of chance practiced relatively modest epistemologies marked by contingency, approximation, fallibilism, pluralism, open-endedness, and the suspension of judgment. What makes the reach of probabilistic explanation so expansive is the looseness of its grasp.

As chance's role grew in the realm of ideas, so too did its cultural work, and not simply because "high" scientific concepts trickled down into popular forums. With the market revolution rolling on in America, and as Jackson Lears has most comprehensively shown, maturing cultural practices increasingly attempted to control and profit from the power of chance. Developments included the expansion of stock markets, the growth of the insurance industry, the spread of numerical literacy and statistical thinking, and the application of probability theory to travel, politics, health, consumerism, and other aspects of daily experience.[7] From Harriet Martineau to Frances Trollope to Dickens, visitors to the United States commented on the "calculating character" of its people, while Tocqueville wrote of Americans in 1840, "Those who live in the midst of democratic fluctuations have always before their eyes the image of chance." An 1847 article in New York's *Merchants' Magazine and Commercial Review* sounded a similar nationalistic note: "We have in the United States . . . become familiar with the doctrine of probabilities. . . . The calculations of the merchant—the harvest of the planter—the fate of a ship at sea—the very existence of the world for another day, are all but probabilities." Around the same time, London's *Morning Chronicle* emphasized the transatlantic scope of the probabilistic revolution: "It is one of the most remarkable developments of modern civilization that the practical importance of the doctrine of chances has obtained universal recognition."[8]

Such exaggerated claims are partly borne out by examples throughout the century, which suggest how probabilistic thinking spread through myriad channels of experience and print culture. Commentators used probability theory to estimate the likelihood of economic panics, train fatalities, extraterrestrial life, and the chances of John Adams and

Thomas Jefferson both dying on July 4, 1826. (Based on one writer's actuary tables, the odds were 1 to 1,721,473,236, significantly less likely than an 1883 assessment following the assassination of James Garfield that both the president and the vice president of the United States would die in the same month every 840 years).[9] Other articles referred to the doctrine of chances when offering advice on lotteries, employment, marriage, child rearing, and crime prevention. So strikingly did the probabilistic revolution play out across the nineteenth century that it is tempting to tell a story of some sweep: as Americans and their transatlantic peers managed chance in the course of ordinary life, they encountered a modernity characterized not only by the rising authority of science and market ideology but also by a paradoxical sense of unprecedented control and unavoidable uncertainty, of empowering knowledge and inescapable risk.

And yet the spread of modern approaches to chance is hardly the whole story, for the probabilistic revolution in the United States, as in Europe, did not proceed unchallenged. Observers condemned gambling and financial speculation as chance upset notions of economic justice grounded in the labor theory of value. Christian writers, especially those drawing on Puritan origins, often called the doctrine of chances "absurd," equated strong beliefs in "blind chance" with atheism and insanity, and went so far as to condemn insurance as an impious attempt to constrain God's will. Following Descartes, Locke, and Kant, almost every metaphysician of the nineteenth century denied the actuality of chance, as did moral philosophers and natural scientists working within the dominant paradigm of the argument from design. Though probability theorists insisted that their methods were compatible with the rational government of God, their assurances failed to mollify many critics, if only because the management of chance could not help but acknowledge chance's wild power to shape individual outcomes. Indeed, objections to chance rose as probabilistic methods were becoming naturalized in many disciplines and social practices, and Peirce was among the first modern thinkers to name chance as a fundamental element of nature (a speculation later corroborated by twentieth-century quantum physics). It is thus possible to find in the rise of chance a cognate version of more familiar falls into modernity: nineteenth-century students of chance, despite their culture's and their own conservative reservations, unleashed a disruptive force of skepticism that no rearguard action could contain.

The triumph of chance over teleology is a compelling (and teleological) narrative, though for critics of nineteenth-century literature coming belatedly to direct engagements with chance, the impressive work of cultural and intellectual historians should serve more as a guide than as a rule. As a figure of uncertainty, chance by definition is devilishly hard to define, let alone fix within the linear plots preferred by most histories of the subject. Forms of chance are widely accepted today—in quantum physics and evolutionary biology, in risk management and informatics, in postmodernism's commitment to aleatory disorder and philosophy's abandonment of metaphysical quests for certainty. Yet for many Americans in the nineteenth century, as well as for plenty of people today, chance remains a nominal concept and its taming a scientific fiction. Everything happens for a reason, one hears, whether that reason is providence or natural law. We only say "chance" when we lack sufficient causal knowledge—when the brain is not wider than the sky, or when we seek to evade the more demanding claims of personal responsibility or God.

Between the true belief and fierce denial of chance is a slippery middle ground that became increasingly contested as the nineteenth century struggled to accommodate new views of chance. For the natural theologian William Paley, chance might cause simple things such as a wart or a pimple but only the omnipotent, omniscient Ruler of a chance-less universe might craft something as complex as the human eye (an argument still maintained today by defenders of intelligent design). For statistical thinkers, chance might govern individual events such as the flipping of a coin, but in the long run proba-bilities abide by set averages that in the aggregate function as immutable laws. As sug-gested by the *Middlesex Gazette*'s account of Diodate Brockway's fall, one can treat both providence and chance as living options, as did Pascal in his notorious wager, or as Mar-cus Schouler more bitterly suggests in *McTeague* (1899) when he mutters, "God *damn* the luck!"[10] Even nineteenth-century probability experts vacillated between competing models of chance: objective views (actual probabilities in nature) versus subjective ones (expectations under conditions of partial knowledge); descriptions of past events versus predictions of future ones; degrees of belief regarding single outcomes versus the mass logic of frequentism (an approach that eventually came to dominate the field but emerged unevenly over the century). Physicists today still disagree as to the scope of chance's purview, while philosophers argue over the relevance of chance in questions of etiology and moral luck. Controversial and broadly applicable, intensely theorized and yet conceptually elusive, chance—like fate and free will—can be a hypothesis too deeply felt for rational adjudication. It even seems beyond apprehension and expression, as sug-gested by references to "blind" and "dumb" luck.[11]

Further complicating matters, chance shares family resemblances with a host of mythic, vernacular, and technical terms: *chaos, fortune, accident, coincidence, contingency, luck, risk, randomness,* both *fate* and *free will,* all of which have been historically imbued with diverse connotations. The ancient goddess Fortuna—sometimes blind or blind-folded, sometimes an angel or a prostitute, sometimes winged or Janus-faced—later takes the shape of Lady Credit, Lady Luck, and (as Susan Mizruchi has recently noted) a vaguely foreign, potential terrorist in a Travelers Insurance Company commercial. In medieval times, vertical wheels of fortune implied equal chances for rising and falling, though the odds on the American game show are much happier and, as suggested by the wheel's horizontal position, have more to do with earthly stakes than the status of one's soul. Dice and cards, symbols of sin in the nineteenth century, are now brightly displayed on the packaging of children's games, while financiers, once seen as masters of the uni-verse, suddenly become deer in the headlights of chance before reverting to the populist stereotype of the parasitic market manipulator, a series of transformations dramatized by Howells, Norris, Dreiser, and Conrad.[12]

One might elaborate a spectrum of attitudes toward chance by parsing various theo-retical positions, though a trip to Las Vegas or a classroom discussion of why bad things happen to good people more viscerally shows how diverse and vexed our lived relations to the possibilities of chance can be. Probabilistic thinking is probably natural—whether one consciously practices it or not, whether the explanation is natural selection, dopa-mine, or neuroplasticity. Adults process language and visual data probabilistically, and infants seem to be intuitive statistical thinkers, while even monkeys are good at playing the odds when sweet, sweet juice is at stake.[13] The management of chance can also seem like second nature in what Ulrich Beck has called a modern "risk society" in which some citizens, directed by institutional structures, have the ironic good fortune of feeling safe enough to worry about their long-term security.[14] Yet as we check the weather report, glance at the latest poll, weigh the cost benefits of bacon versus bran, and estimate what percentage of our students did their reading given that it's Friday and Henry James, we should not too easily take for granted that we have a modern relationship with chance, nor should we too comfortably refer to "we" when generalizing about attitudes toward it. As the historian of science Lorraine Daston has noted, people are everywhere surrounded by intimations of chance and yet there is "nothing self-evident" about it.[15]

It is not simply that probabilistic reasoning is an unevenly distributed skill, or that risk, socially managed and privatized, affects disparate groups disproportionately. Nor is it only that some historical periods and ideologies take chance more seriously than others. What seems to me most intriguing—and less accessible to large-scale historical and sociological studies—is that comportments toward the possibilities of chance vary wildly *within* individuals. An otherwise calculating politician takes a ridiculous extra-marital risk. An investor attributes failure to luck and success to God or merit (or less commonly, visa versa). A person does not know what to think or how to feel when told that a cancer has an 80 percent chance of remission. A professor studies chance for years and still wonders how much he believes in it, finally learning to bracket the question of chance's ontology and ask instead how literary figures, their cultures, and readers embedded within their own historical moments try to make sense of the ambiguities of chance. How we experience the potential meanings of chance is personal, contextual, conflicted, and purposive, and it touches us in profound and quotidian ways. If the rational handling of chance is a sign of modernity, then we have never been consistently modern—just ask a behavioral economist dismantling *Homo economicus* or refer to neuroscience's estimations of the irrational human brain. Or, as the following chapters will argue while trying to restrain disciplinary self-righteousness, consult some nineteenth-century American literature that explores early and as deeply as any other body of work what it means to live with the limits of reason under conditions of aleatory uncertainty. The role of chance did change across the nineteenth century, and its engendering of intellectual and cultural controversies made it particularly animating for literary writers compelled by the psychological, moral, political, religious, and aesthetic consequences of chance. Historians have described the probabilistic revolution, and scientists are exploring how humans process chance, though such work is only the beginning of some stories, not a few of which are literary ones.

Though Dupin solves the case, "The Purloined Letter" (1844) famously ends with uncertainty: the contents of the missive are never revealed (pointing some critics toward the unending referentiality of signs), and Dupin's specific motives remain a mystery (what happens in Vienna stays in Vienna). Poe's story dramatizes epistemological limits while suggesting how the rise of chance might bear on the reading of literature. In Poe's detective fiction, Dupin refers to the "theory of probabilities," the "doctrine of chance," and the "Calculus of Probabilities," which he describes as the "most rigidly exact in science applied to ... the most intangible in speculation."[16] Poe had access to new discourses of chance through many channels, intellectual and popular; and it may matter that a study repeatedly cited by probability theorists of the period demonstrated that the number of dead letters in the Paris post office was so remarkably consistent from year to year as to be predicted en masse, results more or less duplicated by similar studies in London and Washington, D.C. For all its skepticism, "The Purloined Letter" shows that uncertainty understood in aleatory terms can be, to some extent, rationally governed. Inquiry is a game of odds in the story; knowledge is partial but sufficient; Dupin is revealed as both a mathematician and a poet whose probabilistic methods reflect, direct, and exploit the reader's own probabilistic expectations. The management of chance in "The Purloined Letter" is simultaneously a topic and a meta-critical commentary, for if Dupin is a kind of literary critic and the missing letter is a text, then Poe implies that the interpretation of literature involves encounters with chance.

Poe thus hints at a fresh approach to a set of enduring scholarly concerns. Readers of nineteenth-century American literature have long recognized crises of skepticism and belief tracked along multiple axes. Quarrels with an overbearing Calvinist God, the higher criticism's attempts to verify the Bible, the antinomian potential of individualistic faith, the rise of scientific authority in an age of advancing, though by no means dominant, materialism and secularism—all presented challenges to Christian orthodoxies that registered in the literature of the time. Philosophical conundrums also drive nineteenth-century literary skepticism. The psychological and supernatural possibilities of the Gothic undermine enlightenment reason, as do the unbounded subjectivism of romanticism, the affective instabilities of sentimentality, and the epistemological and moral quandaries that roil the literature of slavery and race. Cultural pluralism as experienced in the nineteenth century, as well as the ever-accelerating pace of economic and technological change, further unsettles foundational assumptions, including principles of essential value and teleological progress. Attention to the probabilistic revolution extends, reorients, and departs from these more or less familiar critical narratives as chance comes to mediate both science and skepticism, both faith and unbelief—positions that are typically set in opposition but are surprisingly subtended by the rise of chance.

Literary studies of chance and related concepts have appeared irregularly over the last several decades, making the growing subfield, if one can call it that, more of an archipelago of interests than a centralized area of inquiry. Critics working outside of American literature have pointed in productive directions—Douglas Patey on the rise of probabilism in Augustan aesthetics; Ross Hamilton on accidents replacing essence at the center of modernity; Michael Witmore, Thomas Kavanagh, and Leland Monk on the conjunction of chance and narrative in (respectively) Elizabethan, eighteenth-century French, and modern British literatures. The general consensus is that chance resists integration into totalizing systems of knowledge and judgment and that by dramatizing the play between chance and order, writers meditate on epistemological problems, the navigation of aleatory experience, the role of chance in social practices, and the operations of literature itself. Historical specificity matters in all of these concerns, but while chance has occasioned books in other periods and remains a familiar presence in postmodernism, it has for the most part been only tangentially treated in nineteenth-century literary studies, despite the fact that the rise of frequentism and spread of probabilistic practices made chance a provocative topic as writers and readers faced a newly quantified world to which they were not habituated.[17] Walter Benn Michaels, Wai Chee Dimock, Brook Thomas, and Mizruchi have touched locally on chance in nineteenth-century American literature, while subsequent scholarship with more sustained focus includes Nan Goodman's book on liability law, Eric Wertheimer's deconstruction-inflected work on insurance, and Jason Puskar's forthcoming book on accidents and insurance in the late nineteenth and early twentieth centuries. Such valuable literary criticism tends to center on the postbellum period and socioeconomic formulations of accidents, leaving largely unexplored two lines of inquiry that the following chapters take up.[18]

The first involves the wealth of intellectual contexts implicated in the probabilistic revolution, for while Poe, Melville, Douglass, Thoreau, and Dickinson address chance in social and economic registers, they most strenuously ask how chance alters the dynamics among science, skepticism, and faith, a pursuit that takes them across the Atlantic and into extended intellectual histories, even while retaining more immediate connections to nineteenth-century American life. In today's compartmentalized intellectual culture, one does not expect to find sermons dwelling on probabilism or scientists ruminating on mysteries of fate, nor do studies of aesthetics take much interest in, say, statistics and numerical literacy. Neuroscience and evolutionary theory can reach toward questions of beauty and God, but the authors treated in this book discuss such concerns with refer-ence to their era's own scientific idioms, work that can seem prophetically interdisci-plinary but is better regarded as pre-disciplinary, insofar as probabilism in the nineteenth century spanned intellectual estates only beginning to be subdivided.

A second main contribution of this book is the reclamation of chance's rise before the Civil War. For Andrew Delbanco, James Dawes, Louis Menand, and many of the Ameri-canist scholars mentioned above, it took the chaotic trauma of the Civil War to disabuse Americans of their teleological confidence. Lears more dialectically argues that chance and providence conflict throughout American history, though for him the Civil War remains a watershed moment in which beliefs in chance spread from marginalized groups coded as superstitious to intellectual and cultural elites armed with probabilistic methods.[19] The story of the Civil War as an epistemic rupture has proved durable in American history, stretching all the way back to postbellum thinkers who defined their own modern understandings of chance against a supposedly less savvy antebellum era. Theirs is not precisely an anxiety of influence, though some telling misprisions are in play—from Henry James's rejection of Hawthorne's supposed providentialism, to Howells's caricature of outmoded transcendentalist teleologies, to Twain's mocking of Cooper's probabilistic offenses, to a host of writers who depict the Civil War as a disen-chanting moment when the ostensibly untroubled faith in a chanceless universe all of a sudden falls away. Dividing the century as dramatically as it divided the nation, the Civil War for commentators past and present lets slip the power of chance in America.

The first step in detailing chance's literary influence across the nineteenth century is simply to demonstrate that antebellum authors and their culture reckoned with changing notions of chance. No major writer of the period was an expert in probability theory, but if literary figures (as this book does) eschewed technical mathematics, they self-consciously explored the possibilities of chance and the far-reaching implications of probabilism. While Poe explicitly discusses the doctrine of chances, his contemporaries most often treat its applications (for instance, Melville and oceanography, Thoreau and surveying, Douglass and statistics, Dickinson and eschatology). The chapters that follow report some discoveries in source study and discursive influence, but whether responding to identifiable texts or to a circulating cultural logic, authors found the probabilistic revolution simultaneously enlightening and inadequate in their encounters with doubt.

Their engagements entail remarkable formal performances—from Dickinson's astonishing verse, to Melville's carefully disordered fictions, to the dramatic structures of slave narratives that reenact and strategically frame the fugitive's handling of chance. Nineteenth-century reviewers appealed to probabilities when assessing the realism of characters and plots, a common practice that became more complicated as Aristotelian theories of narrative causation came up against new concepts of chance. Questions of genre, formal unity, and aesthetic value can all involve probabilistic thought. To even have expectations about a plot or line of poetry is, in a basic sense, to read probabilistically; and interpreting a text (as Samuel Johnson knew) is an inherently chancy enterprise, even if modern literary criticism tends to prefer robust rhetorics that avoid qualifiers such as *probably*, *likely*, and *perhaps*.[20] Because probabilities govern relations between readers and texts, realities and representations, changing attitudes toward chance encourage aesthetic experimentation and its attendant meta-critical commentary. So accustomed is our modern age to probabilistic negotiations of uncertainty that it can take less habituated nineteenth-century authors to remind us that, when interpreting literature, we are dealing in chance.

That the rise of chance is most closely associated with the sciences might seem to preclude its literary relevance or reduce it to a foil, a misapprehension attributable to various factors—discipline formation in the nineteenth century and beyond; binaristic views of science and literature from Carlyle to C. P. Snow; sporadic attacks on quantitative science from nineteenth-century literary figures; and the hubris of scientific boosters such as the polymath John Tyndall, who wrote in 1874, "All schemes and systems which thus infringe upon the domain of science must . . . submit to its control."[21] One almost wonders why we needed Heidegger and Foucault to unmask the scientific will to power, especially with Mary Shelley, Hawthorne, and Nietzsche undertaking similar work. Whatever the case, literary scholars schooled in New Critical ambiguity and graduated into post-structural hermeneutic suspicion can still find it tempting, perhaps even psychologically gratifying, to charge science with a naïve and imperial positivism.

Thankfully, scholars are increasingly dismantling hard distinctions between science and literature, particularly in romantic studies, a development simultaneously advanced and complicated by nineteenth-century literary explorations of chance. It is increasingly clear that writers, including reputedly mystical transcendentalists, valued empirical methods and scientific discoveries. But while most scholarship on science and nineteenth-century literature focuses on specific figures, developments, and fields, less attention has been paid to the philosophy of science and the pan-disciplinary spread of probabilism. As if meeting their literary peers halfway on the ground between certitude and doubt, scientists of the period acknowledged theoretical problems of induction and practical challenges to empirical accuracy, making them sensitive to aleatory instabilities and the epistemological modesty they entail. As George Levine has argued, many Victorian scientists regarded positivism as "a deeply skeptical theory of knowledge." They marveled along with romantics at deep time, deep space, the infinite interconnectedness of nature, and the epiphanies of scientific geniuses. But if Laura Dassow Walls has emphasized how Goethe, Von Humboldt, Coleridge, Emerson, and Thoreau celebrated intimations of harmonious order under the logic of analogy, empirical efforts to substantiate such holistic visions involved the gathering and analysis of vast amounts of facts—those demanding quantitative details that require probabilistic management. Dupin is rightfully a probabilist and poet, a maven of induction and deduction, for both scientists and artists confronted the indeterminacies of chance, suggesting that the skepticism of much nineteenth-century literature can be taken to accompany, rather than oppose, the growing authority of science.[22]

In addition to complicating disciplinary categories, chance also unsettles some major literary-historical narratives. German and British romantics find generative power in the interplay of chaos and order, and Eric Wilson has argued that American romantics follow suit in foreshadowing chaos theory.[23] But because European romanticism in important ways predates the growing visibility of the new sciences of chance, it tends to formulate aleatory possibilities in psycho-metaphysical terms under a philosophy of mind. The belatedness of American romantics is thus (for a change) more of a boon than an embarrassment insofar as they are better situated to forge original relations with probability and chance. Transatlantic romanticism remains a powerfully diachronic movement dominated by unidirectional lines of influence from east to west, but a focus on the probabilistic revolution more dialectically connects mid-nineteenth-century American writers with Victorian contemporaries such as Dickens, Mill, Ruskin, Darwin, and George Eliot—all of who encounter (as Gillian Beer has shown) scientific approaches to causality that admit the potential of chance.[24] If scholars of American romanticism once seemed a step behind their British counterparts in matters of transcendental philosophy, they can now admire the progress of their colleagues working at the conjunction of nineteenth-century British literature and science, while still insisting (not too defensively, one hopes) that their objects of study are far from tardy regarding chance—that Poe's critiques of probabilistic reasoning precede and surpass those of *Hard Times* (1854); that Thoreau's scientific aesthetic is more searching than that of *Modern Painters* (1843–60); that Douglass's thinking on probability, race, and liberalism exceeds anything from Mill and Spencer; and that no one, including Hardy, sounds like Melville and Dickinson when writing about chance and God. Following Tocqueville, Lears suggests that the market revolution and frontier ethos made nineteenth-century Americans especially sensitive to chance. This may be right, given that the management of chance takes culturally specific forms, and yet the scientific advances and social practices of the probabilistic revolution were transatlantic phenomena. As with a global economic crisis, chance cuts across national lines.

The rise of chance in the nineteenth century also blurs boundaries between high ideas and everyday life, intellectual and cultural history. Probability theorists in Europe and America took up gambling puzzles, worked for the insurance industry, gave lecture tours, and wrote books and encyclopedia entries for general audiences, while the rise of print culture in the mid-nineteenth century constituted an information revolution requiring the processing of mass facts and inviting probabilistic explanations for the extraordinary events reported every day. Because chance disrupted traditional systems of theology, metaphysics, and natural philosophy, some of the boldest applications of probability theory came from commentators in unofficial forums. The following chapters selectively target discourses that bear on primary texts, including some unexpected archives—gaming manuals, reflections on fishing, sermons on the death of King Ahab, and descriptions of black mathematical genius in the African-American press. Such unstudied sources advance current understandings of chance in U.S. history, pointing toward the raucous emergence of a probabilistic revolution in which literary authors proved especially prescient and, at times, startlingly misguided.

One way to approach their encounters with chance is to think of them in terms of classical pragmatism (including the radical empiricism of William James). While Richard Rorty has famously reformulated pragmatism as an anti-foundational philosophy with little use for scientific methods, the historicist work of Menand and Joan Richardson offers a more empirical account of the movement by attending to scientific affiliations that involve the taming of chance, a rendering of pragmatism also supported by the philosopher Robert Brandom. Pragmatism in the last few decades has expanded opportunistically across disciplines and periods, though the nineteenth-century literary auxiliary of the Metaphysical Club remains a less than pluralistic group dominated by Emerson and Henry James, with occasional invitations extended to Whitman, Dickinson, Thoreau, and Stephen Crane. Such inclusions often follow Richard Poirier in their focus on poetics and style, but when considered as a culturally embedded philosophy of chance attuned to the skeptical potential of empiricism, classical pragmatism becomes a historically proximate, sophisticated, and durable framework in which to discuss issues of doubt and belief across a range of nineteenth-century literary texts. In turn, extending the roots of pragmatism more promiscuously into mid-nineteenth-century literature not only enriches pragmatist genealogies but also reframes—and exposes some limitations of—the thinking of James, Peirce, Dewey, and Holmes Jr., particularly regarding their approaches to moral dilemmas and affective responses occasioned by chance.[25]

Pragmatism can even encourage a literary critic to change his views of skepticism—to turn away from Cartesian doubts about the existence of the object world, to bracket suspicions concerning inter-subjectivity and the commensuration of language with reality, and to take up instead a question of comparable but more personal seriousness: How does one live under conditions of chance? For William James, the rejection of radical skepticism entails a turn toward "concreteness and adequacy, towards facts, towards action, and towards power."[26] A self-regarding scholar (that is, me) might even project a version of his intellectual life across the nineteenth century: an early faith in Enlightenment learning (surely one's classes lead toward Truth) gives way to the romantic valorization of suffering for unattainable knowledge (the Fall into graduate school), which fitfully matures into a pragmatist outlook that more soberly seeks to manage uncertainty without sacrificing the pleasures of wonder—call it a kind of middleclass, mid-life crisis that cheers on Thoreau's extravagant whimsy while keeping an eye on the 401(k). A visit to any Borders bookstore will show that most books on chance are pitched to gamblers and businesspeople, though the probabilistic revolution is about much more than the sweet cash value of instrumentalism. In the hands of some writers, chance retains what Emerson calls a "supersensible utility," for its possibilities are simultaneously enchanting and chilling in psychological, religious, moral, and aesthetic domains.[27] As nineteenth-century authors encounter the possibilities of chance, they struggle between extremes that remain with us today: fundamentalism and relativism, determinism and chaos, hubristic risk management and terror, the rational confidence of the Enlightenment and the debilitating doubts of modernity. If literature can help to navigate these straits, so much the better for those who read in an age of accountability.

The chapters that follow look something like this. Chapter one, "Probably Poe," discusses the spread of probability theory in the 1830s and '40s, paying particular attention to the doctrine of chances in logic and mathematics, as well as to its emerging influence on gaming, sociology, and aesthetics. Poe shows in his detective fiction and beyond that he knows enough about chance to endanger stable epistemologies and literary-critical conventions, especially when he applies probabilistic reasoning to depth psychology and extraordinary narrative events. By tracing the dynamics between odds and the odd, we meet a surprising Poe—one who defends the realism of his fantastical fiction on probabilistic grounds, and whose commitments to chance align him with pragmatism more than deconstruction. Introducing a main claim of this book, Poe shows that the probabilistic revolution and nineteenth-century American literature need not be at odds.

Chapters two and three examine how chance shapes Melville's epistemological and moral skepticism. "*Moby-Dick* and the Opposite of Providence" begins with a deeply historicized account of theo-philosophical approaches to chance in debates over fate and free will, setting skepticism's openness to the possibilities of chance against untroubled accounts of Christian providence. Classical and early modern skeptics form a background for Melville's renaissance of chance, though Melville was also influenced by contemporary science (including meteorology, navigation, and oceanography), as well as by abiding theological anxieties over the seemingly random death of King Ahab. If *Moby-Dick* is a largely negative performance unsettling etiological certitude, chapter three, "Doubting if Doubt itself be Doubting," discusses how *Pierre* (1852) and "Bartleby, the Scrivener" (1853) raise the stakes of Melville's quarrel with causation by exploring the challenge of moral action under conditions of chance. Melville's suspension of judgment regarding chance proves as radical as any political position he might take, and it moves him toward a pragmatism that, more than anything in William James, dwells on the tragic potential of willing oneself to believe.

Chapter four, "Douglass's Long Run," turns explicitly to politics with the question: How does it feel to be a statistical problem? In the tradition of slave narratives, and with some sociological assistance from the black intellectual James McCune Smith, Douglass vindicates the capacities of African Americans to manage the chances of democracy and capitalism. The probabilistic revolution is not usually associated with mid-century debates over slavery and race, but as Douglass's opponents increasingly cite statistics to demonstrate the inferiority of blacks, Douglass answers them in kind, even if it means revising his representative selfhood and deemphasizing the absolutist moral claims of mainstream abolitionism. Before, during, and after the Civil War, Douglass insists that blacks be given an equal chance in the race of life, thus aligning himself not only with the liberalism of Mill and sociological thought of Du Bois but also (as strange as it may seem) with the probabilistic naturalism of social Darwinism and Holmes Jr.

Chapter five, "Roughly Thoreau," focuses on the radical empiricism of *Walden* (1854), Thoreau's journals, and his scientific writings. As an author, philosopher, surveyor, and naturalist, Thoreau comes to accept aleatory uncertainty and its imperatives for the conduct of life, even as—like Ruskin, Darwin, and William James—he engages in the management of chance. Thoreau learns over the course of his career that natural science is not strictly a positivist enterprise but, rather, a probabilistic pursuit in which to measure under conditions of chance is not precisely to know. Thoreau's disciplined commitments to the handling of chance distance him from Emersonian transcendentalism and help him bridge, but not eliminate, the worrisome divide between his science and art.

Chapter six, "Dickinson's Precarious Steps, Surprising Leaps, and Bounds," discusses Dickinson's approach to the limitations of knowledge understood in terms of probabilistic expectation. As chance became increasing visible in American thought and culture, Dickinson pushes beyond a romantic skepticism most powerfully represented by strands of Emersonian thought to challenge the argument from design. Like Thoreau, Dickinson is a philosopher of science whose intellectual and formal experiments trace the dynamics between repetitious and aleatory experience. Painfully and wonderfully aware of the impossibility of perfect prediction, Dickinson's poems enact and theorize chance through its affective correlative, surprise.

Much more might be said at this point, though this introduction will err on the side of brevity, for the study of chance teaches, if nothing else, to be wary of teleological narratives and to practice instead inductive methods, even at the expense of totalities. This seems apposite for a book primarily concerned with individual authors and texts that together constitute a period and even a thesis but ultimately remain unique. Quoting James, "The world is full of partial stories that run parallel to one another, beginning and ending at odd times. They mutually interlace and interfere at points, but we can not unify them completely in our minds."[28] The following stories of chance and nineteenth-century American literature are synergistic but not utterly unified. As readers make (or pick) their way through this book, its claims—once again taking language from James—will, it is hoped, hang together enough to seem plausible, useful, and even satisfying.

CHAPTER 1

Probably Poe

Probability is the feeling of the mind.
> —Augustus De Morgan, 1838

What were the chances of all that happening? Alas, not zero.
> —Jonathan Franzen, *Freedom* (2010)

As something of an orphan in U.S. literary history, Poe deserves some sympathy. The desperate economics of antebellum authorship forced him into a slew of uneven performances, and it was not entirely his fault that his literary executor, Rufus Griswold, set out to damage his legacy. Poe cannot be blamed for the South's losing the Civil War, for T. S. Eliot's genteel discomfort, or for F. O. Matthiessen's relegating Poe to an apologetic, and even guilty, footnote in *American Renaissance* (1941). Nor is Poe responsible for subsequent literary criticism that has been slow to notice that, prior to many of his more respectable contemporaries, Poe wrote provocatively on such flood subjects as transcendentalism, transnationalism, print culture, and race. Poe might qualify as the unluckiest of all American writers were he not such a world-class screwup—if Griswold's animadversions did not have some basis in reality, and if Poe's financial and professional struggles were not often of his own making. Poe's career is one of a frustrated promise that even the French could not redeem during Poe's short life, and yet as maddening as his failings can be, his genius for sparking literary developments is unmatched in American and perhaps world history.

If anyone can lay claim to the title, Poe is the father of the American literature of chance. As an early adopter of probability theory who dropped out of college because of gambling debts, Poe examines the prospects and dangers of chance from a perspective informed by personal experience, scientific knowledge, and artistic intuition. Poe famously sets reason against irrational forces usually formulated as gothic horror, psychosexual anxiety, linguistic indeterminacy, racial panic, or some volatile combination thereof. Less noticed but of comparable weight, the disruptive power of chance is crucial to Poe's writings, particularly his tales of ratiocination—"The Murders in the Rue

Morgue" (1841), "The Mystery of Marie Roget" (1842–43), and "The Purloined Letter." Exploring emergent approaches to chance through his polymath investigator Dupin, Poe deploys probability theory in a number of registers as he comes to anticipate a range of developments in literature and science alike. Locally, Poe's tales of ratiocination confront the challenge of skepticism by working with, not against, scientific and logical discourses of his time. The taming of chance more generally influences Poe's literary practice and theory, vindicating his surprisingly realistic aesthetic as verisimilitude becomes a function of Aristotelian poetics combined with statistical reasoning. Most broadly, as a writer working on the cutting edges of popular culture and struggling in an evolving literary marketplace, Poe both critiques and reflects everyday life during the probabilistic revolution, thus (as odd as it may sound) helping to establish what it means to act rationally in the antebellum United States as some thinkers move tentatively toward more modern, more pragmatist points of view. It has long been recognized that Poe poses some of the hardest skeptical questions. His encounters with chance show that he offers more practical answers than often supposed.

METHOD—IF METHOD THERE IS

D. H. Lawrence once called Poe "almost more a scientist than an artist." He did not mean it as a compliment, and (as "almost" suggests) most readers of Poe do not consider him a legitimate student of science, especially those following the lead of Eliot, who complained of Poe's "lack of qualification in philosophy, theology, or natural science."[1] Poe's early poem, "Sonnet—to Science" (1829), lodges precisely the kind of lament expected from a wildly imaginative romantic best known for the grotesque, arabesque, and supernatural:

> Science! true daughter of Old Time thou art!
> Who alterest all things with thy peering eyes.
> Why preyest thou thus upon the poet's heart,
> Vulture, whose wings are dull realities?[2]

It is strange that Poe later apologized for the poem's echoing of Tennyson, for the sentiments and figures of "Sonnet—to Science" allude with intensely concentrated force to romanticism's quarrels with science—Schiller's critique of a deracinating, disenchanting empiricism in "The Gods of Greece" (1788), Wordsworth's condemnation of murderous dissectors, Shelley's suffering Promethean artists, Keats's description of the peering eyes of the rationalist who dooms the mythic lovers of "Lamia" (1820).[3] Poe's "Diddling Considered as One of the Exact Sciences" (1843) resists science in more satiric terms, redirecting the irony of De Quincey's 1827 essay, "On Murder Considered as One of the Fine Arts" (and echoing an 1835 Blackwood's piece, "The Science of Swindling"). Whereas De Quincey mocks aesthetic overreaching, Poe's essay subverts the totalizing urge and supposed objectivity of science so that any claim to scientific exactitude in the piece is itself an overdetermined diddle, a dynamic also evident in Poe's scientific spoofs from "The Unparalleled Adventures of One Hans Pfall" (1835) to "Von Kempelen and His Discovery" (1849). Such pieces invented fantastical observational reports that some antebellum readers took to be real, suggesting that the authority of science lies not in a rigorously objective method but in what the historian of science Peter Dear has called "socially embedded genres of argument."[4] It is as if Poe proleptically avenges literary criticism for the indignities of the Sokal Affair.

Yet as much as Poe enjoyed satirizing science, and as much as he keeps an anxious eye on British romanticism, he cared enough about current scientific developments to discuss them in informed detail. Poe did well in mathematics at West Point and later pursued interests in astronomy and cosmogony. More empirically, his "Letter to Mr. B—" (1836) praises Bacon for studying the "palpable palaces" of the material world (*PT* 13), a point repeated in his "South-Sea Expedition" (1843) article, which praises "scientific men, imbued with the love of science."[5] In the culmination of his scientific writings, *Eureka* (1848), Poe draws so provocatively on Newton, Kepler, Von Humboldt, Laplace, and others that one reviewer gushed: "Mr. Poe is not merely a man of science—not merely a poet—not merely a man of letters. He is all combined." Writing before Matthew Arnold's "Literature and Science" (1882) and C. P. Snow's "Two Cultures" (1959), Poe pursued his scientific curiosity across nascent disciplinary lines, even as he occasionally charged science with narrowness and hubris. Poe expressed his own more catholic ambitious in an 1848 letter, complaining of "*merely* scientific men . . . who cultivate the physical sciences to the exclusion . . . of the mathematics, of metaphysics and of logic."[6] Of these areas, Poe's metaphysics have preoccupied critical attention, though as John Irwin has marvelously shown, mathematics and logic figure importantly in Poe's writings, especially the Dupin tales.[7]

Highlighting his commitment to logic, Poe referred to the stories as tales of ratiocination. Borges praised "The Murders in the Rue Morgue" as a "perfect specimen" of detective fiction, though Poe's story of a razor-wielding orangutan who clambers through a fourth-story window and kills two women in a seemingly locked room can be seen less as a drama of crime and punishment and more as a narrative thought experiment focused on questions of method.[8] From its expository opening, the tale simultaneously celebrates and delimits the power of rationality: the most difficult mysteries "are not beyond *all* conjecture," though our "analytical" faculties themselves remain "but little susceptible of analysis," so much so that the "very soul and essence of method" take on "the whole air of intuition" (*PT* 397). Poe thus foregrounds the story's interest in what is nominally called intuition, which Poe later refers to as "the process called Intuition" and that which is given "the credit of intuition."[9] Dupin's first intuitive act in the tale is to read the narrator's wildly associative thoughts, a feat so far beyond plausibility as to antagonize some readers and prove a point that Poe made in an 1846 letter: the popularity of "The Murders in the Rue Morgue" comes from its "method and *air* of method."[10] To quote the narrator of the story, doubters may question Dupin's "method—if method there is," but as with scientific hoaxes, chess automatons, P. T. Barnum exhibits, and reality television, it is the cynicism of not entirely disenchanted readers that keeps them reading on (*PT* 402).[11]

As critics note, Dupin's method in solving the Rue Morgue murders is difficult to stabilize in the terms of formal logic.[12] He begins inductively, "scrutiniz[ing] every thing" with a "minuteness of attention" before moving on to a series of "deductions" that lead "*inevitably*" to a "single result" (*PT* 413–16). Though some evidence is withheld or veiled from the reader (most maddeningly, the tuft of hair and the broken nail that only appears to lock a window), Dupin corroborates his suppositions with additional forensic evidence and a planted advertisement, following a general scientific method of observation, hypothesis, and testing. His rational process triumphs in the end, but if Dupin joins the era's scientific consensus by privileging what he calls "*á posteriori*" empiricism over a priori speculation, "The Murders in the Rue Morgue" also registers what Mary Poovey describes as a growing challenge to induction (*PT* 418).[13]

A main narrative in the history of science and chance is the creeping recognition that empiricism is inescapably probabilistic and thus fallible in terms of accuracy, prediction, and logic. Bacon in *Novum Organum* (1620) and Newton in his last version of *Principia* (1687) acknowledged (albeit inconsistently) that the marshaling of facts cannot establish natural laws in any absolute sense, for no amount of data can rule out possible exceptions, howsoever unlikely such black swans may be. The problem of induction becomes more visible in the work of the seventeenth-century philosophers Joseph Glanvill (whom Poe speciously quotes) and Hume, both of whom argue that causation is beyond human certitude insofar as causal claims (one case will follow a like case) are based on the probable correlations of necessarily imperfect analogies (cases can be similar but are never identical). Such empirical skepticism, still at issue in the philosophy of science today, was not a crisis for practical scientists of the eighteenth and nineteenth centuries. Barbara Shapiro's study of London's Royal Society shows that most eighteenth-century natural philosophers were satisfied with the "moral certainty" of highly probable knowledge, though for more theoretically inclined thinkers, the fallibility of induction remained an unsettling concern. Nineteenth-century logicians and philosophers of science such as Richard Whately and William Whewell insisted that supposed inductions actually rely on deductions, for empiricism requires some type of a priori knowledge to form any hypotheses that might allow one to leap from facts to general laws, even if such intuitive assumptions erode claims to scientific objectivity.[14]

Dupin in "The Murders in the Rue Morgue" similarly circumscribes empiricism and induction, mocking the Parisian police for their "vast parade of measures" and anticipating Poe's later complaint about "*merely*" empirical scientists who "chiefly write the criticisms *against* all efforts at generalization—denouncing these efforts as 'speculative' and 'theoretical'" (*PT* 412).[15] Somehow the discrete facts of empirical inquiry must be connected in intelligible causal (and thus narrative) relation, though how exactly Dupin or anyone else manages this feat is by no means clear. As some dubious readers note, Dupin's observations in "The Murders in the Rue Morgue" do not necessarily point to a rampaging orangutan unless one makes a leap in logic that for Whately and Whewell are not inducible from empirical facts. Writing from a Kantian perspective, Whewell asserted in *The Philosophy of the Inductive Sciences* (1840) that facts are ordered by pre-existing, "unconscious" knowledge structures and thus that "there is a mask of theory over the whole face of nature." We can aspire, like Ahab, to strike through the mask and view reality face-to-face, but such desires do not change the fact that we must make sense of facts subjectively. With more epistemological confidence, John Herschel in his influential *Preliminary Discourse on the Study of Natural Philosophy* (1830) and John Stuart Mill in his *System of Logic: Ratiocinative and Inductive* (1843) argued that natural laws can, in fact, be reasoned from observations by analogy, though (following Locke and Hume) they admitted that analogical claims are probabilistic, not absolute.[16] If Herschel recommended a dialectical movement between induction and deduction, his empiricism did not solve the problem of induction and is particularly shaky in the context of Poe's *"very extraordinary"* and *"excessively outré"* tale, for only a highly unlikely combination of events might be analogous to the Rue Morgue murders (*PT* 420, 422). Poe broaches in this way a critical question that remains unresolved: if deduction and induction are insufficient methods, does logic give way to some other mode of knowing, something closer to guessing or intuition?

A potential answer lies for Poe in probability theory. Toward the end of "The Murders in the Rue Morgue" and in the middle of what appears to be the tale's dramatic climax, Dupin reaches the ends of his explanatory power, abruptly cutting short his reconstruction of the crime and refusing to guarantee his hypothesis that an orangutan did the killings. "I will not pursue these guesses," Dupin says, "for I have no right to call them more—since the shades of reflection upon which they are based are scarcely of sufficient depth to be appreciable by my own intellect" (*PT* 425). This admission is astonishing coming from Dupin, who begins the story by reading the narrator's mind and later reflects on his own rational processes with a nearly satiric Cartesian confidence. By having Dupin's reconstruction stop short, Poe frustrates a reader's desire not simply to know but also to have transparently narrated every last gruesome detail of the killings. Dupin may appear less than impressive in this moment, but his sudden epistemological modesty is consistent with the story's opening disclaimer that the highest analytic powers of man are not themselves subject to analysis. If Poe is sometimes dismissed as wildly unsystematic, here he shows some theoretical discipline.

That our most searching intellectual faculties are unknowable suggests a familiar Poe—the marplot of Enlightenment order whose protagonists' insistent claims to logic only highlight the instability of reason (note to self: if you find yourself saying "mad am I not" or "how calmly I can tell you the whole story," you don't sound rational, you sound like a lunatic). Counter-Enlightenment versions of Poe can be associated with gothic, romantic, sensational, and spiritualist traditions. Yet to accept too readily the antirational Poe is to risk at least two errors: to assume hard distinctions between reason and irrationality (a dualism Poe everywhere threatens to dissolve); and to diminish his tales of ratiocination along with much of his critical and creative work, rendering all his talk of induction and deduction—of evidence, method, logic, and science—little more than overlengthy diversions from the irreducible fact of intuition. Doubtlessly, the Dupin tales contain some fraction of fudge, but what seems to be inexplicable guessing or intuition remains open to a measure of scientific explanation. And well before philosophers from Peirce to Karl Popper and Rudolf Carnap identified guessing as a crucial stage in scientific inquiry.[17]

Providing a model for later detective fiction, "The Murders in the Rue Morgue" postpones its final revelations, tempting the reader with red herrings and exhausting every apparent solution: it is not the bank employee, Adolphe Le Bon, who is initially suspected of the crime; the bags of gold do not figure at all; the conflicting witness accounts of foreign tongues offer a tangle of false leads. Only after the reader is brought with the narrator to "the verge of comprehension" does Dupin finally associate his method of inquiry with "the theory of probabilities—that theory to which the most glorious objects of human research are indebted for the most glorious of illustration" (*PT* 421–22).

Dupin's enthusiasm indicates how far the probabilistic revolution had advanced by the mid-nineteenth century. Early pioneers of probability theory include Pascal, Fermat, and Huygens in the seventeenth century, and De Moivre, the Bournoullis, and Bayes in the eighteenth, though as Isaac Todhunter emphasized in his encyclopedic *History of the Mathematical Theory of Probability* (1865), the figure that came to dominate the field was Laplace, who in 1814 published *Philosophical Essay on Probabilities*, an accessible summa of more technical studies that inspired advances within and beyond mathematics. Drawing on Laplace in the 1830s, Charles Babbage built a calculation machine and studied the frequency of letters in his cryptology work, while Siméon-Denis Poisson (a student of Laplace) formulated his law of large numbers in the 1830s, refining frequentist claims that seemingly unpredictable events follow regular laws when viewed in the mass. Adolphe Quetelet, another student of Laplace, helped to found quantitative sociology by applying frequentist thought to human culture, and Herschel and Mill (along with Quetelet and the mathematician Augustus De Morgan) wrote popular works on probability theory in the 1830s and beyond. These theorists of chance generally alleviated but did not solve the problem of induction, for if no quantity of individual facts could verify universal laws, they did improve predictive accuracy so that, in Martin Jay's words, "[T]he bugaboo of skepticism was no longer quite as frightening."[18] It was not simply that increasingly sophisticated formulae solved increasingly complicated puzzles involving dice and cards. Probability theory spread beyond such classical abstract models to include problems in insurance, investment, navigation, meteorology, and jurisprudence (such as how to adjudicate multiple conflicting testimonies, a problem in "The Murders in the Rue Morgue").

In his tales of ratiocination and beyond, Poe refers to the "theory of probabilities" (*PT* 421), the "doctrine of chance" (*PT* 507), and the "Calculus of Probabilities" (*PT* 554), though if Poe was at least somewhat conversant in the field, his sources are hard to pin down. Irwin provides a searching account of Poe's education in mathematics, which gave him the opportunity and expertise to engage advances in probabilistic thought. Poe also briefly mentions in various writings Mill, Laplace, and Johann Bernoulli and specifically refers to Babbage's *Ninth Bridgewater Treatise* (1837), a book that discusses among others mathematicians Laplace, Poisson, and De Morgan. Babbage's influence on Poe is further evident in "Maelzel's Chess-Player" (1836) and the probabilistic decoding of "The Gold-Bug" (1843), and Poe's immersion in antebellum print culture further exposed him to the new sciences of chance.[19] The *Southern Literary Messenger* and *Burton's Gentleman's Magazine* (both of which Poe edited) referred to probability theory, while as editor of the *Broadway Journal*, Poe reprinted probabilistic discussions of insurance and investing from the commercial press of the day. By the early 1830s, The *Encyclopedia Americana* included entries on the doctrine of chances, as did the *Library of Useful Knowledge* and the *Penny Cyclopedia* (for which De Morgan wrote detailed entries). Early accounts of probability theory appeared in influential transatlantic sources such as the *Quarterly Review* and *Edinburgh Review*, while the *American Quarterly Review*, whose editor Poe knew, published a responsible and comprehensive essay, "Doctrine of Probabilities," in 1832.

Far from being neutral disseminators of scientific advances, antebellum newspapers and magazines often resisted the probabilistic revolution, setting the argument from design over and against theories of chance, which were regularly dismissed as "absurd," "stupid," and an "elaborate delusion."[20] Given that Laplace supposedly once told Napoleon that he did not require God as a hypothesis, it is unsurprising that many Americans found French atheism in a science dominated by Frenchmen. John Tillotson's sermon, "The Wisdom of Being Religious" (1664), was frequently quoted in the ante-bellum press as an unanswerable rebuttal to chance: "Was ever any considerable work, in which there was required a great variety of parts, and a regular and orderly disposition of those parts, done by chance? . . . How often might a man, after he had jumbled a set of letters in a bag, fling them out upon the ground before they would fall into an exact poem?"[21] Swift in *Gulliver's Travels* (1726) had satirically responded to Tillotson by describing how Laputans generated books by rolling dice with words on their sides, and Poe also approaches the question of chance as something more than a rhetorical one, as when the narrator of "MS. Found in a Bottle" (1833) "unwittingly" paints "DISCOVERY" on a sail and then wonders more seriously than Tillotson ever did, "Are such things the operation of ungoverned chance?" (*PT* 195).

Chapters two and six will spend considerable time examining Christian attitudes toward chance and efforts to reconcile probabilism with the argument from design; for now, suffice it to say that despite significant objections to the doctrine of chances, some American commentators, including Poe, were not worried about the piety of proba-bility.[22] Quetelet's work appeared in the popular press alongside local news and hu-morous anecdotes, while antebellum pieces discussed probability theory in relation to trade, lotteries, stargazing, travel, and political elections. References run from the infor-mative to the satiric, as when a writer in New York's *Knickerbocker* magazine wondered about the origin of a cheese he had received: "Never having studied Laplace or Quitelet [*sic*], I am not sufficiently skilled in 'the calculus of probabilities,' to say what number of chances to one there may be, that the accompanying cheese was partly made from the contents of that notable 'foaming Shaker pail.'"[23] The prevalence of probability theory in antebellum print culture is difficult precisely to gauge. My sense is that it was not a common topic in the early nineteenth century, but the increasing quantity and sophisti-cation of discussions, as well as the rise of off-handed allusions, indicate that by the 1830s and '40s, probabilism was entering many areas of public life. Poe in "The Murders in the Rue Morgue" does feel compelled to explain the doctrine of chances to his audi-ence; that he does so in passing suggests that he assumes that at least some of his readers were already familiar with the concept.

One achievement of "The Murders in the Rue Morgue" is that it draws on emerging theories of chance for a psycho-mathematical account of intuition that explains how humans act according to probabilities without rationally weighing their chances. We can think of it as a kind of unconscious calculation—a probabilism neither driven by reason nor wholly accessible to it, which is paradoxical only if calculation is defined as a willful intellectual act. Probability thinkers of the nineteenth century acknowledged that feeling, intuition, and the unconscious cannot be divorced from probabilistic determinations. As Laplace wrote in his 1814 *Essay*, "[T]he theory of probabilities is at bottom only common sense reduced to calculus; it makes us appreciate with exactitude that which exact minds feel by a sort of instinct without being able ofttimes to give a reason for it." Mill also referred to probabilism as a "sort of instinct," as did De Morgan, who noted in 1838, "Probability is the feeling of the mind"—a claim that anticipates neuroscientific arguments pioneered by Antonio Damásio, who insists that emotions cannot be separated from reason when individuals encounter uncertainty.[24]

Nineteenth-century probability theorists acknowledged that intuitive forms of knowing were sometimes superior to mathematical formulae and that, because certain causes tend to lead to certain outcomes, humans learn to proceed probabilistically through experience, not ratiocination.[25] For example, I might fold a pair of jacks in poker, not because I have precisely calculated the odds or consciously noticed my opponent suppressing a smile but, rather, because experience has taught me without my knowing that two jacks tends to lose in such circumstances. I might attribute my decision to intuition or common sense—some extra-rational feeling beyond exact definition—but antebellum probability theorists did not invoke transcendent, sentimental, spiritual, or supernatural mechanisms, nor did they have access to natural selection or Malcolm Gladwell's *Blink* (2005). Instead—and as an alternative to the mass logic of statistical calculation—they attributed unconscious calculations to psychological associations that do not render absolute certitude but move one toward probable degrees of belief. Dupin has good reasons for refusing to pursue the "guesses" that are not "appreciable by [his] own intellect." He knows that he cannot know exactly how he knows, but he also knows that his hypotheses are neither random nor entirely inexplicable. We are better probability theorists than we realize and so must attend to those unconscious calculations that often go by the name of intuition, which Poe in a discussion of Laplace in *Eureka* calls the "mathematical instinct" (*PT* 1322).

Unconscious calculation obviously restricts the purview of reason understood as intentional, transparent analysis, thus challenging what is typically thought of as thinking in the nineteenth century and beyond. The orangutan in "The Murders in the Rue Morgue" has learned that when it sees a whip, it is likely to be beaten, a behaviorist response that the antebellum era explained in terms of the association of ideas. Dupin displays his own facility with this psychology when retracing the thought trains of various characters, but just as the orangutan jumps from the lightning rod to the window, Dupin can only imaginatively reconstruct the murders by making what *Eureka* would call "seemingly intuitive *leaps*" (*PT* 1264). Such mirroring challenges easy distinctions between head and heart, human and animal, master and slave. It might even be taken to anticipate current scientific claims about instinctual calculation. Recent experiments in neuroeconomy show that monkeys act with an acute sense of probability, quickly mastering games of chance to maximize their payoff of juice. Other studies argue that humans share with higher primates "basic numerical intuitions" that allow them to calculate quantities quite accurately without using symbolic representations (that is, numbers). Poe was no more a neuroscientist than Proust, but his writings recognize that rational analysis is entangled with experience, emotions, and the primitive brain, all of whose workings are not fully apparent to the self-regarding Cartesian mind.[26]

Unconscious probabilistic thinking is powerful in "The Murders in the Rue Morgue," though importantly Dupin's intuitions are improved by the new sciences of chance. For Laplace and others, intuition can correct mathematics but mathematics also corrects intuition, for experience is not always a reliable guide and feelings are often fallible, particularly in outré or emotionally charged situations or when fine distinctions are required. Poe concurs in "The Murders in the Rue Morgue" when he suggests that analysis and its air of intuition are "much invigorated by mathematical study," an advantage lacking in Dupin's competitor, Vidocq, who is a "good guesser" but is "without an educated thought" (*PT* 412). Dupin in "The Purloined Letter" is revealed to be both mathematician and poet, a pairing also praised in Poe's "Philosophy of Composition" (1846) and his review of Elizabeth Barrett Browning. By improving intuition with the theory of probabilities, Dupin tames the threat of chance, sending the disruptive, improbable orangutan to the Jardin des Plantes—that monument to the argument from design and a favorite example of opponents of chance.

Yet if chance seems contained at the end of "The Murders in the Rue Morgue," it remains a destabilizing presence in the story, suggesting that chance in Poe's mind can be managed but never mastered. Poe's inaccurate rendering of Georges Cuvier's *The Kingdom of Animals* (1817) subverts the argument from design, making a mess of the intellectual foundations on which the Jardin des Plantes was erected. More classically, in Horace's representation of fate, Necessity holds a fistful of nails, symbolizing the inflexible laws of a chanceless, deterministic world.[27] In "The Murders in the Rue Morgue," nails turn out to be fractured as chance irrupts into a seemingly closed system that is not absolutely locked down. Dupin ultimately reestablishes order by synthesizing intuition and analysis, offering a new and probabilistic way to think about the unconscious. The tale's byzantine sexual subtext has led to strong Freudian and post-Freudian readings, though given Poe's own historical moment and the relative dearth of Dupin's interiority, Freud and his followers do not offer much help in accounting for the methods of Poe or Dupin. More historically proximate but also inadequate are traditional romantic theories of the unconscious. Dupin's methods have little directly to do with post-Kantian philosophy, nor does the jaded city-dwelling detective depend upon childlike intuition or inspirational moments in nature. Nor even does Dupin link the unconscious with religious revelation, for God is not a necessary hypothesis in Poe's detective fiction.[28] Instead of these familiar coordinates for depth psychology, Poe draws on his era's sciences of chance to explain how we suddenly find ourselves knowing or, more accurately, making educated guesses. Probabilistic thinking, that feeling of the mind, combines psychological and mathematical accounts of Dupin. It also shows how Poe's tales of ratiocination theorize a response to skepticism by offering a way to determine best inferences and actionable beliefs in the absence of absolute certitude. Unconscious calculations move facts toward generalizations, observations toward testable hypotheses. Dupin in "The Murders in the Rue Morgue" models how one might proceed in the face of doubt, though it is to be expected in a chancy world that his methods are not guaranteed. As with all of Poe's thought experiments, one shouldn't try them at home.

VAST INDIVIDUAL ERROR

In Dupin's next story, "The Mystery of Marie Roget," genius seems thwarted at every turn, in part because Poe attempts to apply probability theory to an actual case—the highly publicized disappearance of Mary Rogers, an attractive young woman living in New York City, whose mutilated body was found floating in the Hudson River in July of

1841. In "Roget," Poe exports the facts of the Rogers case to Paris where Dupin brings his brilliance to bear. Unfortunately for Poe, the real case was solved during the serialization of his thinly fictionalized story, forcing him to work with faulty suppositions already made in print. "Roget" is a desperately improvised narrative that struggles to advance the method of "The Murders in the Rue Morgue" as Poe encounters the failure of what he calls "the doctrine of chance" and "the Calculus of Probabilities" (*PT* 507). Poe's problem, simultaneously epistemological and aesthetic, is that he moves from psychology toward social statistics, from probabilistic degrees of belief about a single event toward a frequentist approach that manages chance as a function of large numbers. "The Mystery of Marie Roget," along with other tales from the early 1840s such as "The Man of the Crowd" (1840) and "The Angel of the Odd" (1844), shows Poe simultaneously critiquing and exploiting statistical reasoning for sensational literary ends.

Historians of science have detailed how Laplace and Poisson influenced early statisticians such as Quetelet, who applied advances in probability theory to the quantitative study of society (what Quetelet called "social physics").[29] Using the law of large numbers, probabilistic thinkers showed how data in the long run regresses to set averages and how phenomena, though seemingly random, ultimately occur in regular frequencies and so are predictable en masse. Frequentism makes excellent sense when, say, flipping a coin: the more times it is flipped, the more likely the distribution of heads will approach 50 percent as aleatory uncertainty is reduced but never entirely eliminated. In his *Treatise on Man* (1835) and numerous studies from the 1830s and '40s, Quetelet extended this logic to various social subjects, formulating what he called the "average man" as a statistical composite or "type" of a population, thus turning probabilistic methods toward romantic interests in national and racial identity. Quetelet's logic may be utterly familiar to modern readers comfortable with statistics and concepts like 2.3 children. But as a formal practice of managing chance variations, and as a way of understanding mass culture, statistical reasoning was relatively new in the mid-nineteenth century and, coupled with the accelerating collection of social data, was taken to have unprecedented explanatory power.

Quantitative sociology arose in Europe, but Americans quickly caught on—in medical journals and political debates, in the continued expansion of the national census, in the growth of the annuity and insurance industries (which increasingly relied on statistics), and in the work of the American Statistical Association (founded in 1840, six years after Quetelet and Babbage started the Royal Statistical Society of London). By the 1840s, statistics pervaded print culture both as elements of arguments and as points of interest. As an 1847 magazine article put it, "The science of statistics may be considered as almost a new one in our country, [but] it has, nevertheless, of late excited much attention, and we see from the reports of Congress and of State, down to the newspaper press, the strongest evidences of its favor and progress." Percy Shelley among others worried about "the accumulation of facts and calculating processes," and not simply because, as Twain would later quip, there were three kinds of lies—lies, damn lies, and statistics.[30] The notion of fixed averages and social types, despite the contrary assurances of quantitative sociologists, implied a determinism based not on providential designs or mental philosophies of the will but on the dismal, inescapable logic of large numbers: if (as Quetelet's studies showed) crime, disease, and out-of-wedlock births occurred with remarkable regularity, then what in the world could a social reformer or self-possessive individual do? Proponents admired the theoretical elegance and practical applications of statistical analysis, but as Poe wrote in a review of James Russell Lowell, "[N]o individual considers himself as one of the mass" (*ER* 815).

Given their commitments to individual freedom, nonconforming genius, and in some cases moral perfectionism, American romantics might be expected to recoil from what Emerson once called "the terrible tabulation of the French statists."[31] From "The American Scholar" (1837) to *Representative Men* (1850), Emerson championed a less quantitative, more heroic theory of representative types. Yet he and other American romantics were ambivalent, if only because many appreciated the idea that—despite the ebb and flow of personal experience—nations, races, and humanity move toward a common telos generally formulated as the One toward which the many inevitably advance. Emerson eventually accepted some of Quetelet's determinism, paying tribute to statistics in "Fate" (1860). As we will see in chapter five, Thoreau worked extensively with data and averages, though he punned by calling them "mean." Whitman ends a long catalog of human types in "The Sleepers" (1855) with the pronouncement, "[t]hey are averaged now," and his 1855 preface to *Leaves of Grass* celebrates an American "largeness" that is "blind to particulars," so much so that the representative poet "is indifferent which chance happens" and finds "the law of perfection in masses."[32] Detaching quantitative sociology from the materialism of Comte, American transcendentalists found in the law of large numbers an analog of—and even a method for approaching—the chanceless domain of higher law.

For his part, Poe in "The Mystery of Marie Roget" is both intrigued and dissatisfied with statistical reasoning. Dupin initially glorifies probability theory: "[M]odern science has resolved to *calculate upon the unforeseen*. . . . *Accident* is admitted as a portion of the substructure. We make chance a matter of absolute calculation. We subject the unlooked for and unimagined to the mathematical *formulae* of the schools" (*PT* 534). Such enthusiasm for science is not atypical for Poe, but it proves hard to maintain in practice as he attempts to account for the Rogers murder using statistical reason. Early in "Roget," Poe asserts that young women disappear with "great frequency, in large cities," suggesting how quantitative sociology emerged with the rise of urban density and bureaucracy as the overwhelming vastness of social experience encouraged numerical representations and modes of analysis (*PT* 510). Critics have noted that Dupin in "Roget" engages in thumbnail statistical thinking: it is "probable" that Roget took "a route of more than average diversity from her accustomed ones" (*PT* 532); experience suggests that "[t]he chances are ten to one" that a spurned suitor returned to New York City (*PT* 537); "[i]n ninety-nine cases from the hundred" intuition is the best guide (*PT* 539); the chances are "one thousand to one" that certain evidence would come to light (*PT* 543).[33] Legal thinkers, particularly in France, had long held that the rational calculation of chances could lead toward truth in matters of criminal investigation. Poe through Dupin does his rational best to deploy probabilistic methods, but for all the tale's loose statistical cogitation, no credible solutions emerge.

By the end of "The Mystery of Marie Roget," Dupin and Poe must settle for indeterminacy as the story concludes with defensive disclaimers instead of self-satisfied revelations. Dupin complains of the law of large numbers: "The practice, *in mass,* is . . . philosophical; but it is not the less certain that it engenders vast individual error" (*PT* 530)—a charge repeated when the story ends by decrying the "mistakes which arise in the path of Reason through her propensity for seeking truth *in detail*" (*PT* 554).[34] Quetelet himself recognized the pitfalls of viewing subjects (as Dupin later echoes) "too closely." "[W]e must study the masses," Quetelet wrote, "with the view of separating from our observations all that is fortuitous or individual."[35] The problem is that the individual case matters most in "The Mystery of Marie Roget," and so Poe comes to side with an opponent of Quetelet—the mathematician and statistician Charles Dupin, who argued in 1836 that social behaviors, including crimes, were so complicated by contingencies that probability theorems could not reliably explain specific incidents. Poe had access to the work of Charles Dupin at West Point, while other theorists by the early 1840s—including Mill, Herschel, and Comte—further questioned Quetelet's bold applications of the law of large numbers to human life.[36] Whether Poe borrowed from them or made his own inferences, *his* Dupin demonstrates in the case of Roget the epistemological limits of statistical reasoning, a critique of probability theory with important aesthetic consequences.

Though symbolists and modernists have extracted artistic dictums from Poe, his fiction and poetry are often at odds with his aesthetic manifestos, which themselves are not always perfectly sincere or internally coherent. Poe's practical criticism is even more turbulent, in part because of personal intrigues: seldom has one reviewer issued so many injunctions with such animus in so short a time. One consistent factor in Poe's astringent literary judgment is his favoring of what "The Mystery of Marie Roget" calls "the unlooked for and unimagined" (*PT* 534). Poe quotes Bacon in his *Marginalia* (1846), "[T]here is no exquisite beauty without some *strangeness* in the proportions," and he goes on to laud in literature the "element of strangeness—of unexpectedness—of novelty—of originality" (*ER* 1381). This aesthetic is manifest in Poe's poetic theory, his obsessions with plagiarism, his reviews of Hawthorne's tales, and his own outré characters and plots. Nonetheless, and with a hypocrisy so brazen as to be almost endearing, Poe in his reviews frequently complains of "monstrously improbable" incidents (*ER* 328), "*ultra*-accident[s]" (*ER* 214), "absurd sacrifices of verisimilitude" (*ER* 154), and "ill adapted and improbable" events (*ER* 350)—sins that Poe's nemesis Thomas Dunn English charged to Poe himself when spoofing Poe's use of probability theory in 1848.[37] As early as 1837, Poe acknowledged tensions between his desires for the strange and the realistic. "Original characters, so called, can only be critically praised as such," Poe wrote, "when presenting qualities known in real life, but never before depicted, (a combination nearly impossible)" (*ER* 976). How one determines what best corresponds to "real life" is, of course, a thorny question, but as Poe pursues his nearly impossible task of writing both plausibly and unexpectedly, he finds potential aesthetic guidance in probabilistic reasoning.

In this Poe was not alone. Following the Aristotelian mimetic tradition, and voicing a widely held sentiment, the common-sense philosopher James Beattie asserted that "Fiction must be Probable, or Plausible," indicating (as Michael McKeon has argued) that in the eighteenth century, historical realism gives way to probabilistic verisimilitude as a standard for novelistic discourse, reflecting a broader intellectual shift from naïve toward more skeptical epistemologies. Douglas Patey has shown along similar lines that

Augustan writers followed classical traditions in understanding literary criticism as "a fundamentally probabilistic affair," though for Patey romantics begin to assert probabilistic perspectives less tethered to the object world (what is likely in nature) and more based on subjective judgments (what feels plausible under conditions established by the text).[38] Either way, chance was generally considered a weak explanation for narrative events in the eighteenth century and beyond. In his influential *Elements of Criticism* (1762), Lord Kames disparaged literature marked by the "vexations of blind chance": "Chance, giving an impression of anarchy and misrule, produces always a damp upon the mind." Antebellum reviewers generally agreed, but while probabilistic verisimilitude remained a measure for fiction in Poe's time, how probability was determined often went unexamined or was simply referred to as common sense, which may have something to do with a Poe complaint from 1841: "There is no criticism in this country—considering that word as the name of a science" (*ER* 161–62).[39]

The probabilistic revolution offered some hope that, if seldom explicitly named, held out the possibility of judging verisimilitude by something more precise than common sense. Citing the "law" that governs "the mass of the population," London's *Court and Lady's Magazine* wrote in 1837:

[A]ll fictions are subject to statistical laws, there are very wide limits of error, but still there are limits; the calculus of probabilities is applied to the measure and effects of action, of feeling, and even of emotion.... [The romancer's] success will be proportioned to the clearness of his perception of [the plot], and his adherence to the mathematical laws of its development.[40]

Five months later, a similar argument appeared in Philadelphia's *Gentleman's Magazine* (later renamed *Burton's Gentleman's Magazine*). William Burton himself probably wrote "Victor Hugo and the French Drama" (1837), which complains that Hugo's work "sets probability at defiance" before proposing statistical reasoning as the proper basis for judging "verisimilitude":

[I]t has been the fashion with novelists and penny scribblers to call upon the world to hold up their hands in wonderment at some circumstance illustrating the hackneyed truism, "Truth is often much stranger than fiction." To be sure it is: it would be exceedingly strange if it were not.... Fiction is based on statistics; it has a calculus of its own, and its estimate of probabilities often presents problems.... [F]iction deals not in the exceptions but the generalities of life[;] it is more or less the estimate of the mean proportional of humanity according to the most approved tables of Quetelet and Babbage.[41]

Michael Witmore has argued in the context of early modern England that Baconian empiricism linked extraordinary experiences with discoveries of natural law; or as Bacon wrote in *Novum Organum*, "[E]rrors of nature, freaks and monsters" serve to "reveal common forms."[42] Quetelet and Burton depart from this logic, advocating a statistical approach in which typicality established by large numbers most accurately indicates plausible truths by averaging out the anomalies of chance. Puritan origins and sentimental repetitions powerfully influence antebellum literary types, though statistical science offers an alternative basis for a more modern, more scientific typology that more readily admits its own constructedness insofar as averages are regarded as aggregative fictions, not ideal representations. Burton and the *Court Magazine* find in quantitative methods a new standard for realism, following Quetelet's claim in *Treatise on Man* that statistical science can lend "powerful assistance" to artists by keeping them "within due limits."[43]

It is highly probable that "Victor Hugo and the French Drama" made an impression on Poe. *Burton's Gentleman's Magazine* negatively reviewed Poe's fantastical novel, *The Narrative of Arthur Gordon Pym* (1838), chastising Poe for "outraging possibility" and foisting "a rapid succession of improbabilities [that] destroys the interest of the reader"— all this despite Poe's prefatory claim that seemingly implausible events have "the better chance of being received as truth" (*PT* 1008).[44] Despite *Burton's* rough handling of *Pym's* verisimilitude, the impoverished Poe served as William Burton's assistant editor from 1839 through 1840 before the alliance ended with a bitter fight in which Poe took exception to the *Pym* review. Shortly thereafter, Poe cribbed some ideas from "Victor Hugo and the French Drama" and began to explore the aesthetic implications of statistical reasoning, simultaneously adopting and proscribing Burton's use of Quetelet.

That Poe was drawn to statistics makes sense for personal and professional reasons. Not only did he have an abiding taste for logic and mathematics, as a struggling author, ambitious editor, shameless self-promoter, and denizen of major cities, Poe was sensitive to the workings of mass print markets, despite—and because—of a deeply held elitism that no amount of financial embarrassment could quell. Poe cited false circulation statistics to exaggerate his success at the *Southern Literary Messenger*; and during his stint at *The Gentleman's Magazine*, the magazine published "Statistics of French Periodical Literature" (1839), an article lamenting the "[t]housands and thousands" of Parisian journalists, "hundreds" of whom starve to death, despite the city's "twenty-seven daily political journals" and "seventy-seven newspapers."[45] Whether or not Poe had a hand in the article and its lengthy table of circulation statistics, he surely sympathized with the plight of fellow writers struggling to negotiate the print-market revolution. So sprawling was antebellum print culture that Poe, like many of his peers, turned to quantitative methods to conceptualize a literary scene that was beyond anyone's comprehension. Poe in 1841 mocked the typical editor who commented on "a flood of publications one tenth of whose title-pages he may possibly have turned over, three fourths of whose contents would be Hebrew to his most desperate efforts at comprehension, and whose entire mass and amount, as might be mathematically demonstrated, would be sufficient to occupy . . . the attention of some ten or twenty readers for a month!" (*ER* 1008). Increasingly embroiled in mass print markets, Poe's very life depended on managing large numbers, which he did most successfully with a carefully strategized sensationalism that may seem to reject but actually reflects the emerging statistical thinking (and feeling) of his time.[46]

Though working within the rational realm of the sciences, early quantitative sociologists were drawn to sensational subjects, if only to advertise their ability to predict the seemingly unpredictable variances of chance. Quetelet, who once aspired to a literary career, gushed in *Treatise on Man*: "Sad condition of humanity! We might even predict annually how many individuals will stain their hands with the blood of their fellow-men, how many will be forgers, how many will deal in poison." Simultaneously noetic and dramatic, such power helped speed the rise of statistics. It may be useful for underwriters and military outfitters to determine regularities in life span and height, but to do so is also to track anomalies—the oldest woman, the tallest man, or (my own childhood touchstones from the *Guinness Book of World Records*) the longest fingernails and the heaviest twins. Such statistical outliers, which Quetelet called "monstrosities," were the singular subjects of Barnum exhibits, but they also help constitute sociological averages and can be fascinating when combined with the force of large numbers.[47]

How enticing and paradoxical are frequent anomalies!—as when Quetelet sorted hundreds of murders by such categories as "Cutting, stabbing, and bruising instruments," "Strangulations," "Cudgels, cane, etc.," "[D]rowning," "Fire," and "Stones."[48] The utility of such distinctions is not readily apparent, which is simply to say that statistics are driven in part by a kind of sensationalism in which the quantification of extraordinary events makes them both less chancy and more interesting—more knowable, familiar, seemingly likely, and thus more emotionally stirring—for to calculate the risks under which one lives is both to tame chance and to acknowledge its power. Ruminating on our current information revolution, Kathleen Woodward calls the feeling "statistical panic": there always seems to be some mass shooting, natural disaster, or recently discovered carcinogen, rendering our relations to risk "strangely unnerving and numbing."[49] Poe's weirdly rational approach to terror is marked by the doubleness that Woodward describes, as are dry antebellum statistical studies whose subjects read like a list of Poe données—suicide, insanity, crime, and death, often tracked by gender, nationality, and race. Quetelet studied the rate of marriage between women in their sixties and men in their twenties, a proposition Poe exploits in "The Spectacles" (1844), and probability theorists often cited a study on the regularity of dead letters in the Paris post office, a subject for Melville in "Bartleby, the Scrivener" (1853) and Poe in "The Purloined Letter." As early as 1717, De Moivre noted that the attractions of the doctrine of chances include "Surprize and Entertainment."[50] This is certainly true for Dupin, who—like many gamblers and readers of detective fiction—indulges in probabilistic thinking in part for pleasure's sake.

And yet, for all its piquant potential and broadening popularity in antebellum culture, statistical reasoning proves an aesthetic liability in "The Mystery of Marie Roget." The story is definitely worth reading, but most students and anthologies prefer Dupin's other tales. Characters in "Roget," including Dupin, lack individuation as personal motives and identities give way to sociological claims about how types—sailors, children, jilted lovers, etc.—tend to behave as a group. As with "The Murders in the Rue Morgue," the tale's patient pacing initially suggests preparation for a stunning conclusion, but the more "Roget" piles on facts and recycles conjectures, the more Poe seems to be stalling, so much that readers may find themselves longing for an overdetermining clue. The investigation—premised as it is on statistical thinking, not on intuitive genius—can even make the evil of the crime feel banal, particularly when it is called an *"ordinary"* case with "nothing peculiarly *outré* about it" (*PT* 519). The story does have sexually charged details; and as David Van Leer and Mark Seltzer point out, the knowledge that young women disappear with great frequency can make "Roget" feel terribly modern, especially in light of the historical fact that Rogers died from a botched abortion.[51]

Nonetheless, Poe fails to vivify characters and actions in a story ruled by large numbers, a problem that Quetelet himself predicted when differentiating the generalities of statistical science from the specificity of literature (a distinction made by other sociologists from Tocqueville to Weber and Durkheim).[52] "It is the social body which forms the object of our researches," wrote Quetelet, "and not the peculiarities distinguishing the individuals composing it.... [T]he literary man and the artist, on the contrary, will endeavour to understand, in preference, those peculiarities which we endeavour to separate from our results."[53] Both Charles and C. Auguste Dupin agree that statistical reasoning can explain the plausibility and even inevitability of monstrosities, but the law of large numbers is not the right tool for analyzing individual subjects, particularly in the hands of an author like Poe, whose best fiction is always to some degree psychological. It is thematically fitting and dramatically unfulfilling that the immense amount of data reported on Roget figuratively drowns her individuality. As suggested by the lingering question of whether the decomposed corpse is even hers, the statistical accounting of the social body effaces the person of Roget.

An earlier Poe story, "The Man of the Crowd," makes a similar point more skillfully, self-consciously exploiting tensions between literary sensibilities and statistical types. The story's narrator begins as a statistical reasoner whose observations of a bustling city street take "an abstract and generalizing turn": "I looked at the passengers in masses, and thought of them in their aggregate relations" (PT 389). Exemplifying Georg Simmel's point that the flaneur is a kind of urban sociologist, the narrator then "descend[s] to details," invoking various social categories—different "classes" of businessmen, the "tribe" of clerks, "gamblers," "Jew pedlars," and so forth (PT 389–91).[54] Not until nightfall does he undertake an "examination of individual faces," ultimately tailing an elderly man who has a random air of "idiosyncracy" (PT 392). The twist is that this seemingly singular individual forever seeks out crowds and remains inaccessible, thus violating the reader's expectation for a dramatic unveiling and prompting the narrator to dub the old man a "type" and name him "the man of the crowd" (PT 396). The man can thus represent Quetelet's average man who is "only the type of a people," a statistical composite with no individual existence outside the law of large numbers (that is, crowds). Such statistical typology departs significantly from the analogical inclinations of romanticism. Wordsworth in The Prelude (1850) calls the blind beggar of London a "type" who teaches that even "freaks of Nature" point to an "ennobling Harmony." By contrast, Poe's urban wanderer remains a dehumanized figure as artificial as the concept of 2.3 children. Quetelet himself called his average man a "fictional being," as did Charles Peirce in his essay, "The Doctrine of Chances" (1878). Like them, Poe recognizes that statistical composites are powerful analytic constructs, though Poe more poignantly realizes that such fictions are not the stuff of literature except by way of irony.[55]

In "The Man of the Crowd" and related stories, Poe shows that Quetelet's "average man" and "social body" are not as knowable as quantitative sociologists may think. In "The Man That Was Used Up" (1839), the artificiality of the average man is figured by General John A. B. C. Smith, whose title, name, and ultimate decomposition suggest that statistical composites literally fall to pieces when one looks for individuals behind the mask of generalities. "The Literary Life of Thingum Bob, Esq." (1844) shifts attention to the publishing industry in that the narrator, a famous magazine editor, is the namesake for a mass print culture that effaces personal identity. "The Man of the Crowd" more seriously dramatizes the epistemological and aesthetic limits of statistical reasoning, for—unlike "Roget"—the primary purpose of the story is *not* to solve the puzzle at hand. Poe announces from the start that some "mysteries . . . will not *suffer themselves* to be revealed," just like a book (Poe repeats twice) that "does not permit itself to be read" (*PT* 388). The unexpected ending of "The Man of the Crowd" enacts the failure of statistical sociology, even as it eschews the stronger moral critiques of, say, Harriet Martineau's *Illustrations of Political Economy* (1832–34), Dickens's *Hard Times*, Melville's "The Paradise of Bachelors and the Tartarus of Maids" (1855), and Stephen Crane's "The Men in the Storm" (1894) and *The Monster* (1898). "The Man of the Crowd" may even comment on the difficulty of gauging popular culture, a problem that Wilkie Collins (that great follower of Poe) addressed in "The Unknown Public" (1858) when arguing that no amount of quantitative research can comprehend "the mysterious, the unfathomable, the universal public."[56] Perhaps "The Man of the Crowd" embodies Poe's worst professional nightmare, as a sharp-eyed observer of urban life watches an unmasterable mass audience dwindle to a solitary and still unknowable figure.

If "The Man of the Crowd" is an allegory for authorial anxiety under the risky and opaque conditions of print culture, it also exacts for Poe a measure of personal revenge— not so much on Quetelet, who makes careful distinctions between art and the new sciences of chance, as on diddlers, who would subordinate imaginative literature to probabilistic methods they do not fully grasp. Five months after William Burton fired him, Poe published "The Man of the Crowd" in the very magazine Burton had recently sold. Poe's story implies how fatuous "Victor Hugo and the French Drama" is, for tales "based on statistics" cannot get at reality, stories using "the tables of Quetelet and Babbage" are not to be read, literature that focuses on large numbers misses the lineaments of the strange, and reviewers who complain of Poe's improbabilities do not recognize that anomalies are not only probable and real but actually constitute averages in the first place. In art as in life, the power of chance cannot be kept within due limits.

Of all Poe's works, "The Angel of the Odd" most aggressively condemns statistical reasoning for too narrowly construing plausibility, a critique that points beyond Poe's writings to broader literary-historical narratives. "The Angel of the Odd" opens with a testy narrator doubting press reports of "odd accidents" and "improbable possibilities." "For my own part," he writes, "I intend to believe nothing henceforward that has anything of the 'singular' about it" (*PT* 757). Enter suddenly the Angel of the Odd, a creature who is made of empty bottles and a keg, speaks in a mock German accent, and whose self-stated business is to "bring about the *odd accidents* which are continually astonishing the skeptic" (*PT* 759). After the angel gets him drunk, the narrator smashes a clock and passes out reading Robert Montgomery's "The Omnipresence of the Deity" (1828), a popular poem that dismisses "dismal Chance" in favor of the argument from design.[57] With providential texts unread and William Paley's symbol for a chanceless universe broken, the story relates a series of terrible, horrible, no good events that, as in "The Murders in the Rue Morgue," dramatize the incursions of chance into a supposedly closed system. A rat steals the narrator's lighted candle, disappears into a hole in the wall, and sets the house on fire. When the narrator escapes via a ladder, he is knocked off by a hog and breaks his arm. His hair is also burned off, ruining his engagement and pushing him to suicide. However, a bird snatches his wig as he goes to drown himself, and while chasing the bird, the narrator runs off a cliff, only to land on a passing balloon piloted by the Angel of the Odd, who forces him to admit "te possibility of te odd" before dropping him down the chimney of his gutted house (*PT* 764). Justifying its subtitle, "An Extravaganza," "The Angel of the Odd" rushes beyond the due limits of probability as causal connections defy belief and prediction. It's just one damn thing after another.

What madcap pleasure there is in "The Angel of the Odd" is on the order of *Tristram Shandy* (1767), Buster Keaton, and Wile E. Coyote. If accidents in early modern literature often signify providence (as Witmore has argued), unlikely chains of unlikely events also have a comic side that does not rely on faith or even the suspension of disbelief but instead takes disbelief itself as its subject and narrative logic.[58] This does not mean that "The Angel of the Odd" utterly lacks a didactic impulse. The culminating irony of the story is that the narrator, in keeping with his refusal to credit improbable events, has recently failed to renew his house insurance. Proponents of insurance in the nineteenth century sought to alter such imprudence, as in an 1847 article quoting the notable political economist J. R. McCulloch:

> [W]hat we call chances, are, indeed, chances to the individual, but are subject to a general law of regularity in the aggregate. 'The number of births, marriages, deaths, . . . and houses burned, and a vast variety of other apparently accidental events, are yet, when our experience embraces a sufficiently wide field, found to be nearly equal in equal periods of time.' . . . Instead of asking why events happen thus regularly, may we not rather ask, why should they not?[59]

"The Angel of the Odd" can feel sophomoric as Poe flaunts his reputation for the Germanic and alcoholic, though the tale, like so many of Poe's fictions, also bristles with meta-critical self-defense. Poe may mock the argument from design by inventing so ridiculous a heavenly agent, and yet the Angel of the Odd reminds the scoffer that improbabilities, even miracles, are possible. Embracing both the radical possibilities of chance and efforts to manage them through insurance, Poe's story is simultaneously a satire on natural theology and a rejection of utter skepticism.

More centrally, "The Angel of the Odd" disrupts normative relations between aesthetics and probability, for the foolish narrator shares the narrow outlook of readers like Burton and Thomas Dunn English, who fail to recognize that singularly unlikely occurrences are within the realm of plausibility.[60] The point can be argued from experience, especially in an information-saturated culture: there always seems to be someone winning her fifth lottery, some professional baseball player hitting his mother with a foul ball, or some Calvinist minister surviving a fall from the rooftop of his church. The point can also be made theoretically. Aristotle in the *Poetics* found much literary license in probabilistic approaches to verisimilitude: "[E]ven an oddity is possible. . . . [I]t is probable that improbable things will happen." Commenting on vast causal chains, Jeremy Bentham in 1825 went so far as to claim that "nothing can happen that is not infinitely improbable," a view Peirce shared when considering endless contingencies: "[E]verything which happens is infinitely improbable." The mathematician John Venn agreed in *The Logic of Chance* (1866) in a section titled, "Extraordinary stories not necessarily less probable." Such openness to chance in narrative matters was largely repressed in eighteenth- and nineteenth-century aesthetics, and yet Aristotelian vindications of improbable plots, even when inexactly formulated as in the *Poetics*, echo across modern fiction.[61]

Examples privileging proximities to Poe might include the following. Balzac's Vautrin from *Père Goriot* (1835) is—like Dupin and their shared historical source, Eugéne Vidocq—a calculator of probabilities who rationally defends the wild possibilities of chance. Following Balzac, Dickens refers to his own mimetic practices as "fantastic fidelity," a defense of the odd that he voices in his prefaces and through his own detective, Inspector Bucket. Collins argued in 1852 that "extraordinary accidents and events" in fiction were as legitimate as "the ordinary accidents and events which may, and do, happen to us all." That same year, Hawthorne in his preface to *The Blithedale Romance* (1852) asked for "license with regard to every-day Probability," in part because "there is as yet no such Faery Land, so like the real world." In "The Art of Fiction" (1884), Henry James asserted that plots are properly driven by "queer elements of the accidental and the arbitrary," while Conrad's narrator in *Lord Jim* (1900) says to Marlow, "It is always the unexpected that happens." This is often the case in postmodern works that draw on Poe's detective fiction. Paul Auster's *New York Trilogy* (1985–86) proclaims in its second sentence, "[N]othing was real except chance," while Tom Stoppard's *Hapgood* (1988) alludes to Poe in its ruminations on the chances of quantum physics.[62] Whether regarding chance as an ontological reality or an epistemological limit, Poe and other writers have sought to liberate imaginative literature from probabilistic constraints, not by rejecting probabilistic verisimilitude as such but by insisting on its extravagant potential. As Dupin says in "The Murders in the Rue Morgue" about the improbability of the gold not figuring in the crime: "Coincidences ten times as remarkable . . . happen to us all every hour of our lives, without attracting even momentary notice. Coincidences, in general, are great stumbling-blocks in the way of that class of thinkers who have been educated to know nothing of the theory of probabilities" (*PT* 421).

Taken together, "The Mystery of Marie Roget," "The Man of the Crowd," and "The Angel of the Odd" might seem to subvert probabilistic notions of realism as understood through statistical reasoning: frequentism does not apply to individual cases; the average man is an impossible character; with everything a viable possibility, no plot twist or readerly expectation is beyond the bounds of legitimacy. Yet Poe's interest in probabilistic aesthetics maintains a commitment to realism, and not simply by making the Hawthornian argument that romances operate by their own rules. Poe's poetic theory generally prefers imaginative freedoms to referents in the object world, but "The Philosophy of Composition" insists with some earnestness on respecting "the limits of the real" (*ER* 24). Poe's comments on fiction sometimes indulge the romantic tendency to valorize subjective effects, though Poe's fictional practices (like his 1841 review of Dickens) vindicate extraordinary characters and plots on realist grounds by insisting that the fantastic is not beyond plausibility, that probability theory rightly construed shows that truth can be originally strange, so much so that we might read Poe's raven as a black swan. For both author and critic, the challenge of literature is not precisely to suspend disbelief but, rather, to expect the unexpected. Poe everywhere tries to surprise his readers—even as he chides them for being surprised, even as he worries (as in his last review of Hawthorne) that under untrammeled conditions of chance *"novelty becomes nothing novel"* (*ER* 580).

THINGS EXTERNAL TO THE GAME

As a taut, intensely meta-critical story that builds on Dupin's previous adventures, "The Purloined Letter" has been taken to be one of Poe's most radically indeterminate texts. Whether formulated in terms of semiotic instability or post-Cartesian paradoxes of the self, readings of the story argue that interpretation can never be complete and that Dupin's methods of inquiry force us to confront the limitations of our own.[63] "The Purloined Letter" is indeed about skepticism broadly construed, though the focus need not be on post-structuralism or even solely on the tale's relation to ideas, and instead can be shifted to everyday practices and a cultural logic of pragmatism, thereby retaining the tale's epistemological modernity without ceding its historical ground. Discussions of chance in the antebellum period help to synthesize these critical imperatives, for as extraordinary as "The Purloined Letter" is, it also participates in popular debates over probabilistic thinking—so much so that indeterminacy and undecidability need not be the final words on the tale.

Perhaps chastened by the debacle of "The Mystery of Marie Roget," Poe in "The Purloined Letter" returns to what worked in "The Murders in the Rue Morgue"—a seemingly closed room, a fully imagined crime, the intuition of a genius, and the application of probability theory to an extraordinary case. What most differentiates "The Purloined Letter" from "The Murders in the Rue Morgue" is that the antagonist is not an orangutan but the Minister D—, a fellow mathematician and poet who makes Dupin's deployment of probability theory analogous to that of a gamer, a dynamic suggested by the inset story of a boy who masters the game of even and odd. Though the boy employs a "principle of guessing," he is not simply as some would have it "'lucky,'" for his method entails the "identification of the reasoner's intellect with that of his opponent" (*PT* 689). The process begins empirically with "observation and admeasurement" but eventually points to something like intuition when the boy says, "I fashion the expression of my face, as accurately as possible, in accordance with the expression of [the opponent], and then wait to see what thoughts or sentiments arise in my mind or heart" (*PT* 690). Barbara Johnson has found in the play between even and odd an unending struggle between symmetrical order and open-ended uncertainty.[64] Yet Dupin's repeated emphasis on "odd" also points toward the odds of probability theory, for we can attribute the boy's success to unconscious calculation, in part because of a possible source text for "The Purloined Letter."

Appearing two years before Poe's story in the South Carolina magazine, *The Magnolia*, "The Philosophy of Chance" (1842) connects the doctrine of chances, intuition, and facial expressions. With nods to Pascal, the Bernouillis, Euler, Gauss, and Laplace, the article glosses the calculus of probabilities, moving from strictly mathematical advances to the sociological applications of Quetelet. The article then discusses how probability theory "extends also to mental phenomena," including "that peculiar kind of sympathy . . . by which the muscles of our face are contracted, when we behold another laugh or yawn." Such mirroring (or aping) allows people to share "[k]indred feelings and sensations" in that their similar physiological actions are associated with similar psychological states. According to the article, these associations are primarily unconscious, coming "not so much to the whole head, but to a certain part, to a particular corner of it, just as one is apt to explore only certain compartments of a bureau for a mislaid paper, where alone some mysterious presentiment tells him that it is to be found."[65] Assimilating probability theory with sentimental philosophy, associationist psychology, physiology, and even phrenology, "The Philosophy of Chance" draws on intellectual discourses familiar to Poe and Dupin. There is no hard evidence that Poe read the article, though both it and "The Purloined Letter" use a missing paper to discuss intuition as a form of probabilistic reasoning that occurs through opaque, unconscious associations between facial expressions and feelings. Both texts also suppose that probability theory operates through and in the body, for unconscious calculation—which directs prediction, hypothesizing, and decision making—is not only a feeling of the mind but also involves physiological processes.

Probabilism is further formulated as a materially embedded practice when "The Purloined Letter" enters into antebellum debates over chance. For Tocqueville, "The whole life of an American is passed like a game of chance," and Jackson Lears has argued that nineteenth-century Americans were especially preoccupied with luck—in part because of the frontier and entrepreneurial risk taking that marked American identity (real and imagined), in part because this ethos became increasingly prevalent with the market revolution, and in part because (Tocqueville notwithstanding) a reactionary strain of rational Protestantism sought to limit the rise of chance. The probabilistic revolution in the United States played out in ideas and culture through a dialectical process in which probability theory shaped and was shaped by its uses in everyday life. For Lears and others, the probabilistic revolution did not commence in the United States until the later nineteenth century, though Poe's references to gaming in his ratiocinative tales represent an important pre-history.[66]

At the start of "The Murders in the Rue Morgue," Poe favorably contrasts whist to chess, primarily because whist (a card game similar to bridge) involves chance and so entails "things external to the game"—the luck of the deal, the accidental dropping of a card, an opponent's unintentional gesture that might serve as a tell (PT 399). Poe continues to subordinate the rectilinear logic of chess to the chanciness of whist, as when "Roget" criticizes the "rectangular precepts of the court" (PT 529) and when the police in "The Purloined Letter" fruitlessly search for the missive by "dividing the surface of the [Minister D—'s] building into registered square inches" that resemble a chessboard (PT 690). "The Purloined Letter" also mentions the "game of puzzles . . . played upon a map" in which one player identifies a word on the map that an opponent must then find (PT 694). The trick, Dupin says, is not to name a small word but, rather, a large one that stretches across multiple grids, for the chesslike mind of a logical opponent will not think outside such boxes.

Dupin's triumph in "The Purloined Letter" vindicates his whistlike methods, which emphasize probabilistic reasoning over rational exactitude. The king and queen of the story can point to either chess or whist, but Dupin knows that the Minister D—must keep the letter "at hand," and he ultimately discovers the missive concealed in a rack of "cards" (*PT* 695). His success is well compensated, for by declining to help until the reward is raised, Dupin takes odds—as in many versions of whist—to maximize his winnings. As in "Maelzel's Chess-Player," Poe's essay exposing a dwarf hidden inside a supposed chess automaton, something odd lurks within what are taken to be square and even models of reason. Fifty years later, Sherlock Holmes worried about such extrarational forces in "The Adventure of the Cardboard Box" (1892)—a story that mentions "The Murders in the Rue Morgue," features a box containing two severed ears, and whose title suggests both the boxes of a chessboard and the playing cards of whist. Though Holmes correctly identifies the murderer in the story, he ends with a haunting question: "What object is served by this circle of misery and violence and fear? It must tend to some end, or else our universe is ruled by chance, which is unthinkable."[67] But is it so unthinkable for Poe? Is Poe, as he is often portrayed, a singular post-Enlightenment thinker prefiguring modern skepticism? Or is he, as has been increasingly recognized, a writer in tune with his era, including his era's increasingly contested but still powerful beliefs in teleological order? Put somewhat differently, should we think of Poe as antifoundational or antebellum? Considering how chance pushed the nineteenth century toward modernity, the most likely answer seems yes.[68]

By contrasting chess and whist, Poe joins in a broad contemporary discussion of chance, even if the debate was not always phrased in explicit philosophical or scientific terms. Reflecting the reformist zeal of the age, an 1836 article from the *Baltimore Monument* warned that chess ruined young morals and minds, as demonstrated by the story of a chess prodigy who became a gambler and was killed in a card game. For the author, the tragic connection was clear: "[B]oth were games of chance." Most commentators, however, followed the lead of Benjamin Franklin's "The Morals of Chess" (1786) and Maria Edgeworth's *Practical Education* (1801) in associating chess with mental discipline, foresight, and rational certitude. Responding to a review of a conduct manual that described gaming as hazardous to children, an 1838 letter to *The American Annals of Education* differentiated "games of *chance* and games of *contrivance*" insofar as the later— including chess and "other games of calculation"—inculcate rational habits. As New York's *Family Magazine* claimed in 1837, "One of the greatest charms of [chess] lies, no doubt, in the circumstance, that whilst man is everywhere surrounded by chance, in this game . . . he has entirely excluded it." It was the exclusion of chance that for many antebellum observers qualified chess as a scientific pursuit.[69]

Whist with its obvious element of chance was frequently contrasted to chess not only as a cultural activity but also as a methodological model. In Charles Lamb's oftreprinted sketch, "Mrs. Battle's Opinions of Whist" (1823), the whist-loving protagonist "could not conceive of a *game* wanting the spritely infusion of chance," so much so that chess inspired her with "insufferable horror and ennui." In his 1838 history of card games, William Chatto quoted the linguist William Jones who during his lengthy travels in India found a version of chess that included dice. For Jones, the introduction of chance "seems to exclude [such] Chess from the rank which has been assigned to it among the sciences, and to give the game before us the appearance of *Whist*." Along similar lines, *Godey's Lady's Book* referred in 1844 to "the science of Chess" and that same year satirized similar claims for whist in a story by none other than (sweet revenge!) William Burton, who created a drunken, pseudo-aristocratic college gambler vaguely reminiscent of Poe. With a burst of sophistry resembling Poe's praise of whist in "The Murders in the Rue Morgue," the villain tries to entice a virtuous freshman into cards: "The abstract contemplativeness of a good whist-player is peculiarly adapted to the formation of a metaphysical state of mind; the 'throws' of a pair of dice are integral portions of sexagesimals, and, therefore, are logistic, if not logical in effect." Burton and others linked whist with gambling, alcohol, licentiousness, and violence, and biographies of Hume associated the game with atheistic skepticism, making much of the fact that Hume played whist on his deathbed instead of turning his thoughts toward God. Whist was seen as a kind of gateway drug, though as the jargon of Burton's villain suggests— and as Poe himself evinces—a minority of voices in Britain and America defended games of chance in scientific terms.[70]

Blackwood's Magazine in 1835 was not alone in referring to "the science of whist." Whist handbooks offered probability tables on the distribution of high cards and suits, as did Jonathan Harrington Green's popular work, *An Exposure of the Arts and Miseries of Gambling* (1843), which combined moralistic condemnations of gambling with probabilistic advice on how to do it well (including pointers on whist, which Green described as "one of the most scientific of all the games"). In an 1875 Piccadilly exhibition that would surely have fascinated Poe, the whist-playing automaton, Psycho, impressed the whist expert William Pole, who described the machine performing the "arithmetic calculations" required by the "'Modern Scientific Game'" of whist. By the time Pole wrote *The Philosophy of Whist* in 1884, it was the presence, not the absence, of chance that legitimized the game as a science:

> It may perhaps be thought that the existence of the element of chance to such a large extent in Whist tends to lower its intellectual character as compared with other games, such as chess. . . . [But] the element of chance, so far from standing in the way of intellectual exercise, is what chiefly gives the opportunity for it. . . . [T]he calculations, provisions, and speculation, arising out of many uncertainties occurring in Whist-play, furnish the most important objects for scientific investigation.

Pole later argued in his *Evolution of Whist* (1894) that "the calculation of probabilities" and the "doctrine of chances" made whist a particularly scientific game, indicating how games of chance became increasingly acceptable in the later nineteenth century, coinciding with the advent of Darwinism, literary naturalism, and pragmatism—traditions that all participate in the probabilistic revolution in America.[71]

Poe's anticipation of such thinking makes him both a part and ahead of his time, for if like many of his contemporaries he contrasts the rational exactitude of chess with the chanciness of whist, unlike most he takes whist as a more accurate model for rational inquiry in an aleatory world, even as he fails to acknowledge consistently that chance can be managed but never mastered. Especially in the first half of the nineteenth century, probability theorists who allowed that chance could influence individual outcomes also paid tribute to what Laplace called "the great laws of nature," including Quetelet who claimed, "[A]ll is lawlike: only our ignorance leads us to suppose that all is subject to the whims of chance."[72] Poe himself writes in "The Mystery of Marie Roget," "[God's] laws were fashioned to embrace *all* contingencies," and he proceeds to misapprehend an example from Laplace, claiming that if two consecutive die rolls turn sixes, the chance of another six coming up is diminished—the so-called gambler's fallacy, which mistakenly holds that past outcomes affect specific future trials (*PT* 553).[73] Poe continues with such teleological reasoning in *Eureka* when announcing that "[t]he plots of God are perfect" (*PT* 1342). The problem Poe names but does not adequately credit is that infinity does not occur within human time, so that two sixes in a row are so infinitesimal a sample as to have no predictive value. That Poe falls into the gambler's fallacy might explain his early exit from the University of Virginia. It also suggests that Benjamin overestimates Poe's rejection of teleological progress, and that Mallarmé understands more clearly than Poe that dice—thrown once, thrown repeatedly, or never thrown at all—will never abolish the power of "CHANCE." As with his aesthetics, Poe's thinking on chance veers between the traditional and radical.[74]

Poe's itinerant faith in perfect plots indicates a recurrent attraction to triumphal Enlightenment logic, even as Poe elsewhere suggests how chance and its role in gaming blur binaristic distinctions between reason and madness. In this Poe joins a strand of literary history showing how rationalists and gamblers alike are susceptible to the fantasy that—given enough patience, methodological discipline, and chips—total order will be realized. Before Benjamin, Samuel Johnson recognized that the capitalist work ethic has deep affinities with the rage for gambling, as when the industrious merchant of *Rambler* 181 (1751) turns his calculative energies to the taming of chance, rolling a die 330,000 times in an effort to master the lottery only to learn after gambling away his life that "few minds [are] sufficiently firm to be trusted in the hands of chance." This is certainly true of Little Nell's grandfather in *The Old Curiosity Shop* (1841), a novel Poe reviewed. And Dostoyevsky, a fan of Poe and another disastrous bettor, also portrays a rational rage for order in *The Gambler* (1866) when roulette players studiously record past outcomes only to turn into frenzied brutes once the wheel begins to spin. Gwendolen Harleth of *Daniel Deronda* (1877) is another risk taker "sanely capable of picturing balanced probabilities" until she painfully learns that "[r]oulette encourages a romantic superstition as to the chances of the game." Much of Poe's work explores instances of what Colin Dayan has called the "convertibility" of reason and irrationality.[75] If Poe never clearly registers the difference between degrees of belief and frequentist methods, he remains sensitive to the world-shaking possibilities of chance, despite—and in powerful ways, because of—his unconsummated pursuit of pure reason. Poe seldom takes half measures or shies from extreme conclusions, and he entertains questions that Laplace, Quetelet, and Sherlock Holmes did not countenance. What if (contra Einstein) God does play dice with us? And what if (contra Emerson) the dice are not loaded but instead are subject to fundamental forces of chance?

Such questions involve Poe in a main narrative of nineteenth-century probability theory: the fitful emergence of what Hacking, following Peirce, calls "absolute chance." Crossing a line that probability science had approached but never explicitly transgressed, Peirce—at his most radical—located chance not in finite subjectivity or disaggregated instances but in the very fabric of the experienced world. Peirce wrote in 1893: "Chance itself pours in at every avenue of sense: it is of all things the most obtrusive. That it is absolute is the most manifest of all intellectual perceptions." Peirce did not envision an utterly random universe in which doctrines of chance have no purchase, but when facing the problem of induction and the threat of determinism, he insisted on "an element of lawlessness in the universe" and a "principle of irregularity, indeterminacy, [and] chance." As suggested by the fact that absolute chance is something of an oxymoron, Peirce was inconsistent in his views on chance and, like Poe, was tempted by teleological order, particularly in his meta-frequentist (and vaguely Hegelian) view that even the variances of natural law tended over time toward unity. Nonetheless, as Hacking writes, "Peirce is the strongest possible indicator that certain things which cannot be expressed at the end of the eighteenth century were said at the end of the nineteenth." Or even in the middle of the century, if we take Poe's detective fiction seriously enough.[76]

To a provocative extent, "The Purloined Letter" precedes and in some ways goes further than Peirce in dismantling mechanistic accounts of the universe without substituting a transcendental telos or foundational system of logic. As brilliant, disorganized, self-destructive theorists who suffered from delusions of grandeur and literally wrote on the verge of starvation, Poe and Peirce felt keenly the discrepancy between their beautiful ideas and imperfect realities. How tempting to attribute life's disappointments to the vicissitudes of chance instead of, say, personal mistakes or a perverse resistance to the systematic order one craves. Perhaps even the intellectual openness that Poe and Peirce exhibit toward the possibilities of chance first required some traumatic aleatory experience to counter the providential and self-possessive ideologies that so dominated nineteenth-century America. To read Poe and Peirce together on chance is to be struck by an array of uncanny affinities. As an alternative to induction and deduction, Poe's sense of intuition, as Nancy Harrowitz and Paul Grimstad have argued, is similar to Peirce's concept of "abduction" (which he also refers to as "guessing").[77] Like Poe and Dupin, Peirce believes that "logic needs the help of esthetics," in part because of "the impossibility of distinguishing intellectual results from intuitional data." Intuition for Peirce is a kind of unconscious calculation—"the feeling of a thought" manifest "in our bodies." Peirce also quotes Poe occasionally in his writings, discusses the search for a mislaid paper in "Design and Chance," penned a copy of "The Raven" in weirdly elongated calligraphy, and exhibited an interest in using probabilistic methods to untangle real world crimes.[78] As thinkers whose commitments to logic push them to the limitations of logic itself, Poe and Peirce acknowledge the extra-rational, intertwined claims of intuition, feeling, and chance.

Most strikingly, Poe and Peirce do not regard a world in which absolute chance plays a role as unthinkable or entirely unmanageable. For Peirce, particularly in his early writings, individuals and societies do best to adopt empirical, fallibilist, pluralistic approaches that rely on probabilistic methods without assuming the static laws of Quetelet and Laplace.[79] "The Purloined Letter" may seem by contrast thoroughly teleological: there is little clue gathering, careful conjecturing, or patient unwinding of a solution, as if Poe has tired of detective fiction even as he is inventing the genre. But if the cocksure Dupin appears to act unerringly, he actually follows a Peirce-like scientific method. Upon entering the apartment of the Minster D—, he initially suspects that the letter is on a table until "long and very deliberate scrutiny" convinces him otherwise (PT 695). He then sees a crumpled letter in a rack of cards and "conclude[s]" that it is the stolen missive, a by now familiar leap in logic we can attribute to probabilistic intuition (PT 696). Yet Dupin's conclusion is really a hypothesis, for he examines the letter more closely "to be sure" and finds it "strongly corroborative of suspicion" before ultimately judging the sum of his evidence and intuition "sufficient" proof. Though his deliberations and inferences are dramatically telescoped (and thus often missed by readers), Dupin in "The Purloined Letter" observes, hypothesizes, and tests, as in "The Murders in the Rue Morgue." Once again he is decidedly effective because he listens to his intuition, not as an infallible revelation that cannot be verified but, rather, as an unconscious but calculated guess that being probabilistic requires corroboration.

Even further, Dupin's methods in "The Purloined Letter" are surprisingly pluralistic. After Dupin condemns the Parisian police for considering "only their *own* ideas of ingenuity" and for having "no variation of principle in their investigations" (*PT* 690), the narrator mentions Dupin's "quarrel . . . with some of the algebraists of Paris" (*PT* 692). Dupin remonstrates that, despite what such algebraists claim, they do not deal in "abstract or general truths," for such truths "are only truths within the limits of *relation*" and therefore must, like the behavior of the Minister D—, be considered "with reference to the circumstances" (*PT* 693). In Irwin's words, Dupin recognizes "the conditionality of many of the traditional certainties in mathematics and logic," but if Dupin's quarrel with pure ideation can push interpretation toward the history of mathematics, it also turns Poe's tales of ratiocination further in the direction of pragmatism.

"The Purloined Letter" invites philosophical inquiry, though what philosophy one uses matters. Post-structuralist readings of the tale tend to emphasize the circulating and unrevealed contents of the missive—when Derrida accuses Lacan of misapplying an essentialist frame, or when Joseph Riddel (drawing on Lacan and Derrida) calls the letter "a sign that is always elsewhere." Following Barbara Johnson, Shawn Rosenheim finds a "semiotic purity" in the story. But if deconstruction more than any other critical tradition has made visible the spectacular linguistic play and irreducible indeterminacies of "The Purloined Letter," deconstructive readings have also (quoting Irwin) induced "intellectual vertigo" and obscured what Stanley Cavell regards as Poe's efforts to leave behind, or at least come to terms with, semiotic forms of skepticism. It is as if Poe reminds us of Hegel's point that skepticism requires some definite content to act upon.[80]

From a pragmatist perspective, one might go so far as to wonder what difference the contents of the purloined signifier might make. As William James wrote in "What Pragmatism Means" (1907), "There can *be* no difference anywhere that does n't *make* a difference elsewhere—no difference in abstract truth which does n't express itself in a difference in concrete fact and in conduct consequent upon the fact, imposed on somebody, somehow, somewhere, and somewhen."[81] "The Purloined Letter" can elegantly prefigure deconstruction, but even when one resists lazy conflations of *différance* and undifferentiated indeterminacy, Poe's story remains more committed to instrumental action and more embedded in specific historical contexts than post-structural readings have allowed. Dupin's methods are remarkably successful in leading to his desired outcome, so much so that to focus too much on aporia is to make the mistake of the Parisian police by overlooking some obvious facts: Dupin solves the crime, takes his revenge, furthers his royalist agenda, and gets paid. This is not to reduce "The Purloined Letter" to some putatively pragmatist cash value, nor is it to follow Rorty and others in aggressively divorcing deconstruction from practical agency.[82] Rather, to stress Dupin's epistemological sufficiency is to return to Poe's claim in "The Murders in the Rue Morgue" that we appreciate methods "only in their effects" (*PT* 397) and that truth is "invariably superficial" (*PT* 412). Because "The Purloined Letter" does not rest its case on foundational or absolute truths, the story never reaches a point of utter skepticism, settling instead for acceptable consequences. Most students in my experience must be reminded to ask the questions that "The Purloined Letter" leaves hanging, for despite the tale's abiding mysteries (the contents of the letter; what happens in Vienna), it concludes with a satisfying enough sense of totality. Uncertainty is unvanquished, but one can still work toward and take odds on truth, even knowing (more like Peirce than Laplace) that the game may take yet another turn.

To do so is to acknowledge a universe of flux, contingency, and chance in which (quoting James) the "only test of probable truth is what works best in the way of leading us." What works for James and pragmatism in general is not the metaphysical supposition that we inhabit a chesslike "block universe," nor do rationalist attempts to model reality sufficiently admit the limitations of knowledge. James writes in "Pragmatism's Concept of Truth" (1907): "To copy a reality is, indeed, one very important way of agreeing with it, but it is far from being essential. The essential thing is the process of being guided. Any idea that helps us to *deal*, . . . that *fits*, in fact, and adapts our life to the reality's whole setting, will agree sufficiently to meet the requirement."[83] In "The Purloined Letter," Dupin copies the seal and address of the stolen missive, though (as Derrida points out) the copy is flawed, indicating the impossibility of perfect representation. On this point, deconstructive and pragmatist readings of "The Purloined Letter" concur: language is not transparent, nor is truth absolute, nor can reality be infallibly modeled. Perhaps neo-pragmatism, as some critics have charged, really is a domestic knockoff of continental theory, whose popularity benefits from its relative accessibility and the ease in which it can be integrated into American nationalist paradigms.[84] One might grant all this and still feel the need to make the not quite provincial point that the American face of Edgar Allan Poe is by no means a solely historicist visage lacking theoretical depth. Rather, Poe's skepticism is transatlantic in its sources and in its affinities with both deconstruction and pragmatism.

A less congenial claim is that post-structural accounts of "The Purloined Letter" miss crucial aspects of the tale, primarily by giving inadequate weight to things outside the text. In order to switch his facsimile with the original letter, Dupin has a confederate stage a ruckus on the street so as to distract the Minister D—, who turns and throws open a window. Representation at this moment in the tale can be taken to point beyond itself, for there are things external to language games that entail what James called "reality's whole setting." In "The Purloined Letter," this reality includes the chaos of the street that enters through the window, as well as the cultural formations of chance in which the story is embedded. Dupin appropriately uses a piece of bread to forge the Minister's "cipher" on his copied letter, for if Poe is punning on the French *du pain* in a moment of semiotic play, he also notes that practical necessities cannot be separated from the symbolic economy of the tale (*PT* 697). For all the fissures, instabilities, and paradoxes of language, Dupin's game has material stakes. Reality in "The Purloined Letter" may be too pluralistically complicated to be comprehensively represented, yet the investigator proceeding with probabilistic caution may find warrantable assertions and courses of action that both James and Dupin term "sufficient." To expect more certainty is to share the rational rage of Parisian policemen, frequentist teleologists, chess players, and pure algebraists who, like Poe in his fits of grandeur, cannot resist the promise of absolute truth. To quote Richard Poirier quoting Frost on Eliot, it is to play at "Eucharist" instead of "euchre."[85]

Clearly Poe does not influence the classical pragmatists as directly as does Emerson, nor does Poe, despite his Boston birth, inherit the New England Mind as anxiously as do some members of the Metaphysical Club. What Poe shares with the first generation of pragmatists, especially James and Peirce, is the recognition that the transatlantic taming of chance constitutes a seismic shift. A major advance in the history of science for Peirce is "[t]he idea that chance begets order," a discovery he attributes to Quetelet, Herschel, and De Morgan, as well as to Darwin, Henry Buckle, and James Maxwell. William James also sees chance as a living option integral to both pragmatism and pluralism, forcing philosophers to "conceiv[e] the more 'true' as the more 'satisfactory'" and to "renounce rectilinear arguments and ancient ideals of rigor and finality."[86] Peirce and James find in probabilistic thinking a way to move beyond absolutism without becoming thorough-going skeptics, an aspect of pragmatism neglected in literary circles since the revival of pragmatism in the 1980s. Rorty's anti-foundationalism is not much concerned with science and probability, nor are Poirier's elegant applications of pragmatism to literary style. Nor, for that matter, is Cavell (pragmatist or not) much provoked by probabilism.

The kind of pragmatism with the strongest connections to Poe (and at issue in the chapters that follow) is more closely described in the historicist accounts of Louis Menand and Joan Richardson.[87] Both scholars study pragmatism's cultural roots and commitments to scientific advances, including the new sciences of chance. Still, Menand's *Metaphysical Club* does not engage in literary criticism, while Richardson focuses on the natural sciences, a subject more central for Dickinson and Thoreau. Richardson and to a lesser degree Menand also join the scholarly majority in tracing the pre-history of pragmatism along Emersonian lines, thereby placing pragmatism in a powerful but less inclusive tradition of New England Puritanism and its discontents. Poe unsettles this narrative with a more catholic, more transatlantic story that the classical pragmatists might have approved given their conviction that ideas are enmeshed in culture, that relations are too interconnected and contingent to circumscribe, and that literature has epistemological capacities that formal philosophy lacks. If most of nineteenth-century American philosophy is mechanistic and teleological, pragmatism—like Poe's tales of ratiocination—accepts the limits that chance imposes on certainty.

As we will see when comparing Melville with James, Douglass with Holmes Jr., and Dickinson with Dewey, what often distinguishes literary treatments of chance from subsequent pragmatist approaches is that literature more vividly explores the everyday crises and emotional comportments occasioned by encounters with chance. Something similar can be said of Poe's writings, for if his tales of ratiocination (like classical pragmatism) seem to me more interested in theorizing than inducing affect, Dupin's navigations through a richly conceived world of chance invite a level of identification and wonder that even James at his most anecdotal and lyrical does not strive for or achieve. That Poe and his literary contemporaries embrace more fervently the lived experience of chance is a claim for later discussion. For now, suffice it to say that if nothing else reading pragmatism into the literature of chance expands pragmatism's explanatory power.

Put broadly in terms of literary form, if Rorty's pragmatism is tonal (irony in the face of skepticism) and generic (philosophy as rhetoric and conversation), and if Poirier's pragmatism most successfully explicates poetics (diction, syntax, rhythm, etc.), then conceiving of pragmatism as a philosophy of chance suggests how verisimilitude (particularly in character and plot) involves a probabilistic epistemology that applies to—and can be enacted by—narrative fictions such as Poe's. Strong readings of Poe tend to set him swinging between Enlightenment hubris and radical doubt. Yet Poe's tales of ratiocination indicate that in addition to dramatizing the shock of skepticism, Poe sought along with others in his culture a more livable, more adequate approach to uncertainty. For all the bets Poe lost in his life, he remained an astute observer of probabilism. The subversive, ironic marplot of rationalism thus becomes a more constructive critic in whose writings intuition looks like calculation, skepticism like science, and radical indeterminacy like James's radical empiricism—insofar as admissible evidence includes feelings beyond the positivist pale, insofar as Poe and James both resist utter doubt, holding instead that minds and experiences (quoting James) "meet in a world of objects."[88] Many mysteries go unsolved in Poe's detective fiction, but Dupin as a realist knows how to get by with fallible methods under conditions of chance. He fails in "The Mystery of Marie Roget," but two out of three isn't bad for Poe, a writer who found many of his ideas unfit for a market economy governed by a probabilistic logic he could not help but admire, resent, and adopt.

Let us conclude by rereading an earlier text often taken as a touchstone for the separation of science and literature. Poe's "Sonnet—to Science" is by no means a love poem, and yet more than many of his romantic forerunners, Poe retains a measure of affection for science, asking of science the not quite rhetorical questions, "How should he [the poet] love thee? or how deem thee wise?" Poe in his sonnet draws from another touchstone poem dramatizing the romantic resistance to science. Keats in "Lamia" mourns the loss of the "Nymph and Satyr," "the Dryads and the Fauns," as the poem laments the "eye severe" of a disenchanting, rectilinear rationalism:

> . . . Do not all charms fly
> At the mere touch of cold philosophy?
> There was an awful rainbow once in heaven:
> We know her woof, her texture; she is given
> In the dull catalogue of common things.
> Philosophy will clip an Angel's wings,
> Conquer all mysteries by rule and line,
> Empty the haunted air, and gnomed mine.[89]

Poe rewrites Keats in his "Sonnet—to Science," setting his own "peering eye" of reason against the "Hamadryad," "Naiad," and "Elfin," and describing science as a "dull" way of seeing that "alterest all things" (PT 38). Yet Poe holds a sense of science's wonder that Keats's poem does not so readily allow. Poe's science may clip an angel's wings, but it itself is a "vulture" of Promethean myth that neither dispels the enchanted past nor renders the world dull through taxonomic exactitude. When restricting the authority of classical learning, Bacon called truth a "daughter of time" in that truth advances, not by sudden revelations, but through the incremental gains of a patient empiricism.[90] Subtly marking a vast cosmological difference, Poe in "Sonnet—to Science" calls science the "daughter of Old Time," a more mythic personification of temporality suggesting that in addition to its Baconian form, science is also a descendant of Chaos and as such an heir to the legacy of chance.

Poe himself bequeathed to a range of authors an interest in literature and chance. His work indicates how the rise of chance spreads, not only in logic, mathematics, and sociology but also in aesthetics, social practices, and popular print culture. Poe is no expert on probability theory, but he intuits implications of chance with a quick and at times confused brilliance that presages the naturalizing of chance across the nineteenth century. In 1880, *Scribner's* published a retrospective on Poe, turning to the probabilistic logic of Francis Galton's heredity studies. Reflecting on Poe's parentage, the article marveled: "The law of chance, that has so much to do with the composition of a man, that makes no two alike, yet adjusts the most of us to a common average, brings about exceptional unions like the one from which [Poe] sprang."[91] With no discernible intention, *Scribner's* echoed a favorite point of Poe: that the law of chance accounts not only for averages but also for lives that are stranger than fiction. Who could predict that an orphan and starving writer would become a figure of such immense literary consequence?

Poe illuminates the changing status of chance powerfully and early, though he is not much interested in approaching the subject from a historical perspective, in part because his writing and reading tend toward the contemporary, especially as he becomes increasingly committed to the popular press. For a deeper history of chance, we turn to Melville, who can be lumped with Poe as a romantic skeptic who died without getting his due, but whose career arc and intellectual development are actually quite opposite to Poe's. Melville generally moves from popularity to obscurity, from prose to poetry, from commentaries on issues of the day to densely historicized ruminations steeped in serious learning. Whereas Poe wonderfully improvises on the cutting edge of the probabilistic revolution, Melville broods with more scholarly patience on longer philosophical and theological trajectories.

CHAPTER 2

Moby-Dick and the Opposite
of Providence

Supposing such an anamoly [*sic*] to exist, an Atheist must be the most miserable of beings. The idea of a fatherless world, swinging by some blind law of chance, which may every moment expose it to destruction, through an infinite space, filled, perhaps, with nothing but suffering and wretchedness, unalleviated by the prospect of a future and a happier state, must be almost intolerable to a man who has a single spark of benevolence in his bosom.

— "The Atheist," *Trumpet and Universalist Magazine*, December 10, 1842

B efore chance became a scientific topic, it was a theological scandal, and prior to that, it was a philosophical concept associated not only with Epicureanism but also with classical skepticism. Nineteenth-century American literary studies tend to follow Stanley Cavell in approaching skepticism as a post-Kantian epistemological challenge, though older forms of skepticism were more broadly relevant in the period as religious and scientific thinkers alike revisited longstanding etiological problems entailing the possibilities of chance.

Melville is often called a skeptic, though the poignancy of the term has gone largely untapped, especially when skepticism becomes loosely synonymous with religious and political iconoclasm. As a handful of his contemporary reviewers noticed, and as bandwagons of modern scholars attest, Melville does have a penchant, perhaps even a compulsion, for upsetting the most sacrosanct assumptions of his time. His father's raving death and his mother's Dutch Calvinism may have instigated his uneasy relations with God, while his maritime encounters with cultural diversity seem more surely to have distanced him from nineteenth-century moral conventions. If, finally, some amount of conjecture is required to portray Melville as a skeptical young man, the contours of his writings more reliably trace his unrelenting and unfulfilled search for belief. Melville's cultural relativism and objections to Christian imperialism appear as early as *Typee* (1846), and his philosophical freethinking is first evident in *Mardi* (1849), an ambitious, awkwardly structured book that stages so wild a speculative trip as to disorient any quest for certainty. The more generically stable *Redburn* (1849) and *White-Jacket* (1850) continue to buck political authority and essentialist conceptions of selfhood, showing Melville to be an insightful and sometimes devastating observer of liberal individualism. Yet as much as Melville's early novels reflect the restless progress of an autodidact who treated all ideas as loose fish, nothing sufficiently readies a reader for the fully elaborated, deeply historicized, syncretic skepticism of his greatest work.

Moby-Dick (1851) has long secured Melville's reputation as a writer who, in Hawthorne's words, could "neither believe, nor be comfortable in his unbelief." Reflecting on his penultimate meeting with Melville on a Liverpool beach in 1856, Hawthorne's now nearly inevitable quote suggests how Melville's theo-philosophical seriousness never resolves itself into conviction, nor do the habits of his subversive imagination turn him into a casual scoffer. While Melville seems vaguely existential in this way, and can even anticipate the rumored end of philosophy in the twentieth century and beyond, Hawthorne most specifically associates his friend with Pyrrhonist skepticism insofar as Herman is taken to disbelieve even the claims of disbelief itself. For all his own sensitivity to crises of faith, Hawthorne could not quite understand how Melville maintained so torturous a suspension of judgment for so long: "It is strange how he persists—and has persisted ever since I knew him, and probably long before—in wandering to and fro over these deserts, as dismal and monotonous as the sand hills amid which we were sitting."[1] Hawthorne's account of Melville's skepticism is personally felt and dramatically rendered, but it remains more intuitively correct than complete, for though Hawthorne bestows some blessings on Melville before sending him on his solitary way, he apparently did not ask nor does he speculate as to the sources and affinities of Melville's doubting. Nor does Hawthorne recognize that Melville's wanderings are not, in fact, monotonous, that the devil of America's greatest skeptic lies in the details.

Just as Poe mediates uncertainty with probability theory, Melville's suspension between belief and unbelief is shaped by the rise of chance. Focusing less on the mathematical and logical discourses that Poe found so provoking, Melville encounters the possibilities of chance as an aspect of skepticism's running battle with teleological concepts of agency, most notably Christian ideas of providence that dominated Melville's era and intellectual heritage. *Moby-Dick* may be about everything, but it seems to me more about *why* than *what*—more about causality than representation, more about etiology than subjectivity, more about Pyrrhonism and its modern iterations than post-Kantian thought and intimations of post-structuralism.

To be sure, Melville's skepticism can lead interpretation into serious engagements with romanticism and its heirs, and *Moby-Dick's* philosophical verve probably has something to do with George Adler, the professor of German who during their 1849 travels sharpened to some unknown degree Melville's appetite for Kant, Schlegel, Hegel, and Coleridge. Yet Melville and Adler did more together than (as Melville put it in his journal) "rid[e] the German horse." They played chess and whist, debated the question of "'Fixed Fate, Free-will, foreknowledge absolute,' etc.," discussed Laplace, and talked about Leibniz's theory that even God is bound by mathematical rules.[2] Chance may or may not have been a topic of discussion, though it figures prominently in the thinking of Leibniz and Laplace and in questions that pervade *Moby-Dick*. Chance is also of concern in books that Melville was reading in the late 1840s, including Cicero's works,

Montaigne's *Essays* (1580), and Pierre Bayle's *Dictionary* (1697, 1702), all of which helped spur the revival of Pyrrhonism in the Early Modern period.[3] Hume's scandalous dismantling of causal certainty further influences *Moby-Dick's* approach to chance, as do scientific advances in navigation, whaling, and oceanography. No single source or context provides the key to the lock of Melville's etiology, though when taken together and combined with his proclivities for religious and philosophical doubt, Melville's multifarious encounters with chance shape the skepticism of *Moby-Dick*. After their visit on a barren Liverpool beach, Hawthorne reported no speculative discussions about self and other, idealism and materialism, language and representation. He wrote instead, "Melville, as he always does, began to reason of Providence and futurity." Melville's disorderly but careful reasoning evinces an exceptional open-mindedness to chance as he interjects a disruptive third term into what William James would later call the "well-worn controversy" over fate and free will.[4]

THE CAUSE OF THE HUNT

I was once asked in a qualifying exam why Ishmael decides to go whaling. In such contexts, the simplest questions can feel threatening: *Did you even start Moby-Dick?* The query was, of course, a friendly invitation to dilate on Melville's book, for Ishmael's multiple explanations of his motives suggest a wealth of interpretive strategies. In "Loomings," Ishmael reports that he has "little or no money" thereby foregrounding socioeconomic themes.[5] He also mentions his "spleen" and "hypos," inviting psychological readings. His thoughts on the inspirational qualities of water underscore his romantic aesthetics and desires, while his reference to Narcissus as "the key to it all" reflects the meta-critical dynamics of the narrative. None of these approaches is mutually exclusive, especially given Ishmael's pluralistic sensibilities; and yet the explanation on which "Loomings" finally dwells threatens to beggar the very question of motive, setting the stage for the emergence of a skeptical Ishmael who is willing to consider the aleatory prospects of that most difficult of all questions: Why?

After cycling through various potential causes in "Loomings," Ishmael ultimately attributes his shipping out to the "Fates," a possibility that, like his earlier nod to "Seneca and the Stoics," indicates an openness (if not yet a capacity) to subordinate himself to a higher power or at least something outside of the self (798–99). Broadly speaking, stoicism does not deny free will but severely restricts it to a person's choice to accept fate gracefully or to rage uselessly against it, a view that made Seneca amenable to later Christian thinkers who wanted to retain classical traditions while following an omnipotent God. As Seneca put it in his *Morals*, a text that Melville owned, "[A] good man can never be miserable; nor a wicked man happy; nor any man unfortunate that cheerfully submits to Providence."[6] Using fate and providence as interchangeable terms, a common practice in antebellum writings and translations, Ishmael gestures toward a determinism that is simultaneously stoic and Christian: "[D]oubtless, my going on this whaling voyage formed part of the grand programme of Providence."[7] Readers on the lookout for Melvillean rebellion will doubtlessly hear some irony in "doubtless," a suspicion that seems justified after Ishmael compares the fates to a "police officer," describes them as "stage managers," and (unable to summon Seneca's cheerful submission) bristles at his "shabby part" in God's play: "I think I can see a little into the springs and motives which being cunningly presented to me under various disguises, induced me to set about performing the part I did, besides cajoling me into the delusion that it was a choice resulting from my own unbiased freewill and discriminating judgment." No miraculous interpositions or arguments from design for Ishmael; providence operates by coercion and deceit.

Ishmael's half-aggrieved, half-ironic musings on providence tend toward impiety in their tone, but his dualistic formulation of fate and free will is entirely conventional for the nineteenth century in that it excludes the possibilities of chance. In this, Ishmael follows other heterodox writers who balked at blithe accounts of providence but still paid tribute to an all-determining God. Thomas Browne in *Religio Medici* (1643), an established influence on *Moby-Dick*, impatiently passes over "the ordinary and open way of [God's] providence" to meditate instead on His more "obscure method": "This we call Fortune, that serpentine and crooked line, whereby [God] draws those actions his wisdom intends, in a more unknown and secret way." Ishmael shares Browne's conspiratorial sense for the devious cruisings of providence; and just as Ishmael shrugs off the "thump and punch" of sea life by appealing to an overmastering God, Browne explains away "the hits of chance" by invoking a providential logic. "Surely there are in every man's Life," Browne writes, "certain rubs, doublings, and wrenches, which pass a while under the effects of chance, but at the last well examined, prove the meer [sic] hand of God."[8] For Browne and Ishmael at the outset of *Moby-Dick*, providence is neither legible nor comforting, but chance remains a privative concept that feels like a physical assault but only goes by the name of fortune. Like the white whale itself, chance simultaneously invites and resists personification: it hits and thumps but has no visage; its brutality feels malignant but is hard to ascribe to an identifiable agent.

The self-proclaimed "chance philosopher" Montaigne is especially sensitive to how the possibilities of chance mark epistemological limits in the course of everyday life. In his essay, "That It Is Madness to Judge the True and the False" (1595), Montaigne instructs his readers "[n]ot to believe too rashly" nor "to disbelieve too easily"— Polonious-like advice but also a skeptical lesson that Melville seems to have taken to heart by the time he met Hawthorne in Liverpool. Melville purchased Montaigne's *Essays* in 1848, giving him access to the skeptical tradition of Carneades, Pyrrho, Sextus Empiricus, and Cicero, all of who took chance seriously enough to withhold their assent to providential claims. Ishmael's numerous descriptions of his motives in "Loomings" follow a main point of Montaigne's: that when "[w]e cannot be sure of the master-cause, . . . we pile cause upon cause, hoping that it may happen to be among them." Montaigne suspects anyone who presumes to understand the serpentine paths of God, in part because he gives chance serious credence, if only within the domain of experience. "[C]hance has so much power over us, since it is by chance that we live," Montaigne writes. Hamlet-like humans must therefore endure what Montaigne calls "the blows and outrages of Fortune," though Montaigne also voices a providential piety that, given the dominant beliefs of his age, may or may not have been deeply held. Like Browne, Montaigne unsettles complacent views of providence by focusing less on benevolent theories of theodicy and more on painful experience. True to his unsystematic spirit and embrace of ordinary life, he advises young scholars worrying over fate and free will to go out and get drunk (a mixing of metaphysics and alcohol to which Melville enthusiastically subscribes).[9]

Holding chance in more sober abeyance, Ishmael in "Loomings" frames the problem of agency solely in terms of fate and free will, an almost universal practice for nineteenth-century theologians and philosophers, as well as for subsequent critics of *Moby-Dick*. And rightly so, at least for the first third of the book, which entertains claims for free will and necessity to the point of parody. The power of fate is everywhere announced in *Moby-Dick's* opening prophecies and rampant foreshadowing—so much so that by the time Elijah says in "The Prophet" chapter, "Any how, it's all fixed and arranged a'ready," a reader seeking a New Critical purchase might think not only of providential programs but also of what is, if only for a time, a generically recognizable novel seemingly shaping itself into a unified, relatively predictable text (892). Against such teleological views, Ahab emerges as a figure of free will and formal heterogeneity, particularly when he sets his Shakespearian self against the fateful white whale. Soliloquizing in "The Sunset," Ahab announces himself as the prime mover of the *Pequod*, boasting that he is both "prophet" and "fulfiller": "What I've dared, I've willed; and what I've willed, I'll do!" (971). Jonathan Edwards might respond, *What willed your will in the first place, hmmm? Did you even start Moby-Dick?* Ahab does not seriously confront such conundrums until much later in the book, and Melville himself will not take on Edwards directly until "Bartleby, the Scrivener." Nonetheless, the dualistic controversy over fate and free will in *Moby-Dick*, so whimsically styled by Ishmael in "Loomings," is more earnestly addressed by Ahab, who presents himself as both a victim of fate and a tower of individual agency, all the while refusing to acknowledge the possibilities of chance.

Ahab's denial of chance is crucial to his psychology and *Moby-Dick's* philosophical architecture. In "The Quarter-Deck," Ahab rejects Starbuck's suggestion that his unmasting is nothing more than the random result of a dumb brute's "blindest instinct"—"blind" being an adjective often paired with chance, and a word etymologically opposed to providence, whose Latin root means foresight (967). In Ahab's mind, the white whale's attack was the "undoubted deed" of some "unknown but still reasoning thing," whether that thing is "the white whale agent" or "the white whale principal" (that is, whether the whale serves the purpose of some prime mover or is itself a freely acting entity). Either way, Ahab requires an intelligent causal force to render his injury meaningful by placing it within *some* design, and by the time "Moby Dick" (chapter 41) arrives, his desire to find a master cause is as fierce as the line is familiar: "The White Whale swam before him as the monomaniac incarnation of all those malicious agencies which some deep men feel eating in them" (989). One question that drives the narrative onward is what precisely such malicious agents might be.

Moby-Dick is too sprawling for a hinge (or as Dickinson might put it, too silver for a seam), but the "Moby Dick" chapter forms a transition, for at the very moment Ahab pledges to dominate all causation, the impossibility of his ambitions shadows forth in the figure of chance. In "The Whiteness of the Whale" (chapter 42), Ishmael begins the uneven process of distancing himself from his captain's insistence on identifiable agency as he plumbs the depths of etiological doubt with the repeated question, Why? Ishmael details the sublime effects of whiteness and tries to isolate the color from the objects it marks, but after exploring a slew of hypotheses as to why whiteness conjures terror, he ends up unable to establish causality, finally associating Moby Dick's whiteness with the "colorless, all-color of atheism" (1001).

It is another famous line, though why whiteness is equated with godlessness is by no means clear. Howsoever much race may figure in "The Whiteness of the Whale," Ishmael is not equating white skin with atheism, for he has already learned from Queequeg that color and faith cannot be directly correlated. Melville seems aware that whiteness combines every color of the spectrum, but Newtonian optics need not conflict with Christian cosmology (in fact, Newton's work with prisms was taken to cohere with the Book of Genesis's "Let there be light" as understood within the argument from design). Ishmael doubts the capacity of words to describe the effects of whiteness, though Christian writings regularly notice the limits of language, so atheism need not lurk here. Something similar can even be said of the chapter's reflections on the brutality of nature. The mystery of iniquity is indeed at issue in Melville's quarrel with God, but plenty of Christians acknowledged the conundrum and, as Michael Colacurcio points out, to worry seriously about theodicy is first to possess some initial inclination toward theism.[10] The link between Moby Dick and atheism may have something to do with Ahab's God-provoking Byronism, and (with or without the footnote to Coleridge) "The Whiteness of the Whale" feels the burden of romantic skepticism in that the senses are susceptible to "subtile [sic] deceits" (1001). Yet suspicions about the accuracy of the senses need not lead to atheism either. Montaigne and Emerson (not unlike Erasmus and Berkeley) demonstrate that doubts about the object world can coexist with and even strengthen Christian faith, particularly if taking one's senses too seriously risks the godless materialism of Flask. "The Whiteness of the Whale" does not ultimately offer anything like a systematic argument, but what most coherently links the color of Moby Dick to atheism is not race, language, theodicy, or perception so much as the absence of any causal logic connecting whiteness to the feelings it brings. For the Christian etiologist, God is always the final answer to questions of causation, but for Ishmael (and the agnostic parent of a toddler), there is no end to "Why?"

And still Ishmael in his "dim, random way" seeks a master cause in "The Whiteness of the Whale" (993). After inductively listing "accumulated associations" that appear to connect whiteness and fear, Ishmael makes the skeptical point that no amount of observed correspondences can guarantee causal links: "To analyse it [the whiteness of the whale], would seem impossible" (994, 997). Against stoics such as Seneca, who wrote in his *Morals* that the "universe is not without a governor; and . . . cannot be the work of chance," classical skeptics saw chance as a valid hypothesis countervailing providential claims. Pyrrho argued, "[T]here is no such thing as a cause," while Sextus Empiricus was more circumspect in his *Outlines of Pyrrhonism*: "[W]e are compelled to suspend judgement concerning the real existence of Cause." "The Whiteness of the Whale" does not go this far in any explicit sense, though Ishmael admits the elusiveness of agency when he wonders, "[C]an we thus hope to light upon some chance clue to conduct us to the hidden cause we seek?" (997). Like the clue-seeking Dupin, Ishmael admits chance into his causal inquiries, and like the dice-throwing corpse in "The Rime of the Ancient Mariner" (1798), the possibilities of chance in "The Whiteness of the Whale" take on a horrifying pallor that signifies in its colorless all-color both an absence and a presence in nature. Whether Ishmael refers to chance nominally or absolutely will remain difficult to say, though even the hint of causal indeterminacy—even a skeptical openness to chance—was daring enough in the nineteenth century to raise the specter of atheism.[11]

Providentialism and absolute chance are by definition mutually exclusive, though to understand the full force of *Moby-Dick's* etiological skepticism is to recognize how nearly unthinkable chance was for many Christians in the antebellum period and beyond. The Unitarian logician, moral philosopher, and biblical scholar Francis Newman wrote in 1838: "The ancients were used formally to class Chance among the causes of things. The moderns have been [so] shocked and disgusted by the use of the argument which Atheists have made, that many religious persons consider the very word an offense, perhaps an impiety." This was especially true in the Calvinist tradition that Melville found so generative. Calvin wrote in a chapter on providence in his *Institutes* (1536), "[F]ortune and *chance* are words of the heathen" referring only to "reason and cause of which we are not acquainted." Though drifting from Calvin in critical ways, Milton's contested *de doctrina Christiana* (first published in 1825) followed the *Institutes* in regarding chance as only a privative concept. For Milton, the line from *Ecclesiastes*, "[T]ime and chance happeneth to them all," is "meant only to exclude the idea of human causation." Nor do biblical examples of the casting of lots as in Jonah imply the existence of chance, for (as Milton quotes from *Proverbs*) "the whole disposing of the lot is of Jehovah." *Paradise Lost* (1667) may have the sore-losing Satan blame chance, and Chance and Chaos may cast shadows over Milton's Hell, but the poem's treatment of fixed fate, free will, and foreknowledge absolute leaves chance entirely out of the question. The Puritan divine William Ames and his disciple in America, John Cotton, continued to deny the actuality of chance, as did Cotton Mather in his *Christian Philosopher* (1721), which brought together Puritan providence and natural philosophy's argument from design.[12]

Most powerfully in American intellectual traditions, Edwards in *Freedom of the Will* (1754) dismissed "such names as *accident, chance, and contingence*," repudiating the creeping libertarianism of his fellow Calvinist Isaac Watts by invoking an infinite regression of causes. Edwards wrote:

> [I]f *the Will designs to choose whatsoever it does choose*, and *designs to determine itself*, as [Watts] says, then it designs to determine all its designs. Which carries us back from one design to a foregoing design determining that, and to another determining that; and so on *in infinitum*. The very first design must be the effect of foregoing design, or else it must be by chance.

As Edwards knew, chance was not an option for Watts or any other God-respecting Christian. For all the strife between libertarians and determinists, and for all the careful distinctions made by "soft determinists" who sought a middle ground, the consensus among Christian thinkers was total: neither Augustinians nor Pelagians, Calvinists nor Arminians, nonconformists nor Anglicans nor Catholics nor deists understood chance as anything more than human ignorance of God's will.[13]

If anything, Protestant denials of chance were more elaborate (and belabored) in the antebellum era—a period that Jackson Lears has called "The Noontide of Providence," and one that applied teleological Puritan hermeneutics to soul and nation alike.[14] Later-day Calvinists echoed Edwards's denial of chance, as did less orthodox evangelists more open to personal agency, including Charles Grandison Finney (who charged that "atheists . . . ascribe all events to chance") and Lyman Beecher (who equated "absurd" beliefs in absolute chance with "atheism"). Unitarian stalwarts such as William E. Channing condemned the moral implications of believing in chance, as did the more radical Theodore Parker, who complained in 1840, "[T]he atheist concludes that the mind and all things spring from senseless nature and chance." Methodists followed Wesley in dismissing chance as a "silly word," and Melville's erstwhile minister (and antagonist) Orville Dewey wrote in 1847: "Events are not blindly and carelessly flung together, in a strange chance-medley: . . . one end, one design, concerneth, urgeth all." Antebellum theologians could refer offhandedly to chance, luck, fortune, and accident, but when seriously addressing questions of agency, they described chance as an atheistic delusion.[15]

The denial of chance in theological circles also held sway in philosophical traditions that shaped mid-nineteenth-century thought. Anthony Collins, a main figure in etiological debates, summarized the state of affairs in 1717: "The questions of Liberty, Necessity and chance have been subjects of dispute among philosophers at all times; and most of those philosophers have clearly asserted Necessity, and denied Liberty and chance." True enough, for Descartes in his search for metaphysical certainty gave no more credence to chance than did Leibniz, while Locke recognized the need for probabilistic reasoning but saw chance as a nominal concept. Referring to Epicurean thought, Lord Shaftesbury derided "the belov'd Atoms, Chance, and Confusion of the Atheists," and when Thomas Reid noted that John Tillotson's attack on chance provided no proof or reasoning, he did so not to challenge the archbishop's claims but, rather, to assert that the chanceless argument from design was a self-evident "first principle."[16] To these mainstream authorities can be added the heterodox thinking of Hume, Voltaire, and Kant, none of whom for all their skeptical potential believed in the actuality of chance. It is hard to overestimate how anathema chance was in the mid-nineteenth century as philosophical and religious authorities charged time and again that believers in chance were "insane" and belonged in a "lunatic asylum."[17] The abundance and intensity of such views indicate the dominance of providentialism in the United States and Britain, but they also suggest that chance was becoming an increasingly viable concept requiring redoubled, if not always discerning, opposition. If science coexisted comfortably enough with Christianity prior to the mid-nineteenth century, the argument from design needed more forceful support as chance began its rise.[18]

Which is not to say that all Christian thinkers simply rejected the probabilistic revolution. Of lasting influence in nineteenth-century America, Joseph Butler's *Analogy of Nature* (1736) and William Paley's *Natural Theology* (1802) followed Locke's *Reasonableness of Christianity* (1695) in using probabilistic logic to ease tensions between empiricism and faith. Butler and Paley admitted that the argument from design could not be absolutely proven, but for them Christianity could be vindicated on the grounds of "moral certainty"—so highly probable a degree of belief as to be for all intents and purposes equivalent to truth. Evangelists and transcendentalists complained that asserting the likelihood of Christianity is not exactly Paul on the road to Damascus, and the cold calculation of rational Christianity was a favorite target of sentimental writers. As we will see in chapter six, ministers worried about Christians applying the doctrine of chances to questions of salvation. But if some religious thinkers believed that dallying with probabilism was playing with the fire of chance, moral certainty remained a popular theological buttress, helping to defend religious faith by marking the limits of empirical authority.[19]

Swayed by the new sciences of chance, some antebellum defenders of Christianity took probabilistic thinking to curious extremes. Some defended the actuality of biblical miracles by pointing to their very improbability, not unlike novelists who vindicated their verisimilitude by claiming that truths were stranger than fiction. Quite differently, in *Probabilities: An Aid to Faith* (1847), Martin Farquhar Tupper (the popular moralist and favorite of Melville's mother) tried to turn the doctrine of chances against Hume when arguing that the Bible's truths are borne out by the "calculation of probabilities." Tupper argued that monotheism makes a stronger case than polytheism, for "if many [gods] are probable, few are more probable, and one most probable of all"—sound logic if one is talking about rolling a six in Yahtzee, though it also implies that black sheep are more probable than white ones. Tupper also took the Old Testament flood to be God's most likely response to human disobedience, much more plausible a punishment (he reasoned) than a plague or flaming comet, both of which have awe-inspiring force but lack the regenerative symbolism of water. Tupper repeatedly warned that probabilistic reasoning is no substitute for heartfelt faith, and yet his book insists that when one thinks about it, the odds of God are pretty good.[20]

An 1847 article, "The Existence of the Deity," in *The United States Magazine and Democratic Review*, took a more quantitative but similarly flawed approach to probabilistic faith. The author recounts a bout with "utter skepticism" brought on by reading "Hume, on the subject of causation"; but after etiological uncertainty leads him to atheism, he is saved by the evidence of godly order that he finds everywhere in nature. This is the basic gambit of the argument from design, though "The Existence of the Deity" attempts to sharpen it mathematically. After noticing that a flower has five petals, five stamens, and a five-part calyx, the author erroneously calculates that the chances of such symmetry are 1 in 125. Casting his eye over a field of flowers, he then marvels at the odds of such widespread coincidence occurring in every single bloom:

> The algebra of an Archangel, with infinite space for his balance-sheet, and eternity for the period of solutions, were insufficient, perhaps, for the overwhelming computation. I would advise the atheist before he dares grapple [with] this argument, to refresh his memory with the doctrine of the calculation of chances, in his favorite La Place [*sic*].

Using a strategy still employed today by proponents of intelligent design, "The Existence of the Deity" asserts the extreme implausibility of the universe's being randomly formed: "[T]he calculation of chances proves most conclusively that to deny [God] is an absurdity a thousand times worse than the ravings of utter madness." Like Tupper, "The Existence of the Deity" puts the doctrine of chances to pious ends, even as it shows how probability theory was often misunderstood by nonspecialists, many of who found that the provisionality of probabilistic knowledge made it readily conformable to preexisting beliefs.[21]

By the time Melville wrote *Moby-Dick*, many Christians were participating in the probabilistic revolution, even as absolute chance remained tantamount to madness and atheism, suggesting its emergence as a living option on the boundaries of conceptual recognition. Melville's sanity and religious faith were, of course, both questioned during his life, and *Moby-Dick* frequently portrays "crazy Ahab" as a godless "raving lunatic" (989). Ahab is indeed an accomplished blasphemer who partakes in the occasional worship of fire, but his biblical rants, dark liturgies, and satanic allusions betray a stubbornly Christian worldview: he believes too much in a master cause, be it Satan or God, to become a full-blown atheist. Like Hawthorne, Melville knows that the most fervent Christian and most tormented sinner can be one and the same, for if Ahab is louder, he is—as we shall see—less of a potential atheist than the random, chance-acknowledging Ishmael, who does not simply rattle the Calvinist cage but also questions the whole framework of providence. In a self-consciously wicked book from a fearless thinker with deep theological learning, Melville's topmost heresy does not only concern the mystery of iniquity.[22] It also involves the almost unthinkable possibility that providence does not exist and that Ahab's insistent denial of chance is the maddest madness of all. As Montaigne joked when arguing that indeterminacy obliges one to rely on probabilities, "To be convinced of certainty is certain evidence of madness."[23] Ishmael is less inclined than Ahab to attack the mystery of causality with a harpoon, but in "The Whiteness of the Whale" he is not yet free of the monomaniacal quest for agency, ending the chapter in his captain's prophetic idiom: "Wonder ye then at the fiery hunt?" The implied answer throws us back on our ignorance: the cause of the hunt is the hunt for a cause.

THE INDIFFERENT SWORD OF CHANCE

Ishmael in "The Whiteness of the Whale" sounds like someone struggling in a qualifying exam. Facing a question with no definite answer, he gropes without much organization through loosely related examples and hypotheses before finally admitting a lack of clarity about everything except an ambient feeling of terror. After "The Whiteness of the Whale," Ishmael learns to be more casual about causal indeterminacy as *Moby-Dick* considers the possibilities of taming—and being tamed by—chance, a recurring concern in the book that has been surprisingly neglected. The fierce denial of chance in the mid-nineteenth century suggests why chance has not been a focus in antebellum literary scholarship generally and Melville studies in particular.[24] Howsoever co-opted Melville may be by the dominant ideologies of his day, he is rightfully taken to be critical of providential faith, including political analogues such as manifest destiny. Yet the intellectual contexts most associated with Melville's culture—Protestant theology, the Scottish Enlightenment, and romantic philosophy—either dismiss chance entirely, severely circumscribe its power, or do not treat its management in a sustained way. Without chance in the mix, individual freedom becomes the only alternative to providentialism, and since Melville is also suspicious of liberal individualism, he can appear to be a strictly oppositional thinker who subverts both fate and free will, both tyranny and liberty, without offering viable alternatives. Melville may not unequivocally believe in chance but neither does he deny it, as seen in the five chapters immediately following "The Whiteness of the Whale." Building toward a crucial passage in "The Mat-Maker," these chapters constitute a more positive, more skeptical perspective on Melville's etiology and the possibilities of chance.

It probably goes too far to argue that "Hark!" (chapter 43) dramatizes the suppression of chance—that the bucket-line of sailors symbolizes a causal chain, and that the unknown noises coming from under the deck (like Poe's dwarf in a chess automaton) represent alien forces of chaos lurking within seemingly rational systems. More surely, "The Chart" (chapter 44) addresses the management of chance by focusing on the epistemological and emotional limits of Ahab's "delirious but still methodical scheme" (1005). Like the portrait of an Enlightenment worthy surrounded by his scientific instruments, Ahab and the setting of "The Chart" bespeak the fixed systems and patient progress of Enlightenment reason: "[S]ea-charts" and "log-books" rest on a "screwed-down table" as the captain "with slow but steady pencil trace[s] additional courses over spaces that before were blank" (1003). Maybe Conrad liked *Moby-Dick* more than he let on, for *Heart of Darkness* (1899) follows Melville in showing how instrumental reason, imperialist maps, and the rage for intellectual order lead finally to madness.[25] To bring the white whale under scientific control, Ahab in "The Chart" employs probabilistic methods based on the idea that stochastic phenomena form predictable patterns when analyzed in mass. Drawing upon a pile of logbooks from "various former voyages of various ships," Ahab assumes that the migrations of sperm whales are "regular" and subject to "periodicalness"; and by "calculating" currents, food sources, and sightings, he hopes to "arrive at reasonable surmises, almost approaching to certainties" (1003–4). Here "almost" points to the incremental and always incomplete work of inductive science, for—as Hume notoriously showed, and as probability theorists reminded their readers—one can refer to all the recorded sunrises in history to reasonably predict that tomorrow will come, but such inferential reasoning brings only surmises that are morally, not absolutely, certain.

Practical scientists of the mid-nineteenth century were not so much troubled by the theoretical limits of induction. When "The Chart" mentions that "carefully collated" logbooks might be used to "construct elaborate migratory charts of the sperm whale," Melville refers to a broad contemporary effort to tame the chances of the sea. Nautical almanacs and books such as William Reid's *Law of Storms* (1838) were based on frequentist logic, as were the efforts of Laplace, Quetelet, the political economist J. R. McCulloch, and the science writer Mary Somerville, who all applied probability theory to statistics on weather and navigation. Most impressively, William Whewell in 1835 headed a massive systematic effort to map the ocean tides, a project involving nine countries, seven hundred tidal stations, and thousands of observers and human calculators working together to infer regular laws from the seemingly unpredictable fluxes of the sea. Thoreau, in *Walden*, knows that sailors, merchants, and maritime insurers must constantly evaluate risk, that there are always "charts to be studied, the position of reefs and new lights and buoys to be ascertained, and ever, and ever, the logarithmic tables to be corrected." *Moby-Dick* does not deal in logarithms, but it does draw on texts steeped in quantitative oceanography, including Charles Wilkes's *Narrative of the United States Exploring Expedition* (1844), a well-known source for Melville.[26]

Under the direction of the U.S. government, Wilkes and his fleet circumnavigated the globe between 1838 and 1842, primarily to establish more accurate maps and lay claims to any undiscovered lands. The expedition was an expression of manifest destiny imposing scientific order over nature. Aware of the errors of past navigators and the complications of ocean surveying, Wilkes was scrupulous about his data, paying close attention to the deviations of navigational instruments and requiring that every officer take his own measurements and perform his own calculations. The infamously autocratic Wilkes can superficially resemble the tyrannical Ahab, but Wilkes's scientific methods were essentially frequentist and, as such, fallibilist and collaborative. He wrote of the expedition's data collection: "[O]ne or two [officers] might fall into error, but it is not likely that many would.... The whole will form a mass of evidence for the use of the government.... I wish particularly to avail myself of the results and observations of all." Like other navigators and surveyors of his time, and as we will discuss in more detail with Thoreau, Wilkes sought to minimize chance deviations with multiple measurements averaged to reduce margins of error, an approach analogous to republican processes in its insistence on both broad-based input and top-down organizational structuring. Wilkes also discussed the possibilities of chance in a chapter on whaling from which *Moby-Dick* draws. "[I]t is believed that the whale-fishery is a mere lottery," Wilkes wrote, "in which success is more owing to good luck than to good management," but "[t]here is, perhaps, no employment on the ocean wherein a sound judgment is more necessary."[27] Implicit throughout Wilkes's *Narrative* is that good judgments entail probabilistic thought.

More explicitly engaged in the probabilistic revolution was a successor to Wilkes, a follower of Whewell and a collaborator with Quetelet—Matthew Fontaine Maury, whom Melville refers to in "The Chart" as "Lieutenant Maury, of the National Observatory" (1004). Nicknamed the "Philosopher of the Seas," Maury was a pioneer of modern oceanography who served as superintendent of the U.S. Naval Observation from 1842 to 1861.[28] Maury's office was tasked with the charting of winds, currents, tides, and whale migrations—hardly a new enterprise, though Maury's efforts in America were unprecedented in scope and detail. Maury compiled data from hundreds of naval logbooks, drew additional information from the Naval National Institute and National Institute for the Advancement of Science (founded in 1848), and also gave free charts to merchants and whalers in exchange for their logbooks at the end of their voyages. Maury's work was an open-ended frequentist project that moved inductively from surmises to certainties, most influentially in his *Explanations and Sailing Directions to Accompany the Wind and Current Charts* (1848), an indispensable book for navigators that Maury continued to update and reissue.

That the revered naturalist Alexander von Humboldt wrote a glowing preface to the book says much about Maury's scientific rigor. In tracing the complex interrelations of wind, air pressure, sea currents, water temperature, salinity, topography, and marine life, Maury wrote: "I set out with no theory.... I set out with the view of collecting facts.... [I]n the manner of doing this, I have been governed altogether by the principles of inductive philosophy." Maury's methods, executed by a weary "compiler" who "wades" through oceans of facts, were indeed informed by Whewell's landmark *Philosophy of the Inductive Sciences*. Yet despite his claim about having no theories, Maury accepted the argument from design. He wrote of nature, "We all know it is perfect:—that in the performance of its manifold offices it is never once left to the guidance of chance—no, not for a moment!" Such conviction wavers, however, if only rhetorically, when Maury turns to the risky business of whaling, writing that whales "chance" to surface, that certain boats are "favored by chance," and that even the data on whale migrations come "by accident or chance." Maury ultimately subordinates such randomness to reason: "In calculating his path through the ocean, [the mariner] has to go into the doctrine of chances, and to determine thereby the degree of probability." Sailing the high seas might be romantic and risky but prudence guided by the new sciences of chance is best.[29]

Even if Melville, as he claims in a footnote, came across Maury's work after drafting "The Chart," Maury and the probabilism he represents illuminate what Ahab's methods are—and are not. Like Maury's weary compiler, Ahab and the "marked chart of his forehead" register the strain of quantitative research (1003): "And have I not tallied the whale, Ahab would mutter to himself, . . . after poring over his charts till long after midnight" (1006). Such reckoning should improve "Ahab's chances," but the problem is that Ahab cannot handle the fallibility of frequentist prediction as he too eagerly, too hubristically anticipates the day "when all possibilities would become probabilities, and . . . every probability the next thing to a certainty" (1005). Ahab is technically correct about the incrementalism of induction, which asymptotically approaches certitude without ever reaching it. Yet given his drive to fix Moby Dick and master utterly the white whale's agency, a reader might wonder if the "next thing to a certainty" will satisfy the monomaniacal and absolutist captain. It does not, not even for a short chapter, for by the end of "The Chart" crazy old Ahab is back, forced raving from his slumber by a "blazing brain" as he staggers about the decks of the *Pequod* like Edwin Forrest in a Shakespeare tragedy (1007). As if Ahab's fever is catching, Ishmael himself then enters into a labyrinth of causal conjectures—wondering about the "agent that so caused [Ahab] to burst," trying to differentiate between "outer" and "integral" causes, and finally comparing Ahab to Prometheus, whose heroic model of knowledge acquisition is a far cry from the bureaucratic, incremental inductions of Whewell, Wilkes, and Maury. As they say in the movies, Ahab is a loose cannon who plays by his own rules. "The Quarter-Deck" shows that he can speak Starbuck's language of scientific and economic reckoning, but "The Doubloon" makes it clear that he is not finally interested in other people's measurements. Like Dupin at the end of the "Mystery of Marie Roget," Ahab tires of large numbers in "The Chart," moving instead toward a more intuitive questing typically associated with romanticism.

Ahab's maddened impatience with charts and logbooks is just the start of his flight from empirical science, for rather than live with the uncertainties of probabilism, he is intent on abolishing them. An early hint of this impulse appears in "The Quarter-Deck," when Ahab rages at the gods: "Swerve me? Ye cannot swerve me! . . . The path to my fixed purpose is laid with iron rails" (972). As Melville may have learned from his reading in Bayle, Epicurus (and later, Lucretius) integrated chance into the fabric of the natural world by arguing in anticipation of quantum mechanics that atoms "swerve" according to chance.[30] Ahab rejects such devious cruising. By nailing the doubloon to the mast of the *Pequod*, he fixes a foremost figure of chance, the flipping of a coin (which Emerson takes to represent skepticism in his 1850 essay, "Montaigne"). Ahab later tramples his quadrant and curses science for its failure to guarantee "where one drop of water or one grain of sand will be to-morrow," yet another reference to induction's inability to absolutely predict future events (1327). Ahab also subordinates science to his imperial person by self-magnetizing the *Pequod's* needle, and even the primitive log and line frustrate him in his search—so much so that by the end of the book, Ahab reaches the atavistic point of sniffing his way toward Moby Dick. The problem with Victor Frankenstein, Rappaccini, and Aylmer is that they expect science to achieve perfection. Quite the opposite, Ahab's perfectionism is precisely what drives him to reject science, for he knows from his struggles in "The Chart" that empirical inductions are probabilistic and thus lead at best to the next thing to a certainty, which for him is not certain enough.

If "The Chart" highlights Ahab's inability to countenance the play of chance, Melville's dialectical imagination offers an alternative possibility as "The Affidavit" (chapter 45) presents Ishmael as a fallibilist foil to the absolutist Ahab. Just as Ahab initially studies former voyages in order to improve his probabilities, Ishmael asserts the plausibility of his narrative by appealing to past instances of whales attacking men and harpooners reencountering whales. But whereas Ahab's tallying gives way to raving, Ishmael is more comfortable with uncertainty, a familiar contrast in *Moby-Dick* criticism that tends to set Ishmael's post-metaphysical pluralism against Ahab's tyrannical metaphysics of presence.[31] Ishmael's corrigibility, however, involves probability at least as much as it does Heidegger and multiculturalism. Shrugging off the burden of absolute proof, Ishmael turns to induction in defending his verisimilitude: "I care not to perform this part of my task methodically; but shall be content to produce the desired impression by separate citations of items" (1009). The joke of "The Affidavit" is that, despite its logically structured argument, Ishmael's methodological looseness only allows him to argue for the "probability" of his tale, which he finds satisfying enough (1011). As with Poe, probabilistic reasoning for Ishmael expands the range of realism, freeing the storyteller to claim plausibility as his fancy runs wild.

When "Surmises" (chapter 46) speculates on Ahab's unfathomable motives, Melville further suggests that causation is beyond rational certitude, a point that comes to a head in "The Mat-Maker" (chapter 47), which names a plot that has been brewing since "Moby Dick" first described the white whale as the incarnation of all malicious agencies. Chapters 41 through 46 do not march toward the telos of "The Mat-Maker," but their recurrent attentions to causal indeterminacy and probabilistic methods culminate when Melville for the first time in the book unmistakably interjects chance into the question of fate and free will. As Ishmael and Queequeg spend a lazy afternoon weaving together on the "Loom of Time," Ishmael conjectures:

> This warp seemed necessity; and here thought I, with my own hand I ply my own shuttle and weave my own destiny into these unalterable threads. Meantime, Queequeg's impulsive, indifferent sword, sometimes hitting the woof slantingly, or crookedly, or strongly, or weakly, as the case might be ... this easy, indifferent sword must be chance—aye, chance, free will, and necessity—no wise incompatible—all interweavingly working together.... [A]nd chance, though restrained in its play within the right lines of necessity, and sideways in its motions modified by free will, though thus prescribed to by both, chance by turns rules either, and has the last featuring blow at events. (1021–22)

It is one thing for Ishmael to employ random methods and take satisfaction in probable truths. It is quite another, especially in the nineteenth century, to offer up chance as a natural force commensurate with fate and free will. With characteristic congeniality, Ishmael sketches a compromise among his three causal elements: chance can be "modified" (that is, managed but not eliminated by human will); it is "restrained" by fated laws (as in frequentist thought); yet it remains a real power that cannot be dismissed as mere ignorance of providential designs. That chance, necessity, and free will "interweavingly" work together may sound ecumenical enough, and most students would rather accept such moderate triangulation than delve deeper into theo-philosophical controversies. *Can we leave causality behind already and talk some more about slavery and race, especially since we feel fairly sure about the right side of these issues?* Moby-Dick is indeed politically prophetic and even potentially instructive, yet given how strenuously Ishmael's captain and Melville's culture deny the existence of chance, the etiology of "The Mat-Maker"—though mellow in tone—is as controversial as anything in Melville's oeuvre. Is Ishmael turning atheist in his acknowledgment of chance? Has he (and maybe Melville) lost his mind?

Some historical coordinates help to elucidate how radical but also how classically grounded the Loom of Time section is. In *Gondibert* (1651), which Melville bought in 1849, William Davenant compares "indiff'rent Chance" to a "Sword" and writes in an adjacent stanza that Melville triple-scored:

> But sure the Heav'nly Movers little care
> Whither our motions here be false or true;
> For we proceed, whilst they are regular,
> As if we Dice for all our actions threw.[32]

Davenant's view that chance is only nominal was, as we have seen, widely held from the seventeenth through nineteenth centuries. However, some classical philosophers afforded chance a more positive role, even if they lacked the mathematical concepts for precisely determining probabilities. For Epicurus (as reported by Diogenes Laertius), "[S]ome things happen of necessity, others by chance, others through our own agency." Cicero in *The Offices*, which Melville bought in 1849, also takes chance as a basic element in life, joining Carneades, Pyrrho, and Sextus Empiricus in suspending judgment regarding causation. Not only is Cicero a manager of chance ("[T]he man of great intellect anticipates the future, calculates the chances, . . . [and] decides how to meet every contingency"), he also employs an extended metaphor that resonates in "Loomings":

> We ought surely to have as much sense as actors who choose not the best pieces but those most suited to their powers. . . . Royalty and command, rank and office, wealth and influence, and the opposite conditions, depend on fortune or on circumstances: but the part that we are to play in the world is the result of our own free choice.

Ishmael in "Loomings" cannot achieve what Cicero calls "indifference to the accidents of fortune," and he cannot quite accept *The Office's* point that there are no shabby parts, only shabby actors.[33] Yet the not-quite-reconciled Ishmael of "Loomings" is not the easy weaver of the Loom of Time. Taking chance as a sword that hits indifferently, Ishmael in "The Mat-Maker" more cheerfully accepts his aleatory lot. Rather than gripe about providential programs or seek the motives of his ever-receding will, Ishmael enjoys a sunny day under chance, if only for half a chapter.

By having the book's first sighting of a whale cut short Ishmael's reverie at the Loom of Time, Melville suggests how hard it is to keep fate, free will, and chance in tranquil equilibrium. With Ishmael dropping his "ball of free will," and with Tashtego's wild cry compared to that of "some prophet or seer beholding the shadows of Fate," *Moby-Dick* returns to the dualistic causation of "Loomings" with a decided tilt toward determinism (1022). So dominant seems this dualistic etiology throughout the book that scholars scarcely mention chance in "The Mat-Maker" at all, even though the power of chance is so forthrightly announced that it remains a living, subversive alternative to overdetermined debates over fate and free will.[34] Staging a renaissance quite different from that of F. O. Matthiessen, *Moby-Dick* looks back toward classical skepticism and its revival in the Early Modern period, suggesting (as Bernard Williams has argued) that current recognitions of chance have more in common with classical worldviews than with Enlightenment thinking.[35]

Things feel differently after "The Mat-Maker" sensitizes readers to the potential of chance. Ishmael increasingly acknowledges chance in his loosely methodical way, as if the narrative's growing focus on actual whaling—the techniques of the chase, the process of rendering, the business of oil, insurance, and navigation—pushes Ishmael toward the kind of probabilistic reasoning that many people employ every day. Prior to "The Mat-Maker," "The Mast-Head" reveals Ishmael's attraction to Cartesian certitude, and it is fitting that in this most abstracted of moods he is dismissive of probabilistic practices—the "'binnacle deviations,' 'azimuth compass observations,' and 'approximate errors'" that (as shown by Maury, Wilkes, and Nathaniel Bowditch) were standard navigational techniques entailing the law of large numbers.[36]

After "The Mast-Head" warns of excessive idealism, and after "The Mat-Maker" names the element of chance, Ishmael is less likely to credit any quest for metaphysical certainty. *Moby-Dick* is not Stephen Toulmin's *Cosmopolis* (1990), but the philosophical outlook of the book is more akin to Montaigne than Descartes. The "genial, desperado philosophy" of "The Hyena" accepts epistemological limits under the risky conditions of whaling (1035). The discussion of dead letters in "The Jeroboam's Story" hints (as we have seen with Poe) at a favorite example of probability theorists. In "The Monkey-Rope," Ishmael resigns himself to chancy contingencies after imagining "a sort of interregnum in Providence" (1135). He even calls whaling an enterprise in which "a *careful disorderliness* is the true method," as if random slackers can be to some degree rehabilitated by getting a real world job (1180; my emphasis).[37] Ishmael will never rise to the careful discipline of Whewell, Wilkes, or Maury, but the more real world experience he has with whaling, the more probabilistic his outlook becomes. He writes that "out of fifty fair chances for a dart, not five are successful," thus two harpoons are recommended for "a doubling of the chances," which is especially important in a dangerous business that threatens a "thousand concurring accidents" (1100, 1102, 1103). Like a theorist of chance, Ishmael even describes "The Grand Armada" as a statistical phenomenon, for though it is "crossed by random whales," the pod circles "one centre," and though it is initially "riotous and disordered," it soon becomes a "systematic movement" as wildness is regularized in the mass (1210–11).

Of special interest is Melville's reference to "analogical probability" in "The Right Whale's Head—Contrasted View." When describing sailors who estimate the age of whales by counting marks on their baleen as if counting rings on a tree, Ishmael writes, "[T]he certainty of this criterion is far from demonstrable, yet it has the savor of analogical probability" (1150). Logicians and philosophers of science from the seventeenth century onward understood that reasoning by analogy, despite potential errors of overgeneralization and specious resemblance, was the only method for inferring natural laws from discrete observations. Ishmael admits that analogies between whales and trees are not "demonstrable" (in the argot of the period, this means apodictically true), but he judges the connection probable enough to be sufficiently compelling, at least in the matter of baleen.

Whether analogical reasoning can justify religious faith is a more momentous question. *Moby-Dick* often subverts biblical literalism, particularly in Ishmael's ironic attempts to vindicate scripture empirically. His theological play has been well documented in regards to Melville and the German higher criticism, though little attention has been paid to Hume, who questioned the authority of scriptural miracles by eroding the grounds of analogical probability. Melville calls Hume in *Redburn* "the most skeptical of philosophical skeptics."[38] Whereas Butler (and later Paley) argued that nature, like a house, presupposes an omnipotent Architect, Hume in *Dialogues Concerning Natural Religion* (1779) pointed out that such claims are only as probable as the analogy, which he took to be a weak one. More notoriously, Hume argued in his *Enquiry Concerning Human Understanding* (1748) that miracles are highly improbable events that cannot be credited through analogical reasoning, if only because the very miraculousness of miracles lies in their violation of analogy. Hume's chapter "On Miracles" follows chapters on skepticism in which Hume shows that causality is beyond human certitude. He concludes: "[W]e have no reason ... to think that our usual analogies and probabilities have any authority. Our line is too short to fathom such immense abysses." Small wonder that the nineteenth century associated Hume with atheism and chance.[39]

Ishmael's reference to analogical probability indicates, if nothing else, that Melville understood the etiological implications of the miracles controversy, as well as the fact that the argument from design—a foundation of faith in Melville's time—ultimately rested on probabilistic ground. Ishmael's speculations throughout *Moby-Dick* explore analogies between, well, almost everything—ships and nations, books and whales, nautical equipment and metaphysical systems, penises and priests, and so on. Such connections point toward Melville's romantic tendency to present all things as a doubloon-like symbol, but they also undermine the argument from design in showing that there are no rational limits to an uncontrollably associative mindset. For Hume, the absence of demonstrable causation frustrates the rage for order: "All events seem entirely loose and separate. One event follows another; but we never can observe any tie between them."[40] Hume's sensibility can describe both causal skepticism and (proto)modern literary forms—picaresque novels with their aleatory plots, impressionistic essays from Montaigne and Emerson, the chaotic poetics of German romantics, and gargantuan pastiches such as *Moby-Dick*. As much as Ishmael attempts to order his experiences through speculative analogies, and as much as *Moby-Dick* is an organic and at times cunningly organized text, its structure nonetheless becomes increasingly loose and separate in its middle sections—as if the naming of chance in "The Mat-Maker" is impossible to unsay; as if, like Ishmael's carefully disordered ways, Melville's narrative wandering is commensurate with experience under conditions of chance. The many readers who confess to abandoning *Moby-Dick* one-third of the way through attest to the fact that the middle of the narrative loses much of its teleological drive. Teachers who assign *Moby-Dick* in its entirety can reassure their students that the end brings the story full circle, though to do so is to take some liberties that the book does not entirely allow.

AT A VENTURE

Here is a fairly conventional way to read the end of *Moby-Dick*. Bursting with hubris and an unwillingness to relinquish belief in his own free will, Ahab is punished for rebelling against providence as represented by the "predestinating" white whale (1405). By contrast, Ishmael submits with some mixture of wisdom and exhaustion to his shabby part in the grand scheme of things, and his survival implies an interlocking set of theological, philosophical, and political injunctions: do not be a blaspheming, absolutist tyrant or allow one to captain your soul or ship-of-state; learn instead to more stoically, pluralistically, and perhaps even piously respect the limits of human knowledge and agency.[41] In such readings, fate trumps free will, while chance has no purchase at all. With the fulfillment of longstanding prophecies, and with so furious a concatenation of symbols as to provide close readers a modicum of job security, "The Chase—Third Day" and the "Epilogue" feel intensely teleological, perfectly figured by the "closing vortex" of the whirlpool that draws everything toward its "vital centre" (1408). Even the coffin that pops up to save Ishmael can smack of formal unity and providential design, vindicating Melville's elaborate foreshadowing and—along with eagles, red flags, Milton, and hammers—completing an array of symbolic and allusive arcs. *Moby-Dick* remains a baggy monster trailing loose narrative strands, but the conclusion of the book seems about as overdetermined as any proponent of fate or formal totality might wish. One would have to be insane to suggest that such things happen by chance.

Or at least one would have to be Melville, for the final two chapters of *Moby-Dick* keep open a possibility that centuries of Western thought tried to foreclose but could not seal off. As providential as Ahab's death seems to be, aleatory instabilities remain at the levels of intellectual argument, literary form, and narrative effect. A well-canvassed but still underappreciated allusion in *Moby-Dick* is Ahab's name, which points to the biblical King of Israel who is punished for warring against God's will.[42] In the King James Bible, Micaiah follows Elijah in prophesying King Ahab's death in battle, but when an unnamed archer kills the disguised king "at a venture" during a tribal conflict whose stakes are far from clear, Ahab's demise lacks what some readers might consider dramatic closure and allegorical neatness (1 Kings 22:34). Yes, the prophecies of Micaiah and Elijah are fulfilled, but the culmination comes quite suddenly and in a context that is confusedly sketched. Yes, the moral is to heed God's command, but the lesson is enacted through an anonymous human agent who draws his bow "at a venture," a phrase that the *OED* defines as "at random" or "by chance." The archer was not even aiming for King Ahab; he just let his arrow fly. Eric Auerbach argued half a century ago that while

classical literature theoretically turns on fortune, chance is not "a living historical reality" because of the narrative clarity and orderly forms of classical literature. By contrast
for Auerbach, the Bible—despite its teleological impetus—allows "random everyday
circumstances" into play, thus creating a productive "antagonism between sensory appearance and meaning."[43] However, we can phrase the antagonism less mimetically and
more causally: Christian theology is teleological, but biblical narrative often feels
weirdly haphazard. Exegetes can work to conform the latter to the former, and in doing
so conform themselves and their readers to their faith, just as scholars can make the New
Critical case for *Moby-Dick's* awe-inspiring totality. But it's hard, at least as hard as finding
Kings a transparently didactic text, for even when compared to other Old Testament
moments—say, David's slaying of Goliath—King Ahab's death can still seem random,
providential frameworks notwithstanding.

Well before and during Melville's time, exegetes worried over this point. When
George Gleig glossed Kings in his popular *History of the Bible* (1835), he wrote simply,
"Ahab was slain by a chance arrow." Gleig did not mean to set chance over providence,
but his mention of the loaded word is telling, especially given that many theologians
insisted that King Ahab was not—they repeated, *not*—killed by chance. In *A Discourse
Concerning the Divine Providence* (1694), William Sherlock admitted that it might appear
that Ahab was killed "by a very great chance," yet "no man will think that prophecies are
fulfilled by chance; and therefore we must confess, that what seems chance to us, was
appointed by God." Matthew Henry's *Comprehensive Commentary on the Holy Bible*
(1706), reprinted at least six times in the nineteenth century, held that King Ahab's death
"seems altogether casual"—that is, by chance—but in actuality was "done by the deter-
minate counsel and fore-knowledge of God." One hundred and fifty years later, the
matter was not laid to rest. In "The Judgments of God Upon the Wicked" (1845), the
Cambridge University preacher James Hildyard said of the biblical Ahab, "[T]he bow
drawn 'at a venture' was assuredly no matter of accident or chance; albeit that the expression of the inspired writer would appear to imply as much." In his catechistic dialogue,
What Is Chance? (1848), G. W. Mylne has his model Christian character deny that Ahab
was killed by chance, while John Dick reasoned in a lecture "On Providence" (1838):
"Chance, indeed, is impossible under the government of God. . . . An arrow shot at random may fall to the ground, or may kill one man as well as another; but in the case of
Ahab, it had received a commission." For Dick and other wary theologians, not all events
can be rightly described as providential, but God's special interposition—as in King
Ahab's example—sometimes makes itself irrefutably known.[44]

The challenge is determining precisely how total and immediate the oversight of
providence is, a question taken up in John Kitto's entry on "Providence" in the *Cyclopedia
of Biblical Literature* (1845), a work Melville owned and almost surely consulted when
composing *Moby-Dick*. Kitto focuses on two familiar and ultimately related objections to
providence: an overarching providence can "interfere with human freedom" and also
"render God unjust in permitting evil to exist." Kitto offers no definite answers to these
problems of agency and theodicy, citing instead the "inscrutable mystery" of God before
referring readers to the seventeenth-century Puritan divine Stephen Charnock as a
helpful source on the subject. Charnock wrote in 1682: "God knows all things that shall
accidentally happen, or, as we say, by chance. . . . [S]uch was that arrow whereby Ahab

was killed. . . . [T]his some call a mixed contingent, made up partly of necessity, and partly of accident." Using chance in a nominal sense and adhering to a so-called compatibilist position, Charnock (like Milton) makes a fine distinction between foreknowledge absolute and fixed fate insofar as God may be the first cause of existence and providentially know the course of all things, but this does not necessarily make him the *immediate* cause of every event. Humans, therefore, possess limited agency, including the potential to sin and be rightfully punished.[45]

Melville and George Adler (who died in a mental asylum after publishing *Letters of a Lunatic* in 1854) mulled over such thoughts as they crossed the Atlantic in 1849. No one knows what they concluded, if anything, about "'Fixed Fate, Free-will, foreknowledge absolute,' etc.," though the ameliorative efforts of compatibilists to salvage some measure of free will sit uneasily alongside strong versions of providence that take God to be omnipresent, omniscient, omnipotent, and omni-benevolent. Melville's copy of *Paradise Lost* indicates as much. At the beginning of Book Ten, God speaks to the angels about the Fall of Adam and Eve, explaining that He Himself "Foretold" the event but did nothing to "necessitate [Adam's] fall" nor "touch with lightest moment of impulse/His free will." Resisting Milton's notion of an all-powerful God who depicts Himself as an innocent bystander, Melville wrote in the margin: "All Milton's strength and rhetoric suffice not to satisfy, concerning this matter—free-will. Doubtless, he must have felt it himself; and looked upon it as the one great unavoidable flaw in his work."[46] Melville respects the achievement of Milton and yet sees his etiology as a dodge: if God knows what will happen, then happen it must, and so man cannot choose to do otherwise. Edwardsian Calvinists avoided Milton's struggles by positing a determinism that goes all the way down. Less theologically coherent but more psychologically sustainable was the view of Unitarians such as Channing, who in his "Remarks on Milton" (1826) could only insist that both providence and free will must somehow coexist in a moral universe, even if Channing found no rational way to explain how such interweaving might work. Francis Newman turned to a familiar example when describing the quandary in 1838: "A certain man drew a bow at a venture, and killed King Ahab. . . . It is certainly impossible to attribute to the Most High a perfect foreknowledge of [such] things, and yet deny that he exercised any sort of superintendence over them."[47] Whether or not Melville came into direct contact with the debates circulating around King Ahab, he recognized that King Ahab figures the crucial challenge that chance poses to providential etiology. Predestinarians and libertarians alike could deny that chance played any role in the arrow shot at a venture. The irony is that the repetition of such disclaimers could exacerbate the doubts they were meant to dispel, especially as chance took on explanatory power outside of theological realms.

That an arrow kills King Ahab makes his case especially poignant. Target shooting was a favorite example for Quetelet, Poisson, John Herschel, George Eliot, and James Clerk Maxwell, all of who—with familiar statistical logic—argued that individual trials are subject to chance errors that in the long run balance each other so that the bulls-eye of a target can be inferred from the errant shots surrounding it. Thomas Huxley (referring to Darwin) and William James (speaking of pragmatism) contrasted the single rifle shot of the absolutist to the "buckshot" and "shotgun" approach of probabilistic methods.[48] When Ahab goes ballistic—threatening to "strike the sun" (967) and pledging to "burst his hot heart's shell" on Moby Dick (989)—he eschews the aleatory deviations and multiple trials of probabilism, wishing not for a shotgun but for a "long gun" to take his vengeance on the heavens (972). Aspiring once and for all to fix the white whale with a single, infallible, teleological thrust, he spits his final line, "*Thus*, I give up the spear!" (1406)—not *Thus, I strike as accurately as possible under conditions of chance, and if this trial proves insufficient, I will continue doing my repetitive, incremental best!* We have seen how Ishmael advises harpooners to better their chances with multiple attempts, and Melville in *White-Jacket* also depicts shooting as a chancy enterprise: "[I]f by good or bad luck, as the case may be, a round shot, fired at random through the smoke, happens to send overboard your fore-mast, and another to unship your rudder, there you lie crippled.... Instead of tossing this old lead and iron into the air, therefore, it would be much better amicably to toss up a copper and let heads win." Recognizing the aleatory nature of missiles, *White-Jacket's* gun crew names its cannon "*Black Bet*."[49]

This is not to say that Melville believes in chance as a fundamental force or that *Moby-Dick's* chance-acknowledging subtext represents his "real" view on causation. *Moby-Dick* neither confirms nor denies that chance has the last featuring blow on events, a suspension of judgment that is hardly a cop-out given the aggressive providentialism of Melville's time. When the prophets' prophesies come to pass and punish the wicked who stab from hell's heart, God's hand may require no advertisement. Except that, like King Ahab's death from an arrow shot at venture, Captain Ahab's end can feel downright odd in its anticlimactic suddenness. It is not that Ahab gets no final speech: he has been giving valedictories for about half of the book, and his last line is so rhetorically juiced as to alert the most tone-deaf of readers. What is strange—and as I take it, intentionally unsettling—is how ignominious his moment of death is: "The line ran through the groove;—ran foul. Ahab stooped to clear it; he did clear it; but the flying turn caught him round the neck, and voiceless as Turkish mutes bowstring their victim, he was shot out of the boat, ere the crew knew he was gone" (1406). Nothing more is seen or heard of Ahab. The passage might allude to threads of fate (see "The Line"), and the lone simile of the scene is provocative, but relative to the ornate style of *Moby-Dick*, the hypotactic description is remarkably reticent—no proliferating language, no meta-critical commentary, any speculative gestures toward providential programs lost in the details of the whale-line, whose jumping of the groove suggests that yarns do not always run according to straight narrative designs. As if a whale is sometimes just a blind brute, and as if biblical kings can indeed die by venture, Ahab is gone ere the crew, the reader, and even *Moby-Dick's* prose seem to know it.

The possibility that chance figures in Captain Ahab's death feels particularly strong when, as the whale-line disappears into the sea, its eye-splice knocks over an oarsman. This detail does not so much speak to the damage that Ahab causes his crew; that trenchant commentary comes moments later when the men look forlornly toward the *Pequod*. The thumping of the anonymous oarsman is a seemingly insignificant fact left out of every cinematic and graphic adaptation of *Moby-Dick* that I have seen (some of which want Ahab, not Fedallah, to resurface bound by his whale-line to Moby Dick in perfect symbolic bondage, indicating that Matthiessen was not alone in wanting more closure in Melville's actual text).[50] The significance of the last featuring blow on the oarsman lies in its very insignificance. If, as Michael Witmore has argued, Calvin ascribes "dramatic irony" to providence insofar as seeming accidents are planned to most fully display God's power, *Moby-Dick* is designedly, ironically undramatic in describing the oarsman's dunking.[51] It is easier to attribute momentous events to God—even tragic ones like fatalities and floods—than to invoke providential explanations for, say, stubbed toes or spilled milk. Melville's indifferent hits of chance are comic in their subversion of totalized order, as if Adam and Eve, with Providence as their guide, accidentally knock loose a coconut that hits a sheep on their way out of Eden.[52] In this sense, the richly foreshadowed death of Captain Ahab does not fulfill in narrative effect the immense teleological momentum built behind it. Theoretically, Ahab meets his fate, but his end can feel kind of random, as if the fulfillment of a prophecy, necessarily imagined beforehand, can never predict the actual experience itself. Even the expected can feel unexpected when it happens, as with the passing of a terminally ill loved one.

Aleatory forces continue to lurk in the "Epilogue" when Ishmael explains how he alone survived by being thrown from Ahab's boat early in the chase: "It so chanced, that after the Parsee's disappearance, I was he whom the Fates ordained to take the place of Ahab's bowsman" (1408). Setting aside its first three words, this sentence announces a totalized, providential conclusion: just as "Loomings" settles on the fates as the reason for Ishmael's departure, the "Epilogue" also invokes the fates to explain how he made it back. Left floating between unknowable depths and unattainable higher laws, Ishmael in the "Epilogue" seems finally to internalize the lesson of stoic submission. For once in his philosophizing life, he eschews speculative reveries, even after witnessing the overwrought allegory that is the apocalypse of the *Pequod*. Ishmael's story even appears to follow the teleological path of a conversion narrative, for unlike Ahab, who cannot quite recant in "The Symphony," Ishmael undergoes a personal transformation in which the recognition of epistemological limits allows the seeker to stop asking unanswerable questions and simply shut up and believe, just as psychological and intellectual exhaustion enables the doubter to give up his willful self. Gesturing toward a main Puritan paradox—the need for the subject to try for salvation within a system that more or less denies humans free will—*Moby-Dick* almost adheres to a providential logic under which the seemingly random hits of chance become a kind of "holy violence."[53]

The trouble with reading *Moby-Dick's* "Epilogue" as a telos is the seemingly casual clause, "It so chanced." The first thing to note about these words is the conceptual instability they generate when combined with the sentence's invocation of the fates. Today, fate and chance are sometimes used interchangeably to indicate causes beyond human control, though notions of chance continue to challenge accounts of determinism.[54] Nineteenth-century writers sometimes conflate fate and chance, but not when etiology is under careful discussion. If Douglas Patey overstates the case that "[p]rovidence and probability" became "adversaries" in the Early Modern period, the tensions he notes are real to the extent that Kitto wrote in his *Cyclopedia*, "As a thing is known by its opposites, the meaning of Providence is elucidated considering that it is opposed to fortune or fortuitous accident." Melville's commitment to etiology makes it unlikely that his juxtaposition of chance and fate in the "Epilogue" is innocent, especially considering that rowing assignments on whaleboats were sometimes determined by lot.[55]

Ishmael's miraculous survival can intimate an interposing providence, though other aleatory associations in the "Epilogue" suggest an opposite explanation. The coffin that saves Ishmael is linked with Queequeg, who holds the sword of chance in "The Mat-Maker" and whom Geoffrey Sanborne has called an "allegorical emblem of Chance."[56] With its cunning springs and pagan designs, the coffin escapes teleological vortices, keeping Ishmael afloat until he is rescued, not so much by a savior sent straight from heaven but by the "devious-cruising" *Rachel* that just happens upon the wrong lost sailor during its methodical searching (1408). All things can always be attributed to Providence, but the end of *Moby-Dick* keeps open the possibilities of chance, abandoning the dualistic framework of "Loomings" and even leaving behind the equivocal interweavings of the Loom of Time as chance subtly supersedes free will as the opposite of providence.

What finally to make of the paradox that the fates chance to save Ishmael is difficult to say, though after depicting the disastrous consequences of Ahab's hunt for a master cause, it seems likely that *Moby-Dick* suggests that the suspension of judgment is prudent in matters of agency and that to deny chance is to put oneself and one's community at risk. Such epistemological modesty sides with aleatory skepticism against prevailing Protestant and American beliefs that for centuries attempted not to suspend but to beggar the question of chance. Blake may need to ask who made the little lamb, but the answer is never in doubt. Children may not always be adequately catechized, but readers of *The Scarlet Letter* (1850) and *Uncle Tom's Cabin* (1852) know who made Pearl and Topsy. Nor does Tillotson in his paradigmatic attack on chance feel the need for open-minded inquiry when causation is at issue:

> Is it not much easier, and more reasonable to say, that the wisdom of God made all . . . things, than to trouble ourselves to imagine how all things should happen thus conveniently by chance? Did you ever know any great work, in which there was a variety of parts, and an orderly disposition of them required, done by chance, and without the direction of wisdom and counsel? How longtime might a man take to jumble a set of four and twenty letters together, before they would fall out to be an exact poem; yeah, or to make a book of tolerable sense, though but in prose? How long might a man sprinkle oil and colours upon canvas, with a careless hand, before this would produce the exact picture of a man?[57]

Rhetorical questions are the very stuff of ideology in that they inculcate and buttress shared assumptions. A fundamental belief of Melville's culture is that chance is beyond belief, a position defended by providential thinkers who demanded assent. As a piece from 1851 put it when condemning "The Atheist, with his doctrine of *chance*": "Is all this harmony the result of mere *accident*? Is the law without the lawgiver—the mechanism without the architect—the creation without the Creator?"[58]

Moby-Dick does not vouchsafe straight answers, but Melville poses questions of his own that are far from rhetorical. What if Ahab's death is at a venture, and chance moves Ishmael's fate? What if indifferent swords give featuring blows, and whales in the sea do not God's voice obey? *Moby-Dick's* refusal to affirm providence places Melville in a tradition of skepticism stretching from the classical Pyrrhonists and Cicero to Montaigne, Bayle, and Hume. This tradition includes Benjamin Franklin—who read Montaigne, Bayle, and Diogenese Laertius; worked in the probabilistic fields of insurance, demography, and lotteries; and inscribed on a memorial to the Calvinist parents whom he left to seek his fortune as a metaphorical orphan, "[D]istrust not Providence."[59] The double negative on Franklin's public monument is cunning. Protestant theology well before the nineteenth century sought to eradicate the possibilities of chance, while philosophy and science attempted to master it under the argument from design. Destiny in Melville's time continued to be a manifest ideology, though less disciplined were some literary authors who imagined all sorts of possible ends. Poe is so infatuated with the odd that he usually forgets to gesture toward God. Dickinson (as we will see) doubts natural theology, particularly in her wonderfully quarrelsome poem, "Bring me the Sunset in a Cup" (1860), which shows how catechistic questions asserting a commonly assumed providence threaten to slide into blasphemy when repeated vehemently enough. *Who laid the Rainbow's piers? Who leads the docile spheres? Who the hell shut the windows down so close my spirit cannot see?*

Even Hawthorne, who on a Liverpool beach admired and pitied Melville's stubborn unbelief, questions the surety of providential faith, especially if the last line of "David Swan" (1837) is somewhat more than rhetorical. Ruminating on the vast contingencies that a storyteller might explore, Hawthorne wonders, "Does it not argue a superintending Providence, that, while viewless and unexpected events thrust themselves continually athwart our path, there should still be regularity enough, in mortal life, to render foresight even partially available?" Hawthorne is as profound a critic of providential justification as America has known, even if (as Sacvan Bercovitch has argued) his works "imply teleology."[60] For Hawthorne, human frailty combined with epistemological limits makes all readings of providence suspect. Perhaps Hawthorne even knew that in the seventeenth century the rational theologian William Chillingworth cited moral certainty in defense of Christian faith, finding considerable more comfort than the so-named Roger Chillingworth in a knowledge that forever escapes certitude.

Moby-Dick, of course, is dedicated to Hawthorne in whose writings Melville found thrilling examples of unspeakable religious speculation. Ranging more wildly through intellectual history, and being more willing to challenge teleological visions at an elemental level, Melville in *Moby-Dick* is more convinced than Hawthorne by the unmasterable power of chance. As he wrote in his copy of *Paradise Regained* (1671), "The greatest, grandest things are unpredicted."[61] No literary text in the nineteenth century draws on the history of chance more deeply than *Moby-Dick*, and yet for all of Melville's learning—or perhaps, precisely because of it—he never takes a clear position regarding the ontology of chance. What seems to interest Melville most is recovering chance as a living option. If *Moby-Dick* primarily does so in theo-philosophical registers, Melville's subsequent writings more centrally explore the moral and aesthetic implications of unfathomable etiology.

CHAPTER 3

Doubting If Doubt Itself Be Doubting

After *Moby-Dick*

Suppose a philosopher to be entirely ignorant of the constitution of the human mind, . . . would he not, as in the case of the doctrine of chances, immediately infer that there must be a *fixed cause* for [the] coincidence of motives and actions? Would he not say that, though he could not see into the man, the connexion was *natural*, and *necessary*?
　　　—Joseph Priestley, *The Doctrine of Philosophical Necessity Illustrated* (1777)

It may be that Melville's happiest days came after completing *Moby-Dick* and before the novel's mixed reviews consigned the book to a purgatory of obscurity that would last through Melville's death.[1] The rise and fall of Herman Melville make for a dramatic story, but if his outlook becomes bleaker and his prose more serpentine as his personal and professional disappointments mount, Melville's writings after *Moby-Dick* do not spin into some tragic decline. The possibilities of chance continue to be aesthetically and intellectually generative for Melville as he extends his thinking on causal indeterminacy to the problem of critical judgment and action. As encompassing a world as *Moby-Dick* is, it lacks a lively, integral sense for the kind of moral complexity that entails momentous decisions made in the face of doubt. Ishmael is obviously beset by uncertainties, but he is generally along for the *Pequod's* ride. Starbuck periodically voices objections, though he, too, is more chorus than actor. As the sole decider of the *Pequod's* course, Ahab sporadically weighs the risks of vengeance against his responsibilities as a captain and family man, while he also acknowledges, if mainly to resent, his epistemological finitude. Yet Ahab's mind is more or less set from the moment we first meet him: death to the white whale is the only motto for a man with little taste for suspending judgments or modifying decisions. The moral structure of *Moby-Dick* is, in the end, more allegorical than psychological, more about the dynamics between positions represented by various characters than about the interplay of duty, desire, and doubt within a single subject.

　　Such is decidedly not the case with *Pierre* and "Bartleby, the Scrivener," intensely psychological texts that, in many ways, echo *Moby-Dick* but also stand as ambitious extensions of Melville's meditations on chance. *Pierre* and "Bartleby" turn with sustained attention to the challenge of what one ought to do under conditions of chance, a question that bears on a set of concerns: Melville's struggles in the literary marketplace, the office of literary criticism, and the difficulty of forming moral judgments when agency is unclear. Drawing on Aristotle, Jonathan Edwards, and the philosophical puzzle known as Buridan's ass, *Pierre* and "Bartleby" continue to pit classical notions of chance against Christian providentialism, though more than *Moby-Dick* they implicate readers in dilemmas of chance as Melville explores the moral consequences and pragmatist limits of aleatory skepticism.

JUDGE YE, THEN, YE JUDICIOUS

As Melville's first extended commentary on sentimentality and print culture, *Pierre* pursues skeptical accounts of causation into affective and vocational domains. As if tracing the end of the American Enlightenment, *Pierre* describes the fall of a Revolutionary family from prominence to disgrace, lightness to darkness, transparency to opacity, and reason to madness. Confronting the animating question of the novel—whether to acknowledge his potential half-sister Isabel to the detriment of himself, his mother, and his fiancée Lucy—the youthful Pierre appears to call forth his most earnest rational energies. The novel canvasses the circumstantial evidence of Isabel's mysterious parentage—so much so that the narrative might well have become a search for her lost provenance. What instead convince Pierre that he is Isabel's half-brother are his overheated transcendental intuitions that Melville sets in opposition to empirical methods. Pierre's "flashing revelations" supersede "inductive reasoning"; his "intuitively certain" feelings overpower the "argumentative itemizings of the minutest known facts"; and he "spontaneously" dismisses "the sordid scrutiny of small pros and cons" on which the novel initially dwells.[2] Pierre and the narrator of *Pierre* share Dupin's disdain for plodding inductions. But whereas Dupin's intuitions are sharpened by scientific methods and prove remarkably reliable, *Pierre* most forcefully shows that epistemologies of the heart (whether transcendental, sentimental, or antinomian) can be devastatingly fallible, a danger that rises when Pierre eschews probabilistic reasoning in favor of spontaneous moral judgments.

Having in his mind settled the factual question of Isabel's origins, Pierre then appears to cogitate at length over what he ought to do. His conversation with the Reverend Falsgrave has all the trappings of ethical deliberation as Pierre's absolutism comes off looking superior to Falsgrave's "moral contingencies" (124). Plotinus Plinlimmon's pamphlet on "provisional" truths gives a stronger account of moral relativism (247). Yet as bracing as such philosophy is, neither Plinlimmon nor Falsgrave sways Pierre, who determines before encountering either man's thinking to become the defender of Isabel. Along the lines of classical tragedy and domestic fiction, Melville sets up a carefully calibrated dilemma: emotion versus reason, sacrifice versus self-interest, conviction versus convention, all arranged in tenuous balance given the uncertain facts of the case. The irony is that the lengthy moral parsing of *Pierre* is after the fact and beside the point, demonstrating—as Oliver Wendell Holmes Jr. would write (and as many a departmental meeting has shown)—that "Philosophy does not furnish motives, but it shows men that they are not fools for doing what they already want to do." The problem, in Samuel Otter's words, is that *Pierre* mercilessly shows that "feelings are a treacherous ground for moral action," especially when the novel continually asserts the impenetrability of motivation and character.[3] With reason relegated to belated justification and with passions running amok, Melville repeatedly returns to an etiological question: why does Pierre feel and thus act as he does?

Herein lies the central ambiguity of a book that doggedly seeks but does not find the master cause that drives Pierre. The narrative voice, which should not be equated with Melville's, announces early on: "In their precise tracings-out and subtile causations, the strongest and fieriest emotions of life defy all analytical insight.... [T]hese are things not wholly imputable to the immediate apparent cause, which is only one link in the chain" (82). Given the novel's barely sublimated sexual energies, we can certainly psychoanalyze Pierre, even if Melville proleptically denies Freud's claim that the unconscious can be structured. Melville also portrays Emersonian transcendentalism as a psycho-philosophy of moods. And yet *Pierre* most explicitly addresses the mystery of motive as a question of causation, orienting—or at least, seeming to orient—the novel's psychological meditations along conventional lines of "Fixed Fate and Free Will" (216).

When *Pierre* refers to the "apparent cause" as "only one link in the chain," and when the novel describes the search for motive as an "endless chain of wondering," Melville echoes the tropes and logic of Jonathan Edwards's determinism (82, 165). Wai Chee Dimock has argued that Edwards's sense of unpredictable affect makes him open to "something like a principle of *tolerable* arbitrariness," though if Edwards acknowledges aleatory experience, he remains at heart a metaphysical opponent of chance. Edwards writes in *Freedom of the Will*, "[H]ere is an infinite number of free acts, every one of them free; and yet not one of them free, but every act in the whole infinite chain a necessary effect."[4] Like Edwards, the narrator of *Pierre* denies that humans are free agents as generally understood, a determinism intimated by a line repeated twice in the novel's opening chapter: "[W]e shall see if Fate hath not just a little bit of a small word or two to say in this world" (17, 20). Subsequent, near-constant invocations of fate seem to make good on the narrator's threat, and following a tradition of influential criticism, we can read the fatalism of *Pierre* as a commentary (intentional or not) on the inescapability of ideology. The language of *Pierre* for Bercovitch is "*too* controlled, over-determined, self-consciously elaborated to the point of impasse," while Myra Jehlen sees the novel as "unreasonably fatalistic," and John Carlos Rowe calls it "*too* coherent and *too* convincing" in its subordination of literature to social forces. These critics and others set *Pierre's* determinism over and against the freedoms of Emersonian self-reliance, and they also register Melville's hints that the pervasive determinism of the novel might itself be overdetermined.[5] When Isabel speaks of her affinities for Pierre, she says, "Fate will be Fate, and it was fated"—a tautology so redundantly played out across the book as to indicate Melville's parody of freewill *and* necessity, Emerson *and* Edwards (189). The problem is that, as with *Moby-Dick*, critical assessments of agency in *Pierre* accept too readily dualisms of fate and free will, for with freedom brutally circumscribed and necessity advertised with suspicious insistence, *Pierre* subtly gestures toward another, almost unspeakable causal explanation.

When Pierre pledges to champion Isabel "through all conceivable contingencies of Time and Chance," the allusion to *Ecclesiastes* marks how vainly he aspires to rise above the aleatory conditions of mortality (128). Like Ahab, Pierre is an absolutist who is satisfied by "nothing but Truth," and yet he cannot help but figure his course as a chancy enterprise (81). "I cast my eternal die this day, ye powers" (129), he announces when pledging himself to Isabel—an image repeated when he "Crosses the Rubicon," recalling Caesar's line, "The die is cast" (216). Paying tribute to the argument from design but doubting its benevolence, *Pierre* suspects that humans are "blinded to the larger arc of the circle which menacingly hems [them] in" (126). Lines like this suggest a nominal view of chance in which humans see the "Finger of God" but cannot comprehend His whole "Hand," though Melville also insinuates that the "hollow of His hand" is empty— that providence is only a delusion (166). Such skepticism admits of aleatory possibilities, as when the narrator quotes *Hamlet* (1603) on the workings of "mischance" and follows Shakespeare in linking such sentiments to Montaigne (162). Or when the narrator asks the loaded question, "With the lightning's flash, the query is spontaneously propounded—chance, or God?" (133). Only after Pierre's individual agency is crushed and fate seemingly takes over the novel do the submerged possibilities of chance arise as a threatening hypothesis.

As if limning the psychology of Christian etiology, Pierre's capacity to suffer for his convictions makes him loath to acknowledge chance, as seen in the chapter where he, Isabel, and Lucy happen upon a painting exhibition. Entering the show on a "sudden impulse," always an inauspicious sign for Pierre, he finds an extraordinary Italian portrait included among the lesser works "[b]y some hocus-pocus of chance, or subtly designing knavery" (405–6). The painting is of an anonymous man who uncannily resembles Isabel, implying that she might as well be descended from a swarthy foreigner as from Pierre's Anglo-American father. Isabel is mystically moved by the portrait, but Pierre peremptorily dismisses the likeness as "one of the wonderful coincidences, nothing more" (409). Aristotle in his *Physics* defines chance as "coincidence," by which he means two phenomena occurring together with no intentional or causal connection. Aristotle also closely associates chance with "the spontaneous," a word that transcendentalists used to describe inwardly-inspired ascensions to knowledge, though one that Aristotle employs to indicate causes that are "indeterminate and opaque."[6] Melville combines both meanings of chance insofar as *Pierre's* spontaneous emotions have no discernible cause. Up until the art exhibit, Pierre had pledged to master contingency and chance, but when faced with the countervailing evidence of the portrait and its "subtile and spontaneous" effects, he initially invokes the logic of coincidence as an avoidance strategy, a dodge that Isabel points out: "Oh, by that word, Pierre, we but vainly seek to explain the inexplicable." Pierre, however, cannot countenance the possibility that he and Isabel are connected inexplicably by chance, that all his circumstantial proofs, intuitions, and sacrifices are nothing more than coincidental. "Let us begone," he abruptly concludes, "and let us keep eternal silence." Sex is the most popular taboo in *Pierre*, and the repression of race has received some attention, but chance—that byword for atheism and madness—also dare not speak its name.[7]

Just as Melville never clarifies relations between Pierre and Isabel, *Pierre* is less concerned with the ontology of chance than with the challenge of judgment and action under conditions of causal uncertainty. After fleeing the painting gallery for a sailing excursion, Pierre confronts the devastating second thought sparked by the Italian portrait. Recollecting his spontaneous emotions with anxiety, he wonders painfully late in the game, "How did he know that Isabel was his sister?" (409). As an aspect of skepticism, fallibilism can be seen as a cowardly evasion of commitment, though rigorously applied it risks nothing less than the acknowledgment that one's whole life is in error. When Pierre thinks again about Isabel's origins, this time he does not rely on spontaneous intuitions, for he evaluates the "entirely inconclusive" evidence in a startlingly new way. With odd and unconvincing abruptness, the narrator notes that for all Pierre's transcendental enthusiasm he is actually "uncompromisingly skeptical" and "skeptical of all tendered profundities," a revelation of his character promptly displayed when for the first sustained time in the book Pierre probabilistically considers his chances (410–11). Pierre worries that Isabel's history seems "less probable" when "[t]ested by any thing real," though he also finds some "corroboration" that she did in fact travel overseas, "the most surprising and improbable thing in [her] whole surprising and improbable story" (412). Pierre does not invoke the calculus of probabilities to determine the likelihood of Isabel's history, but when facing the quandary of chance or fate, coincidence or design, he proceeds if only momentarily in the manner of a probabilistic skeptic.

Pierre's brush with the rational weighing of chances is fleeting but profoundly unsettling, if only because it suggests that Pierre's growing fatalism is actually a choice that recoils from the possibilities of chance. Returning to his dismal quarters after the art exhibition and sail, Pierre finds two letters that speed him to his end—a rejection from his publisher, and a joint challenge from his cousin Glen and Lucy's brother Fred. As with Ahab's madness in the "The Chart" and the first sighting of whales in "The Mat-Maker," the missives move *Pierre* from the management of chance toward violent, impatient determinism. "Now I go out to meet my fate, walking toward me in the street," Pierre declares, "[T]he fool of Truth, the fool of Virtue, the fool of Fate, now quits ye forever!" (414–15). The bloody course that follows seems laid on iron rails, yet so quickly and fervidly do Pierre and the narrator embrace fate as an all-explanatory force that one wonders if their insistence is an overdetermined attempt to avoid the emotional and intellectual demands of fallibilism and the endless unknowing of the skeptic. This seems especially likely given that the novel ultimately returns to causal uncertainty. Pierre says in prison: "Here then, is the untimely, timely end;—Life's last chapter well stitched into the middle! Nor book, nor author of the book, hath any sequel, though each hath its last lettering!—It is ambiguous still" (418). The most important ambiguities of *Pierre* will not be resolved by a paternity test, for nothing can trace the unending causal chains that bring Pierre so precipitously to murder and suicide. *Pierre* thus follows *Moby-Dick* in foregrounding causal questions best answered not with absolutist ardor but with the suspension of judgment. More originally, and as suggested when Pierre compares his life to a disordered book, *Pierre* explores more deliberately than *Moby-Dick* how the possibilities of chance bear on aesthetics and authorship.

As seen in chapter two, *Moby-Dick* confounds teleological expectations of unity. Ishmael revels in his random methods; Melville demonstrates that the messiness of reality cannot be contained by literary forms; and the ship's carpenter can stand for a typical reader when he complains about turning Queequeg's coffin into a lifebuoy: "I don't like this cobbling sort of business. . . . I like to take in hand none but clean, virgin, fair-and-square mathematical jobs, something that regularly begins at the beginning, and is at the middle when midway, and comes to an end at the conclusion" (1354). This speech may seem banal to the point of parody, though Melville may very well have in mind Aristotle's claim in the *Poetics* that a plot should constitute a *"whole . . . which has a beginning, a middle and an end."* As distinct from eighteenth-century pseudo-Aristotelian unities of time and space, and different from Coleridge's organic theory of parts representing wholes, Aristotle's *Poetics* defines narrative unity in terms of causal relations:

> A *beginning* is that which itself does not follow necessarily from anything else. . . .
> Conversely, an *end* is that which does itself naturally follow from something else. . . . A
> *middle* is that which itself comes after something else, and some other thing after it.
> Well constructed plots, therefore, cannot either begin at a *chance* point or end at a
> *chance* point.

Even when praising the "Astonishment" brought on by events that are "contrary to expectation," Aristotle holds that narratives should abide by at least the appearance of causal logic. For Aristotle, unexpected but seemingly plausible events "will be more astonishing than if they come about spontaneously or by chance, since even chance events are found most astonishing when they appear to have happened as if for a purpose. . . . [and] are not thought to occur at random." Aristotle does not distinguish between objective and subjective notions of chance, between absolute chance and aleatory experience, nor does he define what exactly constitutes the appearance of purposiveness. Nonetheless, his emphasis on causal continuity was a widely accepted aesthetic standard for eighteenth- and nineteenth-century critics, including the influential Archibald Alison who set "Design," "Uniformity," and "Regularity" over and against the baneful effects of "Chance." As a cobbled-together book more like Queequeg's coffin than a fair-and-square mathematical job, *Moby-Dick* resists the tyranny of unity, dramatizing its lack of clear causality in a loosely structured plot.[8]

Pierre continues such experimentation, not only pushing novelistic genres to barely recognizable extremes but also mocking the idea of formal unity understood as causal continuity.[9] The chain of Pierre's motives remains untraceable, and his character is inconsistent (and meta-critically announced as such), just as his life remains a jumbled book whose last chapter is stitched into the middle. The "Young America in Literature" chapter flouts narrative conventions of totality and linearity: "I am careless of either," the narrator proclaims, "I write precisely as I please" (286). No doubt a rejoinder to reviewers who decried the heterogeneity of *Moby-Dick*, *Pierre* savages arbiters of "'Perfect Taste'" who superficially valorize "euphonious construction," "pervading symmetry," and "high judicious smoothness" (287). So enthralled are such critics by Aristotelian unities that they forget Aristotle's vindication of the unexpected, celebrating instead the young Pierre as a poet who "never permits himself to astonish," a standard Melville everywhere violates.

It is not simply that incest and suicide are shocking or that characters are frequently described as "astonished"; much more than *Moby-Dick*, *Pierre* dramatizes how chance shapes the creation and reception of literature. Charlie Millthorpe's writings reflect his "random thought" (328), and Plinlimmon's pronouncements are "taken down at random" and published (339). Pierre's literary influences are "randomly acquired by a random but lynx-eyed mind" (330), while his opus is represented to readers by the "random slips" from a manuscript that he "randomly correct[s]" (353, 394). Chance also governs literary acclaim, for in the narrator's view, "Merit" accounts for only the "one thousandth part" of popular success with "nine hundred and ninety-nine combining and dovetailing accidents for the rest" (393). As an author whose work was both praised and vilified, and whose reputation underwent drastic changes, Melville follows Poe and anticipates Howells in *A World of Chance* (1893) by dwelling on the capriciousness of reviewers and print markets (a capriciousness borne out by the radically conflicting contemporary opinions of *Pierre*).[10]

Just as Pierre's disregard of potential coincidences leads to his deadly embrace of Isabel, Pierre's disregard of chance in the matter of authorship more or less guarantees his professional failure, suggesting that Melville's quarrel with the literary marketplace is also a quarrel with probabilistic business practices. In a letter to his British publisher Richard Bentley, Melville described *Pierre* as "calculated for popularity," though Melville, like Pierre, could not finally subordinate his artistic vision to a marketing strategy.[11] In contrast to Fanny Fern's Ruth Hall (who masters the business of letters) and Millthorpe (who is both a literary mercenary and a lawyer engaged in the probabilistic work of mortgages and bonds), Pierre labors over an iconoclastic manuscript "of all things least calculated for pecuniary profit" (392). Pierre's imprudent approach to literary professionalism fits romantic images of authorship—from Byron's aristocratic disdain for his audience, to Emerson's serene insouciance, to Hawthorne's impractical artists of the beautiful, to an 1859 article in *Russell's Magazine*: "[The artist's] inspiration must come from within, it must be spontaneous and irresistible; there can be no consideration of profit or loss—no calculation of chances."[12]

Refusing to game the literary market, Pierre aspires to perfection with Ahab-like rigidity as imprisoned at his desk—"squared to his plank"—he tries to eliminate caprice from his creative process (351). As not a few academics can attest, the urge to write a flawless book can be debilitating. It is as if Pierre read the part of "Self-Reliance" (1841) about shunning mother, father, and brother when genius comes to call and skipped over Emerson's subsequent sentence about the saving power of Whim. Or perhaps Pierre read only the beginning of "Experience" (1844) with its dreadful stair of skepticism and never got to the parts where Emerson praises surprise, thrives by accidents, and simultaneously invokes and circumscribes the glittering power of chance. Melville himself does not make—in fact, he exposes—Pierre's mistake of denying chance, but neither does he follow Emerson in celebrating whim and inconsistency. The "Young America in Literature" chapter may rise briefly to transcendental breeziness, but *Pierre* as a whole is unrelentingly gloomy. Lacking Ishmael's random playfulness, if it wasn't for bad luck, Pierre would have no luck at all.

Perhaps the most tragic aspect of the novel is that Pierre is arguably justified in refusing to suspend the judgments that damn him. That is, even if he were more open to chance in the epistemologically modest manner of a skeptic, he still might have rightfully acted as he did and suffered the same consequences. Pierre is naïve, self-absorbed, and sexually interested, but Isabel, half-sister or not, can certainly use an advocate. Pierre, of course, might have made himself morally useful without breaking Lucy's heart, living in sin, and killing his poor mother. Then again, is there not something redeeming in offering up a full measure of charity instead of allowing self-serving uncertainties to paralyze one's nobler instincts? Perhaps, except that Pierre's ostensible sacrifices can still be read as more self-interested than noble in that he aspires to be both Christ and an idolized husband of two. We might indict Isabel as a manipulator or condemn the social systems that pressure Pierre, but no one forces him to write an unprofitable book, and pistols don't kill cousins, people do. As such deliberations suggest, whether or not one gives Pierre the benefit of the doubt is the novel's most decisive question, for it is impossible to engage the book intellectually or emotionally without entering into such judgments. With an astonishingly subtle and ironic design, *Pierre* thus puts a skeptical reader in the hypocritical position of not entirely understanding Pierre and yet judging him harshly for not suspending his judgment in matters he does not entirely understand. Put differently, it is difficult to suspend our judgment anymore successfully than the impetuous, self-righteous Pierre. As with "Bartleby" and "Benito Cereno" (1855), *Pierre's* portrayal of a flawed protagonist struggling with epistemological and ethical conundrums invites would-be superior readers to confront their own flaws as the judges themselves are dragged to the bar. Melville in *Pierre* surely thumbs his nose at the moralists who tasked him from *Typee* onward, and "The Young America in Literature" chapter does take specific aim at the Duyckincks and their circle. But *Pierre's* design upon its audience is much more than a bitter, self-regarding satire shoehorned into an otherwise sentimental parody, for the novel tangles readers in ambiguities as Melville shows that for Pierre and readers of *Pierre* the suspension of judgment under conditions of chance is both prudent and impossible.

In the final few paragraphs of the novel, Fred and Millthorpe figure Melville's imagined audience by discoursing upon the Shakespearian carnage, but after all their tearful condemnation and sympathy, Isabel gets the final word: "All's o'er, and ye know him not!" (420). The uncertainties of the novel do indeed make judgment fraught, though the impulse for critique remains irresistible, if only because the narrator twice double-dog dares us, "Judge ye, then, ye Judicious" (200, 201). In the end, we are left with no reliable standards of judgment. What moral frameworks possibly obtain if humans lack free will or if agency is untraceable? What judgments can be defended in a world of contingency or, in a more current idiom, moral luck? *Pierre* does not definitively answer such questions except to suggest that readers (especially literary critics) might do well to try and suspend some judgments so as not to resemble the "painstaking moralist" who "complacently expatiates" over *Hamlet* (200). Perhaps Melville is thinking of readers like Samuel Johnson, who—finding "little purpose" in the play's final violence, and complaining of a lack of Aristotelian unities—objected to *Hamlet's* disregard of "poetical justice" and "poetical probability" alike.[13] Pierre himself is no better a critic, reducing *Hamlet* to the aphorism, "[A]ll meditation is worthless, unless it prompt to action." In the face of doubt, he and the narrator repeatedly insist that "vital acts" are superior to "bodiless thoughts" (241). If their subordination of ideas to deeds proves overzealous, it also indicates Melville's impatience with the limits of deliberation, thereby marking his own unease with skepticism and potentially aligning him with an emerging philosophical movement—pragmatism, though of a less progressive sort.

William James did not have *Pierre* in mind when he noted that absolutist metaphysical systems begin to falter "about 1850," but as a philosopher who advocates action as a response to aleatory uncertainty, James illuminates a pragmatist path that *Pierre* considers but does not quite take.[14] As with Poe, direct connections between Melville and pragmatism are tenuous from the perspective of source study. When James attempted unsuccessfully to synthesize his ideas in a unified "System der Philosophie," he joked that the motto of his never-finished book should be a quote about Ahab from "The Chart": "God help thee, old man, thy thoughts have created a creature in thee; and he whose intense thinking thus makes him a Prometheus; a vulture feeds upon that heart for ever; that vulture the very creature he creates."[15] James also discussed *Moby-Dick* with Holmes Jr. and read *Typee* and *Omoo* (1847) at bedtime, while John Dewey mentions Melville after the Melville revival of the early twentieth century. Outside of these instances, any commerce between Melville and the first generation of pragmatists must be taken to occur along lines of intellectual affinity and common cultural influence. As James's quote from "The Chart" suggests, pragmatists suspected along with Melville that quests for certainty are doomed; and just as Melville could neither believe nor be comfortable in his unbelief, James steered between what he called "the opposite dangers of believing too little or of believing too much." "The Doubloon" chapter of *Moby-Dick* can be taken to dramatize James's *A Pluralistic Universe* (1909), and Ahab's search for the white whale is aptly described by James in "The Mad Absolute" (1906). "Benito Cereno" might as well be titled, "A Certain Blindness in Human Beings" (1899), while *Pierre* anticipates "The Sentiment of Rationality" (1879) insofar as intellectual processes are governed by feelings whose origins cannot be traced. Melville and James also share views on aesthetics, as when James writes in resistance to Aristotelian unities, "The world is full of partial stories that run parallel to one another, beginning and ending at odd times."[16] Most central to the purposes at hand, Pierre and the narrator of *Pierre* advance the pragmatist point that risky action, not the suspension of belief, is the best response to chance.

To be sure, James does not champion action indiscriminately or set it in direct opposition to intellection: he is aware that rash behavior can lead to brutal consequences, and he is quick to make the Emersonian point that thought can be a form of action. For James, decisiveness guided by probability and restrained by fallibility is prudent in a pluralistic universe whose aleatory nature—or less radically, appearance—should be emboldening, not cause for inaction. Especially under the influence of Rortian antifoundationalism, pragmatism can seem like an aggressively skeptical philosophy, though at the heart of James's great essay "The Will to Believe" is an impatience with what he calls the "[p]aralysis" of "pyrrhonistic sceptic[ism]," "intellectual scepticism," and "moral skepticism." Like *Pierre*, "The Will to Believe" admits certain epistemological problems: we make decisions according to *"passional nature,"* not on *"intellectual grounds,"* while "[n]o concrete test of what is really true has ever been agreed upon." At the same time, James objects to what he sees as the passivity, cowardice, and "excessive nervousness" of the skeptic, particularly in matters of faith. James invokes Pascal's wager to show that religious belief can be justified probabilistically, and he argues that we should take "the chance of guessing true," that we should "run the risk of acting as if

[our] passional need . . . might be prophetic and right." James concludes that some judgments cannot be suspended and that some risks are unavoidable, ending "The Will to Believe" with a quote from the jurist Fitzjames Stephen:

> We stand on a mountain pass in the midst of whirling snow and blinding mist, through which we get glimpses now and then of paths which may be deceptive. If we stand still, we shall be frozen to death. If we take the wrong road, we shall be dashed to pieces. We do not certainly know whether there is any right one. What must we do? "Be strong and of a good courage." Act for the best, hope for the best, and take what comes. . . . If death ends all, we cannot meet death better.[17]

It is a shame that James ends his essay with the gung-ho buoyancy of an inferior writer. If only he could have read Frost's "The Road Not Taken" (1916) for a deflating, mock-heroic description of how we justify decisions made under conditions of doubt.

Passages like the one concluding "The Will to Believe" make pragmatists susceptible to the charge that they lack a sense of tragedy, though in "The Will to Believe" and elsewhere, James acknowledges what he calls "radical evil." In language that Melville would have approved, James knows that in the course of experience "[s]ome part of the ideal must be butchered," and in a later essay that discusses "How We Act on Probabilities," James notes that no amount of insurance and statistical reasoning can fully indemnify humans from risk.[18] Like John Stuart Mill, to whom *Pragmatism* (1909) is dedicated, James was for an extended period in his life debilitated by the threat of determinism. Indeed, the corrigible, unsystematic nature of James's thought may have come from his incapacity to reconcile the theoretically formidable arguments of determinism and his passional need to believe in free will. Forced to choose between debilitating ideation and loose experience, James opted for the later. Yet even if pragmatism is not blithely unconcerned with violence, despair, alienation, and other tragic aspects of life, the therapeutic assurances of "The Will to Believe" sound facile alongside *Pierre*.

Though Melville and James both subvert rationalism and dismantle absolutism, *Pierre* has precious little faith in action based on passional nature. Not only does Melville dwell on what happens when someone feels and acts precipitously, he wonders whether we have free will, something James more or less takes for granted. In "The Will to Believe," it is belief and not will that James feels to be under siege, and when James insists that we have "the right to choose [our] own form of risk," he sounds more like an investor flourishing in rising markets than the victim of a hurricane, war, or financial crisis who has risks imposed upon him.[19] In *Israel Potter* (1855), Melville exposes the social contingencies of chance by contrasting Potter, a hapless sufferer of aleatory forces, with Benjamin Franklin, who comfortably profits from them. The novel even imagines a Jamesian pragmatist in the risk-embracing John Paul Jones, who ruggedly navigates the "half-disciplined chaos" of the world by employing a "straggling method" that is simultaneously calculating and open to chance.[20]

Unlike Franklin's, Pierre's social freedoms serve to undermine the philosophical hypothesis of free will and James's enthusiastic approach to chance. As he is tossed by his feelings and thrown by coincidence, Pierre's economic and cultural capital do not alter the fact that he does not fully choose or comprehend the risks that eventually bring him down. Nor is he able to think probabilistically when confronted with emergencies. Nor can a reader end the novel with Stephen's stiff upper lip: "If death ends all, we cannot meet death better." Unable to look away from the destructive contingencies that James (like Emerson) sometimes acknowledges but often tonally discounts, *Pierre* suggests that in a chancy world there are worse things than the skeptic's paralysis, that the perfectly balanced Memnon Stone of the novel might offer a more prudent example for living than the tortured Enceladus rock driven into the earth.

Perhaps Melville's own declining family history, refigured and embellished in *Pierre*, made him a better witness than the first generation of pragmatists to the tragic possibilities of chance. James did suffer psychic episodes; Peirce did drive himself into poverty; Holmes did endure the horrors of war; and Dewey was the son of a grocer. Still, brilliance, effort, and fortunate circumstances helped James, Holmes, and Dewey achieve worldly success, while even Peirce recognized at some level that his trials were of his own making. None of the pragmatists experienced the sense of shrinking opportunity that Melville surely felt imposed upon him as the eleven-year-old grandson of a Revolutionary hero and son of a once prosperous merchant thrown suddenly into dependence on relatives during an unpromising economic time. Whatever the cause of Melville's world vision, and whether or not he sometimes thought of himself as a victim of chance, his skepticism in *Pierre* rejects certitude in a manner that the pragmatists can help to describe, but his misgivings about individual agency, progressive history, and creative destruction put him ahead of the Metaphysical Club—insofar as Melville better preempts twentieth-century critiques of pragmatist optimism, insofar as he offers pragmatist lessons for a twenty-first century injured by passional declarations of moral clarity and impetuous underestimations of risk.[21] Rorty has called pragmatism a philosophy of hope. Melville expands the range of emotional comportments one might bring to conditions of doubt, construing from aleatory uncertainty a philosophy of possibility that includes with hope the brutal potentials of *Pierre*.

As Hawthorne recognized on that Liverpool beach, Melville finds no comfort in his unbelief. He even has qualms about believing too much in skepticism, as implied by a line he marked in *Don Juan* (1819–24) when Byron writes in regard to Pyrrho and Montaigne, "I doubt if doubt itself be doubting."[22] Pierre would probably have been better off if he doubted a little longer and willed himself a little less fervidly toward passional belief. But as if to warn against *Pierre's* skeptical warnings, and as if to temper his proleptic challenge to James, Melville doubts the wisdom of doubting by imagining an extreme case of suspended judgment. His name is Bartleby, and his corollary is a lawyer.

"BARTLEBY" AND BURIDAN'S ASS

When James at the end of "The Will to Believe" refers to a man on a mountain pass who must decide between indistinguishable options, he responds to—or more accurately and characteristically, leaves behind—a paradox often attributed to Jean Buridan, the fourteenth-century French philosopher. The most popular version of Buridan's thought experiment is this: a hungry ass is placed equidistant between two identical piles of hay, and because the animal cannot determine a preference for either, it therefore cannot choose between them and eventually starves to death. At stake is the etiologial question of whether subjects can act freely when faced with indifferent options, or in the terms of "Bartleby" (and Jonathan Edwards): Is choice possible without preference? "Bartleby" ultimately takes no clear position on the question of liberty and necessity, and like *Moby-Dick* and *Pierre*, the tale muddies the waters further by introducing as a third element the possibilities of chance. But whereas the cautionary examples of Ahab and Pierre assert the wisdom of suspending judgment under aleatory conditions, "Bartleby" marks the self-imposed limits of Melville's skepticism, not only because the scrivener's refusal to affirm anything leads to an asslike demise but also because the probabilistic thinking of the tale's lawyer-narrator proves inadequate to Bartleby's case. The lawyer of "Bartleby" is comfortable enough as a prudent manager of chance until he comes across the problem of one unmanageable scrivener.

The paradox that came to be associated with Buridan has a rich philosophical history: food versus drink (Aristotle), two equally enticing dates (the Arabic philosopher Ghazâlî), two equal portions of food (Aquinas), a dog placed between two dishes (Buridan himself; where the ass comes from is unclear), a "Gammon of Bacon" versus "a Bottle of Wine" (Montaigne, with typical gusto), the band Devo (whose 1980 song "Freedom of Choice" refers to a dog who starves between two bones). Bayle included a thorough entry on Buridan's ass in his dictionary; and by the nineteenth century, De Quincy referred to the puzzle as a "philosophic commonplace." Yet if Buridan's ass was familiar enough, it remained a controversial topic. Buridan, Isaac Watts, and Kant (among others) used it to argue in favor of free will: because it is absurd to starve in the midst of food, subjects must therefore possess some power to choose that is independent of any preference. That is, even lacking external motivating factors, people enjoy some internal faculty of choice. On the side of necessity, Leibniz argued that entirely identical options simply do not occur in nature, while Schopenhauer (whom Melville almost surely did not read until after writing "Bartleby") refuted libertarian interpretations of Buridan's paradox by arguing that all apparent choices are always and forever predetermined.[23]

Schopenhauer's determinism is akin to that of Edwards, whom the lawyer of "Bartleby" conspicuously consults along with Joseph Priestley's associationist defense of necessity. In a section of Edwards's *Freedom of the Will* titled "Concerning the Will's Determining in Things which are Perfectly Indifferent in the View of the Mind," Edwards rejects Watts's argument that choice without preference is a proof of free will. Edwards dismisses as sophistry thought experiments premised on "two cakes, two eggs, etc., which are exactly alike," and he argues that if a "hungry man" chooses between "two sorts of foods," then by definition he is not indifferent but rather expresses a preference.[24] For Edwards, there is no choice without preference, and because preferences entail the infinite regression of desires—we cannot will our will, for some other motivating force must always lie behind our willing—no executed desire is entirely free, leaving God as the primary cause of all things.

Edwards's determinism proved a durable metaphysical argument, but it does not solve the problem of Bartleby's inaction for the lawyer or for literary critics, if only because Melville does not follow Edwards in dispensing with the problem of Buridan's ass. Edwards might take "I prefer not" to indicate an actual preference (I do not want to cross-check documents or travel to Europe, thank you very much), but it can also indicate the absence of any preference whatsoever (I am perfectly indifferent toward every option). Thus, Bartleby can stand for an Edwardsian subject bound by a necessitarian chain of preferences, or he can be an exception to Edwards's deterministic rule—a man who, because he has no preferences whatsoever, is unbounded by regressing causal chains. Melville's potential irony only heightens such uncertainty, for—like Buridan's ass—Bartleby can be seen as an absurd figure undercutting whatever claim he is taken to represent, or he might be an exaggerated but earnest example intended to highlight some human condition (what Dickens called an "extreme exposition of a plain truth").[25] As an indifferent, immobile, "mulish" character who starves to death in the midst of food, Bartleby can stand in for Buridan's ass by raising fundamental etiological issues without offering a definitive interpretation (647). Buridan's ass may simply offer a new philosophical coordinate for a familiar problematic in "Bartleby," but while scholars have long recognized in Melville's tale the conflict between fate and free will, the *"luny"* figure of Bartleby read through Buridan's paradox disrupts traditional, dualistic views of causality by conjuring the possibilities of chance (645).[26] Or as the grub-man puts it as Bartleby wastes away, "He's odd, ain't he" (670).

Before and during the nineteenth century, Buridan's ass impelled some thinkers toward chance. Thomas Gataker's heterodox Puritan treatise, *Of the Nature and Use of Lots* (1619), controversially argued that a man choosing between two identical knives might rightfully rely on chance to make his decision. Faced with equal desires for bacon and wine, Montaigne asserted that choices without preference can be made by "some outside impulse, incidental and fortuitous." As reported by Bayle, Spinoza also took "lot or chance" as a legitimate way to escape the paralysis of Buridan's puzzle, and though it is less likely that Melville knew of Caleb Pitt's *An Essay on the Philosophy of Christianity* (1824), the book indicates how chance in the nineteenth century made inroads into Protestant thought. In attempting to finesse Edwardsian determinism, Pitt invoked "a hungry ass between two bundles of hay, equally inviting," holding that "if the agent is pressed to act, chance action takes place by mere volition." Widely considered a sign of atheism and insanity, chance nonetheless proved difficult to exclude from Buridan's finely balanced dilemma, even in pious antebellum discussions of what happens when one prefers not.[27]

If Bartleby can represent Buridan's ass and the possibilities of chance that it unleashes, the lawyer more centrally dramatizes the quandary of living with causal uncertainty. As Dan McCall has shown, part of the genius of "Bartleby" is that even resistant readers come to resemble the lawyer-narrator by imposing their own interpretive agendas onto the ambiguous scrivener.[28] It is as if Melville presages the dilemma of modern English majors: conjuring fears of a dead-end cubicle job ("Bartleby, the Temp"), the story helps budding literary critics imagine themselves as lawyers. We can mock the lawyer's self-satisfied tergiversations, but the reader's identification with the lawyer, howsoever partial and reluctant, is necessary for the story's success. As Colacurcio has argued of Melville's short fiction in general, the question is not how we are to solve unsolvable humanitarian problems but, rather, "How are we to compose our affect when the case proves itself beyond our competence?"[29] Entangled in unanswerable questions of agency, "Bartleby" is about, among other things, the moral injunctions of chance.

The lawyer of "Bartleby" plays a starring role in Melville's post-metaphysical follies: rationalists, overconfident in their methods and betrayed by their all too human flaws, realize late that the Age of Reason is over and that someone must turn out the lights. For post-structuralist critics, the figure of Bartleby dismantles Enlightenment dualisms—yes and no (Deleuze and, briefly, Derrida), being and nonbeing (Agamben).[30] Yet like "The Purloined Letter," "Bartleby" need not take the linguistic turns of such readings, whose focus on the epistemological implications of the scrivener deemphasize the lawyer's own struggle to act under deeply felt imperatives. For all of his old-fashioned ways, the lawyer is not intellectually unprepared for a modernity that includes the taming of chance. His recourse to Edwards and Priestley, though thematically illuminating, is so out of character as to suggest that he has reached a point of desperation in trying to diagnose Bartleby. More likely to read a newspaper or commercial magazine than two dusty tomes on determinism, the lawyer is at heart a probabilistic thinker who approaches Bartleby as a problem of fate, free will, *and* chance. Doing "a snug business among rich men's bonds and mortgages," the lawyer—like *Pierre*'s Charlie Millthorpe and Hawthorne's Governor Pyncheon—is a calculating manager of risk in a speculative economy (635).[31] While nineteenth-century defenders of such financial speculation pointed to its social benefits, the shrillest antebellum critics of Wall Street saw in it the threat of chance. As one wrote of speculators in 1834, "The numerous believers in what is familiarly called the doctrine of chance, may be startled at being told that they are worshippers at the shrine of. . . . Fortune, Chance, [and] Luck."[32] It is a charge that the narrator of "The Lightning-Rod Man" (1854) makes against the Franklinesque traveling salesman, even as the narrator himself dabbles in classical learning and pagan allusion.

The lawyer of "Bartleby," who never quite makes it to church, would be scandalized by the accusation of worshiping chance. He considers himself an "eminently *safe* man" and is repeatedly pleased with his "prudence" (635–36). He weighs the "probable effects" of the scrivener's poor diet and worries (quite correctly, it turns out) about "the chances that [Bartleby] will fall in with some less indulgent employer" (646–47). After finally bringing himself to evict Bartleby, he applauds his own "masterly management" of the situation, though doubts creep in when he returns to the office "arguing the probabilities *pro* and *con*" of whether Bartleby has actually left (658–59). Such deliberation follows a celebrated strategy of Franklin, who in a widely quoted 1772 letter to none other than Joseph Priestley described his method of listing each "*pro*" and "*con*" when facing difficult choices. Franklin wrote, "[T]ho' the Weight of Reasons cannot be taken with the Precision of Algebraic Quantities, yet . . . I have found great Advantage from this kind of Equation, in what may be called *Moral* or *Prudential Algebra*."[33] Franklin is too practical to worry over a paradox in which pros and cons exactly balance in the manner of Buridan's ass (or for that matter, *Pierre*'s Memnon Stone), but he knows that even the most rational minds sometimes struggle to determine preferences. The narrator of "Bartleby" learns a similar lesson, though he becomes less sanguine and prudent than Franklin. Anxiously calculating probabilities on his way back to the office, he overhears two men taking "odds" on an election and—Poor Richard be damned—offers to bet, even though he does not know the grounds of the wager. When he finds that Bartleby has not left the building, he feels like a man struck by "summer lightning," another sign that he has lost the risk-management skills exemplified by the salesman of "The Lightning-Rod Man"

(659). As noted at the start of "Bartleby," the lawyer was "a Master in Chancery" but that position is "now extinct," preparing the way for a modern tale in which chance will not be mastered (636).

The lawyer's loss of his probabilistic bearings might not surprise a behavioral economist, and similar falls are dramatized at length in Howells's *The Rise of Silas Lapham* (1885), Norris's *The Pit* (1903), and Dreiser's *The Financier* (1912). Also uneasy with the extremities of the market revolution but more committed to skeptical philosophy, "Bartleby" shows how the lawyer comes to share the paralysis of his scrivener, thereby recalling another use of Buridan's ass, which was deployed to satirize the indifference of skeptics. Sextus Empiricus associated skepticism with "'Equipollence'" (defined as "equality in respect of probability and improbability"), and he advocated epistemological and emotional comportments of "Suspense," "Quietism," and "moderate feelings in respect of things unavoidable." Skeptics, that is, prefer to prefer not. The lawyer of "Bartleby" similarly strives for "tranquillity," aspires to be "entirely care-free and quiescent," and does his best to feel moderately about Bartleby's plight, which he tries to view as an unavoidable misfortune (668). The narrator also owns a bust of Cicero, and his deliberative style links him not only to the skeptical Franklin but also to Pyrrho himself, who (as reported by Bayle) weighed all arguments according to "pro and con."[34] Buridan's paradox can discredit such methods by pushing conflicting desires and ledgerlike deliberations to an absurd equipollence, which is why Montaigne dismissed Buridan's ass when denying that skeptics were paralyzed by a lack of preferences. Nonetheless, notions of ridiculously indifferent skeptics persisted through the nineteenth century, particularly in the oft-cited anecdote that Pyrrho's friends had to move him out of oncoming traffic so that he would not be run over.

On this point Melville expresses some doubts about skepticism. It is not simply that the debilitated Bartleby can be taken to caricature Pyrrhonic equipollence. Nor is it only, according to Agamben's argument, that the scrivener takes up a classically skeptical position by refusing to affirm the existence of anything. Nor does Melville's critique of skepticism only concern the lawyer's practical inability to feel tranquil or sustain his suspension of judgment. Nor is it even that Melville is extraordinarily sensitive to the cognitive dissonance of philosophizing in general and skepticism in particular: funny how the lawyer withholds his judgment and action just when it suits his self-interest best. All of the theses are true enough, but the deepest thrust of "Bartleby," as I take it, is that the rational management of chance, classical or modern, unleashes its own set of risks. As in *Moby-Dick* and *Pierre*, etiological uncertainty is at the center of "Bartleby." The difference is that "Bartleby" is a counter cautionary tale that dramatizes, not the imprudence of absolutism, but the dangers of not believing fiercely enough. In this Melville debunks an ambition of skeptics burnished by modern science and the market economy: that probabilities can be so accurately weighed and that chance and its consequences can be so effectively managed as to eliminate the need for anything like faith. One hardly expects Ahab or Pierre to act with the prudence of a Maury or Franklin, but the lawyer of "Bartleby" is a more calculating candidate who still cannot handle chance—either from a psychological perspective (he remains haunted by the unknowable causes of Bartleby's condition), or from a moral and political one (he is unable to save the scrivener or convince himself and most readers of his virtue). Buridan's paradox cannot be escaped by offering Bartleby a more satisfying job or purchasing better meals for him in prison. Beyond the reach of pros and cons and probabilism, Bartleby remains "unaccountable" (662). As my wife sometimes tries to tell me, not all problems are meant to be strategically solved.

By the end of "Bartleby, the Scrivener," the lawyer partially accepts the aleatory threat of Bartleby even as he struggles to manage him, mainly by attempting to understand the scrivener within a statistical paradigm. That Bartleby's malady may originate in the Dead Letter Office strengthens interpretations that focus on print culture or take linguistic turns, and Marxist readings find support in Bartleby's work history (if labor conditions are taken to dehumanize him, he cannot be congenitally or randomly damaged). Dead letters can also join screens, walls, and blindness as tropes for failed intersubjectivity. But if etiology matters in the story, and it desperately does, dead letters highlight the tense interplay between chance and law, anomaly and pattern. As discussed in chapter one, probability theorists found that the number of dead letters in the Paris post office varied little from year to year, indicating that even seemingly aleatory events can be explained by statistical logic.[35] With exemplary teleological fervor, the *Christian Observer* in 1856 integrated such thinking into Christian cosmology by quoting from the president of Princeton, James McCosh: "The events of providence . . . appear to us very much like the letters thrown into a mailbag. . . . [E]very occurrence, or bundle of occurrences, is let out at its proper place. . . . [W]ho is so blind as not to perceive, that not one of the events or issues associated with, or growing out of any one of the thousand letters and parcels in the mail-bag had its origin in chance?"[36] Who indeed could be so blind? Some critics argue that we are not supposed to wonder about the causes of Bartleby's condition.[37] Yet in "Bartleby" it is next to impossible to repress the question *Why?* The lawyer's line about Bartleby sleeping with kings and counselors is not convincing enough to put the story to rest. God may work in mysterious ways, and professors can annoyingly insist that a masterfully proleptic Melville ironically undermines any confident thesis about "Bartleby" that a student might hope to defend. But still, I mean, what is it with the guy? Maybe he's gone off his meds.

Having exhausted Edwards and Priestley, the lawyer's hypothesis about the Dead Letter Office is less diagnostic than frequentist, less about identifying the causes of Bartleby's particular dysfunction and more about taming en masse the mystery of agency that the scrivener so stubbornly represents. If Bartleby as an individual remains unaccountable, when taken in bulk—"Dead letters! does it not sound like dead men?" (672)—statistical thinking blunts his aleatory threat by reducing him to what Melville in *Moby-Dick* calls "the dead level of the mass" (949). The lawyer's attempt to view Bartleby as a function of large numbers is not entirely unjustified, for while the refrain about having no preference is most famous, the scrivener also insists no less than three times, "I am not particular" (666–67).

As with "The Mystery of Marie Roget," taking Bartleby as a general type is disconcerting in terms of the sheer quantity of suffering implied, but large numbers make it easier to call a problem unavoidable and hold at a distance more intimate claims. As deployed by Malthus and Quetelet, statistics might predict the number of starving people, murderers, and forgers per year, and both thinkers were accused of a complacent determinism that Dickens caricatures in *Hard Times*—when Louisa Gradgrind only understands human pain in terms of sociological percentages, and when Tom Gradgrind excuses his robbery probabilistically ("So many people are employed in situations of trust; so many people, out of so many, will be dishonest"). From the "statistical despairs" of *Aurora Leigh* (1856) to the "rise of bread and fall of babies" in Melville's "The Paradise of Bachelors and the Tartarus of Maids" (1855), dismal sociologists and political economists were charged with lacking benevolence, a determinism (as Catherine Gallagher has argued) that has analogs in overdetermined fictions of the time. Nineteenth-century data-gathering organizations could worry that "duties to the poor" were hard to define under the "artificial and complicated" state of modern capitalism, and Oliver Wendell Holmes Sr., whom Melville knew, could formulate what Jane Thrailkill calls "statistical pity" by putting medical data to sympathetic purposes. Still, "Bartleby's" addendum on the Dead Letter Office is more like "The Man of the Crowd" in showing that quantitative sociology and the probabilistic logic that supports it do not say enough about chance, psychology, and (for Melville much more than Poe) moral imperatives. Six hundred dead dragoons aside, ours is in fact to wonder why as we watch the scrivener perish. If so, "Ah Bartleby! Ah, humanity!" does not signal the lawyer's ascension up some ethical scale toward the embrace of universal humanity; rather, his final line suggests a retreat into comfortable, abstracted determinism. One death is a tragedy but a million are a statistic. Can't we just, like Hurstwood in *Sister Carrie* (1900), look at the numbers in the newspaper from a comfortable chair? For the lawyer-narrator—a better person than most, it should be said—the answer is ultimately no. He may wish to fix or forget about Bartleby, but he is forced to recognize that his snug probabilities cannot indemnify the claims of one unaccountable man—unaccountable meaning beyond quantification and causal explanation alike.[38]

None of which should suggest that Melville prefers sentimental benevolence to probabilism.[39] The narrator of "Cock-A-Doodle-Doo!" (1853) unconvincingly laments the "hundreds" of locomotive and steamship deaths that he reads about in the newspaper.[40] But if he responds insufficiently to large-scale tragedies disseminated through print culture, his face-to-face encounters with individual suffering also show him quite capable of withholding his succor in favor of personal comfort. As in "The Piazza" (1856), replacing abstractions with intimate experience makes more barefaced but does not overcome self-interested philosophizing. And if the lawyer of "Bartleby" looks bad for suspending judgment in the face of moral uncertainty, just wait for Amasa Delano. *The Confidence-Man* (1857) continues to press the limits of both skepticism and benevolence, for while epistemological suspicion in the novel seems a whole lot smarter than faith, one cannot laugh too hard at charitable inclinations nor entirely blame a tubercular man for coughing up some cash in the name of hope. In *Billy Budd* (1891, 1924), Captain Vere is likened to Montaigne as a prudent thinker free from bias, but when faced with a murderous "accident" at sea, causal uncertainty causes him to lose both his sympathy and his skeptical equipollence. Like Lemuel Shaw in the sensational 1850 Webster murder case, Vere will not consider the possibilities of chance; or as "Billy in the Darbies" puts it, "O, 'tis me, not the sentence they'll suspend."[41] Vere might have done better to suspend his judgment and wait for a more official trial, though it is clear enough that additional evidence and deliberations will not put the case beyond chance's doubt, for nothing can unerringly trace the chain of Billy's or Claggert's motives.

In Melville's theaters of suffering, action is demanded, but directions are not included. Agency is simultaneously unknowable and central to the moral decisions of characters and the critics who would judge them. No amount of commentary on King Ahab's death by venture will make Melville march cheerily with providence. No amount of psychological, political, or literary analysis will lay bare the ambiguous desires of Pierre or the social forces that move him. No reading in Edwards or quantitative sociology will bring Bartleby into the realm of accountability. In Melville's mature fiction, fate, free will, and chance are somehow interwoven, and the skeptic is probably prudent to admit that the threads are too devious to disentangle. Yet Hawthorne recognized on a Liverpool beach not only Melville's twisting between belief and unbelief but also that he was "too honest and courageous not to try to do one or the other." Unlike Bartleby and Buridan's ass, Melville knows that some choices cannot be deferred, if only because (as James came to emphasize) not choosing is itself a decision and action. Melville nearly annihilates the neutral ground that the skeptic tries to occupy, though he also points out that skepticism can be wise in a risky and uncertain world. In the end, nothing precludes a skeptic from suspending judgment about even the suspension of judgment. But does this realization offer sufficient guidance for what we ought to do? Is it explanation enough for the things we lose? Melville does not unequivocally answer yes because the costs of indecision can be high. The consequences, of course, extend to social domains, though in much of Melville's work readers by design must actively forge connections between epistemological and specific political crises. Such is not so much the case with Douglass, who insists that certain beliefs are right and that the time for action is now. Political activism and polemic rhetoric are not usually associated with skepticism, but Douglass's career shows how a partisan can come to wield the sword of chance.

CHAPTER 4
Douglass's Long Run

I tremble for my country when I reflect that God is just: that his justice cannot sleep for ever: that considering numbers, nature and natural means only, a revolution of the wheel of fortune, an exchange of situation, is among possible events: that it may become probable by supernatural interference!
—Thomas Jefferson on slavery, *Notes on the State of Virginia* (1785)

I could see that the scientific task of the twentieth century would be to explore and measure the scope of chance and unreason in human action, which does not yield to argument but changes slowly and with difficulty.
—W. E. B. Du Bois, *Dusk to Dawn* (1940)

R ace relations in America have long been entangled with the possibilities of chance—the risk of personal violence and social upheaval, the struggle for equal opportunity, the desire to both deploy and limit the claims of scientific reason. Jefferson's *Notes on the State of Virginia* is a founding document of American racism that most convincingly shows how race is too politically charged, intellectually overdetermined, and psychologically freighted for anything like objective discussion in the American Enlightenment and beyond. An avid measurer of animals, plants, and landmasses, Jefferson provides detailed statistics in *Notes* to counter the Comte de Buffon's assertion that the climate of the Americas is degenerative, even as Jefferson feels himself obligated to acknowledge the inferential limits of his sampling. But when Jefferson takes up the subject of American Indians (initially lumping them under the category of "Animals"), he suddenly turns to unsupported generalizations, depicting the country's indigenous peoples in a mode of romantic racism. Scientific reason and epistemological modesty further give way to pejorative fantasy when *Notes* discusses African Americans in its notorious fourteenth query. Though Jefferson admits a "great allowance" for climate and culture, and concedes the difficulty of empirically gauging mental and moral capacities, nothing deters him from concluding that blacks lack the intelligence and emotions of whites, have no artistic sense, and stink. Jefferson's representations reflect and authorize racist beliefs of the time, though as our epigraph suggests, his thinking on slavery and race could not decouple doubt and conviction, science and supernaturalism, probability and providence as he indiscriminately fears the retributory power of "numbers," "fortune," "nature," and "God."[1]

Poe's "The Murders in the Rue Morgue" expresses a related sense of panic. Part of the horror of the story is that an orangutan does the killing, conjuring white American anxieties over rapacious, semi-human blacks.[2] As in all of Poe's racially inflected fiction, "The Murders in the Rue Morgue" does not explicitly address political conditions in the United States, nor does it make any serious effort to imagine the experiences of racial others. Perhaps Poe was too busy with theories of chance to be bothered with such imaginative leaps, and perhaps Melville, for all his insights into antebellum race relations, is also guilty of some elision. Queequeg holds the sword of chance in *Moby-Dick*, and the racially ambiguous Isabel is subjected to probabilistic parsing in *Pierre*, but Melville—like Poe—is primarily interested in how chance affects his protagonists and their semi-autobiographical trials. Whether they do so successfully or not, whites in the work of Melville and Poe remain the primary potential tamers of chance.

More directly concerned with how the probabilistic revolution relates to slavery and race in the nineteenth century are a host of African-American writers, foremost among them Frederick Douglass and James McCune Smith. As an alternative to the providential arguments of abolitionists and slavery proponents alike, debates over chattel bondage and racial equality increasingly involved scientific adjudication, beginning most dramatically in the 1830s and '40s and continuing through the century and beyond.[3] In the tradition of Jefferson's *Notes*, many pseudo-scientists of the era justified racial oppression in the emerging and overlapping fields of polygenesis, phrenology, craniology, and later eugenics. Literary scholarship has been drawn to these discourses, not only because of their historical significance and interpretive use but also because their claims have the advantage of being morally and intellectually discredited. The strangeness of nineteenth-century racial science makes it especially compelling in the classroom and print, if only because it does not need to be analyzed seriously as science and also allows for some pleasant presentist condescension: *How thoroughly blinded by racism would one have to be to believe this crazy stuff?* Less interesting to literary and cultural studies have been more legitimized nineteenth-century scientific approaches to race, including the work of sociologists and political economists who employed probabilistic methods. Participating in the rapidly expanding efforts of quantitative race commentary, African-American thinkers fought to turn chance to their advantage, arguing that blacks had the capacities to thrive under the aleatory conditions of modernity. Especially in McCune Smith's journalism and Douglass's writings in and around the Civil War, African-American authors insisted under a probabilistic logic that everyone deserves an equal chance to manage chance. This may seem utterly unremarkable today, for if Americans disagree on definitions and methods, most support what they call "equal opportunity" (a phrase habitually invoked by both opponents and supporters of affirmative action). However, the case for this kind of fairness was not widely and self-consciously made until the mid-nineteenth century, as some reformers pursued racial justice not so much by asserting moral absolutes but by deploying a kind of probabilistic liberalism bolstered by new concepts of chance. The sciences in America have a long history of mismeasuring human potential, but the sciences of chance, in addition to their pernicious forms, also have a progressive politics grounded in African-American thought, including the slave narrative tradition.

PROVIDENCE AND IMPROVIDENCE

In his preface to James Albert Ukawsaw Gronniosaw's 1770 slave narrative, the Methodist hymnist Walter Shirley wrote of Gronniosaw's eventful life: "Shall we in accounting for it refer to nothing higher than mere chance and accidental circumstances? Whatever infidels and deists may think; I trust the Christian reader will easily discern an all-wise and omnipotent appointment and direction."[4] By juxtaposing providence and chance while offhandedly dismissing the later, Shirley took up an orthodox position: the illusion of chance, howsoever powerfully experienced, is nothing more than human ignorance of God's providential design. In celebrating the divine government of God, Shirley followed Gronniosaw's text, for like Britton Hammon, Phillis Wheatley, John Marrant, Ottobah Cugoano, Olaudah Equiano, Boston King, and Lemuel Haynes, Gronniosaw often praises providence as an all-determining causal force. The religious convictions of these early black Atlantic writers differ, as do their specific views on how much and in what way God's will requires human cooperation. Yet their emphasis on providence accords with a growing body of scholarship that takes Christianity in general and pre-Jacksonian Calvinism in particular less as an impediment to and more as a complex foundation for a politically organized radical abolitionism.[5] The transatlantic antislavery movement was driven by dissenters and evangelicals; slave narratives drew on Christian literary forms such as sermons, hymns, and conversion narratives; formal and informal black religious institutions gave shape to abolitionist activism. As an expression of Enlightenment piety and reason, Shirley's question was confidently rhetorical: no one could possibly lift "mere chance" above providence when accounting for improbable journeys from chattel bondage to redemptive freedom.

Given the Christian beliefs of abolitionist audiences, patrons, editors, and amanuenses, it is possible to question the spiritual convictions that many slave narratives announce (though interestingly enough, critics are less likely to doubt the Christianity of white abolitionists, who also had rhetorical and self-interested reasons for expressing their culture's dominant faith).[6] Setting aside this issue and noting how deeply felt Christianity clearly was for many abolitionists, slave narratives after 1825 largely share the providential worldview of their black Atlantic forerunners—from the religious revelations of William Hayden, Sojourner Truth, and "Old Elizabeth," to more conventional invocations of godly grace from Mary Prince, Josiah Henson, and John Thompson, to even the relatively secular narratives of ex-slaves like Moses Grandy and William Grimes, both of whom focus on economic agency while still thanking God for their salvation. When Alexander Crummell in 1861 included "Butler's Analogy," "Paley's Natural Theology," and "Wayland's Moral Philosophy" on his list of great works, he indicated how central the argument from design remained for many Anglophone black intellectuals even after the emergence of Darwinism.[7] As might be expected, antebellum slave narratives tend to be powerfully teleological at the levels of both plot and cosmology, not simply because they would never have been published if their authors had not attained freedom but also because providentialism can account for all events, good and bad, under its totalizing logic.

Yet for some African-American writers of the period, providence raised as many questions as answers. It was not only that defenders of slavery invoked God with their own teleological fervor or that ambivalently antislavery writers such as Jefferson, Hawthorne, Lincoln, and Melville often turned to providence as an excuse for not taking more assertive abolitionist stands.[8] As rhetorically invigorating, morally enlivening, and personally sustaining as it was for many black abolitionists, faith in providence could attenuate (or more subtly, complicate) political activism in the name of God's will. Robert Alexander Young's tonally militant "Ethiopian Manifesto" (1829) ultimately exhorts readers to stand and wait for a messiah with "webbed and bearded" toes, while Hayden (who purchased his own freedom) advises slaves to work diligently for their masters, assuring them "that they will be treated with kindness, and rendered still more happy in the bondage in which Providence has seen fit to cast their lot." Against such views, William Wells Brown and Jacob Green assert God's opposition to chattel bondage as a basis for the right to rebel against masters, while the eponymous hero of Martin Delany's *Blake* (1861–1862) answered William Cowper's hymn, "God Moves in a Mysterious Way" (1779), with the retort, "He moves too slow for me." As Eddie Glaude Jr. has emphasized, Henry Highland Garnett came to eschew the kind of Christian teleology that David Walker had fashioned into a powerful political rhetoric. Yet even Garnett participated in a robust tradition of liberationist Christianity that called upon and credited God while simultaneously being careful, in Douglass's words, not to "shuffle our responsibilities onto the shoulders of providence."[9]

A related complication of providential thinking involves the problem of theodicy, for if (as in the Isaac Watts hymn that Henry "Box" Brown quotes), "There's not a sparrow or a worm/O'erlooked in [God's] decree," then how does one justify the shocking cruelties that slave testimonies increasingly cited? The ex-slave John Thompson quoted Cowper's hymn: "Judge not the Lord with feeble sense,/But trust him for his grace/Behind a frowning providence/He hides a smiling face." Such views can be comforting and are in keeping with Augustine, Luther, Calvin, Wesley, and Whitefield. But the fugitive Moses Roper could not help but expose how painful such teaching could be, writing near the end of his 1837 slave narrative, "[I]f the all-wise Disposer of all things should see fit to keep [my family] in suffering and bondage, it is a mercy to know that he orders all things well, that he is still the Judge of all the earth, and that under such dispensations of his Providence, he is working out that which shall be most for the advantage of his creatures." For their part, William and Ellen Craft in *Running a Thousand Miles for Freedom* (1860) explicitly rejected such patient piety, mocking the anti-abolitionist minister Orville Dewey (whom Melville, Margaret Fuller, and the ex-slave Samuel Ringgold Ward also heartily despised) for arguing that the slave's "personal rights ought to be sacrificed to the general good." The Crafts responded by advocating more human agency and a less convenient, less complacent faith. If Doctor Dewey was so sanguine about the sacrifices of slaves, they wrote, then he ought to switch places with one. As with other writers working in the shadows of determinism, such as Hawthorne, Emerson, Stowe, Dickinson, and Elizabeth Stuart Phelps, slave narrators found providentialism simultaneously attractive, troubling, and needful of justification. The difference is that ex-slaves often have a sharper eye for the social uses and abuses of Christian teleology. Bearing on both their souls and their liberty, providence was personal and political.[10]

If potential quietism and problems of theodicy pressured beliefs in godly design, "mere chance"—as Shirley's preface to Gronniosaw's text suggests—presented a more fundamental threat by challenging not just the pace or justice of providence but also its very existence. Charles Buck's *Theological Dictionary* (1800), reprinted over fifty times before the Civil War, cited the belief in chance in its definitions of "Atheism" and "Unbelievers," holding that "[a]ccident, and chance … are no other than names for the unknown operations of Providence." As seen in chapter two, Buck's position was widely held, though many slave narrators from the antebellum era found chance difficult to dismiss or bracket—so much so that the emphasis on providence in many of their texts can be read as compensation for the fact that, in Lydia Maria Child's words, the slave's "happiness, nay, his very life, depends on chance."[11]

The association of chance and slavery has deep roots in classical thinking (as Bernard Williams has argued), a dynamic that carries forward into the American nineteenth century. As property with virtually no civil rights under a volatile market economy in which agricultural labor generally flowed from exhausted soil to recently acquired territories, and which included the domestic sale of over 1 million slaves between 1790 and 1860, slaves were especially vulnerable to chance, a recurring problem on which narratives dwell. Wells Brown laments the "uncertainty of a slave's life," while Josiah Henson emphasizes the "cruel caprices and fortunes" of chattel bondage.[12] In almost all slave narratives, masters, homes, and work environments unpredictably change, punishments and rewards are randomly dispensed, and families are sundered because of unexpected deaths, accidents, mood swings, and—with telling repetition—debts incurred from horseracing, poker, dice, and stock speculation. Even supposedly providential paths to liberation are marked by potential incursions of chance when fugitives or pursuers stumble or are lost, weather foils or abets an escape, and risky appeals are made to strangers who turn out to be slave-catchers or Quakers. Some slaves even won lotteries that helped them purchase their freedom, as in the cases of Hayden and the rebel Denmark Vesey. Such lucky and unlucky events are often ascribed to providence, but many are also attributed to chance or left ambiguously open as literary and intellectual structures fail to account for aleatory experiences. Thus, many slave narratives are not as teleological as they present themselves to be, for as much as paratextual materials and retrospective authorial comments assert providential order, texts remain riddled with intimations of chance that cannot be entirely contained.

Such is the case of rougher slave narratives like those of Austin Steward and Leonard Black that surprise their readers with random events and sudden dislocations of time and space. Events succeed events with little causal explanation and few transitions except for a "later" or "then." Characters, even family members, appear and vanish with no introduction or valediction. Ideological coherence is limited by the dearth of explicit causal analysis, and there are few unifying formal features such as foreshadowing, extended metaphors, and patterns of allusion. As John Ernest has argued using chaos theory, the interplay between confusion and order can realistically depict the slavery experience, a productive way to think about less canonical slave narratives (and postbellum oral histories) that resist the urge for coherent self-construction that marks so many early American autobiographies. In refusing to explain away the extremities of chance, slave narratives bolster Paul Gilroy's still provocative point that blacks are "the first truly modern people."[13]

More sophisticated slave narratives bring more formal structure and ideological design to the experience of bondage, though many do not deny the claims of chance so much as self-consciously manage them. Solomon Northup's dictated narrative, *Twelve Years a Slave* (1853), describes how Northup, a freeman kidnapped and sold into bondage, confronts his abusive, axe-wielding master:

> It was a moment of life or death. The sharp, bright blade of the hatchet glittered in the sun. In another instant it would be buried in my brain, and yet in that instant—so quick will a man's thought come to him in such a fearful strait—I reasoned with myself. If I stood still, my doom was certain; if I fled, ten chances to one the hatchet ... would strike me in the back. There was but one course to take. Springing towards him with all my power, and meeting him full halfway, before he could bring down the blow, with one hand I caught his uplifted arm, with the other seized him by the throat.[14]

This sounds like a scene from Sir Walter Scott or, more accurately, James Fenimore Cooper. As Nan Goodman has argued, Cooper's sea captains (like later sailors from Richard Henry Dana Jr. and Melville) do not exemplify raw strength and daring-do so much as prudence, calculation, and foresight, reflecting a growing emphasis on the prevention of accidents in nineteenth-century legal discourse.[15] Elsewhere Poe offers Dupin as a probabilistic hero who makes a point of avoiding danger, and even the spontaneous Whitman writes in his 1855 preface to *Leaves of Grass* that "[e]xtreme caution or prudence" are "parts of the greatest poet."[16] Northup does display his physical prowess, and the blow-by-blow description of his battle is thrilling. But just as a film cuts to the action hero's face to show him or her assessing a complicated threat before launching into the fray, Northup makes sure to identify his "thought" as a "man's"—to display his ability to deliberate ("I reasoned with myself"), estimate his odds ("ten chances to one"), and act accordingly (choosing fight over flight, not as a beast but as a rational thinker who acts in marked contrast to his master, who is "[f]rantic with rage" and "maddened beyond control").[17] Under risky conditions, Northup evinces his intellect not by exhibiting pure reason or adhering to moral principles but by thinking and acting probabilistically.

Though by no means their only priority, the vindication of black intelligence was a main goal of many slave narrators and the people who read them. What is less obvious is how the conflict over black mental equality forced participants on both sides of the slavery debate to consider what it meant to be rational. Did outwitting a master indicate superior intelligence, slave trickery, or mere animal cunning? Did slaves offer resistance as rational agents or, as they were sometimes portrayed, as disobedient children and pets, unreflective savages, religious zealots, pawns of white influence, or desperately reactive victims? How one answered such questions mattered a great deal as probabilistic thought became increasingly associated with higher orders of reasoning in the eighteenth and nineteenth centuries. Patricia Cline Cohen has argued that in nineteenth-century America, numeracy became seen as a standard for intelligence, economic competency, and republican citizenship.[18] The rise of probabilism helps to explain why Northup so carefully performs his ability to weigh his chances, and it also suggests why some defenders of slavery did not simply insist that blacks were stupid but more specifically argued that the African "mind" lacked probabilistic capacities.

The argument generally involved mathematical acuity, decision making, and foresight, particularly as calculative thinking became increasingly important under the market revolution. Jefferson wrote of blacks in his fourteenth query, "[O]ne could scarcely be found capable of tracing and comprehending the investigations of Euclid," an attitude that persisted through the nineteenth century as when Benjamin Peirce, ex-president of the American Association for the Advancement of Science, wrote to his son Charles in 1860: "No pure blooded African had ever yet become a mathematician. . . . Hence it follows that races differ." Whether focused on theoretical or applied mathematics, such charges denied the ability of blacks to prosper under modern capitalism, emphasizing—as Walter Benn Michaels and Ian Baucom have argued—that slaves were typically subject to, not participants in, the speculative and thus probabilistic financial transactions that constituted the international slave trade. Slavery advocates charged time and again that "the negro" fails in "determining the proper course for himself," is "incapable of comprehending the wants of the future," and suffers from "that want of foresight, so characteristic of the negro race." When the pro-slavery theorist Thomas Dew claimed that blacks lack the "cold, contracted, calculating *selfishness*" of whites, he simultaneously appealed to romantic racialism and denied Africans the political and economic self-interest at the center of possessive individualism.[19]

Such was the view of George Fitzhugh, who more insistently than anyone in the antebellum era set slavery over and against capitalism. Fitzhugh wrote in *Cannibals All!* (1857), "He who is capable of foreseeing by his intellect, is naturally a master," and by contrast he invoked the vulnerability of blacks in the "chance-dealing and advantage taking" world. Fitzhugh elsewhere wrote that in the North, "[T]he negro . . . finds, with his improvident habits, that his liberty is a curse to himself," thus slaves need a master "whose skill and foresight . . . shall shield him from the consequences of his own improvidence." From minstrel stereotypes of carefree, childlike blacks, to allochronic portrayals of African culture, to plantation myth descriptions of slavery as a patriarchal institution that protected its charges from the market economy, a main assumption was that blacks did not have the capacities to meet the probabilistic demands of modernity. Supposedly lacking in providence (literally, the power to look forward), African Americans were repeatedly described as "improvident," thereby excluding the entire race from religious, national, and economic narratives of progress. Even Stowe in *Uncle Tom's Cabin* largely accedes to the assessments of Dew and Fitzhugh when Augustine St. Claire contrasts the "tropical warmth and fervor" of Africans to the "calculating firmness and foresight" of Anglo-Saxons, a claim Stowe repeats in her own voice when interjecting that blacks "are not naturally daring and enterprising." In their own ambivalent resistance to the market revolution, domestic and sentimental abolitionists often denied blacks the capacity to tame chance.[20]

In response, more radical abolitionists committed to racial equality argued in favor of black providence. Articles in the antislavery press cited Hannibal, Benjamin Banneker, and the French meteorologist Lislet Geoffroy as examples of black mathematical genius, and they continued a tradition begun by Banneker by refuting Jefferson's *Notes*. One writer argued that not only could blacks understand Euclid but that Euclid himself was an African, while the African-American orator Maria Stewart referred to Africa as "the seat, if not the parent of science." The antislavery press circulated anecdotes of black autodidacts and savants—the chess prodigy Paul Morphy, whom some suspected of having African blood; a ship's cook who navigated by chronometer and lunar distance "holding a chicken in one hand, and a butcher knife in the other"; the Virginia slave who could quickly calculate in his head the number of seconds in someone's life (and who after being "corrected" by a white skeptic armed with paper and pencil, humbly pointed out that his ostensibly superior auditor had neglected to take leap years into account). An article in *The National Era* claimed that the "faculty of calculation, or mental arithmetic, is not uncommon among slaves," while James Holly in *A Vindication of the Capacity of the Negro Race for Self-Government, and Civilized Progress* (1857) praised the leaders of the Haitian Revolution for managing the contingencies of chance. Similar claims for foresight and the probabilistic reasoning it entails appear in Wilson Armistead's *A Tribute for the Negro* (1848), H. G. Adams's *God's Image in Ebony . . . Demonstrative of the Mental Powers and Intellectual Capacities of the Negro Race* (1854), and Wells Brown's *The Black Man: His Antecedents, His Genius, and His Achievements* (1863). In these books and others, black intelligence is measured in part by the ability to strategize and calculate under conditions of uncertainty. More specifically than Wheatley, they argue that Africans are sons of science, too.[21]

Northup's account of his probabilistic reasoning is but one example of a slave narrator who refuses to be a passive victim of chance. As he contemplates freedom, Henry Bibb "count[s] the cost" while considering his "fearful odds," and he decides to flee only after concluding that his "chance was by far better among the howling wolves in the Red river swamp, than before [his master]." Bibb continues to strategize probabilistically when eluding a group of slave catchers: "I thought my chance of escape would be better, if I went back to the same side of the road that they first went, for the purpose of deceiving them; as I supposed that they would not suspect my going in the same direction that they went." Bibb does not hide a purloined letter in plain sight or play a round of even and odd, but he does exemplify a kind of game theory, foreseeing the likely moves of his opponents, whose own rational choices are premised on their predictions of Bibb's probable moves. This antagonistic, contingent, aleatory dynamic is also evident in Harriet Jacobs's *Incidents in the Life of a Slave Girl* (1861) when Linda Brent acts "with deliberate calculation" and decides to "match [her] cunning against [her master's] cunning" by hiding right under his nose. Brent violates Flint's probabilistic expectations (as in fantastical fiction, the expected and unexpected begin to slide into each other), and her success subverts two related beliefs of the time: that neither women nor African Americans were capable of managing chance. Drawing on slave narratives, and contra the comments of St. Clare and Stowe herself, *Uncle Tom's Cabin* also describes the foresight of black agents when the slave trader Haley tries to catch Eliza with the ostensible help of Sam and Andy. Forced to evaluate the tricksters' advice when facing a fork in the road, Haley tries to "strike the balance of probabilities between [their] lies of greater or lesser magnitude," only to lose the game of they-think-that-I-think-that-they-think when Sam and Andy tell him the truth. Here a white man proves unable to master probability, a point Stowe also makes with Mr. Shelby and the shiftless John

Cripps of *Dred* (1856), both of who prove incompetent managers of chance in their speculative enterprises.[22]

In sentimental discourse, identifying with the subjectivity of another leads to sympathetic relations, but in probabilistic games of escape, seeing the world from another's point of view is to have power over that person. This is why Douglass (contra Jefferson's *Notes*) worries that some masters can "read, with great accuracy, the state of mind and heart of the slave, through his sable face." It is also why he refuses to divulge his means of escape in his first two autobiographies, choosing instead to reverse power relations and force his opponents to experience the "frightful risk" of uncertainty. From "Box" Brown's "calculating the chances of danger," to the Crafts who (misquoting Shakespeare) remind their readers to "judge of probabilities," to the Georgia fugitive John Brown, who makes a "calculation to run away" and "turn[s] over in [his] mind the chances," slave narrators seldom depend utterly on providence or see the world as so random as to be beyond human manipulation.[23] Instead they make the most of their limited knowledge and agency and run the risks of escape. That they must highlight their ability to judge and manage chance testifies to a racist ideology that denied them such capacities, and that their highlighting must be highlighted today suggests that probabilistic thinking is something modern readers take for granted in human beings. Enduring a burden of proof that in the twenty-first century is borne by monkeys, toddlers, and defendants claiming insanity, slave narrators must demonstrate that they can assess the probable outcome of their actions.

In doing so they invite their readers to identify with slaves not only through emotional sympathy (how would I feel to be a slave?) but also by participating vicariously in probabilistic decision making (what would I do in such circumstances?). These two modes of identification can be set in opposition and coded by gender (say, the affective sympathy of Hester Prynne versus the calculating identifications of Roger Chillingworth), but they are by no means mutually exclusive. Poe, avoiding Descartes's error, argues that probabilistic decision making involves both emotion and logic; "Bartleby" shows how difficult it can be to separate economic and sympathetic modes of judgment; and *Ruth Hall* (1854), for instance, indicates that a woman's acute business strategies can also serve benevolent, domestic purposes. Ex-slaves often attribute their momentous decisions to something beyond calculative reason, as when "Box" Brown is inspired to mail himself to freedom only after he prays. Hoping to move as many readers as possible, slave narratives appeal to both the heart and the head, though there is at least one critical difference between the well-covered topic of sentimental power and what might be called strategic identification. It is widely noted that the sympathy generated by slave narratives risks occluding the agency of slaves, linking sentimental claims for black humanity to the inhumane abjection of blacks and providing little sociopolitical direction on how to overturn the slave system. Strategic identification emphasizes instead the intelligence and free will of slaves, who most forcefully impress their humanity on readers not by suffering but by weighing their chances.

For better and worse, such instrumental reasoning can be easier on readers (as well as writers), allowing them to focus on the mechanics of an escape rather than attempt to occupy (or fully expose) the emotional state of a slave. To the question at the end of *Uncle Tom's Cabin*—"But, what can any individual do?"—slave narratives answer "*feel right*" but also offer more practical, contingent, and strategic responses.[24] What should be done depends on a range of circumstances that cannot be fully canvassed, including geography, topography, weather, opportunity, provisions, the chances of success, and the consequences of failure. By thinking through these probabilistic challenges as such, slave narrators vindicate their full humanity by vindicating their capacity to manage chance, a political and aesthetic strategy played out, not only at the level of character and plot but also in terms of reader responses.

By emphasizing the chanciness of their experiences, slave narrators reduce expectations for formal unity and lessen the potentially dulling effects of ideological and generic predictability. They also make their stories dramatically compelling through strategic identification. When students lose their critical distance and react to a slave narrative by announcing, "I would have stolen a horse" or "I would have hit that overseer with my shovel," they display a productive imaginative engagement that vindicates the designs of the text. A teacher who finds such identifications naïve can steer discussion toward slave codes and the mind-forged manacles that slave narrators like Douglass expose so well, but an instructor might also eventually learn to ask, "What do you think made you respond to the text in that way?" It is fitting that Equiano, a cagey calculative thinker, translates "Olaudah" as meaning not only "fortune" and "vicissitude" but also one who is "well spoken," for to make vivid a slave's negotiation of chance is to artistically draw in a reader.[25] As I try to convince my wife, solving problems, as opposed to sharing feelings, is another way to care.

BALANCING PROBABILITIES

As seems so often the case with Douglass, the treatment of chance in his writings is simultaneously representative and extraordinary. From his earliest letters and *Narrative of the Life of Frederick Douglass* (1845) to his journalism and the last edition of *Life and Times* (1881, 1892), Douglass retains a commitment to providential explanation very much in keeping with abolitionist traditions begun in the eighteenth century. The antislavery movement in antebellum America was Christian in all its forms—gradualist and radical, nonresistant and militant, colonizationist and assimilationist, segregated and mixed. But while Douglass throughout his lengthy career makes religious arguments and preaches with jeremiad intensity, he also voices a counter-impulse that acknowledges the power of chance. Frustrated with the practical results of providentialism, and following his friend James McCune Smith, Douglass increasingly deploys a more empirical reformist logic as an alternative to Christian teleology. Statistical sociology and the probabilistic thinking it entails become powerful tools for Douglass, even if they oblige him to recast his carefully fashioned representative self.

Douglass's *Narrative* does not directly examine relations between providence and chance, but it does intimate the probabilistic approaches that become more prominent in his writings. As Houston Baker first argued at length, the *Narrative* is marked by tensions between providential moral claims and possessive liberal individualism.[26] When speculating why he was the only slave chosen to move from the Lloyd plantation to Baltimore, Douglass writes: "I may be deemed superstitious, and even egotistical, in regarding this event as a special interposition of divine Providence in my favor. But I should be false to the earliest sentiments of my soul, if I suppressed the opinion" (36). Douglass admits the potential fallibility of his feelings, and the *Narrative* is, of course, unforgiving of slaveholding Christianity, but in this instance Douglass's faith in providence accords with the evangelical abolitionism of his sponsor William Lloyd Garrison and the American Anti-slavery Society.

None of which precludes the *Narrative* from acknowledging the claims of chance. Douglass notes that when running away, "[T]he chances of success are tenfold greater from the city than from the country" (49), and though the "odds were fearful," he decides to leave the "stern reality" of chattel bondage for the "doubtful freedom" of flight (73–74). Douglass is personally and painfully aware of the aleatory conditions that slaves endure, yet here and elsewhere he links slavery with "immutable certainty" (29) and escape with "doubtful liberty" (74). Just as Bibb calls his escape a "dangerous experiment," Douglass refers to his first failed effort as a "test," urging his co-conspirators that "half was gained" simply by embracing the risks of escape, regardless of the outcome (75).[27] Douglass thus associates manly courage and political freedom with the acceptance of chance, as does James W. C. Pennington, one of Douglass's early sponsors, in *The Fugitive Blacksmith* (1849). Pennington writes of his decision to flee:

> It is impossible for me now to recollect all the perplexing thoughts that passed through my mind. . . . The bare possibility [of being caught and sold South] was impressively solemn; but the hour was now come, and the man must act and be free, or remain a slave for ever [*sic*]. . . . I considered the difficulties of the way—the reward that would be offered—the human blood-hounds that would be set upon my track—the weariness— the hunger—the gloomy thought. . . . But, as I have said, the hour was come, and the man must act, or forever be a slave.[28]

Like Pennington, Northup, Bibb, and Jacobs, Douglass in the *Narrative* gives the lie to racists such as Fitzhugh. Describing his personal trials of resistance less as spontaneous acts of flight and more as calculated risks, Douglass shows himself to be a rational agent able to live with—and willing to die for—the foreseeable but unguaranteed chances of liberty.

In his second autobiography, *My Bondage and My Freedom* (1855), Douglass more explicitly though still ambivalently discusses how freedom demands the handling of chance. He again calls his selection to go to Baltimore "a special interposition of Divine Providence," but he also expresses more significant doubts that require more careful assurances (213). Douglass complicates his claim to godly favor by identifying and then rejecting aleatory explanation: "Viewing [the selection] in the light of human likelihoods, it is quite probable that, but for the mere circumstance of being thus removed . . . I might have been wearing the galling chains of slavery. I have sometimes felt, however, that there was something more intelligent than *chance*, and something more certain than *luck*" (212). Douglass acknowledges the difference between divine governance and human notions of chance, in this instance privileging providence over chance while also demonstrating that he recognizes probabilistic thinking as a living option, a design he continues to elaborate in *My Bondage and My Freedom*.

As in the *Narrative*, Douglass in 1855 describes plantation discipline as a totalizing system, but *My Bondage and My Freedom* more thoroughly exposes how the teleologies of slavery are false—inadequately enforced by physical and mental violence, subverted by "The Vicissitudes of Slave Life," and actively manipulated by strategizing slaves (236). Douglass again formulates his first escape attempt as a choice "between certainty and uncertainty," choosing the unknown potential of freedom not in an act of blind faith but, rather, in the manner of "men of sane minds" who "conjecture the many possibilities" (311–12). The nineteenth century used "conjecture" as a scientific term denoting probabilistic judgment, and more than in the *Narrative*, Douglass details in *My Bondage* the many contingencies of his plan—weather conditions, the probable detection of a canoe, the "chance of being regarded as fishermen" (313).[29] Douglass adds in his "Letter to His Old Master" (1849), reprinted in the appendix of *My Bondage*: "The probabilities so far as I could by reason determine them, were . . . ten chances of defeat to one of victory" (413). Douglass describes at length his "doubts, fears and uncertainties" in the face of such desperate odds (310). Yet if he presents his deliberative self as less heroic than a protagonist from Scott or Cooper, or for that matter "The Heroic Slave" (1853)—and if *Life and Times* attributes his eventual escape "to good luck, rather than to bravery" (643)—Douglass asserts that his management of chance is nonetheless a sign of his manhood: "To balance probabilities, where life and liberty hang on the result, requires steady nerves" (314). As both artist and abolitionist, Douglass in *My Bondage* renders his probabilistic struggles as compellingly as language and policy permit, and he also explicates the meaning of his trials: they affirm a distinctively modern sense of manhood in that Douglass triumphs, not by extinguishing uncertainty but by acting rationally under its threat.

More can be said about Douglass's vacillation between chance and providence in *My Bondage and My Freedom*. He admires how Henry Harris resisted his captors, giving Douglass the opportunity to destroy a forged pass: "I never see much use in fighting, unless there is a reasonable probability of whipping somebody. Yet there was something almost providential in the resistance made by the gallant Henry" (318). Douglass's "almost" can stand for a larger ambivalence. At times he practically paraphrases Cowper, one of his favorite poets, as when he writes, "The allotments of Providence . . . often conceal from finite vision the wisdom and goodness in which they are sent" (370). At other times, probabilism comes to the fore, as when Douglass attends to odds and contingencies in the language of "chance," "probabilities," and "luck."

Even the form of Douglass's second autobiography reflects tensions between teleology and chance. The style is more predictable than that of the *Narrative*, more characterized by the balanced rhythms, smooth pacing, and organizational symmetries of nineteenth-century high eloquence, and this mature style, like Douglass's refined image on the frontispiece, assures the reader of his eventual rise. Yet *My Bondage and My Freedom* is also enriched by surprising stylistic disruptions—inserted quotations from the *Narrative* that disrupt the even surface of the text; self-conscious infelicities of diction and tone (especially when describing violence); Douglass's refusal to follow the generic convention of detailing his successful escape; an ending that has the tenor of summation but remains stubbornly open-ended. If slave narratives conclude more or less with liberty and more or less take antislavery stands, their endings are seldom as overdetermined as the autobiographies of great men or the imagined resolutions of novels, for the most explicit purpose of slave narratives is to garner support for an ongoing cause whose victory is far from assured. The last chapter of *My Bondage and My Freedom* is titled "Various Incidents," as if the drive for narrative closure cannot contain the possibilities of uncertain political struggle.

Douglass's hesitant turn toward probabilism in *My Bondage and My Freedom* reflects broader cultural suspicions not so much about the existence of providence as about the usefulness of teleological argument in settling political disputes. Like many thinkers of his era, Douglass was frustrated with the slavery debate, which was mired—and had been mired for decades—in mutually exclusive providential claims. Part of the problem was that competing assertions relied on untestable assumptions, whether they came from higher law abolitionists such as Garrison, Stowe, Thoreau, Charles Sumner, and William Seward or from pro-slavery theologians and philosophers such as James Thornwell, William Elliott, and William A. Smith.[30] As is often the case in protracted arguments, partisans complained of their opponents' tautologies while at the same time asserting their own. Sumner in an 1850 Massachusetts Supreme Court case criticized segregationists for judging individuals "a priori," while Thoreau marveled in 1851 in response to pro-slavery calls to annex Cuba: "How often the Saxon man talks of carrying out the designs of Providence—as if he had some knowledge of Providence and [God's] designs." Conversely, an anti-abolitionist critique reprinted in *Frederick Douglass's Paper* contrasted its own "inductive system" to that of abolitionist "fanatics" who presumed "to explain a priori the mysterious ways of the Infinite." Among those who characterized abolitionists as dangerously abstracted theorists, Fitzhugh adopted the conservative empiricism of Burke: "[I]t is much safer and better, to look to the past, to trust to experience, to follow nature, than to be guided by the *ignis fatuus* of a priori speculations." An 1857 article in *The National Era* agreed from the opposite side of the issue, admitting that "theories have always failed in practice" and insisting that "we [abolitionists] need not a perfect system, but a remedial method adapted to conditions, accidents, and incapacities, which are not the subjects of absolute law." Decades of gridlock in the slavery crisis were turning some Americans from ideologues into pragmatists.[31]

In accordance with Jacksonian anti-intellectualism, and in rough anticipation of pragmatist philosophy, debates over the practicality of deductive reasoning also emerged in the black press in the United States and Canada. An 1854 article in Mary Ann Shadd's *Provincial Freeman* praised the power of deduction: "Philosophy . . . arranges every science, [and] marshals all the principles of general knowledge." Editors routinely encouraged metaphysical study, and one article traced the origins of Western philosophy to Africa, arguing that Pythagoras and Plato "went to Ethiopia and Egypt, and sat at the feet of black philosophers." Yet as much as writers in the black press acknowledged the authority of metaphysicians, moral philosophers, and theologians, and as much as they deployed absolutist claims against chattel bondage and racism, they also doubted the transformative power of teleological reasoning. Like Booker T. Washington half a century later, some simply saw learned theory as a distraction. An 1848 piece in Douglass's *North Star* complained: "[W]e have reached after [education's] flumeries [*sic*] and its pageantry to the neglect of the reality. . . . [I]nstead of merchants and mechanics, we have moralists and philosophers." In 1852, *Frederick Douglass's Paper* expressed more positive fears that "the philosophers, in their many and mazy speculations, are forever leading us out to sea." As early as 1841, an article in *The Colored American* made a similar charge when writing of racial injustice:

> It is not a metaphysical question, and therefore bars that straining and effort after theories. . . . [W]e have seen much argument, a vast deal of theorizing, and much eloquence displayed. There has been no little of ethical and philosophical knowledge made to bear upon the question. Nearly all this we [consider] extraneous. The disquisitions upon morals that have been published, from Cicero to Paley, and from him to Wayland, can aid but little in telling it. And much less dependence can be placed upon subtle speculations or wire-drawn theories, drawn though they be from the abstruse Plato, or the transcendental Kant.

Demonstrating both knowledge of and dissatisfaction with metaphysics, the article rejects the two dominant schools of antebellum philosophy: Scottish realism (represented by Paley and Francis Wayland) and idealism (both Platonic and Kantian). The writer appeals instead to "practical mind[s]" and deliberations based on "facts"—a position shared by an 1847 prospectus printed in *The Liberator*, which asked readers to support *The U.S. Statistical Journal* as a way to bring quantitative objectivity to the slavery controversy. Though moral absolutism continued to be prominent in *The Liberator* and every other abolitionist venue, the slavery debate increasingly turned to the supposed objectivity of science. When disputants locked in irreconcilable conflict repeatedly invoke unprovable a priori claims, some people look for alternative methods of adjudication and persuasion. (One might cite the transition from the idealism of George W. Bush's "moral clarity" to the more technocratic pragmatism of Barack Obama).[32]

Douglass participated in his era's shift from teleology toward empiricism, and not only by turning uncomfortably to natural science in "The Claims of the Negro Ethnologically Considered" (1854). In 1851, he joined Thoreau in complaining of religious leaders calling for the annexation of Cuba: "[S]uch divines may be expected to see the hand of Providence as well in a war with Spain as in a war with Mexico: for both of which they will not fail, through the misty mazes of theology, to trace responsibility to the throne of Heaven." Douglass later said of pro-slavery opponents, "It is in vain to reason with them," and he charged that anti-abolitionist logic moved speciously "from premise to conclusion." Yet Douglass also recognized that antislavery tautologies were failing in theory and practice. One can find as early as the *Narrative* an emphasis on situational ethics that conflicts with Garrisonian moral absolutes, while Douglass justified his decision to accept his manumission in 1846 with deeply reasoned arguments emphasizing action philosophy over theoretical consistency. "What to the Slave is the Fourth of July?" (1852) laments the insufficiencies of deductive logic as forcefully as any text of the time, and Douglass wrote when advocating black manual training in an 1853 open letter to Stowe: "I have, during the last dozen years, denied before the Americans that we are an inferior race; but this has been done by arguments based upon admitted principles rather than by the presentation of fact." Clearly Douglass's own formidable example of achievement was not enough to sway the nation. How to vindicate black equality with broader factual proof became a driving question that Douglass took up with the assistance of James McCune Smith.[33]

Smith was a prominent black intellectual whose accomplishments are still being assessed, most notably by John Stauffer.[34] Smith held three degrees from Glasgow University and was a successful physician in New York City. He was also an active political abolitionist who published on a range of topics related directly and tangentially to slavery and race—from Haitian histories and antislavery editorials, to literary sketches and aesthetic commentaries, to scientific pieces on phrenology, climatology, mental philosophy, cosmology, and medicine. Smith believed in the divine government of the universe but generally eschewed providentialism and abstraction. After the *Dred Scott* decision, he wrote a frustrated essay titled, "Reforms are Mere Acts of Intellection" (1858), and he denied in 1864 that slavery would be vanquished by godly intervention. "[W]e believe that the age of 'miracles is past,'" Smith wrote, "And, we fail to see in the history or character of the American people any special attraction for a special providence."[35] Abjuring teleological assertions, and resisting the abstract Comtian sociology of pro-slavery thinkers such as Fitzhugh and Henry Hughes, Smith pioneered an empirical abolitionism that drew from the emerging probabilistic sciences, particularly quantitative sociology.

Ralph Ellison wrote in 1964, "Since its inception, American social science has been closely bound with American Negro destiny," though Ellison, like most modern commentators, did not date this dynamic until after Emancipation. Susan Mizruchi's *Science of Sacrifice* (1998) begins its groundbreaking study of literature, sociology, and race in the postbellum period, focusing especially on Du Bois, while Oz Frankel has pushed inquiry somewhat earlier, showing how the American Freedmen's Inquiry Commission, founded in 1863, ended up using its statistical surveys to reinforce racist categories. Yet if postbellum statistical studies of the race problem were unprecedented in scale and theoretical sophistication, they have roots in the antebellum slavery debate, which occurred alongside the disciplinary formation of sociology. Thomas Dew drew from Malthus and the 1830 census in his landmark pro-slavery article, "Review of the Debates in the Virginia Legislature" (1831–1832). As Samuel Otter has shown, abolitionists surveyed African-American communities in and around Philadelphia beginning in the late 1830s. The 1840 national census was especially controversial for indicating that free African Americans died younger than slaves and were more likely to suffer from physical disabilities, pauperism, insanity, and "idiocy." The *Southern Literary Messenger* and John Calhoun happily interpreted such results as proof that blacks were unfit for modern capitalism, while the Mississippi Senator Robert Walker used the census data (as well as figures from Quetelet) to argue for the inferiority of blacks in his popular pamphlet, "Letter on Texas Annexation" (1844). In response, Edward Jarvis, president of the fledging American Statistical Association, exposed inaccuracies in the 1840 census data, pointing out that some towns reported numbers of mentally ill blacks that exceeded their total black populations. Even as statistical sociology struggled to establish itself as an objective science, it was from its origins entangled in political agendas (as suggested by the etymological root of statistics in the state).[36]

McCune Smith entered the fray over the 1840 census in "Freedom and Slavery for Afric-Americans" (1844), a series of articles published in *The New York Tribune* (and reprinted by *The Liberator, The National Anti-Slavery Standard,* and *The Cincinnati Weekly Herald and Philanthropist*). Though beginning from an objective quantitative position— "Figures cannot be charged with fanaticism"—Smith argued that racism and passing corrupted the census data and overstated the problems of free blacks. In "Freedom and Slavery for Afric-Americans" and beyond, Smith did not deny the value of statistics so much as insist with technical rigor on their proper collection and use. In an 1846 article on life insurance, Smith referred to statistics from Quetelet while explicating probability theory, and in 1853 he chaired a National Convention of Colored People committee whose mandate was to assemble a statistical report of all free African Americans. The ambitious project was never completed, but Smith gave a paper on improving the census to the American Geographical Society in 1854. He wrote the introduction to *My Bondage and My Freedom* the next year, describing Douglass as a thinker who preferred "induction" to "deduction" and calling him a "Representative American man," not only in the Emersonian sense of a paragon but also in the terms of Quetelet's average man insofar as Douglass was, in Smith's words, "a type of his countrymen" (132–33). Around this time, Smith was also publishing "Heads of the Colored People" (1852–1854), a series of literary sketches for *Frederick Douglass's Paper* that focused on social types, not unlike the sociological taxonomies of Dickens's *Sketches by Boz* (1833–1836) and Poe's "The Man of the Crowd." From medical studies that looked critically at sample sizes to complaints about Jefferson misrepresenting racial types, Smith condemned what he called "clumsily contrived statistics," a problem evident in racist works of the time by Josiah Nott, George Gliddon, Hinton Helper, and Thorton Stringfellow. The difficulty, as Smith repeatedly showed in his writings, is that facts are subject to error and racist manipulation.[37]

Smith's best efforts to put statistics to abolitionist ends appeared in *The Anglo-African Magazine,* an intellectually ambitious, short-lived monthly that he helped to edit with Thomas Hamilton in 1859. Douglass described the magazine in *Douglass's Monthly* as "devoted to Literature, Science, Statistics, etc.," and Douglass reprinted one of Smith's longest articles, "Civilization: Its Dependence on Physical Circumstances" (1859). By looking at the "mass of population," praising Laplace, and referring to Quetelet's studies, Smith used the logic of large numbers to attribute racial differences to environment, not immutable physiological traits:

> [W]e speak of man, not the individual, but in the aggregate. Take one hundred thousand men in a given portion of the globe, and another hundred thousand in another, and differently, climated portion of the earth. Obtain the average strength of each party; and it will be found that the party which produces the greater physical, will also produce the greater intellectual power. It will also be found that this stronger party will live in the climate the better fitted to develop physical vigor.

Here Smith adopts a frequentist outlook to counter essentialist claims of black inferiority, a strategy he further pursues in "A Statistical View of the Colored Population of the United States" (1859), a series of articles that praise Quetelet and quote from his *Treatise on Man*. Like Delany's eponymous hero in *Blake* (who serves as an unofficial census taker for the circum-Atlantic black community), and like Frank Webb (who in *The Garies and Their Friends* [1857] invokes statistics to defend the success of free blacks in the

North), Smith recognized the need for African Americans to harness the power of science and participate in their own statistical representation.[38]

Douglass concurred in his own editorial work, for if he registers some doubts about straying from moral suasion, he follows McCune Smith and larger trends in transatlantic print culture as his papers begin regularly quoting statistics in the late 1850s. Douglass reports data on free and enslaved blacks, interprets census figures, reprints Lord Brougham's statistical analysis of West Indian emancipation, and covers Delany's participation in the 1860 International Statistical Congress in London (which sparked a minor controversy when Delany's presence prompted the official U.S. delegate to walk out). Douglass himself would eventually address the 1879 American Social Science Association, though more important than his interest in statistics is the changing methodological outlook they imply.

Douglass's "Self-Made Men" (1859), his most repeated lecture, moves away from the representative manhood Douglass champions earlier in his career and instead begins to theorize individual and racial uplift in terms of chance and large numbers. The most surprising aspect of the speech is that Douglass does not discuss his life story; it is as if Barack Obama gave a talk on groundbreaking political leaders without ever referring to himself. Douglass's fame as a self-made man surely made his self-regard implicit in his speech, though a deeper reason is his growing discomfort with the metonymic logic of representative selfhood. Douglass begins "Self-Made Men" by stating that the subject of great men encourages a "tendency to the universal," but he quickly insists on the diversity of human nature, which has "extremes and ends and opposites" that cannot be "reduced to fixed standards." Like Emerson, Douglass aspires to a selfhood that enjoys both universality and flux, both representativeness and exemplarity. More sociologically, Douglass recognizes that humankind in the mass is so varied as to be beyond representation by any single individual, a realization that crystallizes for Emerson somewhere between "The American Scholar" (1837) and *Representative Men* (1850).[39] As much as the romantic selfhood of the early Emerson and Carlyle loom over Douglass's speech, Douglass defends his own contribution with a telling metaphor:

A thousand arrows might be shot at the same object, but, though united in aim, they might be divided in flight. Some fly too high, others too low. Some go to the right, others to the left. . . . Nothing was more natural or instructive than to walk among these fallen arrows, and estimate the probable amount of skill and force requisite to bring each to its place. (3:292)[40]

As discussed in chapter two, target shooting was a favorite example of nineteenth-century probability theorists. In his preface to *Treatise on Man*, Quetelet explained the logic of frequentism: "We aim at a target—an end—marked by a point. The arrows go to the right and left, high or low, according to the address of the shooters. . . . [I]f they be sufficiently numerous, one may learn from them the real position of the point they surround."[41] "Self-Made Men" suggests along with Quetelet that numerous trials from manifold sources best approximate truth. Just as the average man is a useful fiction, there is no single representative man, even if a candidate happens to be regarded as a representative of his race.

Having framed his lecture as part of a probabilistic process governed by statistical logic, and as if haunted by that life-shaping moment when he alone was chosen to move to Baltimore, Douglass takes up the question of how significantly chance figures in the making of self-made men. Douglass initially denies that man is "a being of chance": "I do not think much of the accident or good luck theory of self-made men." Yet he also admits that self-making is a kind of "solecism," and he goes on to praise men who "made the most of circumstances, favoring opportunities, accidents, chances, etc." (3:293). It is shocking that Frederick Douglass, who rivals Benjamin Franklin and Abraham Lincoln in the canon of self-made American men, would come to refer to self-making as a kind of oxymoron. For Douglass, self-made men take advantage of chance by rising with luck and pluck, circumstances and individual agency. And Douglass predictably emphasizes the latter: "[W]e are stingy in our praise of merit, but generous in our praise of chance"; "[W]e may explain success mainly by one word and that word is WORK! WORK! WORK! WORK!" "Self-Made Men" is a conventional motivational speech well designed for consumption on the lecture circuit, except that aleatory anxieties continue to unsettle the bromides that would guarantee success to those who strive. Like Poe and Melville, Douglass does not deny chance, especially in an unequal society in which accidents of birth, including racial identity, capriciously skew life opportunities. The best that Douglass can offer his audience under such conditions is an imperfect frequentist promise: "Science is diffusing its broad, beneficent light," so much so that "dependence upon chance or luck is destined to vanish." The end of chance, for Douglass, comes through repeated efforts, science, and free will, not through what he calls "supernatural interference," thus placing him on a secular, capitalist trajectory somewhere between Franklin and Weber.

The chanceless order that Douglass envisions is fundamentally a meritocracy in which accidents of birth and color do not govern one's chances for individual success. Antebellum abolitionists occasionally argued for what they called "equal chances," and Douglass certainly fights for what we call equal opportunity throughout his long career. What makes "Self-Made Men" a remarkable performance is that Douglass's maturing political philosophy complicates the representative racial selfhood that, as Robert S. Levine has shown, defines so many of Douglass's efforts before the Civil War.[42] Douglass continued to be seen as an exemplar of his race and continued to craft his reputation as such, but "Self-Made Men" pushes against the limits of representative politics by favoring diverse historical examples over autobiographical exemplarity, the management of chance over supernatural interference, and the well-ordered society of utilitarianism over the heroic selfhood of romanticism. Douglass never stops advocating individual effort and strenuous self-cultivation, but he increasingly recognizes the probabilistic influence that social conditions have on aggregate populations.

It is a subtle but important change in Douglass's thinking. The *Narrative* presents his move to Baltimore as a special interposition of providence. *My Bondage and My Freedom* more seriously engages the unsettling possibilities of chance. In response to the failure of moral suasion and providentialism, and following the lead of Smith's statistical reasoning, "Self-Made Men" addresses individual uplift as a probabilistic challenge, acknowledging the accidents of social disparity and recommending the management of chance in two ways: individuals must make the most of their chances, and societies must equalize opportunities, not because of some Kantian or Rawlsian concept of justice but because diverse participants—multiple archers—lead to better outcomes. Douglass recognizes the dangers of representative selfhood, for his example can (and continues to) be used for conservative purposes: *Why all the complaints about unequal opportunities? Douglass pulled himself up by the bootstraps, why can't everyone else?* As much as Douglass has personal and strategic reasons for explaining his success as testaments to providence and merit, he also has reasons for presenting himself as an extraordinarily lucky case. To be a powerful African American under nineteenth-century U.S. racism is to be in a disturbingly basic way an unrepresentative figure. Douglass never cedes his title as spokesman for his people, but he learns to rely less on this self as he elaborates what might called his "probabilistic liberalism" during and after the Civil War.

GIVE THEM A CHANCE!

In August of 1860, Douglass published "The Prospects of the Future," an editorial containing as despairing a passage as he would ever write:

> The great work of enlightening the people as to the wicked enormities of slavery, is well nigh accomplished, but the practical results of this work have disappointed our hopes. The grim and bloody tragedies of outrage and cruelty are rehearsed day by day to the ears of the people, but they look on as coolly indifferent as spectators in a theatre. . . . They commend the iron-linked logic, and soul-born eloquence of Abolitionists, but never practice the principles laid bare by the one, or act upon the motions called up by the other. . . . You cannot relate a new fact, or frame an unfamiliar argument on this subject.—Reason and morality have emptied their casket of richest jewels into the lap of this cause in vain.[43]

Eight years earlier, "What to the Slave is the Fourth of July?" had offered Douglass's morally enlivening eloquence as an alternative to failing discursive arguments, but "The Prospects of the Future" despairs of logic *and* eloquence, rational *and* moral authority, as Douglass contemplates the apparent futility of his life's antislavery work, so much that for the first time in his life he seriously considered emigrating. Within a year, the attack on Fort Sumter brought Douglass new optimism and helped him move toward an abolitionist approach enslaved neither to first "principles" nor "iron-linked" laws but based instead on his recurrent belief that "[m]utability is the law for all" (4:244). Douglass's Civil War writings by no means renounce providence, deduction, or moral absolutes, for he continues with some frequency to ally abolitionism with the "*changeless laws of the universe*" (3:508). Such views accorded with the teleological convictions shared by Northerners and Southerners, blacks and whites, during and after the Civil War, and David Blight has emphasized that Douglass sometimes saw the war as part of a legible godly design.[44] Yet as the fighting ground on and Douglass struggled to put emancipation at the center of the conflict, more than ever before he tired of deducing his case from absolute principles, turning instead to a different set of intellectual habits—fallibilism, pluralism, experimentalism, induction, open-endedness, and the management of chance.

Douglass wrote after the attack on Fort Sumter: "We are living in troubled times, on a mighty stream afloat, without pilot, rudder or chart.... We live but today, and the measureless shores of the future are wisely hid from us" (3:425). Without rejecting wise providence, Douglass acknowledges an uncertainty that points him toward epistemological pluralism. "*It takes two men to tell the truth*" (3:363), Douglass wrote in 1861, a claim he extended five years later when advocating suffrage for African American men: "One man may tell a good deal of truth; one race may tell, perhaps, a large amount of truth; but it takes all men, of all classes, of all cliques and conditions in life to tell the whole truth" (4:125). Again, Douglass does not renounce "whole truth," but he denies that any one person can know it, even a representative man. To think otherwise is hubris, for as Douglass wrote in 1867, "I know of no greater misfortunes to individuals than an over confidence in their own perfections, and I know of fewer misfortunes that can happen to a nation greater than an over confidence in the perfection of its government" (4:149–50).

Such fallibilism coming from Douglass is both fitting and surprising. Given his pluralistic outlook in "Self-made Men" and beyond, he cannot help but recognize that his own truth-claims are subjective, partial, and therefore open to revision, a corrigibility he demonstrates at various points in his career when adjusting his views on the Constitution, violent resistance, and Abraham Lincoln. At the same time, Douglass remained a fierce proponent of African-American rights whose rhetorical and intellectual style conceded little to his enemies. The challenge is to understand how Douglass squares uncertainty and conviction. How can he seem both a skeptic and a believer, both a pluralist and a partisan?

An answer that underscores Douglass's political and philosophical development is that he recasts reform as an experiment that leads to, not presupposes, truth. Douglass frequently referred to the war as a "school" (4:4), "lesson" (4:14), and "test" (4:31); and in 1863, he pressured Lincoln to take the risk of mobilizing African-American troops: "Give them a chance! Give them a chance! I don't say they are great fighters. I don't say that they will fight better than other men. All I say is, give them a chance" (3:567). Early in his career, Douglass tended to deduce equal rights from iron-linked universal laws, but here he appeals to chance and experiment, not claiming to know the capacities of blacks nor arguing from first principles, but suggesting instead that equal opportunity must precede reliable knowledge, for men and nations learn better from the trials of experience than from deductive philosophizing. Douglass wrote in 1864, "[M]ost men [are] taught by events" (4:108), a claim he extended in *Life and Times*: "[Men] are taught less by theories than by facts and events" (775–76). He also wrote in "The Mission of the War" (1863): "Speaking in the name of Providence, some men tell us that slavery is already dead.... I do not share the confidence with which it is asserted. In a grand crisis like this, I prefer to look facts squarely in the face."[45] Statements like this vindicate McCune Smith's claim in his introduction to *My Bondage and My Freedom* that Douglass prefers induction to deduction, hard facts to speculative theories.

The challenge is that for experience to fulfill its explanatory potential in the matter of race, it must be free from overdetermining social biases that, like a priori assumptions, literally prejudge the possibilities of truth. Just as Smith worried about the racist inferences drawn from skewed statistics, Douglass complained in 1862 that blacks "have been weighed, measured, marked and prized—in detail and in the aggregate," but unlike whites subjected to quantitative sociology, they have not had "an equal chance to live" (3:502–3). In an era that often attributed the disparate conditions of races to more or less immutable natural differences (sometimes rooted in climate, sometimes in the body and mind), Douglass needed to make a probabilistic point that today is almost always conceded in theory but seldom acted upon with sufficient political conviction—that a general lack of opportunity for any segment of the population leads to an aggregative dearth of achievement. The heroic overcoming of long odds makes for rousing personal narratives, but heroism in itself is an insufficient and even damaging basis for social policy as Douglass suggests when acknowledging that the self-made man is actually a solecism. From a probabilistic point of view, equal opportunity—that is, equal chance—allows truths to be known in the long run, and so the most reliable course for a nation beset by warring assumptions about black capacities is to turn toward the authority of mass facts fairly determined over the course of what Douglass calls the "republican experiment" (4:150). As a speaker memorializing the fallen African-American soldiers of the famed Massachusetts Fifty-fourth proclaimed, "They ask[ed] only a chance to prove their manhood ... to establish our claims to be recognized as men worthy of a chance in the wide world."[46] Most abolitionists interpreted the Civil War through the lens of moral absolutism (God's truth goes marching teleologically on), and most Americans of the time judged racial capacities without regard to disparate opportunities. Keeping alternative explanations open, Douglass asserted the need to tame unequal chances—not in the name of higher law but for the sake of legitimate experiment, not under the banner of heroic selfhood but in the logic of large numbers.

This logic can be taken as a kind of liberalism, though Douglass's relation to liberalism has been difficult to stabilize and can be further destabilized still. While political philosophers from Charles Mills to Bernard Boxill to Peter Myers have associated Douglass with a liberal tradition drawn from Locke and natural rights, literary critics such as Russ Castronovo and Arthur Riss see Douglass as more skeptical of and even resistant to such thinking. Liberalism for Douglass, however, can also be understood less in terms of possessive individualism and abstract models of selves and rights, and more as a probabilistic political theory most powerfully represented by John Stuart Mill. Douglass hardly abandons Lockean political discourse, but as he fights for "fair play" and "an equal chance in the race of life," especially during debates over reconstruction, his writings reflect an emerging alignment of probabilism and modern liberal theory (4:202; 4:566).[47]

Douglass demands in "What the Black Man Wants" (1865) that Americans "try the experiment" of equal opportunity:

> Do nothing with us! If the apples will not remain on the tree of their own strength, if they are worm-eaten at the core, if they are early ripe and disposed to fall, let them fall! I am not for tying or fastening them on the tree in any way. . . . And if the Negro cannot stand on his own legs, let him fall also. All I ask is, give him a chance!" (4:68)

Before the war, Douglass had used falling apples to compare the inevitability of abolitionist victory to the absolute laws of Newton and the argument from design. In "What the Black Man Wants," apples figure lynching and even racial extinction while also paying tribute to Darwinian principles marked less by benevolent natural laws than by strife and probabilistic selection. So open is Douglass, at least rhetorically, to whatever outcome experimentation might bring, he wrote in 1870, "If [the Negro] can stand up, well. If he falls down and disappears, I have sometimes between tempted to say, Equally well" (4:262). Dew and Fitzhugh followed Burke in setting tradition and experience over theoretical speculation, but Douglass shows how a political philosophy of experience can justify radical reform, for freedom and equal opportunity are fundamental to Douglass, not so much as absolute ideals from which to deduce political arguments but, rather, as necessary conditions for the proper adjudication of social arrangements. Equal chances are necessary for valid experimentation and hence knowledge, not only in the individual cases of slaves who, for instance, are forbidden to read but also for a nation whose progress toward whole truth must include as many perspectives as possible.

Douglass's philosophical pluralism thus works in concert with his political goals and also accords with his rhetorical practices as a writer and orator. Douglass deployed hybrid styles and tonal ranges while working in a wide variety of genres—classical oratory, forensic argument, autobiography, fiction, and even poetry.[48] Like a novelist, he inhabits multiple perspectives and adopts the idioms of manifold parties while alluding to a wealth of literary traditions and displaying his skills as an impersonator. Douglass does not, like Emerson, enact subjective flux at the level of sentence and diction, but his strategic shifting of modalities and dialectical habits of thought show him taking up the challenge of asserting personal convictions in a pluralistic world. Between 1855 and 1881, Douglass moves away from autobiography, focusing his energies on editorials and speeches that draw less on individual subjectivity and more on the authority of large numbers. Smith should have known better than to call Douglass "a type of his countrymen," but if statistical composites can never be embodied by a single individual, Smith's inclination was right in that one of Douglass's singular achievements is his ability to speak many voices.

The most realized statement of Douglass's pluralism is "Our Composite Nationality" (1869), a speech whose political and epistemological claims acknowledge the need for America as a nation to better manage chance. Douglass briefly invokes "eternal, universal, and indestructible" laws when calling for equal civil rights regardless of color or creed, but then he quickly changes course, "So much for what is right, now let us see what is wise" (4:252–53). Having bracketed absolutism in favor of practicality (or as we will see, utilitarianism and pragmatism), "Our Composite Nationality" returns to its thesis that in the long run diversity is a noetic and material advantage for America and the world. Douglass writes, "It is by comparing one nation with another, and one learning from another, each competing with all, and all competing with each, that hurtful errors are exposed, great social truths discovered, and the wheels of civilization whirled onward" (4:241). Rejecting on the one hand "universal conformity" and on the other heroic models of manhood that Douglass associates with Carlyle, "Our Composite Nationality" offers a postromantic worldview: "All great qualities are never found in any one man or in any one race" (4:255). Hero worship and Anglo-Saxonism may inspire some Americans, but truths are best approached through multiple perspectives.

"Our Composite Nationality" can certainly be read as a foreshadowing of modern multiculturalism, though Douglass is not primarily animated by tolerance, and even freedom in his speech seems less a self-evident good than a means to utilitarian progress.

Douglass's focus on competition and the "fitness" of races is part of his abiding laissez-faire individualism and one reason opponents of race-based preferences sometimes cite Douglass for support, including more conservative African-American thinkers such as Booker T. Washington, Benjamin Brawley, and Clarence Thomas, all of whom quote from "What the Black Man Wants" when arguing that African Americans must stand or fall according to their own merits (4:255).[49]

If Douglass cannot be entirely contained by any political philosophy, "Our Composite Nationality" is best understood as a work of pluralism informed by probabilistic logic. Douglass writes, "The theory that each race of men has some special faculty, some peculiar gift or quality of mind or heart, needed to the perfection and happiness of the whole is a broad and beneficent theory, and, besides its beneficence, has, in its support, the voice of experience" (4:255). This passage implies an essentialist racial "theory" but calls on "experience" to validate such claims, suggesting that what people suffer and do, as opposed to what the "are," should premise notions of racial identity.[50] Most centrally in "Our Composite Nationality," Douglass understands race at the level of mass society. He refers to "aggregations" to argue that America should mind the law of large numbers and give Chinese immigrants full rights, for racial variety and a diversity of gifts makes for a stronger nation (4:241; 4:249). As in "Self-Made Men" and Quetelet's *Treatise on Man*, "Our Composite Nationality" argues that the greater the number of participants, the better the chances for getting at truth.

The connection between Douglass's statistical reasoning, his support of equal chances, and his defense of racial diversity is part of an emerging nexus of liberal ideologies that Smith and Douglass helped to synthesize. Historians have begun to trace rich transatlantic connections in nineteenth-century Anglo-American liberalism, but if Leslie Butler has recognized slavery and race as key sites of interaction, the spread of liberalism in mid-century African-American thought remains for the most part unstudied.[51] In a profoundly suggestive paragraph from his essay, "On the Fourteenth Query of Thomas Jefferson's Notes on Virginia" (1859), Smith reflects on one of his earlier articles from that year, "Civilization: Its Dependence on Physical Circumstances." Smith asserts that he wrote "Civilization" prior to reading two major works of the time with which the article has strong affinities—the first volume of Henry Buckle's *Civilization in England* (1857), and John Stuart Mill's *On Liberty* (1859). Mill, who engaged probability theory in his *System of Logic: Ratiocinative and Inductive*, applied emerging sciences of chance to his political philosophy. Attacking a priori reasoning as "an instrument devised for consecrating all deep seated prejudices," Mill—a staunch abolitionist who was in the minority of English thinkers supporting the Union during the early stages of the Civil War—argues in *On Liberty* that cultural diversity and "fair play" help speed the pace of social progress. Smith in his article on Jefferson quotes Mill on how European countries flourish because of "their remarkable diversity," and Smith mentions Mill's citation of Wilhelm Von Humboldt, the political theorist whose posthumous *Spheres and Duties of Government* (1854) championed "diversity" and "unfettered freedom." Like his glorified naturalist brother, Alexander, Wilhelm generally rejected invidious racial distinctions, forging a link between the empirical sciences, political liberalism, and anti-racist thought. Smith's position in "Civilization" is quite similar to those of Mill and Von Humboldt. "[Wherever] institutions favor a free admixture of human thought," Smith writes, "there, civilization advances; but, wherever human institutions isolate human thought, keep soul from communion with its fellow soul, there progress ceases." At a time when many white Americans argued that national strength depended on racial purity, Smith helped theorize a counter-argument that variety is a positive good.[52]

Buckle is another coordinate for the conjunction of probabilism, liberalism, and anti-racism in mid-nineteenth-century British and American thought. An autodidact, poly-math, and chess champion turned historian, Buckle in the first volume of his *History of Civilization in England* provides a framework for applying probability science to history, invoking (among others theorists of chance) Quetelet, Mill, and John Herschel. Buckle saw history as a huge data sample from which to infer frequentist laws, and he called on "statistical evidence" and the "doctrine of chance" to reveal "the undeviating regularity of the moral world." More specific to African-American rights, Buckle followed Mill in resisting scientific racism, quoting from Mill's *Principles of Political Economy* (1848): "'[O]f all the vulgar modes of escaping from the consideration of the effect of social and moral influences on the human mind, the most vulgar is that of attributing the diversities of conduct and character to inherent natural differences.'" Like many thinkers of his time, Buckle did not make consistent distinctions between biology and culture, but he did view diversity as an advantage, and in a review of *On Liberty* he staunchly advocated social "experiments" and individual "eccentricities." For society to advance in the long run, the odd must get fair play.[53]

The influence of Smith—and through him, Mill and Buckle—is apparent in "Our Composite Nationality," as when Douglass writes, "The voice of civilization speaks an unmistakable language against the isolation of families, nations and races" (4:254). Early in Douglass's career, romantic individualism tends to stand in dialectical tension with communitarian politics. "Our Composite Nationality" helps reconcile these urges by praising a society of diverse individuals operating under the auspices of equal opportu-nity, laissez-faire economics, and social Darwinism (particularly as presented by Herbert Spencer, whose *Social Statics* in 1851 also helped to combine liberalism and probabilistic logic). Not unlike Lincoln's growing commitment to equality under the logic of fair chances, Douglass's contribution to modern liberalism can thus look something like this.[54] Beginning in the late 1850s and with increasing specificity, Douglass argues that a well-ordered society must minimize the unequal chances of racism so as to maximize the benefits of diversity. Of course, classical and enlightenment thinkers had long favored the free exchange of differing opinions in the public sphere. But nineteenth-century lib-eral theorists attributed social progress not simply to the weighing of abstract ideas in neutral deliberative contexts but also to the social and even biological conditions under which ideas are formed, circulated, practiced, and evaluated. Theirs is a more expansive account of how diversity works in the world; and much more intimately than their trans-atlantic counterparts, Smith and Douglass formulated their probabilistic pluralism in the crucible of American struggles over race, putting color at the center of modern liberalism at a time when the U.S. lacked a coherent theory with which to manage its composite nationality. In doing so, Douglass steers away from natural rights and contract theory, opting out of what the political theorist Charles Mills has called "The Racial Contract" and resisting any Rawlsian notion that an objective, original position can be salvaged from the accidents of history.[55] After frustrating decades in the slavery debate, Douglass doubts that racial controversies can be adequately adjudicated by deductive reasoning and a priori assumptions. Instead, he argues that truth-claims emerge through experiment, in experience, and over the long run, but only if individuals within a composite population have an equal chance to rise.

If "Our Composite Nationality" and Douglass's postbellum thinking are potentially imperialistic and unapologetically capitalistic, they present a formidable case for racial equality under the aegis of a liberalism so broadly accepted in twenty-first-century America as to be nearly self-evident. That Douglass supports equal opportunity may seem utterly predictable today; and modern readers, while admiring Douglass's courage and language, can be nonplussed by such ideas. It is now for many obvious that racism is wrong and equal opportunity fair and productive. However, throughout the nineteenth century, *Webster's American Dictionary of the English Language* defined *chance* in descending order of emphasis as an "unknown cause," "fortune," "luck," and only lastly "opportunity." Douglass's project is in part to insist on the probabilistic logic of opportunity, and attention to Douglass's intellectual affinities and specific historical struggles suggests how difficult it was during his long life to convince nonbelievers why exactly equal chances should be extended to a diversity of peoples. It might require changing not only opinions about race but also habits of thought, approaches to evidence, and theories of national progress. It might also require a self-made man to rethink the political preconditions for large-scale racial uplift and to call for a liberalism grounded in probabilities, not contracts or moral absolutes.

RECONSTRUCTING BLACK PRAGMATISM

Fallibilism, experimentation, induction, open-endedness, pluralism, and other aspects of probabilistic thinking not only characterize the writings of Douglass in and around the Civil War, they are also hallmarks of pragmatism. From a broad intellectual-historical perspective, this is probably no coincidence. Before Buckle and Quetelet influenced the classical pragmatists, they influenced Smith and Douglass, and William James dedicated *Pragmatism: A New Name for Some Old Ways of Thinking* (1907) to the memory of Mill. Cultural pluralism in the United States is often traced to James through Horace Kallen and (less directly) Du Bois and Alain Locke, all of whom turned James's radical empiricism toward the subject of composite nationality. Douglass extends this genealogy of pragmatist pluralism into the mid-nineteenth century, anticipating the moment when, in Susan Mizruchi's words, "America's self-consciousness about its extraordinary diversity" came to the national fore.[56] There are good reasons Douglass has not been studied as a pragmatist in any sustained way. His work had little if any direct impact on the first generation of pragmatists, and he has not figured in the rise of neo-pragmatism, which itself is only occasionally interested in race. Scholars who have called Douglass a pragmatist do so in passing and in vernacular reference to his growing real politik, while Douglass, for all his theoretical acuity, does not identify himself as a philosopher.[57] To think of Douglass in terms of pragmatism is to join a growing number of scholars in conceiving of the tradition as a culturally embedded discourse shaped by the slavery crisis and the Civil War.[58] Douglass can be understood in this way as a transitional, hyphenated figure—a proto-pragmatist who marks a political option available to and yet not taken by members of the Metaphysical Club, among them Oliver Wendell Holmes Jr., who stands as an instructive foil.

Looking back with some embarrassment on the antislavery zeal of his youth, Holmes recalled in 1919, "Then I was in with the abolitionists, some or many of whom were skeptics as well as dogmatists."[59] Like Douglass, Holmes was a Garrisonian idealist who lost some faith in higher law, though Holmes's fall from grace was more precipitous and his renunciation of absolutism more severe. As Menand has emphasized, the unpredictable violence of the Civil War disabused Holmes of perfectionist confidence, teaching him that one must fight and sometimes die for convictions even while recognizing that they might be wrong.[60] From Holmes's fallibilist, dutiful perspective, skeptics who do not believe enough are as misguided as dogmatists who believe too intensely, for neither allows countervailing experience to adjust faulty worldviews. Holmes wrote bluntly, "Absolute truth is a mirage" (*EH* 107), and he called the search for higher law "churning the void in the hope of making cheese" (*EH* 116). Like his father, who applied frequentist analysis to puerperal fever and wrote as the Autocrat of the Breakfast Table that "most of our common, working beliefs are probabilities," Holmes Jr. was a probabilistic thinker and (following Mill) a self-proclaimed "*bet*tabilitarian" who saw life as a series of wagers (*EH* 108).[61] Holmes famously emphasized "experience" over "logic" in his theory of culture and law (*EH* 237), just as Douglass named "experience—slave experience" as the basis of his own "political philosophy" (4:160). Like Douglass, Holmes was also sensitive to the conditions that make experience most enlightening, thus he defended free speech, fair play, and social experiments, even those he personally considered inane.

The kind of experiments that Holmes and Douglass especially valorized were risky, strenuous, and militant, for while James sometimes saw the Civil War as a tragedy caused by absolutism, Douglass and Holmes were more likely to see it as a chance to put truth-claims through the most telling of inductive trials. In language that Douglass also employed, Holmes appreciated the "lessons," "school," and "test" of the war.[62] And in the same way that Douglass struggled to give African-American soldiers a chance, Holmes celebrated "the chances of war" as the path to fullest manhood (*EH* 88). Particularly striking is that neither man believed that commitment requires certainty or that partisanship precludes pluralism. As we have seen, Douglass warned against overconfidence and could bring a fallibilist comportment to the war, while for Holmes the value of a soldier's sacrifice lay precisely in its uncertainty. Holmes wrote in his celebrated Memorial Day address, "The Soldier's Faith" (1895), "[I]n the midst of doubt, in the collapse of creeds . . . the faith is true and adorable which leads a soldier to throw away his life in obedience to a blindly accepted duty, in a cause which he little understands, in a plan of campaign of which he has no notion, under tactics of which he does not see the use" (*EH* 89). For both men, doubt should not slide into quietism, nor should conviction lead to fanaticism. Rather, aggressive experimentation—what Holmes called "a leap in the dark"—can be deadly for individuals but is ultimately most productive for nations in a chancy world.[63]

The irony is how differently Douglass and Holmes understood the lessons of the Civil War—so much so that given their political proclivities, emphasizing similarities can seem downright perverse. Holmes's Memorial Day addresses elide moral distinctions between the Union and the Confederacy, a main feature of the Lost Cause myth that furthered intersectional reconciliation among whites by repressing the ongoing racial injustice that survived the Thirteenth, Fourteenth, and Fifteenth Amendments.[64] Douglass fought furiously against such mythologizing in speeches such as his own Memorial Day address, "There was a Right Side in the Late War" (1878), a position he supported by pointing to the Union victory as evidence of slavery's unfitness. As a young soldier, Holmes asserted "the right of our cause" in an 1862 letter to his antislavery family, predicting that slavery would be defeated "in the long run," even if defenders of freedom had "a better chance" in times of peace.[65] Already for Holmes probabilistic thinking was overtaking providential belief. He almost never mentions chattel bondage in his Civil War letters or journal, and as a Supreme Court Justice, he generally proved unsympathetic to African-American rights and the pernicious effects of racism. Swayed by the social Darwinism of his era, Holmes appreciated (without fully endorsing) the racist theories of Oswald Spengler. And as Nan Goodman has shown, Holmes's legal views of liability, which helped relieve individual actors from moral responsibility, cohered with larger cultural efforts to absolve whites of damages resulting from racism.[66] In his notorious opinion in *Buck v. Bell* (1927), Holmes upheld state statutes for forcibly sterilizing people judged mentally, physically, or morally inferior. These laws were applied disproportionately to blacks under the logic of eugenics, a movement pioneered by Francis Galton, cousin to Darwin and an expert in statistical probability who, in *Hereditary Genius* (1869) and later works, used frequentist methods to prove the ostensible inferiority of blacks when considered as an aggregate people. For all his pluralistic methods and self-advertised preference for experience over abstraction, Holmes's participation in the probabilistic revolution led to political positions strikingly different from those of Douglass.

Part of the reason is that Holmes had less patience. He wrote in *Buck v. Bell* that "[t]hree generations" were sufficient evidence of irredeemable inferiority, and in allowing the de facto disenfranchisement of African Americans in Alabama in his *Giles v. Harris* (1903) decision, Holmes disregarded the legacy of slavery and was uncharacteristically willing to let egalitarian theory trump actual racist practices (*EH* 104). Douglass developed a more powerful sense of how long the long run of racial justice could be. In 1859, he responded to charges of black inferiority by advocating "fair play . . . for a reasonable time," though for him this would come to mean something more than a mere three generations. Douglass wrote in 1870 that whites could support black schools and churches "for a hundred years to come" and still "they would not then have given fair play to the negro."[67] Before the Civil War, Douglass lacked patience for gradualist abolitionism, but after emancipation he was more likely to urge fortitude in the cause of racial uplift, even to desperate African-American exodusters fleeing the terrorism of the post-Reconstruction South. One weakness of pragmatism is that its open-endedness makes it hard to know when to end an experiment or social practice—a tragic dynamic when experimentation comes with high human costs, and one the Supreme Court will no doubt encounter again in its ongoing oversight of race-based preferences.[68]

Another reason for differences between Douglass and Holmes involves attitudes toward science and race. Holmes firmly believed in scientific progress, predicting that biology and political economy would come to adjudicate all social questions, whereas

Douglass had seen enough abuses of statistical sociology and racial pseudo-science to seek political and legal protections from such ostensibly objective disciplines, even as he attempted to refute racism on its own quantitative ground. Of course, when considering Holmes's views on race, it is hard to avoid an explanation that he himself suggests: that theoretical arguments are always driven by instinct and conditioning, that reason does not generate convictions but merely justifies them after the fact, and that social Darwinism and eugenics in the case of Holmes may have simply provided available justifications for a more visceral racism.

Holmes's racial politics can be considered an anomaly within pragmatist traditions, though how unrepresentative his racial thinking is remains a complicated and not always flattering line of inquiry. Peirce was not much interested in politics, but he was hostile to abolitionism and racial equality, despite his philosophical appreciation of "multitude and variety," while Dewey, for all his dedication to social justice, is strangely uncommitted to issues of race. James, a main source of cultural pluralism as a theory, presents an especially tangled case. As Ross Posnock has emphasized, James's influence was crucial for Du Bois, Locke, and later black intellectuals, yet it is hard to talk about James's racial progressiveness without a series of "yets." James publicly opposed the lynching of African Americans, yet this can say as much about his dislike of violence as his commitment to racial equality. He was certainly supportive of Du Bois, yet he shied from his former pupil's radicalism. James donated money to Booker T. Washington's organization after sharing a podium with him, yet he did so with some romantic condescension, telling Washington of his hopes that African Americans will "build up a tribal life, so to speak, based on moral realities and simplicities, and divorced from the shams and vanities that are eating into the heart of the wealthy white civilization around them." James certainly held antislavery views and occasionally praised the courage of abolitionists, yet he also kept his distance from civil rights reformers during and after the Civil War— using Wendell Phillips and the abolitionist movement as cautionary examples of absolutism, and saying remarkably little about Garrison's politics in a letter to Garrison's son (a childhood friend of James) upon the famous liberator's death. As George Fredrickson has argued, James disagreed with Holmes's strenuous views of the Civil War; yet Menand is right that James resembles Holmes in largely ignoring slavery and race as a major issue in the national conflict, even in his dedicatory speech at the Robert Gould Shaw Memorial in 1897, James's most explicit (and strangely belated) commentary on the greatest event of his age.[69]

How to make sense of pragmatism in terms of race has been a difficult question for modern scholars. The point here is not to damn Holmes and Peirce for their racism or to chide Dewey and James for their tepidness. Nor is it to follow Stanley Fish in arguing that pragmatism can be put to so many potential uses as to have no politics at all. Nor even is it to mention except in passing that, as Toni Morrison and Cornel West have discussed, race is a singularly powerful source of contradiction for many American thinkers, a subject on which intellectual coherence founders and the will for democracy fails. James Kloppenberg has shown how pragmatism is deeply enmeshed in late-nineteenth and early-twentieth-century progressivism.[70] With their sense that truth seeking is grounded in social practices and that solutions are best sought pluralistically, classical pragmatists might be expected to join in their era's struggles for racial justice. They did not, nor did many of their heirs, ironically confirming the pragmatist point that some amount of culture-based blindness in humans is impossible to overcome. For Benn Michaels, pragmatism—particularly that of Kallen—managed to combine philosophical pluralism with a cultural pluralism based on racial essentialism, a curious combination in that an anti-absolutist philosophy helped invent a politics of absolute identity. West also focuses on pragmatist inconsistencies regarding race, noting that though Dewey, Sidney Hook, and C. Wright Mills disapproved of racist practices, none saw racism as a central problem in America, a critique West extends to neo-pragmatists. More positively, West, Eddie Glaude Jr., and a 2004 essay collection seek to redress such failings by reconstructing a pragmatist tradition more engaged with the critical issue of race.[71] Douglass has been entirely absent from these debates, but his example points to an alternative, racially committed genealogy of pragmatism, just as pragmatism offers a vocabulary and grammar with which to talk about Douglass's probabilism.

Like Quetelet, Mill, Buckle, Darwin, Spencer, James, and Holmes, Douglass came to recognize the insufficiencies of teleology and absolutism, which increasingly turned him toward utilitarianism, liberalism, social Darwinism, and what came to be called pragmatism. That Douglass joins in these mainstream interlocking traditions attests to his postbellum shift toward political and intellectual centers, though the intensity of Douglass's dedication to racial justice distinguishes him from many white peers who share similar post-metaphysical beliefs and sympathize with antislavery and anti-racist positions without lending significant support. More compatible with Douglass are fellow African-American writers who share both his commitment to civil rights and his dissatisfaction with the politics of absolutism. Ida B. Wells, a discriminating supporter of Douglass, used statistical suasion in her anti-lynching campaigns. Trained in logic, Anna Julia Cooper distrusted teleological reasoning, charging in *A Voice from the South* (1892) that "ready formulated theories and preconceptions" preclude "all candid and careful study" of race in the United States. For Cooper, national progress is best achieved "through the co-existence of radically opposing or racially different elements," a pluralism that Pauline Hopkins expresses in *Contending Forces* (1899) when Will Smith, the novel's hero, paraphrases Douglass ("Ultimately this nation will be composite") and proclaims that if the black race is truly inferior, then it must be "exterminated" over time. The probabilistic revolution of the nineteenth century is generally associated with masculine-coded spheres, though Wells, Cooper, and Hopkins suggest that women writers also adopted probabilistic pluralism.[72]

This was not always the case with many postbellum black intellectuals, including at times Douglass himself. Delany, Crummell, and other black nationalists often saw U.S. race relations as too vicious to be harmonized in a composite nationality, and attitudes toward Chinese immigrants in African-American culture were seldom as liberal as those of Douglass, whose own views on American Indians in "Our Composite Nationality" fall easily into stereotypes of the vanishing race.[73] Though Cooper cited statistics and appealed to experience, she also saw quantitative empirical methods as an "absurd" way to gauge the promise of African Americans. Locke agreed, beginning *The New Negro* (1925) with the sentence: "In the last decade something beyond the watch and guard of statistics has happened in the life of the American Negro." This recalls Douglass's 1862 complaint that African Americans "have been weighed, measured, marked and prized—in detail and in the aggregate." As both subjects and practitioners of statistical sociology, black thinkers in the wake of Douglass saw large numbers as a double-edged sword.[74]

No one demonstrates this better than Du Bois, whose explorations of cultural and philosophical pluralism in many ways begin where Douglass's leave off. Du Bois may have had Douglass in mind when he criticizes the dream of a "conglomerate America" in "The Conservation of Races" (1897), and Du Bois's satirical story, "The Black Man Brings His Gifts" (1925), takes aim at Douglass's hope in "Our Composite Nationality" that each race has "some peculiar gift or quality" that the nation should learn to appreciate. "The Black Man Brings His Gifts" is careful to enumerate African-American contributions to the life of the country, but when the whites of the story plan a pageant to celebrate their town's diversity, most cannot talk about the community in the aggregate without repeatedly adding, "not counting the black people." Mizruchi has shown how Du Bois's relation to quantitative sociology is dynamic and profoundly vexed. In *The Philadelphia Negro* (1899), Du Bois turns to statistics for "a fair basis of induction," and he denounces racist claims based on "fantastic theory, ungrounded assumptions or metaphysical subtleties," joining other thinkers of the time who linked racism with faulty abstractions. Du Bois further complains in *The Souls of Black Folk* (1902) that whites judge blacks "a priori," though he also recognizes that chance imposes its limits on the less prejudiced claims of empiricism.[75]

In an essay in Rayford Logan's *What the Negro Wants* (1944), a title echoing Douglass's "What the Black Man Wants," Du Bois's "My Evolving Program for Negro Freedom" sketches a post-positivist sociology that admits the possibilities of chance. Du Bois recalls how in Atlanta in 1910, after witnessing the aftermath of the Sam Hose lynching and sitting on his porch with a shotgun in his lap, his "whole attitude toward the social sciences began to change." It was not simply that his studies "represented so small a part of the total sum" of African-American experiences, or that they "were so far removed in time and space as to lose the hot reality of real life." As Posnock has argued, Du Bois realized that his empiricism must be radical in a political and pragmatist sense—that (in Du Bois's words) a person "could not sit apart and study *in vacuo*," that "[f]acts . . . were elusive things: emotions, loves, hates," and that "there was so much decisive truth missing that any story . . . would be woefully incomplete." After Du Bois's soul-searching admissions of contingency, extra-rationality, and pluralism, "My Evolving Program for Negro Freedom" describes a fortunate fall into chance:

> I saw rhythms and tendencies; coincidences and probabilities; and I saw that, which for want of any other word, I must in accord with the strict tenets of Science, call Chance. I went forward to build a sociology, which I conceived of as the attempt to measure the element of Chance in human conduct. This was the Jamesian pragmatism.

In a moment palpably registering the danger of sudden, random, racist violence, Du Bois acknowledges with some hesitation a pragmatist belief in the possibilities of absolute chance. Moving beyond a frequentism that would render experience legible and predictable through aggregative numbers, Du Bois hears the lower frequencies of an aleatory universe not unlike Ellison, who (as Kenneth Warren has argued) realized that quantitative methods always fail to represent the more spiritual, indeterminate experiences of folks.[76]

Douglass never got quite so far. He did not have the chance to study with James at Harvard or witness the rise of quantum physics, nor did he place so much faith in quantitative sociology (and history) as to become disillusioned with it. Like Du Bois, Douglass acknowledged the power and potential abuses of the new sciences of chance, and he was frustrated by absolutist beliefs that make it difficult to argue rationally about race. Accepting the risks of probabilistic thinking, Douglass is an early voice of black pragmatism, a tradition most prominently represented by West, though Douglass is not mentioned at all in *The American Evasion of Philosophy* (1989). The original cover of West's book is dominated by a spreading tree figuring the history of pragmatism, and given the pluralistic nature of the tradition, as well as West's own inclusive formulation, it is surprising that the lower branches of the tree—labeled as James, Peirce, Dewey, and Du Bois—all sprout from the thick trunk of Emerson. It appears as if American antifoundationalism cannot help but claim the most familiar of foundations. Except that when looking more closely at the cover, one notices multiple, unnamed roots descending from the trunk of Emerson to an unidentified book whose pages spread beneath the tree. Can these roots be reclaimed? Must they all lead toward Emerson? And are they rightly grounded in a book—as opposed to, say, a newspaper, a magazine, or something less iconic like a speech, a culture, an experience, or a series of transatlantic influences and routes? West does not press a monolithic narrative; his subtitle is "A Genealogy of Pragmatism." An alternative history might feature Douglass, who participated in a shift toward chance that includes the emergence of pragmatism, a movement that James recognized as a new term for old methods already in play. Because chance itself cannot be mastered, it can encourage an open-mindedness that resists prejudgment in general and racial prejudice in particular. Facts do not tell the whole story for Douglass, but he increasingly approaches politics as an art of the probable. Who knows if Thoreau, an admirer of Douglass, would have also moved from higher law abolitionism toward a more empirical postbellum politics. Thoreau left many projects unfinished at his death in 1862, but about the same time Douglass began using probabilistic logic, Thoreau also gravitated toward encounters with chance—not so much in the domain of politics or sociology but in the field of natural science (itself hardly disconnected from race).

CHAPTER 5
Roughly Thoreau

Well, that often comes over me with overwhelming force; but at other times, it seems to go away.
  —Charles Darwin, on the feeling that the universe is intelligently governed, 1882

[A]ttempts to catch the regularities of Nature . . . can never hope to attain more than a somewhat close approach to the truth.
  —Charles Peirce, unpublished manuscript, c. 1895

T he foregoing chapters can be categorized by disciplinary affinity: Poe deals with logic and mathematics; Melville delves into theology and metaphysics; Douglass's commitments most powerfully intersect with statistical sociology and political philosophy. None of these writers is primarily concerned with how chance operates in the natural sciences, the domain that literary critics usually have in mind when referring to the disparate bodies of scholarship lumped together under "literature and science." As a canonical writer and accomplished naturalist, Thoreau has been an organizing figure in this area of study, though his participation in the probabilistic revolution has gone virtually unnoticed, despite the fact that his writings explore the relations between empiricism, beauty, and chance. Thoreau tends to encounter chance less as a question of causality and more as a challenge to scientific accuracy, for if he celebrates whimsy and anomaly throughout his work, he also tries to make sense of random variations by employing the law of large numbers. For Thoreau, chance and its management take two related forms: mensurative errors that can be minimized by averaging masses of data, and unpredictable natural phenomena that can be explained by an empirical skepticism shared by Darwin and William James. The aggressively individualistic Thoreau may seem an unlikely practitioner of aggregative, quantitative methods, but as he follows Douglass in moving from romantic subjectivity toward statistical thinking, he finds in the approximate claims of large numbers a way to both esteem and control the power of chance, which comes to play an unsettling, generative role across his diverse writings.

No nineteenth-century author pursued probabilistic inquiry at more personal cost than Thoreau. Poe pushes the theoretical limits of probabilism, and his life exemplifies the human costs of risk. Yet if Poe tried to game the literary marketplace while posing as an expert crime solver and cryptographer, he never took up real-world probabilistic projects with sustained or systematic attention. Melville's fiction more self-consciously shows how demanding it is to live according to probabilities, for if Ahab's absolutism and Pierre's rashness make them ill-suited for handling chance, even the prudent lawyer of "Bartleby" succumbs to exasperation when his scrivener evades probabilistic control. Douglass for his part is intensely dedicated to the long run of racial justice, though he, too, tires of probabilistic reasoning when he insists on obligations that cannot be deferred and dwells on moments of moral transformation. Scientific commentators in the nineteenth century also emphasized sudden epiphanies of knowledge—Archimedes in his bathtub, Galileo on the tower of Pisa, Newton under the apple tree. Scientific discovery does depend on flashes of insight, though less romanticized assessments from the nineteenth century portray science as a long-term enterprise based not so much on spontaneous leaps of logic as on systematic consistency, emotional stability, and the incremental progress of empiricism and induction.[1] Which is to say that nineteenth-century philosophers of science advocated a methodical ethos and style. Poe, Melville, and Douglass variously acknowledge the patience required to manage chance, but no literary figure internalized such discipline more faithfully than Thoreau.

In a journal entry from 1851, Thoreau admired the skill of a local stonemason: "[B]y patience and art he splits a stone as surely as the carpenter or woodcutter a log. So much time and perseverance will accomplish."[2] It is fitting that Thoreau appreciated patience, for modern scholarship has been slow to realize that the full force of his literary achievements cannot be felt without attending to his scientific work. No one denies that around 1850 Thoreau increasingly focuses on his naturalist studies, and scholars have long noted that Thoreau sometimes worries about the compatibility of science and art. A major change over the last two decades is the critical reevaluation of Thoreau's empirical commitments. His naturalist research can no longer be dismissed simply as a sign of waning creativity, nor can his significant imaginative contributions be limited to literature strictly defined. Philosophically, Thoreau seems less enamored with idealism and more anticipatory of something like pragmatism, while his naturalist writings, rooted in the object world, have been fundamental to the rise of ecocriticism.[3] With more emphasis falling on his post-*Walden* writings, some of Thoreau's best readers have narrowed the gap between his transcendental and his scientific impulses: Thoreau maintains a "delicate equilibrium" between the two; he takes science to be "inextricable from other kinds of knowledge"; his "higher empiricism" and "empirical holism" seek (if not always achieve) a "synthesis" of imagination and fact.[4] Yet even as an emerging critical consensus makes science safe for literary readers of Thoreau, it tends to conflate his empirical researches with blunt scientific positivism.[5] Thoreau's naturalist study does indeed temper the subjective instabilities inherent to transcendental philosophy, but it also leads to a different kind of uncertainty within scientific domains. As much as the hyperactive dialectical play between idealism and materialism structures his thinking, Thoreau's empiricism in both theory and practice opens its own path to skepticism.

From Thoreau's surveying to his recording of blossoming dates to his tracking of lake levels, snow depths, and tree sizes, his naturalist studies are marked by an obsession with measurement that was a growing feature of the physical sciences in the early nineteenth century.[6] Thoreau's measuring garners some curious facts—the longest whisker of a deer mouse (1 5/8 inches), the number of herbaceous flower species that bloom before May (22), and—quite startling to picture the effort required—the number of grubs in a box of acorns (865). Emerson's 1862 eulogy for Thoreau recalls his friend's "natural skill for mensuration," but when Emerson concludes his influential sketch by comparing Thoreau to an edelweiss hunter, he presents Thoreau less as a rigorous naturalist and more as a quester for symbols of beauty and virtue, less as an expert on Concord's ecology and more as a romantic hero of the Alps. We might expect this of Emerson, whose own empirical attentions tend to drift toward mythical and metaphysical abstractions. When Emerson writes in "Experience" (1844) that the fall into skepticism makes us "suspect our instruments," he does not refer to literal problems of calibration but, rather, to the illusions and moods that make subjectivity so fraught. Even when "The Transcendentalist" (1842) celebrates "finer instruments" such as rain gauges, thermometers, and telescopes, Emerson takes them as symbols for the "few persons of purer fire kept specially as gauges and meters of character," as "spiritual compass[es]" and "superior chronometers."[7] Binaristic formulations of transcendentalism and science have for generations gone too far, but there are real reasons Emerson and his circle have been defined against empiricism, both Lockean and Baconian.

More productively than any of his peers, Thoreau complicates this oversimplification by showing how nineteenth-century science addresses skepticism by facing the uncertainties of chance. Thoreau is a methodical, enthralled observer of the play between pattern and anomaly who attempts to contain chance within natural law even while reveling in the unpredictable wildness of nature. In *Walden* and beyond, Thoreau regards mensuration as at once less precise and more powerful than does Emerson, in part because Thoreau does not suspect his instruments in a radically subjective mode. Thoreau does face throughout his career epistemological conundrums associated with subject-object dualism, but instead of plunging into Cartesian vortices and wrestling with skepticism after Kant, he increasingly dedicates his lifework to the collecting and ordering of material facts, a task that leads to uncertainty in its own right given the inexactitudes of mensuration, the probabilities of inferential reasoning, and the chance variations of natural phenomena. By accepting the discipline of an empirical skepticism that diminishes but does not eliminate chance, Thoreau approaches natural laws as nearly as he can. If his encounters with chance are less explicit than Poe's, less dramatic than Melville's, and less politically charged than Douglass's, they are more fundamental to his everyday experience in an array of registers. As a philosopher, surveyor, woodsman, natural scientist, and artist, Thoreau patiently and joyfully moves toward knowledge of nature, approximate though that knowledge must be.

AXES AND KNIVES

The first step in recovering Thoreau's empirical skepticism and its acknowledgment of chance is to distance Thoreau from transcendental philosophy as represented by Emerson and Kant. Of Thoreau's many mensurative projects, his most conspicuous is his map of Walden Pond, which appears in *Walden* to challenge idealist accounts of romanticism in general and transcendentalism in particular. Students faced with a true/false quiz on *Walden* can be tempted to deny that Thoreau finds the pond 102 feet deep: surely the mystical philosopher of subjectivity and selfhood would not reduce his best trope to a number; surely the fuzzy professor of literature would not stress so factual a case. At least one antebellum reader of *Walden* took Thoreau's survey of the pond as a satire of naive empiricism.[8] Yet as much as *Walden* mocks the counting of cats and puns on the positivism of "supernumerary sleepers," Thoreau in his book as well as his life gathers data along with his huckleberries.[9] Thoreau was noting by the early 1850s that his empiricism and idealism are not always in accord, and we should probably read *Walden* (in Lawrence Buell's words) less as a paragon of formal and intellectual unity and more as "a richly tangled expression of [Thoreau's] conflicting priorities." *Walden* is a transitional book insofar as Thoreau reworked its drafts at the same time he was reshaping himself as a naturalist during a period of institutional and conceptual upheaval in the natural sciences as a whole. Yet if Thoreau never shies from contradiction and often feels himself in opposition, he and his readers cannot be kept from aspiring toward some greater coherence.

By measuring Walden in "The Pond in Winter," Thoreau reminds his impertinent neighbors that his project is not simply a summertime idyll but also a trial set under the harshest environmental and epistemological conditions. The three winter chapters of *Walden* outweigh its single chapter on spring, for if ecstatic moments of rebirth make for better motivational slogans, Thoreau knows that most of life is spent in the more dormant, more ordinary stretches between. Echoing the tropes of sleep and dislocation with which Emerson opens "Experience," "The Pond in Winter" begins with a groggy, sputtering skepticism: "After a still winter night I awoke with the impression that some question had been put to me, which I had been endeavoring in vain to answer in my sleep, as what—how—when—where?" (253). Whereas Emerson's struggles with such queries are painfully protracted in "Experience," the very next sentence in "The Pond in Winter" finds so immediate a consolation for its confusion as to practically render Thoreau's sleepy doubts moot: "But there was dawning Nature, in whom all creatures live, looking in at my broad windows with serene and satisfied face, and no question on *her* lips." It is almost like a sexual dream, except that Thoreau is waking to the real.

As if mocking the endless involutions to which epistemology is susceptible, the opening brush with radical skepticism in "The Pond in Winter" is superficial by design. Thoreau's list of questions—what, how, when, where?—are unmoored from any concrete experience, and his response to one of philosophy's most enduring problems is so casual as to amount to a joke: *How do we know that the world is not actually a shadow or dream, that we can trust our perceptions? How do we resolve the epistemological problems unleashed by Descartes, Hume, Kant, and. . . . Hey look, what a beautiful day!* Keats may remind us that this is all we need to know, and an (old school) environmentalist can add, *Honor thy Mother.* But while Thoreau appears to be evading philosophy by invoking a personified pantheism, he actually condenses a conventional argument of the Scottish Common Sense school, which held against Berkeley and especially Hume that the radical skeptic has no defensible warrant to suspect the object world in the first place. Hume and the Scottish realist Thomas Reid agreed that perceptions cannot be absolutely verified, but they differed over how much assurance might be taken from everyday experience. The exchanges between Hume and the school of Reid were frequently paraphrased in antebellum philosophical discourse (which consistently declared Scottish realism the victor), and by starting with the "impression" of having skeptical questions put to him, Thoreau in "The Pond in Winter" invokes the crux of the debate.

Hume took "impressions" as fundamental to perceptions, but he refused to make either correspondent to any external reality. He wrote in *Treatise of Human Nature* (1739):

> As to those *impressions*, which arise from the *senses*, their ultimate cause is, in my opinion, perfectly inexplicable by human reason, and 'twill always be impossible to decide with certainty, whether they arise immediately from the object, or are produc'd by the creative power of the mind, or are deriv'd from the author of our being.[10]

In response to Hume's suspension of judgment, Reid asserted an epistemological realism that attempted to preempt the doubts of radical skepticism. It is true, Reid argued, that we cannot be absolutely certain as to the origins of our perceptions, but that is not sufficient reason not to take them as accurate. Invoking Aristotle's metaphor of the mind as wax that registers impressions from nature, Reid argued that "material impressions" represent things that "really do exist," for experience all but proves that each impression comes "from the mint of Nature," "bears her image," and should be taken "upon trust." Melville's counterfeiting Confidence Man can smirk at such trusting views, but Thoreau—who elsewhere in *Walden* describes objects in the world as "coins from heaven's own mint"—is satisfied enough by Reid's feminized nature to get out of bed and go on with his day (78). Just as Reid insists, "It isn't in my power to get rid of my belief in external objects," Thoreau cannot quite come to question his senses: "I can almost say, Walden, is it you?" (175).[11]

Like his transcendental cohorts, Thoreau is often taken to reject (or at least depart from) the Scottish Common Sense that dominated his era, though the main difference between "The Pond in Winter" and Reid's school may be more about style than system.[12] Reid and his followers called Hume's doubts absurd, but they hurt their case by attacking repeatedly and at length an argument that they claimed to be beyond their powers of belief. Thoreau more convincingly dismisses Humean skepticism by moving beyond it as blithely as he does: *Of course, we have doubts, my skeptical friend, but there is dawning Nature. What is really left to argue?* As if preempting those who find Thoreau's speculations too flighty for philosophical consideration, the opening of "The Pond in Winter" shows how writing can be a kind of philosophy—how Thoreau's tonal insouciance enacts a realist epistemology more effectively than more serious discursive efforts. As Montaigne wrote in his essay, "We Can Savour Nothing Pure" (whose title might explain Thoreau's hankering to eat a woodchuck), "The high inquisitive opinions of philosophy prove unsuited in practice. . . . We must manage the affairs of men more rough-and-readily, more superficially, leaving a good and better share to the rights of Fortune."[13] *Walden's* rough style—its conversational rhythms, Yankeeisms, brusqueness, and humor— indicates what Cavell calls a "presumption of intimacy" that makes *Walden's* appeals to ordinary experience difficult to deny in good faith.[14] Thoreau does not need to answer ungrounded queries such as "what—how—when—where?" What matters most is the attitude and communal sensibility that he brings to such questions, for the assurances he senses but cannot logically guarantee come not from some higher authority that proves that the real world is actually real. He finds instead in nature a serene and adequate response to generalized threats of skepticism. "The Pond in Winter" will eventually come to ask harder, more empirical questions of Walden, but Thoreau takes up the inquiry in the course of daily life, not in the dreamy realm of the philosophical skeptic who, as Peirce would later complain, speculates "without stirring from [the] sofa."[15] When the reclining Thoreau voices abstracted doubts, he signifies little except the bootless confusion brought on by pure intellection, a winter discontent that lasts only as long as his questions lack specific content.

The surest statement of Thoreau making what he calls in his journals the "transition from dreams to waking thoughts, from illusions to actualities" (X:141) is the sentence beginning the second paragraph of "The Pond in Winter": "Then to my morning work" (253). By this Thoreau means locating the frozen pond, digging through its layers of snow, and chopping a hole in the ice for fresh water. Such duties are probably best taken literally, given the chapter's embrace of the real, though *Walden* has already imbued Thoreau's labors with dense philosophical associations. *Walden* everywhere shows that the urge to analogize is irresistible to the point of instinct—so much so that a reader may realize, like Frost's speaker in "The Ax-Helve" (1917), that to talk about tools is to talk about a kind of knowledge best known by the work it performs. The first thing Thoreau grabs in "The Pond in Winter" is his axe, which he values precisely for its imprecision. One might think the penknife a more attractive tool for so careful and cutting a wordsmith as Thoreau, but Thoreau is refuting a common belief that Emerson also rejected in "The American Scholar" (1837)—that the thinker is as poor a substitute for a worker "as a penknife for an axe."[16] Inverting this analogy, "The Pond in Winter" sets the winter fisherman's axe over and against the finer instrument of the naturalist: "The latter raises the moss and bark gently with his knife in search of insects; the former lays open logs to their core with his axe, and moss and bark fly far and wide" (254). Just as *Walden* earlier recommends that students not be given penknives and instead learn to smelt their own blunter blades, it is the imprecise, axe-wielding fisherman who catches the worm, not the book-trained, circumspect scientist.

Thoreau's preference for the rough tools of woodcraft further suggests that he, for all his transcendental inclinations, retains an affinity for Scottish realism. Kant in his *Prolegomena to Any Future Metaphysics* (1783) sided with Hume against the Common Sense school represented by Reid's disciple James Beattie, who had accused Hume of an overly abstract method that Beattie invidiously compared to a "needle's point" too fine to analyze the actual world.[17] Kant wrote in defense of Hume's precision and abstraction:

> Hammer and chisel are perfectly fine for working raw lumber, but for copperplate one must use an etching needle. Likewise, sound common sense and speculative understanding are both useful, but each in its own way; the one, when it is a matter of judgments that find their immediate application in experience, the other, however, when judgments are to be made in a universal mode, out of mere concepts, as in metaphysics.

Like Emerson in "The Transcendentalist," Kant begins with a basic distinction between realism and idealism, and he takes idealism for a finer instrument, setting the exactitude of transcendental analysis over and against the rougher hewn, experiential claims of

Beattie and Reid. Kant defends metaphysics as a discipline of "mere concepts" in part because he recognizes the limits of empiricism and induction. Experience cannot establish universal truths, offering instead only probabilistic guidance, a Humean point that Kant emphasizes in the *Prolegomena*:

> I must forbid only two things: first, the playing of *probability* and conjecture, which suits metaphysics just as poorly as it does geometry; second, decision by means of the divining rod of so-called *sound common sense*, which does not bend for everyone, but is guided by personal qualities.[18]

If romanticism in general and *Walden* in particular undertake what Cavell has called "the Kantian project to answer skepticism," important differences remain.[19] Just as "the fine long needles" of Poe's Parisian police are inferior to Dupin's probabilistic methods, Thoreau subordinates Kantian exactitude to a more approximate, probabilistic, Lockean knowledge consistent with Scottish realism. Grounded in experience, committed to induction, and accepting the need to trust impressions and moral certainties in the face of abstract doubts, Common Sense philosophy believes in a nature that one cannot absolutely know. This helps explain why Thoreau at the climax of "Ktaadn" (1848) celebrates "the *actual* world! the *common sense*!" while still retaining skeptical doubts (*"Who are we? where are we?"*).[20] As the opening of "The Pond in Winter" insists, the realist who cannot fully answer all questions can still trust in the object world.

Not only is the axe mightier than the penknife in "The Pond in Winter," Thoreau also recuperates Kant's disparaging comparison of Scottish Common Sense to a "divining rod." Kant's point is well taken insofar as the supposedly self-evident principles of Scottish realism aspire to universality but take personal experience as a basis for noetic authority. Simplistically rendered, as it often was by Reid's followers, Common Sense philosophy can seem naively intuitional and transparently tautological. Thoreau's epistemological realism, however, follows Reid in recognizing its premises as such, as when Thoreau writes in "The Pond in Winter," "After a cold and snowy night [the pond] needed a divining-rod to find it" (253), a reference recalling a famous passage from "Where I Lived and What I Lived For":

> The intellect is a cleaver; it discerns and rifts its way into the secret of things. I do not wish to be any more busy with my hands than is necessary. My head is hands and feet. I feel all my best faculties concentrated in it. My instinct tells me that my head is an organ for burrowing, as some creatures use their snout and fore paws, and with it I would mine and burrow my way through these hills. I think that the richest vein is somewhere hereabouts; so by the divining-rod and thin rising vapors I judge; and here I will begin to mine. (88–89)

The whipsaw contradictions of this passage blur distinctions made by Kant in the *Prolegomena* and Emerson in "The Transcendentalist," in that reason and instinct, human and animal, mind and body, idealism and materialism are simultaneously inverted and mixed. The abstract "intellect" may be a "cleaver" as discerning as a penknife or etching needle, but Thoreau is committed to his using his head as a blunter, more material "organ for burrowing," thus thinking becomes an action that occurs in the messy object world. When he writes, "I think that the richest vein is somewhere hereabouts," Thoreau is not thinking like a Cartesian cogito but, rather, thinking as in hypothesizing and estimating: *I think there's a lake about a mile down the road.* It is hard to imagine Kant or Descartes launching their systems from such approximate ground as "somewhere hereabouts." It is easier (with some provocation from Cavell) to notice that Thoreau participates in a "widespread dissatisfaction with thinking" that anticipates Nietzsche, the pragmatists, and Heidegger (who once said, "Thinking is a handicraft").[21] Disclaiming apodictic conceptual processes and purely objective starting points, Thoreau is left to "judge"—for Locke and his followers, a term denoting probabilistic beliefs adopted in the absence of certainty. That Thoreau judges with a divining rod further admits approximate knowledge with two puns: to divine is to conjecture, and a rod is a unit of measurement that was generally understood in Thoreau's time but had no exact value. In "The Pond in Winter," one should not look up to ideals but, rather, point down like a divining rod toward facts. Using tropes—themselves rhetorical tools that loosen hard equivalencies between signs and things but remain (in Thoreau's linguistic theory) grounded in natural relations—Thoreau argues that one must think with an earthly imprecision that Kantian and Emersonian idealists discount.[22]

Which is not to argue that *Walden* lacks what Buell calls a "passion for accuracy."[23] Thoreau wields his hoe with discrimination; he admires the solid, single blow from a hammer; and his natural descriptions have a fine detail that can be overrated (as we will see) but not ignored. At the same time, *Walden* registers the difference between an exactitude that exists only in abstraction and the accuracy of experienced workers who use their tools well in the world. Celebrating his intellectual and physical labors— and maybe taking a dig at his axe's lender, the famously abstracted Bronson Alcott— Thoreau is proud to return his borrowed axe "sharper than I received it" (36), just as he earlier boasts in *Walden* that his "sight has been whetted by experience" (6). Avoiding falls into the radical skepticism made possible by transcendental idealism, Thoreau offers his woodcraft as both a metaphor and a method for roughly but expertly knowing the world. After reporting in "The Pond in Winter" that Walden is "exactly one hundred and two feet" deep, Thoreau immediately qualifies his exacting figure (256): because water levels shift, five feet or something thereabouts might be added to his measurement (just as a point might be added to a true/false quiz after some student lobbying).

The limits of mensuration pervade "The Pond in Winter" as Thoreau imagines the prospects of absolute truth but constantly returns to the estimations of experience. He surmises that the depth of Walden might be calculated from its shoreline and that there might be a "formula for all cases," including questions of human "character" (259–60). Yet while Thoreau wonders how universal laws might govern both natural and moral domains, he premises his conjectures of such laws on the fact of Walden's depth, a figure that he repeatedly adjusts in his journals and further destabilizes in the "The Pond in Winter" as he modestly aspires not to know but rather to see "how nearly [he] could guess" the laws of Walden's bottom. For a chapter dedicated to empirical accuracy, "The Pond in Winter" remains provisional in both content and tone—marked by questions, subjunctives, and conditionals that do not invalidate Thoreau's skill for mensuration but do highlight the necessity of approximation, even (or rather, especially) for the patient empiricist.

ERRORS AND AVERAGES

In an undergraduate essay from 1837 in which Thoreau quarreled with Paley's confident natural theology, he wrote, "What is more common than error."[24] Thoreau's fallibilism is especially evident in "The Pond in Winter" when he moves from sounding the depths of Walden to surveying its ice and shore, thereby shifting attention from metaphysical foundations toward the textures of everyday life. For Emerson, Dickinson, Frost, Stevens, and Plath—and even for more trusting neighbors such as Longfellow and Whittier—winter in New England is the most wonderful season for epistemological crises. Thoreau may have a mind of winter, but more than might be expected, he finds Walden's frozen surface largely reassuring. Not only does the ice form a convenient platform from which to drop a plumb line and weight, its "general regularity" (258) provides an even surface for a tripod mounted with a level or theodolite (a surveyor's tool that measures horizontal and vertical angles, thus allowing for trigonometric calculations of distances). The challenge comes when Thoreau in the course of his measurements learns that the ice is not exactly ideal. It is "undulated," and its "fluctuation," though "almost infinitesimal," causes variations of several feet when Thoreau measures trees across the pond (261). Poe, whose artillery training at West Point involved much trigonometry, makes a similar point in "The Gold-Bug": a small error at the point of observation is magnified when the target is far away, an apt metaphor for the problem of divergent subjectivities between and even within individuals, for in "The Gold-Bug," even the small parallax between the left and right eye spells the difference between failure and success. If Ishmael in his Cartesian reveries at the masthead disregards "'binnacle deviations'" and "'approximate errors,'" Thoreau is more attentive to margins of errors and the probabilistic minimizing of chance.

Thoreau's empirical skepticism begins with facts on the ground. After noting the fluctuations of Walden's ice and thus admitting the inexactitude of his surveying, he wonders, "Who knows but if our instruments were delicate enough we might detect an undulation in the crust of the earth?" (261). Thoreau recognizes that his knowledge of nature is premised on his knowledge of the ground from which he views it. Yet as much as he seeks a *"point d'appui,"* his question about finer, more delicate instruments seems ultimately more wistful than serious, particularly given that his reading in Charles Lyell's *Principles of Geology* (1830–33) and his firsthand observations of erosion around Concord and Cape Cod convinced him that the surface of the earth is under constant change (88).[25] Emerson in "Self-Reliance" exults in the looseness of our footing, happily informing the naive materialist that the earth is really a molten ball whirling through the galaxy. "The Pond in Winter" makes a somewhat different point with its fluctuating ice, for Thoreau's outlook is less cosmological than empirical, less interested in asserting the Emersonian self as an epistemological principle in a universe of flux and more committed to the artful science of surveying as a method for rough measurement.

Thoreau began his work as a surveyor at a time when the practice was being rapidly modernized. In the eighteenth century, surveying typically required expensive equipment and rare expertise, but as the United States furiously added new roads, mines, canals, railways, and territories, surveying instruments and training became more accessible, particularly for smaller scale projects that (unlike geodetic surveys) do not take the earth's curvature into account.[26] The U.S. Coastal Survey, established by Thomas Jefferson in 1807, was finally funded by Congress in 1832 with much imperialistic fanfare as the United States more clearly defined its boundaries even as it aggressively expanded them. Surveyors continued to accompany exploration parties and divide territories and townships into grids, while in established areas such as Concord new surveys were required for estate divisions, construction projects, and the marking of wood lots, as well as to update older surveys outdated by the drift of the magnetic north. Melville was not alone in considering surveying as a potential vocation, for the barriers to professional entry were low and surveyors had become a cultural type romanticized for their woodcraft adventures, as in Cooper's novel, *The Chainbearer* (1845).

Considering his passion for mensuration, topography, and exploration narratives, it makes sense that Thoreau eventually took to surveying. In an early journal entry from 1837, he wrote under the heading "Measure": "Not the carpenter alone carries his rule in his pocket—Space is quite subdued to us. The meanest peasant finds in a hair of his head, or the white crescent upon his nail, the unit of measure for the distance of the fixed stars" (1:17). Thoreau liked the idea that man is the measure of all things, but his early gestures toward egoist subjectivity give way to a growing objectivity. *Walden* mocks holy men who measure empires with their bodies, and when *Cape Cod* (1855) describes a man who uses his foot and extended leg to measure the width of streams, Thoreau advises the man to carry a string so as to ensure the consistency of his leg's angle. More committed to accuracy, Thoreau marked inches on his walking stick and surveyed the topography on his travels in New England, a hobby he enjoyed until surveying became his main source of income in 1849. Soon thereafter he was calling his day job "insignificant labor," resenting its coarse economic uses and the time it took from his writing (5:244). Rick Van Noy argues that Thoreau came to see surveys as inadequate representations of nature and that this realization indicates his growing resistance to "scientific positivism."[27]

Walden's desire to speak "*without* bounds" does register an extravagant impulse, though surveying for Thoreau is not entirely confining or naively positivistic, if only because it offers a sophisticated model for managing the uncertainty of chance errors (289). Cavell has argued in regard to Cartesian epistemology that skepticism becomes a threat only when thinkers aspire to a kind of absolute knowledge that has little bearing on ordinary experience. By contrast, surveying—with its magnification of small errors and the real-world consequences thereof—is a practice that does not invent skeptical problems but, rather, encounters them in everyday life. As dramatized in Borges's "On Exactitude in Science" (1946) and Thomas Pynchon's *Mason & Dixon* (1997), a main irony of surveying is that the pursuit of perfect representation is inevitably self-defeating when pushed to extremes, a point Emerson missed when writing in his eulogy that Thoreau "could easily solve the problems of the surveyor, but . . . was daily beset with graver questions."[28] "[G]raver" shows that Emerson gets one of *Walden's* favorite puns, but Emerson ultimately underrates how challenging and inspiring the science of surveying can be.

As enthusiastically as mid-nineteenth-century surveying manuals celebrated their technical and trigonometric precision, they were forced to admit that "chance errors" came from a distressingly large number of sources: temperature and moisture affected the length of measuring chains; levels and theodolites from even the best manufacturers varied to surprising degrees; iron deposits and solar flares compromised compass readings. Alternatively, taking direction by the stars was subject to its own set of random variations, in part because measuring the distance between the polestar and magnetic north required an error-prone process involving theodolites, boards, poles, candles, and string. Ignoring or approximating the curvature of the earth further diminished the accuracy of surveys, especially given that the earth is not a perfect sphere. More locally, a surveying manual that Thoreau owned warned that "broken and uneven ground" could frustrate the most skilled surveyors, while other texts noted the difficulties caused by "undulations and inequalities in surface."[29] Surveying manuals did offer imperfect solutions such as calibration, overlapping triangulation, and repeated measurements, but surveyors had no *point d'appui*, no way of knowing for sure which instrument should calibrate which or which measurement was the best standard. The quandary has analogs in radical skepticism, as when Emerson complains in *Nature* (1836), "I cannot try the accuracy of my senses." But just as Common Sense philosophers, in Kant's horrified words, took "the judgment of the multitude" as a basis for truth, surveyors managed their fallibility not with self-reliance or pure reason but with probabilistic methods that by averaging masses of data controlled for chance variations.[30]

The law of averages (another name for the law of large numbers) is a tenet of frequentist thought incipiently formulated by Jacob Bernoulli in the seventeenth century, though not widely used until refined by Siméon-Denis Poisson's law of least squares in the mid-1830s. The law of averages acknowledges that individual trials are subject to chance variations, but it assumes that variances over the long run occur with regular frequencies, thus rendering outcomes predictable en masse as variances cancel each other out. As Bernoulli and Laplace both noted, the law of averages is a common sensical method used informally in the course of everyday life, though for a modern observer to track its rise as a technical practice in the nineteenth century is to witness the surprisingly labored exposition of a seemingly obvious mode of thought. Texts on probability theory written for educated audiences lavished explanations on how to calculate basic averages, and they defended in detail the most mundane premises (for instance, just because a tossed coin lands on heads twice in a row does not mean every subsequent flip will do the same). One reason for such scrupulousness is that the general public was leery. As Augustus de Morgan summarized objections in his popular *Essay on Probabilities* (1838), many people saw probabilism as "not practical," "irreligious," "not true," and an inducement to gambling. To demonstrate the reasonableness and utility of their work, probability theorists emphasized the law of errors, a specific application of the law of averages that helped establish margins of error. In doing so, they addressed an empirical problem that was becoming increasingly visible with advances in technological and quantitative precision: repeated measurements of a single object can produce, as Quetelet put it in his own popular monograph, an "astonishing" and "embarrassing" diversity of results.[31] Scientists and surveyors of the nineteenth century hardly discovered the fallibility of measurement, but as they mapped the stars, earth, and oceans; established metrics with unprecedented accuracy; and deployed new formulas and instruments in coordinated governmental projects, they were especially sensitive to how chance errors frustrate desires for factual truths.

Thoreau had access to the fundamentals of probability theory through Richard Whately's *Elements of Logic* (1826), and his amateur interests in mathematics and astronomy no doubt exposed him to the law of errors and averages. A more practical and surely powerful influence was his experience as a surveyor faced daily with what surveying manuals called "probable errors" and "uncertain chances." An 1839 article bragged that surveyors were experts in "the calculus of probabilities," while William Gillespie's popular *Treatise on Land-Surveying* (1851) is one of many antebellum manuals that taught Poisson's law of least squares.[32] Before Benjamin Peirce and his son Charles brought their probabilistic genius to the U.S. Coastal Survey, surveyors were using the law of averages and errors to reduce the threat of chance, even as their aspirations to perfection highlighted the approximate nature of their work.

Like the transcendentally influenced insurance executives Wallace Stevens and Charles Ives, Thoreau encountered chance in both his day job and his art, and he understood that ideas of absolute order cannot account for the variances of the natural world. Thoreau wrote in an 1850 handbill advertising his services, "LAND SURVEYING of all kinds, according to the best methods known; the necessary data supplied, in order that the boundaries of Farms may be accurately described." A cagey businessman when it suited him, Thoreau emphasized his precision before adding in smaller print, "Areas warranted accurate within almost any degree of exactness."[33] Thoreau's "almost" indicates both a desire for exactitude and an admission that exactitude is impossible. The materialist may crave absolute title to his land (one thinks of the "worldly miser" in "Walking" [1862] of whom Thoreau writes, "[T]he Prince of Darkness was his surveyor").[34] But "The Pond in Winter" eschews Faustian dreams of mastery and settles for the very human minimizing of error:

> If we knew all the laws of Nature, we should need only one fact, or the description of one actual phenomenon, to infer all the particular results at that point. Now we know only a few laws, and our result is vitiated, not, of course, by any confusion or irregularity in Nature, but by our ignorance of essential elements in the calculation. Our notions of law and harmony are commonly confined to those instances which we detect; but the harmony which results from a far greater number of seemingly conflicting, but really concurring laws, which we have not detected, is still more wonderful. The particular laws are as our points of view, as, to the traveller, a mountain outline varies with every step, and it has an infinite number of profiles, though absolutely but one form. Even when cleft or bored through it is not comprehended in its entirety. What I have observed of the pond is no less true in ethics. It is the law of average. (259–60)

Moving from absolutist ambitions to a more modest probabilism, this self-consciously unlyrical passage describes a way for empiricists to work under pluralism and chance. Obviously, we do not know "all the laws of Nature," even if Thoreau takes seriously the possibility that we can. Nor do we entirely know one fact, even if some day we "should." Thus, for "Now"—a word that often shakes American transcendentalists free from sleepy abstractions—we must work with what partial information is available, "vitiated" and "confined" though it is. Solace for our epistemological limits takes two forms for Thoreau: the assurance that nature ultimately has no "irregularity" (a main premise of the law of averages), and the "wonderful" realization that our imperfect understandings pay tribute to nature's great scope. For Thoreau, wonder is more picturesque than sublime, more associated with William Gilpin's aesthetic of "roughness" than with the theories of Kant or Burke, and yet the passage above is not content to end with Gilpin's subjective, psychological feelings of beauty.[35] Repeating a point more elaborately made in "A Walk to Wachusett" (1843), "The Pond in Winter" mentions "instances" in which we see objects clearly, even though nature possesses a "far greater number" of perspectives and an "infinite number of profiles." Here radical subjectivity threatens to fragment into pluralistic confusion until Thoreau invokes the "the law of average" to stabilize the mass of kaleidoscopic possibilities. The ascertaining of a single absolute truth might someday serve as a *point d'appui*. Until then, the best a limited observer can do is rely on the law of averages to combine our varying views of nature's shifting landscape. The law of averages also suggests that after multiple failures a single effort may one day strike truth. Either way, the pursuit of natural law requires repetition and patience.

A subsequent passage in "The Pond in Winter" shows how Thoreau's epistemological roughness can be a beautiful thing, for—to borrow a pun repeated in *Walden*—Thoreau esteems nature so highly in part because he can only estimate it. At the end of the surveying section in "The Pond in Winter," Thoreau realizes that by cutting holes to sound Walden, he changes the level of the ice, thus suggesting before Heisenberg that pure objectivity is impossible when observations change the status of the observed. Yet any skeptical worries that Thoreau might have are compensated by aesthetic wonder:

> When such holes freeze, and a rain succeeds, and finally a new freezing forms a fresh smooth ice over all, it is beautifully mottled internally by dark figures, shaped somewhat like a spider's web, what you may call ice rosettes, produced by the channels worn by the water flowing from all sides to a centre. Sometimes, also, when the ice was covered with shallow puddles, I saw a double shadow of myself, one standing on the head of the other, one on the ice, the other on the trees or hillside. (262)

This passage feels Emersonian in that a lengthening lyricism attempts to override a philosophical impasse, and it may refer to the seminal moment in *Nature* when Emerson walks ecstatically among puddles in the snow. But whereas Emerson when faced with a lack of foundations exhorts the poet to flow and not freeze, Thoreau enacts a more "mottled" negotiation of fact and eternal flux. The "dark figures" that he admires in the ice conjure both the quantifying urge of science and a tropological opacity that refuses to be fixed. Compromising Thoreau's observational and linguistic precision, the figures are only "somewhat" like a spider's web and "may" be comparable to rosettes. Yet if Thoreau admits that his analogies are imperfect—that the infinite number of nature's profiles cannot be brought into harmonious oneness—the plurality of channels all flow toward a "centre," just as multiple observations regress asymptotically toward a mean under frequentist law.

Absolute certainty will not be attained, nor will Walden be definitively measured, but Thoreau's "double shadow" that ends the surveying section of "The Pond in Winter" is not like the skeptical specters of Plato's cave, Poe's raven, or Benito Cereno's "Negro." Nor is it one of the deceptive "double images" that philosophers invoked to subvert perceptual accuracy.[36] Nor even is Thoreau's imposition of twin selves onto nature entirely concerned with questions of romantic subjectivity that critics so often emphasize.[37] Thoreau's double shadow can point to a moody psyche whose participation in subject-object dualism destabilizes scientific positivism, yet it also repeats what I take to be the central point of "The Pond in Winter": dark figures may flummox or enchant the idealist and can mark the limits of quantitative science, but the empiricist knows that the shadow of skepticism is cast on the object world. Surveyors face grave epistemological problems, but existence is not one of them. As the elusive meanings of the pond open skeptical possibilities in an aleatory mode, Thoreau responds by appealing to the law of averages—good news when an observer of Walden (or *Walden*) accepts the beautiful necessity of estimation.

FISH AND GAMES

If *Walden*'s epistemological inquiries were limited to the history of ideas and the philosophy of science, it would make some sense for "The Pond in Winter" to end with Thoreau's double shadow on the ice. Having sounded the skeptical depths of the pond and dwelled more positively on its surface, Thoreau might continue his climb into the chapter "Spring"—moving up the cut in the railway bank, through "rambles into higher and higher grass" (284), up toward his concluding vision of the sun as a "morning star," thereby leaving behind empirical incrementalism in the leap toward transcendental truths (297). Thankfully Thoreau is never so predictable. Though *Walden* gives a general impression of ascension and is drawn toward higher truths, it also exhibits local variations as if under the loose rein of frequentist law. Poe, Melville, and Douglass can present similar dynamics in that the impetus for totality exists in dialectical tension with acknowledgments of pluralism, open-endedness, uncertainty, and chance. The final few pages of "The Pond in Winter" continue to elaborate Thoreau's empirical skepticism, but by moving from his solitary surveying to the one hundred ice harvesters who cut Walden into blocks, Thoreau engages the challenge of chance in economic and social registers.

Implicitly contrasting his deep studies of the pond to the ice cutters' superficial skimming, Thoreau appears to distinguish his own business at Walden from their vulgar commercial ambitions. Even so, and as with the railroad and telegraph, the ice cutters are not the straw men imagined by readers who want a fiercely anti-capitalist, ecocritical Thoreau, for with a subtle self-criticism more open-minded than anxious, Thoreau compares the ice cutters' labors to his own. When describing their stacked blocks of ice as "held fast by chains and stakes like corded wood," Thoreau recalls the stakes and chains of surveyors who also divide nature into grids (262). When the ice cutters fail to master the pond—when tools break, workers fall into the water, and much of the stacked ice melts away—Thoreau's tone does not wax triumphant, if only because he himself has experienced what it means to err on the ice. After comparing the ice cutters to images in a farmers' almanac, a genre with which *Walden* has affinities, the section ends, "Perhaps I shall hear a solitary loon laugh as he dives and plumes himself, or shall see a lonely fisher in his boat, like a floating leaf" (265). Just as the ice cutters are at the mercy of chance in the form of accidents, weather, and financial markets, loons and anglers represent for Thoreau the difficulty of prediction under conditions of chance.

The laughing loon in "The Pond in Winter" echoes an earlier scene from the chapter "Brute Neighbors," in which human reason proves unable to master nature's whimsy. After a loon appears on Walden Pond, hunters armed with fine instruments ("patent rifles" and "spy-glasses") come "two by two and three by three" until there are "at least ten men to one loon," and yet still the loon evades the numbered hunters, long odds, and Thoreau's own quantifying urge (210). Thoreau describes his probabilistic attempts to predict the loon's surfacing as a game of checkers. And like Poe in his critique of the Parisian police, Thoreau shows that dividing the world into squares is too rational a method, not only for surveyors and the ice entrepreneur who hopes (checker-like) "to cover each one of his dollars with another" but also for authors who factitiously model nature with two-dimensional checkerboard metaphors (263). Despite making multiple observations of the loon, Thoreau continues to "miscalculate[]" where the bird will appear, a failure that brings more wonder than frustration as the loon violates Thoreau's checkerboard image by sailing beautifully off into the distance (211). *Walden* ultimately leaves its unpredictable brute neighbor at large as Thoreau fails to fix and so esteems all the more the untamable wildness of nature. Perhaps this is why Ginger Nut calls Bartleby the scrivener "*luny*."

Something similar can be said of fishing—a complicated practice for Thoreau, and one that became increasingly subjected to probabilistic thinking in the antebellum period. Fishing is one of Thoreau's favorite tropes for truth seeking; and even when he writes in the "Higher Laws" chapter, "I cannot fish without falling a little in self-respect," the line suggests that the angler's experience in nature provides a helpful check to egoism (192). Thoreau elsewhere describes fishing as a lesser order pleasure when compared to naturalist observation, and—like Henry Ward Beecher in "Morals of Fishing" (1855)—Thoreau disapproves of angling as a blood sport. Thoreau has no patience for materialists who "[do] not think they were lucky or well payed [*sic*] for their time unless they got a long string of fish" (6:245), suggesting that his modulated views of fishing involve the relation of economics and luck.

As a proponent of the labor theory of value, and sharing the moral (if not epistemological) anxiety brought on by the spread of financial speculation, Thoreau is wary of modes of acquisition that in his mind rely too heavily on chance—lotteries and gambling, land speculating and stock-jobbing, even slaveholding and politics, which he referred to as gambling.[38] Thoreau wrote in 1852 regarding the California gold rush: "[S]o many are ready to get their living by the lottery of gold digging without contributing any value to society. . . . I will resign my life sooner than live by luck" (4:317). Thoreau was hardly alone in resenting the growing influence of market forces, but unlike most nineteenth-century opponents of gambling and financial speculation, he recognized the pervasive reach of chance into even artistic endeavors. "The humblest thinker who has been to the mines sees and says that gold digging is of the character of a lottery," Thoreau wrote, "Still—he buys a ticket in another lottery nevertheless, where the fact is not so obvious" (4:372). For Thoreau, fishing is more acceptable than gold mining insofar as it renders legitimate use value, yet it does not guarantee compensation for the laborer, in that "The fisherman . . . has sent out a venture—He has a ticket in the lottery of 'fate'" (4:338).

What finally redeems fishing for Thoreau is that its unpredictability can be to some degree managed, for if angling was not subjected to the rigorous methods that Matthew

Maury brought to whaling, fishing in the mid-nineteenth century was increasingly seen as a scientific enterprise involving probabilistic skill. New York's *Spirit of the Times*, a popular magazine of gaming, woodcraft, and frontier life, noted changing attitudes toward outdoor sports in an article from 1841: "Racing, hunting, coursing, shooting, [and] fishing, . . . are so systemized; everything belonging to them is so exactly regulated." To those relishing freedom in natural spaces, this may sound like a complaint, but the author was actually pleased that angling was becoming "a matter of taste and science." Izaak Walton's *Compleat Angler* (1653), which Thoreau read, was a frequently updated classic showing how fishing could entail scientific attention to classification, habitat, and behavior, so much so that an 1842 review essay in the *North American Review* praised a new edition of Walton and three other books for treating fishing "like a science." To control the proverbial chances of fishing, antebellum anglers pursued what was called "the science of the rod," while one review even invoked the "doctrine of chances" as a way to understand fishing failures and successes.[39]

Attitudes toward the science of fishing were mixed, though even negative narratives indicate its rise. The Walton-worshiping scholar of Washington Irving's "The Angler" (1819–1820) is outfished by a boy with a bent pin for a hook, while the learned Dr. Battius in Cooper's *The Prairie* (1827) shows that natural philosophy is no substitute for experience in matters of the rod and gun. Also exhibiting a Jacksonian anti-intellectualism, and participating in a subgenre of frontier literature, a humorous 1848 piece in *Spirit of the Times* recounts how a greenhorn "assisted by mere chance" outfishes his more knowledgeable guide, thereby demonstrating that no system brings "infallible certainty" to angling.[40] More technical commentators acknowledged the "accidental" nature of fishing but insisted that probabilism could help manage the "mischances" of the sport. Humphry Davy—the famed chemist, president of the Royal Society of London, and a passionate poet and angler—admitted the power of both science and chance into his meditation on fishing, *Salmonia* (1840). More philosophical idyll than intestinal disease, *Salmonia* reflects on "chains of causes and effects so wonderfully and strangely linked together," suggesting that science can improve results but never master the chances of fishing. Similarly, William Chatto's *The Angler's Souvenir* (1835), a book that Thoreau owned, ends with a dispute as endemic to fishing as tall tales and tangled lines. After Chatto's narrator attributes a poor fishing performance to the kind of bad luck one has at "cards or any game of chance," his wife replies: "There is no such thing as luck. It is your lack of skill."[41] Fishing success for Chatto and others lies somewhere between certitude and chance. Now and in the antebellum era, the best policy is to manage the chances of angling as skillfully and stoically as one can, an ethos that for Thoreau no less than Hemingway extended from fishing to life.

Nowhere is Thoreau's dedication to probabilism clearer and more troubling than in the "Baker Farm" chapter of *Walden*. Thoreau's views of Irish immigrants are sometimes respectful in his journals, though his brutal depiction of John Field in "Baker Farm" exposes some social and racial insecurities.[42] Published at the height of Know-Nothing nativism, the chapter anxiously seeks to differentiate Thoreau from the Irish squatters at Walden: *his* cabin is not a filthy shanty; *his* simplicity is not poverty; *his* heroic self-cultivation is not Field's degraded "'bogging'" (184). Fishing is another way for Thoreau to distinguish himself from Field and his ilk.[43] Thoreau writes of fishing with Field,

"[H]e, poor man, disturbed only a couple of fins while I was catching a fair string, and he said it was luck; but when we changed seats in the boat luck changed seats too" (188). Thoreau says in "Higher Laws" that he has a "skill" and "instinct" for fishing, the latter of which slips easily into race (192). Thoreau wrote in a journal entry from the mid-1840s: "The instincts . . . are perhaps the mind of our ancestors subsided in us. The experience of the race" (2:146). Thoreau also mentions the poor woodcraft and farming of the Irish—how one can tell from its mangled stump that an Irishman chopped down a tree, and how an Irish farmer plows his field by beating his horse in the face. "Baker Farm" makes clear that Field is a fool for using worms to catch shiners to catch perch. What makes Field a bad angler—in New England, at least—has something to do with his race, as when Thoreau calls him "born to be poor, with his inherited Irish poverty . . . not to rise in this world, he nor his posterity, till their wading webbed bog-trotting feet get *talaria* to their heels" (188). The alterity of the Irish in "Baker Farm" is aggressively embodied as Field and his family are depicted as behaviorally and biologically foreign to Thoreau's native land. There is a reason besides the National Rifle Association why political candidates are prone to pose with rods and guns: managing the chances of the outdoors is a sign not only of rugged masculinity or Mama Grizzly womanhood but also of an inherited understanding of the local grounds in "real" America.

For Thoreau, Field's failure as a fisherman points toward a racialized incapacity to manage chance. Thoreau notes twice that Field is "without arithmetic" and seems incapable of comprehending Thoreau's lessons in economy (186). Following stereotypes of the superstitious Irish, whose Catholicism repulsed many rational Protestants, Field does not even recognize fishing as a skill, mistaking his poor technique for bad luck. As discussed in chapter four, pro-slavery thinkers argued that blacks lacked the mental abilities to manage chance and, thus, were unfitted for democratic capitalism. In a journal entry on which "Baker Farm" draws, Thoreau similarly casts Field as a passive victim of chance who "sits there with his shiner bait and his alder rod to see what his luck will be this time" (2:210). Thoreau by contrast makes his own luck, for not only does he have a racial instinct for angling, but he also improves his probabilities with scientific reason—studying fish in the wild, reading in ichthyology, and consulting with experienced anglers. Refusing to let the example of Field dampen his fishing pleasure, "Baker Farm" celebrates the management of chance: "Go fish and hunt far and wide day by day. . . . There are no larger fields than these, no worthier games than may here be played" (186–87). Thoreau cannot abide gold mining and financial speculation, which he associates with rampant luck, but fishing for him and many of his contemporaries involved similar encounters with chance as the probabilistic revolution swept over Wall Street, Main Street, and the outdoors. In the end, Thoreau takes what consolation he can in playing games of chance better than ice cutters, loon hunters, and Irish fisherman.

AN UNFINISHED LIFE OF SCIENCE

Thoreau's probabilistic thinking is exercised in his surveying and fishing, and it accords with *Walden*'s empirical skepticism as expressed in "The Pond in Winter." The management of chance has a much weightier presence in Thoreau's naturalist researches, which he began in earnest in the early 1850s and continued until his death in 1862. Thoreau's scientific labors—the collection, aggregation, and collation of naturalist data—are everywhere evident in his later journals, later essays, and the book-length manuscripts he was composing at his death, the posthumously titled *Dispersion of Seeds* and *Wild Fruits*, both of which point toward a natural history of Concord that Thoreau sometimes called his "Kalendar." Representative of this uncompleted project is Thoreau's "Pond Kalendar," a table tracking the freezing and icing out of local ponds between 1845 and 1862. Thoreau wrote in the margin: "I calculate in spring of 60 that Walden freezes on av. December 25. F.H.P. [Fair Haven Pond]—about December 2d" (6:308). Like the "almost" of his surveying handbill, Thoreau's use of averages and underscoring of "about" indicate that knowing the natural world entails probabilistic approximations based on masses of data, an outlook crucial not only to Thoreau's science but also to his aesthetics. Thoreau's later writings can provide what most readers seem to want— precise descriptions of luminous moments in the woods. Yet it is bracing to realize how seriously—and how ambivalently—Thoreau deploys the power of generalization as he submits his multiple observations to the logic and language of large numbers.

The first challenge in understanding Thoreau's naturalist work is that his goals are never explicitly stated. Emerson in his eulogy referred mournfully to Thoreau's "broken task, which none else can finish," and Ellery Channing, who often accompanied Thoreau on his rambles, noted that Thoreau realized too late in his life that he needed to coordinate his many observations. Tempering the disappointment of Emerson's eulogy, Channing punned on Thoreau's open-ended roughness when he wrote, "[N]o man had a better unfinished life." But while Channing celebrated his friend's "art of science" and recalled how he "impaled [his facts] on the picket-fences of order, and coined a labeled scientific plan," neither Channing nor Emerson described what Thoreau's plan was or how he might have completed it.[44]

Laura Dassow Walls has best explained the contexts and goals of Thoreau's naturalist studies. In accordance with the *Naturphilosophie* of Goethe, Schelling, Coleridge, and Emerson, and more poignantly resembling what Walls calls the "empirical holism" of Alexander von Humboldt and Darwin, Thoreau believed that nature's complex relations form a harmonious unity and that dense ecological webs are revealed by linking multiple observations of flora, fauna, climate, and topography across history.[45] Walls discusses how Thoreau "wove [chance] into the fabric of his life and journal, amassing happenstance toward its accumulation into pattern"; and just as Humboldt and Darwin invoked the doctrine of chances when inducing natural laws from vast quantities of facts, Thoreau turned to probabilism and the law of averages in his meditations on nature's variability. Thoreau understood along with Quetelet and Poe that norms and outliers are mutually constitutive, and he acknowledged along with Melville and Douglass that probabilistic methods move toward certainty without ever reaching it. Yet more remains to be said about Thoreau's attitude toward chance, for not only does it help to locate him within (and beyond) the natural sciences of his time, it also shows how his empirical holism is experienced as a kind of skepticism.[46]

We know that Thoreau lived during a formative period in the history of the natural sciences.[47] Modern disciplines were being increasingly defined by specialized argots, instruments, methods, and professional organizations. More controversially, the teleological assumptions and static taxonomies of the argument from design came under growing pressure from thinkers emphasizing nature's ongoing and sometimes catastrophic changes: Laplace and William Herschel in astronomy, Lyell in geology, Robert Chambers in his popular *Vestiges of the Natural History of Creation* (1844), and Erasmus Darwin, Lamark, Alfred Russell Wallace, and Charles Darwin in what is now called biology. These men had their own significant disagreements about the pace and mechanisms of natural change, and their breaks with the argument from design are not as neat as sometimes supposed. Paley's *Natural Theology*, that bulwark of rational Christianity, admitted that "chance" ("the operation of causes without design") might produce "a wen, a wart, a mole, a pimple" (though he insisted, "never an eye"), while even supposed heretics such as Chambers paid tribute to the "designs of Providence."[48] For those who were convinced of instabilities in nature but did not abandon teleological ideas of order, the challenge was to account for variation and accident without wholly giving in to chance, to square causal uncertainty and unruly empirical evidence with eternal natural laws.

The law of averages was an attractive solution, for if naturalists were slower than mathematicians, sociologists, and political economists to embrace new theories of chance, they assumed that seemingly random phenomena follow fixed principles in the long run. Drawing on advances in probability theory, natural philosophy in the early nineteenth century increasingly became a quantitative science.[49] Chambers referred to Charles Babbage's work to bolster his claims of "statistical regularity," going so far as to write in *Vestiges*, "Man is now seen to be an enigma only as an individual; in the mass he is a mathematical problem."[50] Even conservative proponents of the argument from design believed in the power of large numbers, including the Harvard naturalist Louis Agassiz, who collected vast samples of common species, a project in which he enlisted Thoreau (and later the young William James).

Agassiz and others situated chance variations within stable systems of natural law, though more radical—and enlightening for Thoreau's naturalist work—is Darwin's extension of frequentist logic into matters of speciation. Gillian Beer and Joan Richardson show how Darwin in the Galápagos experienced a Miltonic sense of "Chaos and Anarchy": as with Melville in "The Encantadas" (1854), the alien, brutal environment of the islands unsettled easy beliefs in natural theology. The sheer quantity of facts that Darwin gathered on his travels further threatened confusion, though by applying what was called "botanical arithmetic" to his profusion of zoological observations, Darwin established averages and charts to track the divergence of species. Darwin never employed advanced probability formulae, as do some modern evolutionary biologists, and he never went so far as the philosopher Daniel Dennett in thinking about natural selection as a mathematical algorithm. Darwin did know of the probabilistic revolution through Quetelet, Herschel, Spencer, Whewell, his cousin Hensleigh Wedgwood, and especially Malthus; and it may matter that Darwin read Montaigne's *Essays* during the long gestation of *On the Origin of Species* (1859). As the historian of science Gerd Gigerenzer and his co-authors put it, "Chance was one of Darwin's greatest problems."[51] Darwin conceived of natural selection according to random variations and the chances of survival, and when arguing (without the aid of Mendelean genetics) that physical characteristics are inherited, he appealed to the "doctrine of chances." Though many nineteenth-century observers did not place Darwin's theories in direct opposition to Christianity, an 1860 review in *The Boston Investigator* was not alone in noting how crucial chance was to *On the Origin of Species*:

> [Darwin's] facts are overwhelming and most curious. How small when you see it, and yet how grand is the law. . . . Nature forever selecting and perpetuating the most suited varieties; the doctrine of chances determining who shall people the earth. . . . I feel half grieved for it; for I should like to believe in more direct personal action or interposition of a Deity.

This early commentary, like the Duke of Argyll's anti-Darwinist *Reign of Law* (1868), emphasized a point sometimes forgotten today: Darwin's greatest divergence from Christian cosmology is more directly about chance than the Book of Genesis, more fundamentally about the argument from design than about angels, apes, apatosauruses, and the age of the earth.[52]

Darwin himself was uncomfortable with the possibilities of chance, both for scientific and religious reasons. In an 1860 letter to Asa Gray, the Harvard botanist who influenced Thoreau and was privy to Darwin's theories by 1857, Darwin wrote, "I am inclined to look at everything as resulting from designed laws, with the details, whether good or bad, left to the working out of what we may call chance."[53] This statement gestures toward Paley's position that chance is nominal or limited to mere details, but while Darwin largely suspends his judgment, chance was a topic he could not ignore, if only because he faced an accusation routinely encountered by theorists of chance—that to admit even moments or degrees of randomness is to enthrone blind chance, as suggested by John Hershel who famously referred to natural selection as "the law of higgledy-piggledy." Such charges indicate how profoundly Darwin's thinking challenged scientific conventions in the nineteenth century, for despite Darwin's frequent disclaimers, many believed that he (in the words of Thomas Huxley) "attempted to reinstate the old pagan goddess, Chance."[54] Darwin was right in *The Descent of Man* (1871) to worry that his book would be judged irreligious. He proleptically praised "that grand sequence of events, which our minds refuse to accept as the result of blind chance," but he wrote privately a year earlier, "I cannot look at the universe as the result of blind chance, yet I can see no evidence of beneficent design, or indeed of design of any kind, in the details." Darwin recognized but never reconciled himself to the radical aleatory implications of his work. On his deathbed, he reportedly said of the belief that the universe is intelligently governed, "Well, that often comes over me with overwhelming force; but at other times, it seems to go away."[55] Darwin's uncertainty marks the single most important shift in nineteenth-century intellectual history: the argument from design is self-evident until it is not.

Darwin's struggle with the possibilities of chance is in part a matter of quantity, of trying to conceptualize deep time and its vast stores of phenomena, all of which are in theory measurable and interconnected under the logic of empirical holism. Darwin wrote in the conclusion to *On the Origin of Species*: "[We] hide our ignorance under such expressions as the 'plan of creation,' 'unity of design,' etc.," but in actuality "[t]he mind cannot possibly grasp the full meaning of the term of a hundred million years; it cannot add up and perceive the full effects of many slight variations, accumulated during an almost infinite number of generations."[56] Too much perspective can be downright dispiriting for the probabilist whose samples are too small to infer larger designs with certitude. And if the greatest naturalist in history cannot handle nature's immensity, how is a moonlighting local surveyor to make good? Anxieties about superabundant data were widespread during the information revolution of the nineteenth century, but Darwin, whose linguistic subtlety should not be underrated, offers some comfort for the patient empiricist overmatched by nature's largesse. To admit ignorance of "full meaning" and "full effects" is not necessarily to admit intellectual failure but, rather, to admire the grand scope of nature and the achievement of partial understanding—a rough, fallibilist, modest epistemology evident in Darwin's habitual framing of his claims as theories and probabilities. As Beer has shown, Darwin's discoveries forced him to confront the limitations of language, including the inescapability of metaphor and the inability of words to figure natural profusion.[57] Thoreau encounters similar challenges in his own scientific work, though more deeply than Darwin his experiences as a naturalist shape his relations to writing.

Long before pouring over *On the Origin of Species*, and even before admiring Darwin's *Voyage of H.M.S. Beagle* (1846), Thoreau recognized that empirical holism entailed encounters with skepticism and chance. The point is so basic that it bears emphasis: Thoreau appreciates the "infinite novelty" of nature, and like any good scientist, is attuned to variations and anomalies; but without the law of averages to aggregate his data and help hypothesize governing laws, Thoreau's scientific observations remain nothing more than a mass of random facts, while his explanatory efforts cannot make the leap from natural history to natural science (IX:5). Thoreau was fairly consistent in his faith that regular frequencies emerge over time. "It takes us many years to find out that Nature repeats herself annually," he wrote in 1860, "But how perfectly regular and calculable all her phenomena must appear to a mind that has observed her for a thousand years" (XIII:279). The difficulty, as Darwin also understood, is that life is comparatively short. Thoreau wrote in *Cape Cod*, "Any conclusions drawn from the observations of a few years, or one generation only, are likely to prove false."[58] Such intense awareness of life's brevity lies at the heart of Thoreau's mourning work—from the elegiac reflections of *A Week on the Concord and Merrimack Rivers* (1849), to *Walden's* insistence that we should live before we die, to Thoreau's naturalist observations that take nature's measure while knowing that full knowledge remains beyond reach. Some critics have emphasized that Thoreau desires to step outside of time, but his patient scientific labors show him accepting his temporal limitations while minimizing the potential of sampling error, itself an aspect of chance.[59] Thoreau's naturalism is less about transcendence than about the unavoidable uncertainties of experience. As he writes in *Walden,* to talk too much of heaven risks disgracing the earth.

For Emerson, no stranger to the demands of waiting, the "scale on which [Thoreau's] studies proceeded was so large as to require longevity." What Emerson does not say is that no amount of data can change probabilities into the fullest of truths, and that no one, not even a long-lived Thoreau, could have finished the task he took up. In "I reason, Earth is short" (1862), Dickinson surmises that in heaven, "Somehow it will be even—/Some new Equation, given," but both she and Thoreau realize that for the mortal empiricist, final accountings are not to be had. Nature's wholeness can be faithfully pursued, but it can never be comprehensively reckoned—a lesson implicit in the unfinished opuses of

Humboldt, Coleridge, Joseph Banks, Henry Buckle (whom Thoreau read near the end of his life), and Agassiz (who never finished his massive effort to catalog all animal life in the United States). Romantic philosophy is one way to counter beliefs in scientific objectivity and certitude, if only because observation can never disentangle itself from the participating "I." Yet even when subjective instability is bracketed, as seems increasingly the case with Thoreau, the practical burden of sheer factual volume and the theoretical problem of induction force holistic empiricists to admit what Thoreau in *Walden* calls "the narrowness of my experience" (3). Cavell has argued that Thoreau's appeals to patience recommend that we attend with rigorous receptivity to the unfolding of our relations in the world, and Wai Chee Dimock discusses Thoreau's sense of deep time in terms of global literary history. Thoreau's patience should also be understood within a scientific framework in which the quantity of empirical facts is as unsettling as the quality of subjective observation. The British physicist and popularizer of science John Tyndall wrote in 1854 that science requires of its practitioner "the loyal surrender of himself to Nature," an approach that almost sounds like transcendental abandonment, except that it prioritizes methodological consistency and material facts.[60]

Thoreau in his journals largely surrenders the impulse to synthesize his many observations, a resistance to scientific perfectionism with far-reaching aesthetic consequences. For the lover of inspired natural description, Thoreau's discretion is not a problem, for vivid passages from the journals can be excerpted and anthologized without regard to any overarching vision except that of a series of finely crafted entries loosely bound by personality, comportment, and style.[61] For readers seeking more textual and intellectual unity, it is harder to appreciate the journals—even those after 1850, when Thoreau stops excising sections and begins to treat his journals more as a self-standing work, even if the interplay of pattern and anomaly can simultaneously structure Thoreau's reactions to nature and a reader's response to the journals themselves. Thoreau writes that "regularity and permanence make phenomena more interesting to me," and he is stimulated by the repetitious symmetries of leafs and lakes, skeletons and nests, the slope of mountains and the transit of stars. At the same time, he is equally inspired by extraordinary phenomena that he "chances" upon—a towering aspen, a seldom seen lynx, a weasel bringing down a hawk. In meta-literary terms, Thoreau praises the seasons as a "rhyme" that nature "never tires of repeating" (IX:168), but he elsewhere happily dissolves regular prosody into something like free verse: "Finer than the saxon arch is this path running under the pines roofed not with crossing boughs but drooping ice-covered twigs in irregular confusion" (5:416). In moods of heightened receptivity, Thoreau finds wonder in both order and chaos.

As discussed in chapter one, probability theory shows the ordinary and extraordinary to be mutually constituted; but if the more controlling, more defensive Poe argues that one should expect the unexpected, Thoreau works to experience the obverse paradox of being regularly surprised, as when *Wild Fruits* describes being "annually surprised" by the yearly appearance of grasses.[62] Particularly in his later years, Thoreau labored to maintain a sense of discovery during his repetitious researches: "To conceive of it [a natural object] with a total apprehension I must for the thousandth time approach it as something totally strange" (XII:371). The episodic form and immediacy of the journals reflect Thoreau's efforts *not* to regularize the data he was regularly collecting, as when he writes, "A journal is a record of experiences and growth, not a preserve of things well done or said. . . . The charm of the journal must consist in a certain greenness, though freshness, and not in maturity" (VIII:134). This is the romantic Thoreau who preaches carpe diem, though he also at times is dissatisfied with his uncoordinated observations: "Most that is first written on any subject is a mere groping. . . . It is only when many observations of different periods have been brought together that [the writer] begins to grasp his subject and can make one pertinent and just observation" (XI: 439). The journals are full of memorable moments strikingly rendered in present tense verbs. It is Thoreau's later manuscripts that bring a more systematic—and ironically, a rougher—representation of facts.

On first blush, *Wild Fruits* appears to share the journals' dedication to immediately apprehended experience as Thoreau catalogs in rich detail various species of flora around Concord. Thoreau's description of saw grass is just one example of the remarkable prose-poetry that appears in *Wild Fruits*: "Its long, slender, seedy spikes, growing low and spreading almost horizontally, seen after the fields have been mowed, remind us of early autumn."[63] Much is admirable here—the initial soughing of *l*'s and *s*'s, the sudden shooting upwards of the velar *k* in "spikes," the expansive spread of low, long vowels preparing us for their cyclical mowing, the gradual introduction of a human perceiver whose moody impressions do not prejudice description because they make themselves belatedly known, as if Thoreau self-consciously delays the inevitable imposition of a lyrical "I." Other passages in *Wild Fruits* are similarly crafted as Thoreau seeks a language that he elsewhere calls "nutty"—dense, precise, sensuous, and grounded in material realities (4:8). Buell calls this aesthetic "literary realism" in part because the ecological observer resists the pathetic fallacies to which romanticism is prone.[64] Yet for all its careful fidelity to nature, *Wild Fruits* retains a certain unreality insofar as each entry does not describe an actual berry or plant but, instead, constructs a composite drawn from Thoreau's many observations as indicated by the book's frequent use of approximating terms such as "about," "around," "probably," "usually," and "say." As much as an imagist might appreciate the lapidary language of *Wild Fruits*, and as easy as it is to forget that the book is dealing in generalizations, Thoreau distills abstract types from large numbers, offering up imaginary plants to better account for real gardens.

In doing so, he practices and theorizes what might be called a statistical aesthetic. During the writing of the manuscript that would become *Wild Fruits*, Thoreau contrasted "scientific" and "poetic" language in a lengthy journal entry:

> [T]he truest description, and that by which another living man can most readily recognize a flower, is the unmeasured and eloquent one which the sight of it inspires. No scientific description will supply the want of this, though you should count and measure and analyze every atom that seems to compose it. (XIV:117)

This passage appears conventionally romantic in that inspired experience eloquently rendered supersedes Linnaeus-based botany understood as a discipline of disarticulation. Yet as the entry further unfolds, Thoreau admits the power of scientific aggregation when he writes that to represent the "uniformity where Nature has made curves," it is "indispensable for us to square her circles" (XIV:120). Thoreau knows from charting and averaging his data that checkerboard metaphors and composite types do not exactly correspond to nature, whose curves—like a Gaussian graph of variations—cannot be figured by a single number. Thoreau's computations in his journals and uncollected manuscripts show him cavalierly approximating the averages of rainfall, snow depths, lake levels, and the like. Only occasionally does he carry his averages into decimals or fractions, most often dropping remainders or using plus and minus symbols to indicate his approximations.[65] As representations that balance chance variations against each other, averages are useful fictions that Thoreau does not mistake for hard truths. The quantitative thinking required by averages can also be potentially disenchanting, as when Darwin complained about his loss of "the higher aesthetic tastes" (particularly for British romantic poetry) and worried that his mind was becoming "a kind of machine for grinding general laws out of large collections of facts."[66] Thoreau similarly tires of the aggregative grind, but if his journals in precept and practice resist the flattening out of experience, in *Wild Fruits* and elsewhere Thoreau finds statistical reasoning aesthetically stimulating, not unlike a contemporary who also attempted to bridge the divide between romantic art and quantitative science.

Thoreau and the early Ruskin share many affinities—from their youthful admiration of Humboldt and Lyell, to their researches on the margins of professional science (particularly botany), to their search for what Ruskin called a "unison of artistic sensibility with scientific faculty." Ruskin has been taken to influence Thoreau's aesthetic of careful observation, though given Ruskin's championing of J. M. W. Turner's proto-impressionism, his realism is by no means positivistic or naïve.[67] In volume one of *Modern Painters* (1843), which Thoreau read in 1857, Ruskin addresses the question of specificity versus generalization by attending to the "scientific accuracy" available through large numbers. Ruskin departs from the consensus led by Joshua Reynolds, who (in Ruskin's paraphrase) advises artists "to neglect *specific* form in landscape, and treat its materials in large masses, aiming only at general truths." By contrast, *Modern Painters* recommends a style that focuses on the "specific character of the given object," which may seem antithetical to statistical reasoning except that "specific character" for Ruskin does not refer to individual phenomena. Ruskin writes:

> The true ideal of landscape is the expression of the specific—not the individual, but the specific—characters of every object, in their perfection; there is an ideal form of every herb, flower, and tree: it is that form to which every individual of the species has a tendency to arrive, freed from the influence of accident.[68]

Ruskin's ideal is not that of Plato; it is closer to what he and Quetelet call a "type"—a composite that, under the law of averages, cancels out chance variations ("accidents"), even as it acknowledges their presence.

Ruskin ultimately values both chance and its taming. He writes in the second volume of *Modern Painters* (1848) that the "pleasures of sight" are lost "when, instead of being scattered, interrupted, or chance-distributed, [natural elements] are gathered together, and so arranged to enhance each other as by chance they could not be." For Ruskin (as for Poe, Quetelet, and Thoreau), "Both the frequent and the rare are parts of the same system." It is the patient observer of multiple specimens who can discern unreal but representative averages that are specific but not found in the world. "There is no bush on the face of the globe exactly like another bush," Ruskin writes, "[a]nd out of this mass of various, yet agreeing beauty, it is by long attention only that conception of the constant character—the ideal form—hinted at by all, yet assumed by none, is fixed upon the imagination for its standard of truth."[69] Thoreau was a better naturalist than Ruskin; he seldom used loose terms such as "bush" and was much more receptive to the Darwinian revolution. Thoreau also spent more time in the field, which may be why he wished that *Modern Painters* was "a more out-of-door book" (X:69). *Wild Fruits* beautifully realizes Ruskin's aesthetic by grounding its natural descriptions not in vague generalities or singular euphoric examples but in the specific character common to a species as ascertained through the patient apprehension of large numbers.

Like *Wild Fruits*, "The Succession of Forest Trees" (1860) approaches nature probabilistically, though as Thoreau's most accomplished ecological text, the lecture is less about aesthetic representation and more about proto-Darwinian mechanisms. First presented to the Middlesex Agricultural Society, "The Succession of Forest Trees" draws from *The Dispersion of Seeds* to reconcile "accident" with "Nature's design."[70] Suggesting how the ordinary and extraordinary are subtended, Thoreau first caricatures himself as an "oddity" and "queer specimen" come finally to join the herd ("Every man is entitled to come to Cattle-Show, even a transcendentalist"). He then asserts his authoritative knowledge of nature, not one premised on superior subjectivity as is often the case in his early works but, rather, one based in the empiricism of surveying, which Thoreau evokes with three puns: "[A]n upright man is the best *ruler*"; "I have some *title* to speak"; "I need offer no apology if I invite your attention, for the few moments that are *allotted* me, to a purely scientific subject" (my italics).[71] Thoreau's speech may disclaim his literary commitments, but the literary retains claims on his language.

Having embraced mensuration over metaphysics and distanced himself from his reputed idealism, Thoreau begins the main portion of his lecture, which explains why pines grow in the place of harvested oaks and why oaks replace harvested pines. Thoreau describes how chance events—a windblown seed, an animal burying a nut—contribute along with the chances of survival to "the regular succession of forests."[72] Sharpened but not instigated by Thoreau's recent reading of *On the Origin of Species*, "The Succession of Forest Trees" draws on years of observations to weigh the chances of seeds surviving over the long run of natural selection. Thoreau disparages those holding the then prevalent view that plants grow "spontaneously" (that is, without seeds), likening such believers to "farmers' sons" who "stare by the hour to see a juggler draw ribbons from his throat." This metaphor reflects Thoreau's animus toward his audience and his own oratorical capitulations; and it also suggests that romantic, self-reliant spontaneity—an important concept for Schelling, Coleridge, and Emerson, as well as for Thoreau in more speculative moods—cannot satisfy the empiricist who seeks the laws of creation in the object world, not the self. Such laws are discovered by attending to what Thoreau in a draft of his lecture calls *"little things."*[73] Like Darwin, who was wary of broad theorizing and pursued intensively specialized studies, Thoreau understands in "The Succession of Forest Trees" that empirical holism, for all its intellectual expansiveness, requires a narrow focus for the short-lived naturalist who thinks globally but must act in local fields.

Thoreau's acceptance of such scientific discipline is one narrative in a career characterized less by radical change than by incremental and incomplete adjustments. In an 1844 journal entry in which Thoreau aspires to study "the whole order of nature," he exults, "What young experimentalists we are!" (1:496). By the early 1850s, Thoreau more soberly regarded the holistic work he had recently begun: "But this habit of close observation—In Humboldt—Darwin and others. Is it to be kept up long—this science" (3:331)? For the rest of his life, Thoreau answered affirmatively, and one question is how he kept on saying *yes*, particularly when faced with Darwin-like fears that naturalist data erode aesthetic sensibilities and that quantitative methods can never master chance. Thoreau wrote in an 1851 entry that has become a touchstone for scholars:

> I fear that the character of my knowledge is from year to year becoming more distinct and scientific—That in exchange for views as wide as heaven's cope I am being narrowed down to the field of the microscope—I see details not wholes nor the shadow of the whole. I count some parts, and say "I know." (3:380)

Partiality can indeed be disappointing for a transcendentally inspired holistic empiricist. But even worse than the narrowness of experience is the hubris of saying *I know*, for if Thoreau cannot stop the counting of parts any more than he can wish himself into omni-science, he can resist not only transcendental perfectionism but also the delusions of comprehensive knowledge that were rampant in nineteenth-century science. Thoreau charged that "Science affirms too much," and he was repulsed by the arrogance of Agassiz (5:159). As Emerson put it in his eulogy, Thoreau "seemed haunted by a certain chronic assumption that the science of the day pretended completeness."[74] Even *Walden* for all its vatic ambitions accepts the narrow condition of living in the "angle of a leaden wall" (293). Here Thoreau does not hope to know nature comprehensively, for he realizes— gradually and at some cost—that such a goal is theoretically and practically impossible. Instead, Thoreau learns to seek connections in nature while saying *I don't know*, a bearing that allows him to continue the unfinishable project of empirical holism by acknowl-edging but not being debilitated by the shortness of life.

Thoreau's empirical holism in practice requires a skeptical outlook in which probabi-listic thinking replaces positivism. Many Victorians in the tradition of Comte and Mill recognized the limits of the empiricism they championed.[75] So, too, did Thoreau, who— like Darwin—knew that no mortal collector can fully apprehend nature's laws. But if for Darwin the fallibility of inductive science encourages public modesty and not a little private hand wringing—and if, as Beer seems correct in arguing, Darwin is not especially interested in "self-help"—Thoreau's philosophy of science can be therapeutic for his readers and himself, making it difficult to distinguish among his ethos, style, and scien-tific method. Hume's point that experience cannot assure the sun's rising becomes for Thoreau an opportunity. The conclusion of *Walden* envisions the sun as a "morning star" announcing "new, universal, and more liberal laws" that no amount of empirical study can predict (288). This openness to chance and the wonderful unknown is also evident when Thoreau pledges in *Walden* to "cut a broad swath and shave close" (82). To work broadly with large numbers is to use the law of averages, but such rough methods only shave close to truth like an asymptote approaching its limit. If, for Ahab, the next thing to a certainty is not good enough, for Thoreau it is inspiring, if only because (quoting Beer again) "[t]he Darwinian world is *always capable of further description*."[76] In this way, the romantic quest for a synthesis that seems forever approaching but forever out of reach is analogous in feeling but different in premise and method from the unending labors of the empirical skeptic.

Standing near the top of the mountain in "Ktaadn," Thoreau exults in "*Contact!*" as an alternative to the "myriad of particular things" unnaturally disarticulated as in naturalist displays. Yet contact is still not unification, not precisely the achievement of wholeness and loss of boundaries, forcing Thoreau in even this most ecstatic instance to celebrate a "forever untamable *Nature*" "made out of Chaos and Old Night."[77] Using similar Miltonic language in the Galápagos, Darwin remains uneasy with the possibilities of chance. More joyfully, Thoreau pleasures in axes, loons, the uncertain sport of angling, and the labors of a natural science that seeks, as Thoreau wrote two years before his death, "an end which is never attained" (XIV:117). Faced with an unfinishable task, Thoreau accepts both chance and the limits of his knowledge: "I never studied botany, and do not today systematically, the most natural system is still so artificial. I wanted to know my neighbors, if possible,—to get a little nearer to them" (IX:157). For a writer who tried to be a good neighbor—who appreciated proximity, occasional contact, the roughness of averages, the estimations of "almost," and the unpredictable variations of nature—shaving close is less a tragic admission of imperfection than a practical response to the challenge of chance, even if Thoreau learned from his brother's unlucky death that shaving close can consume lives already too brief.

SUMMING UP

Now a hard question: was Thoreau's work worth it? Does the disciplined acceptance of empirical limits make a decade of data collection well spent? Or might one wish from Thoreau, say, more lyrical essays, a fuller elaboration of his political philosophy, or even some version of *Walden II* that people might actually want to read? The naturalist writer John Burroughs, one of Thoreau's heirs and a sensitive reader of *Walden*, saw Thoreau as a "victim" of his journals (which Burroughs called that "hungry, omnivorous monster"), lamenting that the "vast mass of facts and figures was incapable of being generalized or systematized." Burroughs was wrong insofar as Thoreau's data have been productively used by the biologist Richard Primack to substantiate and advertise the case for global climate change and its specific effects on Concord's ecology. Thoreau now contributes to environmental consciousness as a measurer as well as a muse, and yet the value of Thoreau's naturalist work can still be in and of itself disappointing.[78]

The primary challenge for Thoreau, as Burroughs recognized, was moving from facts to generalizations, from data to natural laws. Scholars have inferred how Thoreau in the last years of his life began to compile his vast stores of information using a multi-step and not always uniform process. After integrating his field notes into his journals, Thoreau transferred data into lists organized by date, before creating tables that tracked his facts across what is most often a nine-year period (1852 to 1860). Of these unpublished tables, two that have been labeled "Fall of Leaf" and "Earliest Flowering of April Flowers" are the most focused and manageable examples. Each row heading names a species of tree or flower; each column heading refers to a successive year; and Thoreau fills in the grid as best he can with the month and day on which a particular species leafed out or blossomed. Thoreau's scrawl can be exasperating, and both tables include some tangential categories, but on the whole they make good sense. They allow one to compute average dates of phenomena (as in the "Pond Kalendar" and *Wild Fruits*), and in doing so they prepare the way for an analysis of the life cycles and ecological relations of trees and flowers (as in "The Succession of Forest Trees").[79]

By contrast, the majority of Thoreau's tables cover specific months across nine years. These monthly tabulations were most likely intended for the synthetic "Kalendar" project, and they are intensely committed to empirical holism in that they are not limited to specific genera or species but to a multitude of what have been labeled "General Phenomena." These tables contain conventional naturalist data on such things as rainfall, snow packs, and the arrival of birds, as well as blossoming and leafing-out dates, but they also include idiosyncratic observations cataloged according to month and day: "some boys have bathed," "a washing day," "notice skunk cut buds," "woodchoppers' axes," "end of sauntering walks," and so on. Such phenomena are not unrelated to the environment (bathing indicates warmer weather; washing days suggest dry and breezy conditions). Thoreau even shows a proto-ecological sensibility by including human behavior in the web of Concord's environment. That said, the "General Phenomena" tables lack a clear principle of exclusion, include highly subjective and contingent observations, and suggest that Thoreau collected his data without a specific hypothesis or plan. Unless the plan was to discover how everything related to everything in Concord during each month—a goal faithful to the premises of empirical holism (as well as Jamesian radical empiricism), but one that leads to the omnivorous collection of facts of which Burroughs, Emerson, and even Channing complain. Emerson's eulogy may seem unforgiving in its assessment of Thoreau's unfinished scientific task, but Thoreau's tables suggest that the empirical commitments that sharpen his prose and make his thinking so powerfully dialectical also threaten to become a kind of mania—reckoning for reckoning's sake.[80] The more narrowly focused *Wild Fruits* and "The Succession of Forest Trees" represent Thoreau's naturalist researches in aesthetically pleasing and scientifically viable ways, though for most of Thoreau's naturalist observations the sum is less than the parts, requiring later scientists such as Primack to make meaningful analyses. Too often the facts distilled in Thoreau's tables lose their freshness without gaining explanatory force.

The greatest value of Thoreau's naturalist work may in the end be primarily about his observational and compositional habits and the ethos they entail—a possibility Burroughs suggested when writing that Thoreau's "science is only a handmaid to his ethics," and one that recent critics have traced along spiritual, humanist, and ecocritical lines.[81] The bearing of this chapter has been somewhat different, for among other lessons Thoreau's naturalist writings suggest how to live with the uncertainty of unfinishable empirical projects (or more simply, how to live with life). Tending toward epistemological realism and worked out in his everyday practices, Thoreau's probabilism makes approximate sense of unpredictable, fallible, and multifarious experiences. Thoreau responds to skepticism, not by subordinating the object world to some higher or ideal order, but by taking up what both the radical skeptic and the proponent of intelligent design lack: an empirical research agenda. One need not be a biologist, positivist, or utilitarian to appreciate such things. It might be nice to have a purpose-driven life without succumbing more than necessary to teleology.

That Thoreau's research agenda is overly ambitious highlights a crucial aspect of his work, in that his attitude toward the approachable yet unreachable knowledge of nature (as well as the nature of knowledge) helped him to ease the perfectionist anxieties that wracked so many American transcendentalists. The pursuit of higher truth, utopian society, ideal friendship, and ceaseless self-cultivation can be, as Emerson writes in "The Transcendentalist," so "exacting" as to threaten despair. The breaking of so many transcendental hearts and minds does not, of course, have a single cause; but the struggles of Fuller, Channing, Alcott, Jones Very, and others of the Concord circle can be taken in part as symptoms of unrealistically pure expectations. Moral perfectionism certainly has the advantage of inclining subjects toward growth, yet the most productive transcendentally influenced writers developed strategies to survive their own best hopes. Fuller moved away from perfectionist philosophy and dreams of literary immortality into the messier, more practical realms of journalism. Hawthorne, like Poe, remained fascinated by but deeply suspicious of utopian projects. Even though he was more attracted than Thoreau to Kantian exactitude, Emerson's (paradoxically willful) whimsy tempered his demands on the world and himself. In "Self-Reliance," Emerson aspires to be God in nature but is prepared to be a weed by a wall. He comes to terms with chance in the interest of self-preservation, urging readers (and himself) not to expect perfection but, rather, to emulate the rough "sturdy lad" who has "not one chance, but a hundred chances" and "like a cat, falls on his feet." For Emerson, those who use "all that is called Fortune" have "chained the wheel of Chance"—not necessarily stopped its workings, but measured and therefore tamed it with the tools of a surveyor. Kant and Locke may form the two most prominent poles of Emerson's early double consciousness, but we should not forget about Montaigne, whom Emerson praises for a "wise skepticism" which recognizes "that there is no practical question on which any thing more than an approximate solution can be had."[82]

More than Emerson (who in the following chapter will continue to both acknowledge and deny chance), Thoreau found in probabilistic thinking a way to diminish the threat of perfectionism. He wrote in the early 1840s as he desperately sought some calling: "Every man's success is in proportion to his *average* ability. The meadow flowers spring and bloom where the waters annually deposit their slime, and not where they reach in some freshet only" (2:61). This passage can comfort a literary critic attempting to make meaningful generalizations about an author of vast inconsistency and scope. Who knows but that Thoreau might even console perfectionist students unhinged by a "B." Like low-stakes journal exercises that have more insight and passion than anxiously polished final papers, Thoreau suggests that our capacities are best revealed in the long run, when the law of averages has time to work and single trials do not dominate outcomes or perceived potentialities. Thoreau wrote in *Walden*, "In the long run men hit only what they aim at" (24), and he recommends that we "try our lives by a thousand simple tests" (9). As a romantic, Thoreau embraces the possibilities of failure and the promise of future success. As a probabilistic thinker, he values the cumulative weight of every day's experience without dwelling too much on any single case such as, say, an erroneous measurement, an unsuccessful day of fishing, or a poorly received first book. Thoreau believes in singular moments of inspiration, but he increasingly conceptualizes such moments within a broader process involving multiple trials and errors—which is to say that Thoreau applies the logic of large numbers to his artistic as well as his scientific work.

When Thoreau speaks of successes and failures, longstanding aims and unending experiments, he is often talking about his writing, which comes to embrace the generative potential of chance. Among eighteenth-century aesthetic condemnations of chance is a comment on process from Pope: "True ease in writing comes from art, not chance,/As those move easiest who have learned to dance." Thoreau's own early attitudes toward his craft can be perfectionist, purist, and rigid: "Nothing goes by luck in composition—it allows of no trick" (1:276); "Good writing . . . will be obedience to conscience. There must not be a particle of will or whim mixed with it" (1:233). For Robert D. Richardson, the young Thoreau rightfully worried that his style was too mechanical; and Fuller made a similar point in her capacity as editor of *The Dial*, hoping to "melt" Thoreau's poetry and eliminate from his prose "the grating of tools on the mosaic."[83] Thoreau was an extraordinarily patient reviser, and as *Walden*'s parable of the artist of Kouroo suggests, perfectionism for him retained some attractions. Yet part of Thoreau's triumph in *Walden* and beyond is his openness to incursions of chance. Stylistically this is manifest in his sudden tonal shifts and playful turns of digression and whimsy. As dramatized by the fox-chasing hound in *Walden* who is finally disappointed to find his quarry shot dead, Thoreau knows that a rambling, open-ended hunt is more satisfying (and probably more epistemologically responsible) than the linear pursuit and ultimate fulfillment of a teleological goal. What feels free and loose to some readers, of course, is assiduously crafted by Thoreau—not only meta-critically observed (hound as author and/or audience), but also encouraged by Thoreau's writing process, which moves away from the chanceless rigor of his early years.

Describing a moment of writer's block, and wondering about the unpredictability of artistic inspiration, Thoreau wrote in his journal in 1851:

> I bethought myself while my fire was kindling to open one of Emerson's books which it happens that I rarely look at—to try what a chance sentence out of that could do for me. Thinking at the same time of a conversation I had with him the other night—I finding fault with him for the stress he had laid on some of Margaret Fuller's whims. . . . The first sentence which I opened upon in his book was this.—"If, with a high trust, he can thus submit himself, he will find that ample returns are poured into his bosom, out of what seemed hours of obstruction and loss." (4:202)

Waiting for his creative fires to rise, Thoreau takes his chances with a kind of bibliomancy that leads to Emerson's "Literary Ethics" (1838), a happy coincidence in that the essay recommends "spontaneous sentiment" to authors who "grind and grind."[84] As if to reward his abandonment to chance and chasten his resistance to whim, the passage that Thoreau lights upon teaches submission to aleatory experience.

That Thoreau took such lessons to heart is suggested by another journal entry: "Perhaps this is the main value of a habit of writing—of keeping a journal. . . . Having by chance recorded a few disconnected thoughts and then brought them into juxtaposition—they suggest a whole new field in which it [is] possible to labor and to think" (4:277–78). For Thoreau, chance operates in the domain of the real, as when he writes, "I have never met with anything so truly visionary and accidental as some actual events" (3:94–95). And chance benefits the author who courts its appearance over the long run of experience and composition: "There is always some accident in the best things, whether thoughts or expressions or deeds. . . . What we do best or most perfectly is what we have most thoroughly learned by the longest practice, and at length it falls from us without our notice, as a leaf from a tree" (XII:39). What Thoreau does—not perfectly, but "most perfectly"—is write, and his practice at it was long. The paradox that he notes here and elsewhere is that fortunate accidents are best encouraged through discipline, a fitting belief for a thinker dedicated to large numbers as a way of managing the uncertainties of chance. The advice is ultimately familiar enough: write regularly to increase your chances for extraordinary work. For Thoreau, this compositional strategy coheres with a probabilistic outlook that helps him bridge potential and very real gaps between his science and art.

It is in some ways surprising that Thoreau of all American romantics is most committed to the law of large numbers: no author of the period—or any period, for that matter—is a more stubborn, nonconforming individualist. In 1840, Thoreau defined genius against the masses by mixing the dictions of statistics, art, spiritualism, and surveying: "Only *meanness* is mediocre—*moderate*—but the true *medium* is not contained within any *bounds*" (1:153). Such punning continues in *Walden's* complaint that "we live meanly; . . . it is error upon error" (82), while Thoreau later laments that "the public demand an average man,—average thoughts and manners,—not originality" (VII:79). Yet no matter how mean Thoreau finds the methods of Quetelet and Darwin, he wrote approvingly in 1854, "It is remarkable how the American mind runs to statistics" (8:68). Nor did he exempt himself from the impulse, aspiring in *Walden* to "reduce [life] to its lowest terms, and, if it prove[s] to be mean, why then to get the whole and genuine meanness of it" (82). A journal entry from 1851 can stand as a summation indicating the simultaneous commitment and chagrin of an idealist moving toward probabilism. "I am getting used to my meanness," Thoreau wrote, "getting to accept my low estate" (4:141). This is not to argue that Thoreau is an unequivocal proponent of probabilism and large numbers, but neither should his empiricism be defined against his sensitivity to epistemological limits.

To think of Thoreau's science as an aspect of and not an alternative to his skepticism helps to locate his work more firmly within a pragmatist tradition. Cavell's rightfully esteemed *Senses of Walden* (1977) has inclined some scholars to regard Thoreau as a pragmatist, though his standing as such remains tenuous. As much as Cavell's work on Thoreau shares the pragmatist view of truth seeking as an open-ended, experiential pursuit, Cavell does not identify himself as a pragmatist nor have literary critics much advanced his claims in regard to Thoreau, finding (like Cavell himself) that Emerson is a more compelling founder of post-metaphysical philosophy in America. That *The Senses of Walden* in Thoreau scholarship is more often cited than engaged may have something to do with Cavell's far-sightedness and the intensity of the claims he makes on his readers, but it also has something to do with Thoreau, who becomes less interested in linguistic aspects of intersubjectivity as his writings turn toward natural science. If Cavell is wary of pragmatism's scientific commitments (particularly in regards to Dewey), it may be those very commitments that make Thoreau most like a pragmatist.[85]

As with Poe, Melville, and Douglass, any argument in this direction cannot rest its case on immediate influence. William James might be expected to have some commerce with Thoreau: his father knew Thoreau; James himself was acquainted with *Walden* and *A Week on the Concord and Merrimack Rivers*; and James was also dedicated to the natural sciences, most centrally in the 1860s and '70s when he accompanied Agassiz on an expedition to Brazil and taught comparative anatomy at Harvard. Yet James almost never mentions Thoreau, and when he does refer to *Walden* in *Varieties of Religious Experience* (1907), he quotes Thoreau in a highly transcendental mood, despite the fact that both men share more empirical outlooks derived from similar scientific experiences. Thoreau came to mistrust Agassiz's hubris and erroneous claims for biological stasis, sympathizing instead with the views of Darwin (and his American defender, Asa Gray). James also sided with Darwin and Gray against Agassiz, the break coming during his trip to Brazil, where James witnessed (like Humboldt in South America and Thoreau in the "Spring" chapter of *Walden*) the "bewildering profusion and confusion of the vegetation, the inexhaustible variety of its forms and tints." Encountering a natural largesse that escapes static taxonomies and quantitative control, James the young naturalist came to a conclusion that James the philosopher would later generalize: Agassiz's errors stem from the fact that "[h]e wishes to be omniscient." Acknowledging the overwhelming interconnectivity of nature and recognizing the impossibility of comprehensive holistic knowledge, James—like Thoreau—came to embrace the contingency and partiality of experience in a pluralistic world. As with Thoreau, this entailed for James an open-mindedness to the possibilities of chance. Because the monistic universe of Agassiz and others is in theory fully cohesive and predictable, James in a letter to the idealist philosopher F. H. Bradley defined "'Chance'" as "*identical* to pluralism."[86]

That James in his letter puts "Chance" in quotations shows that he was also open-minded toward the hypothesis of higher law, whether understood in terms of philosophy, religion, or natural science. Like Thoreau, James as a young man admired the grand vision of Humboldt, and James described the world as a web in which "each part hangs together with its very next neighbor in inextricable interfusion." What turns James away from empirical holism is his recognition that ecology—and later, the multiverse—is too bewildering, profuse, and fluid for the designs of Humboldt, Agassiz, and at times Thoreau. The best one can hope for is a rough understanding improved by an appreciation of nature's pied beauty, whose fickle contingencies hints at "*conjunctive relations*" that humans cannot fully grasp. James writes: "[T]he study of facts is the only way of getting even approximate answers"; "[A]s the sciences have developed farther, the notion has gained ground that most, perhaps all, of our laws are only approximations."[87] Preferring the rough tools of experience to the finer instruments of metaphysics, James's career suggests that one path to pragmatism leads through natural science disabused of its positivism.

Peirce—who wrote an early paper, "On the Theory of Errors and Observation" (1870)—also realized that "experience never can show any truth to be exact." As seen in chapter one, Peirce situates pragmatism within the probabilistic revolution, and he models his early theories of truth and method on the law of averages and errors. Whereas Peirce shares with Poe a psycho-mathematical account of chance and intuition, his key commonality with Thoreau is a deep recognition that induction can only asymptotically approach natural law. Peirce does draw on the *Naturphilosophie* of Schelling and can display significant Kantian tendencies, but he also has (as Hilary Putnam emphasizes) strong affinities for epistemological realism, including Scottish Common Sense.[88] In empirical matters, Peirce remains a close-shaving anti-perfectionist: "Try to verify any law of nature, and you will find that the more precise your observations, the more certain they will be to show irregular departures from the law. . . . Trace their causes back far enough, and you will be forced to admit they are always due to arbitrary determination, or chance."[89] As a brilliant, unmanageable, and theoretically inclined member of the U.S. Coastal Survey, Peirce's knowledge of probabilistic mathematics far exceeded Thoreau's. Yet Thoreau is guided by a main premise of pragmatism's rough epistemology, for like James and Peirce, but with a stauncher commitment to the long-term prospects of empirical fieldwork, Thoreau accepts the conditions of chance and approximation as he works toward natural law.

A few final points of comparison place Thoreau in a pragmatist tradition that looks less like a philosophical genealogy and more like an ecological web of discursive influences and relations. In "The Will to Believe," James subordinates metaphysics to empiricism, for although metaphysicians promise "bottom-certitude," they are constantly adjusting their opinions.[90] Peirce adopts similar imagery when writing of scientific method: "Even if it does find confirmations, they are only partial. It is still not standing upon the bedrock of fact. It is walking upon a bog, and can only say, this ground seems to hold for the present."[91] One of *Walden*'s best jokes concerns a traveler who is assured by a local boy that a certain swamp has a hard bottom. When the man, taking the boy at his word, sinks deeply into the bog and complains that the boy has misled him, the boy says of the swamp's purported hard bottom, "[Y]ou have not got half way to it yet" (294). The rise of neo-pragmatism has lead to backformations in which classical pragmatists are regarded as anti-foundational thinkers. James and Peirce certainly and often rebelliously resist the dominant metaphysics of their time, but their fallibilist, inductive, probabilistic practices do not preclude the living option of hard bottoms. Like Thoreau, they do not deny that a *point d'appui* might exist, but their empirical approaches remain asymptotic, like a person who moves repeatedly halfway toward a wall (or hard bottom) without ever making definite contact. Channeling Peirce, Susan Howe hints how Zeno's paradoxes allow one to maintain both skeptical methods and absolutist hopes, to be "half-enchanted" by the desire to "prove fallibilism to be fallible."[92] *Walden*'s joke about hard-bottomed bogs points to a similar epistemological poise. Thoreau recognizes simultaneously the need for patience, the personal toll such waiting can take, and—most remarkably—the pleasure a laughing reader and writer can take in our struggles with uncertainty.

Joan Richardson and Elisa New have begun to reconstruct an American literary pragmatism grounded in empirical approaches to nature.[93] Among the shared intellectual influences that inform both Thoreau and pragmatism is the rise of a naturalism increasingly attuned to empirical skepticism. Such skepticism involves science more directly than romantic philosophy, aleatory uncertainty more than subjectivity. Yet when confessing a dormant perfectionist desire for what he called "the idea of continuity," Peirce in 1892 refused to make science and transcendentalism mutually exclusive:

> I was born and reared in the neighborhood of Concord,—I mean in Cambridge,—at the
> time when Emerson, Hedge, and their friends were disseminating the ideas that they

had caught from Schelling.... [T]he atmosphere of Cambridge held many an antiseptic against Concord transcendentalism; and I am not conscious of having contracted any of that virus. Nevertheless, it is probable that some cultured bacilli, some benignant form of the disease was implanted in my soul, unawares, and that now, after long incubation, it comes to the surface, modified by mathematical conceptions and by training in physical investigations.

Here Peirce suggests that mathematics and empiricism might connect in largely unacknowledged ways American transcendentalism and what would soon be identified as pragmatism. As Peirce wrote in an unpublished manuscript: "One of my earliest recollections is of hearing Emerson deliver his address on Nature.... [W]e were within hearing of the Transcendentalists, though not among them."[94] Thoreau's differences with Emersonian idealism were more intimate than those of Peirce, and—more than any of the early pragmatists, including the vocationally challenged young James—Thoreau worked out for himself the claims of radical empiricism in the field of natural science. Better than James and Peirce, Thoreau knew what it was like to leave the transcendent circles of Concord for the natural history museums and scientific libraries afforded by Cambridge and Boston. He also knew what it was like to return to his native woods in pursuit of the thankfully unfinishable task of taming chance in the wild. And as Thoreau unevenly sauntered from transcendental philosophy toward empirical skepticism, another solitary nature lover traversed similar ground between romantic philosophy and Victorian science.

CHAPTER 6

Dickinson's Precarious Steps, Surprising Leaps, and Bounds

I do not know that knowledge amounts to anything more definite than a novel and grand surprise on a sudden revelation of the insufficiency of all that we had called knowledge before.
—Thoreau's *Journals*, February 27, 1851

You certainly can't avoid approaching it [literature] without a certain set of expectations. But a lot of the time what you're hoping for, if only subconsciously, is to have those expectations upset. You would like to be swept off your feet. You would like to be plunged into doubt.
—Richard Rorty, 2002 interview

Thoreau's astringent commitments to science sharpen his sense of surprise, in that his repetitious observations of diverse natural phenomena help him estimate natural laws while still esteeming extraordinary variances. In both his scientific and his literary work, Thoreau's negotiations of the one and the many become less governed by romanticism's metaphysical holism and more influenced by Victorian approaches to quantification and probability. Thoreau's empirical skepticism runs deep, as suggested by the tentative negations of his epigraph, which show him to be wary about claiming knowledge of a knowledge that remains unavoidably unpredictable and vague. Thoreau's openness to surprise expands his descriptive capacities by enlivening his appreciation for the interplay of repetitious and unexpected experience, a dynamic evident at the level of his sentences and throughout his nature writings that were becoming increasingly admired in the last few years of his life.

In an *Atlantic Monthly* article from 1861, Thomas Wentworth Higginson praised Thoreau's nature writing, lifting its power to render nature anew above the widely praised efforts of Emerson and Ruskin. The next year Higginson wrote his "Letter to a Young Contributor" (1862), piquing the interest of Emily Dickinson and instigating their oddly fruitful relationship, though Dickinson differed from her ostensible mentor regarding the compatibility of literature and science. Higginson's interests in both art and natural history did not prevent him from rejecting what William Whewell and the present-day biologist E. O. Wilson term "consilience" (for the logician Whewell, a pre-disciplinary "convergence of inductions"; for Wilson, "the linking of facts and fact-based theory across disciplines"). In "Literature and Art" (1867), Higginson joins Matthew Arnold, Henry Adams, and John Burroughs in contrasting art and science; for while Higginson concedes that science is destined to dominate modern civilization, he still insists that "[b]eyond and above all the domain of use lies beauty." In "A World Outside Science" (1892), Higginson selectively quotes Wordsworth on the antithesis of science and poetry, and he continues to draw a "boundary-line" between the "measurable" tests of scientific method and the "intuitive and inspirational" realm of art.[1] Yet if Higginson became increasingly anxious about what he took to be the thoroughgoing positivism of science, Dickinson—as is so often the case—saw more clearly into the matter. Dickinson's rambles were never as literal as Thoreau's, nor did she keep anything like an Amherst "Kalendar," but Dickinson shares Thoreau's understanding of the explanatory power and limits of science, in part because her empirical vision is attuned to the imaginative possibilities of chance. More poignantly than Poe's methodological explorations, Melville's moral and epistemological provocations, Douglass's political deployments, and Thoreau's naturalist studies, Dickinson wonders how it feels to experience chance.

What is it like to have one's naked soul scalped? To break through a plank in reason? To be arrested by a sunset or a bird taking flight? Dickinson's poems are full of surprises—from formal inventions that violate expectations of totality, syntax, and sense, to gender assertions that belie the conservative surface of her life, to antinomian revelations for which no believer or doubter can fully prepare, to moments when perceptual and rational faculties are all of a sudden overwhelmed. Denise Levertov has said, "I think that anyone who cares for the work of Emily Dickinson at all, cares for the experience of surprise," a point Dickinson herself suggested when she compared the feeling of poetry to having the top of her head taken off.[2] It is not simply that Dickinson is technically innovative, thematically iconoclastic, or dialectically inclined. More meta-critically, she enacts a theory of surprise—one that shows how experience leads to skepticism (not confidence), how surprise might (or might not) be poetically rendered, and how it feels to abandon one's self to chance (and the moments that frame its appearance).

Dickinson, of course, is hardly alone in associating poetry with surprise. From Sidney and Pope to Wordsworth and Eliot, poets have praised the delightful, unexpected, spontaneous, and shocking effects of their craft; while symbolists, Dadaists, and Language poets take chance as both a subject and a source for creative expression. Literary scholars have begun to study what Philip Fisher has called "an aesthetics of surprise" that goes beyond familiar versions of the sublime to include a family of affective responses such as astonishment, estrangement, and wonder. For Fisher, surprise accompanies extraordinary ascensions toward knowledge in both aesthetic and scientific domains. It is an affect of skepticism in that the subject simultaneously feels the power and provisionality of intimated truths. With a similar epistemological comportment and more focus on Dickinson's historical moment, Christopher Miller has reconstructed a discourse of surprise drawn from Addison, Burke, Adam Smith, Samuel Johnson, and most fully elaborated by British romantics, who (in Miller's words) find in surprise "a peculiar mixture of knowing and not-knowing." With special emphasis on romanticism,

Fisher and Miller forge connections between uncertainty, affect, and aesthetics. Yet if romanticism valorizes the unpredictability of chaos, spontaneity, free play, and the sublime, Dickinson's work may be best understood as a post-romantic reaction against such formations.[3] As sensitive as she is to post-Cartesian doubts and the multilayered psychology of selves behind selves, Dickinson often proceeds with an empirical skepticism less grounded in romantic philosophies of the mind and more interested in surprise as an affective correlative of chance. Dickinson recognizes that surprise is conditioned by expectations imperfectly inferred from repetitious experiences as her poetry theoretically sketches and poetically exploits what she calls "not precisely knowing/And not precisely knowing not."[4]

ROMANTIC EMBARRASSMENTS

To think of Dickinson as an empirical skeptic influenced by the rise of chance and probability is to distance her from romantic philosophical contexts that often dominate Dickinson criticism. Nothing in Dickinson has received more attention than what she calls "the Outer" and "the Inner." From a psycho-biographical perspective, this dualism can point to tensions between sociality and solitude, convention and rebellion, appearance and emotional reality, while cultural critics find analogs in gender constructions, domestic space, privacy, and publication concerns. Though by no means incompatible with such interests, epistemologically inclined approaches to Dickinson usually view the Outer and the Inner in terms of romanticism's division and potential synthesis of self and other, mind and body, artistic imagination and nature. Early critics describe a stubborn split between Dickinson's interior and exterior worlds, analogous though they may be, making her a poet of radical subjectivity and skeptical alienation—accounts overdetermined, as Virginia Jackson has argued, by the "lyricization" of poetry and literary criticism during the nineteenth and twentieth centuries.[5] More recent studies of Dickinson's epistemology track a more dialectical figure who encounters the object world with committed, if provisional, realism—a shift that accords with the increasing emphases on Dickinson's cultural contexts and the materiality of her manuscripts.[6] In disentangling American literature in general from romantic philosophical traditions, Elisa New argues that Dickinson participates in an anti-idealist and even anti-theoretical tradition: "Perceptual rather than conceptual, tending to lyrical rather than narrative or philosophical expression, the literature of experience achieves not an explanation of its own effects (poetics) but a closer relation with affect itself."[7] What follows only partly concurs, for while Dickinson is indeed a poet of experience who remains wary of transcendental idealism (including that of Emerson), her poetry does not divorce perceptions from conceptions, lyricism from philosophy, and explanation from affect. Dickinson's skepticism can be productively associated with Cartesian problematics, but the romantic play of Inner and Outer does not adequately account for a recurring empiricism that entails intensely theorized concepts of chance.

Dickinson's reading in romanticism can be difficult to source, though we know that Keats and Carlyle were favorites and that she knew something of Goethe, Coleridge, Wordsworth, De Quincey, Emerson, and Thoreau. The erstwhile transcendentalist Higginson provided an additional conduit to romantic philosophy, as did occasional references in the novels, periodicals, and newspapers that Dickinson read.[8] Dickinson's poems are sometimes powerfully shaped by subject/object negotiations, as indicated by "The Outer—from the Inner" (1862; F450), a seemingly archetypal work of romantic skepticism:

> The Outer—from the Inner
> Derives it's magnitude—
> 'Tis Duke, or Dwarf, according
> As is the central mood
>
> The fine—unvarying Axis
> That regulates the Wheel—
> Though Spokes—spin—more conspicuous
> And fling a dust—the while.
>
> The Inner—paints the Outer—
> The Brush without the Hand—
> It's Picture publishes—precise—
> As is the inner Brand—
>
> On fine—Arterial Canvas—
> A Cheek—perchance a Brow—
> The Star's whole secret—in the Lake—
> Eyes were not meant to know.

Opening with post-Kantian subjectivity, the first three stanzas of "The Outer—from the Inner" hold romantic instabilities in check: shifty perceptions are governed by a "central mood"; subjective dizziness indicates an "unvarying Axis"; the Inner sloppily, superficially "paints" the Outer without entirely obscuring a more essential "Brand."[9] Symbolically fluid and conceptually repetitive, the first three stanzas' robust sense of personal identity both generates and mitigates perceptual doubt, a dynamic driving much romantic writing, including that of Emerson.

Mood, axis, and painting are all main tropes in Emerson's essay "Experience" (1844): "Life is a train of moods"; "We must . . . possess our axis more firmly"; we look through "many-colored lenses which paint the world their own hue." "Experience" can be associated with the "noble doubt" of *Nature* as to "whether nature outwardly exists," though less noticed is that when Emerson struggles with skepticism, he struggles with both illusion *and* chance, subjectivity *and* causality, even if the former topics hold more sway over the rhythms of his thought.[10] "Experience" begins with a lack of discernible causal order as we suddenly find ourselves on a set of stairs without knowing where they come from or lead. Emerson finds the resources to celebrate his sense that "Life is a series of surprises," though he also criticizes classical skeptics who turn "exalted Chance into a divinity." Moving from dialectics toward synthesis, Emerson eventually accepts aleatory experience ("I worship with wonder the great Fortune") but only after refiguring Chance as a more benevolent, recuperative deity worthy of human devotion. "Experience" ends with tentative faith in a teleological, if presently mysterious, design: surely we will witness the unification of outer reality and inner thought; surely, to invoke the aesthetic terms of Kant, what appears to be purposeless will turn out to be purposive insofar as the world exists to realize the unification of genius and power. As a kind of jeremiad for the skeptically wayward, "Experience" begins with a conspicuous lack of design and ends with a promise of visible order rendered in totalizing rhetoric. As in "Self-Reliance," "Montaigne," and "Fate," Emerson begins by taking chance seriously before managing to move past its most radical implications.[11]

Like "Experience," "The Outer—from the Inner" swings between order and chaos, suggesting that Dickinson can be taken as a philosopher of moods in an Emersonian tradition. Yet again the gravitation of Concord's Sage seems to pull all of his New England contemporaries toward him, though as scholars have increasingly pointed out since the disestablishment of the American Renaissance, we should be wary of placing Dickinson too comfortably in a transcendentalist orbit.[12] Whereas "Experience" ends by declaring a unilateral truce with a skepticism it cannot vanquish, "The Outer—from the Inner" veers from its stabilized subjectivity toward a recalcitrant, unpredictable object world that belies any promise of unity. If the generic nouns of Dickinson's first three stanzas conjure an interior symbology of ideas, "Brand" and the only run-on stanza in the poem introduce (literally as an afterthought) a more somatic referent in "Arterial Canvas"—skin. Fittingly, this move toward the boundary between Inner and Outer comes at the moment Dickinson describes a blush, for surprise can be a kind of intellectual embarrassment, one way to feel when we recognize that our conceptions are insufficiently in touch with reality. Or, as Hume put it when encountering perceptual skepticism after Descartes, "[H]ere philosophy finds herself extremely embarrassed."[13] The inadequate thought in "The Outer—from the Inner" is its initial assertions of an imperial romantic subjectivity. As much as consciousness might like to think itself in concert with the universe, and as much as the inner conceives of itself as a regulating axis or determining mood, surprise registers on the exterior blushing face as well as in the incommensurate mind, on both the feeling, feminine, undisciplined "Cheek" and even "perchance" on the rationalist "Brow." Whereas the lack of a thesis statement in "Experience" introduces a bewilderment that moves fitfully toward self-trust, the early axiomatic confidence of "The Outer—from the Inner" sets the stage for an epistemological failure at which the poem under Dickinson's knowing hand is self-conscious enough to blush.

What to make of a blush is no simple question and helps to measure the connection and distance between romantic and empirical skepticism. As Christopher Ricks has described it, blushing can figure romantic philosophical interests in the interplay of body and mind, innocence and knowledge, solipsism and intersubjectivity. This is especially true for Keats, who despite his reputation for sensuality tends to thematize blushing in psychological terms. Just as Schiller in *On Naïve and Sentimental Poetry* (1795) describes the knower as being "startled at himself," and just as Wordsworth in "Surprised by Joy" (1812) reacts to his own emotional states by diving deeper into self-reflection, Keats's embarrassments (quoting Ricks) stem from an "intense self-awareness and a richly co-operative creative subconscious."[14] Similarly, "The Outer—from the Inner" can be taken to enact a concept of "unconscious production" passed from Fichte and Schelling to Coleridge and Emerson: because post-Kantian subjects unknowingly participate in the construction of the object world, they come to recognize their creative force only in startling moments of synthesis.[15] Yet for all their efforts to achieve a kind of oneness that renders subjects and objects commensurate, romanticism ultimately subordinates the Outer to the Inner as surprise is both experienced in and instigated by the mind under the aegis of philosophical idealism.

As animating as this romantic epistemology can be, it is hardly the only approach to surprise. Not unlike modern neuroscientists who measure startle reflexes in terms of facial expressions, blinking, and neural activity, nineteenth-century scientists studied blushing and embarrassment from inexact empirical perspectives.[16] In *The Physiology or Mechanism of Blushing* (1839), Thomas Burgess argued that God intended "arterial blood" to "paint" the face so as to encourage sympathy between humans, and he wrote in a chapter titled "The Poetry of Blushing," "[S]uch adaptation and harmony of arrangement as here evinced, could never be the effect of *chance*; on the contrary, in every link of the chain which combines all the organs engaged in the production of [blushing], there is a palpable evidence of *Design*." A frequently reprinted article in the antebellum press reinforced (and actually predated) Burgess's book, concluding, "A single blush should put the infidel to shame, and prove to him the absurdity of his blind doctrine of chance." Nonetheless, Darwin in *The Expression of the Emotions in Man and Animal* (1872) denied such providential interpretation, indicating how blushing continued to be seen as an embodiment of aleatory experience—a somatic sign of our susceptibility to chance and surprise, and a potential threat requiring rational explanation or at least containment within social and narrative structures.[17]

Jane Austen's treatments of blushing are exemplary, for although she enacts (in Miller's words) "a phenomenology of surprise," surprise in her novels remains a temporary condition on the way toward more or less unified endings characterized by comprehensive knowledge. The logician Richard Whately referred to Austen's probabilities when reviewing *Northanger Abbey* (1803, 1817) and *Persuasion* (1817): "[Their] compactness of plan and unity of action . . . is generally produced by a sacrifice of probability: yet they have little or nothing that is not probable."[18] Here Whately marvels at Austen's ability to produce surprise without spoiling verisimilitude or totality. With a repetition indicating her meta-critical awareness, Austen's novels are full of blushes and embarrassments that show how difficult it is for characters to manage chance, even as Austen herself in her plots and comments carefully calibrates probabilities. The young Catherine Morland of *Northanger Abbey* frequently colors when her probabilistic reasoning proves false, showing her inability to manage "the terrors of expectation" dramatized in Dickinson's *Northanger Abbey*–inspired poem, "One need not be a Chamber—to be Haunted" (1862; F407).[19]

By contrast, the older Anne Elliot of *Persuasion* tends to blush when her most desired expectations come to pass. Color is a sign of Anne's self-consciousness and passion, but it also shows how she has painfully learned that probabilistic thinking is risky, most tragically in her prudent but ultimately regrettable rejection of Captain Wentworth's youthful courtship. Marking the difference between *Northanger Abbey*'s degrees of belief about single instances and *Persuasion*'s attention to repeated experience, Anne is a more mature, chastened fallibilist who bears the skeptical burden of expecting the unexpected, a condition that Dickinson describes in "Wonder—is not precisely knowing" (a poem to which we will return). Like George Eliot (whom Dickinson read avidly) and Henry James (who follows Eliot in linking gambling, marriage, the "calculation of chance," and the "calculation of probabilities"), Austen never forgets that courtship entails at some stage what she calls in *Pride and Prejudice* (1813) "determining probabilities."[20] Austen displays through her characters' blushing the affective power of chance, and yet like Emerson and Burgess, she ultimately domesticates chance within designs that place inner states and outer realities in happy, unembarrassed union. Readers close her books with the satisfying feeling that future surprises are not looming.

For anyone hoping for similar closure in "The Outer—from the Inner," embarrassment only becomes more acute in the poem's final lines. Stopping with "Brand" would make for an elegantly figured if mundane account of subjectivism, while ending with "Brow" might bring a romantic synthesis tempered only by the unsettling possibilities of "perchance." Most challenging, however, are the actual final two lines, which remain as tricky as their syntax: "The Star's whole secret—in the Lake—/Eyes were not meant to know." That what seems the object ("secret") and subject ("Eyes") can be both "in the Lake" may conjure romantic oneness—the achievement of some absolute "whole," as when Thoreau goes fishing in the sky. Yet the claim that "Eyes" (and, of course, I's) are "not meant to know" demands more provisional interpretation in that it is unclear who does not intend eyes to know, whether the eyes do in fact know, and what such knowledge might consist of. As in "The Brain—is wider than the Sky" (1863; F598), seemingly legible formulations of romantic epistemology finally collapse into confusing contingencies.

This is not because Dickinson is incapable or uninterested in making philosophical sense. Allen Tate was right that she conflates emotion and reason, but he was wrong in paying what was already in 1936 a familiar backhanded compliment: "[Dickinson] cannot reason at all. She can only *see*."[21] Taking up Majorie Perloff's point that literary theorists have neglected Dickinson, scholars are increasingly insisting that the limitations of reason in her poems do not represent a lack of logic or vision so much as a postmetaphysical stance.[22] The attitude toward romanticism in "The Outer—from the Inner" is one of unending embarrassment—of feeling conspicuous (like a duke or dwarf), published, branded, and eyed at the moment of one's epistemological inadequacy. In some Dickinson poems, precipitants of surprise can be named—an Indian summer with an actual date, a real bullet that clipped a real person. More often, as in "The lovely flowers embarrass me" (1864; F808) and "His Cheek is his Biographer" (1879; F1499), external coordinates for surprise remain unidentified and so make the speaker's critical inadequacy our own. What is the "whole secret," where is the "Lake," and who are the "Eyes" and the "Star"?

Dickinson is among other things a poet of ideas, but such unanswerable questions show her discomfort as such, for as much as some of her poems occupy transcendental or idealist perspectives, their self-consciously displayed inability to know nature exposes the limits of a romantic subjectivity that undervalues the material world. To follow New's general line of argument, the ending of "The Outer—from the Inner" is instructively ungrounded, and the passive phrasing of the poem's first line purposefully makes the external object the subject of the sentence, grammatically signaling that the Outer comes first, despite the Inner's belated assertions of primacy. To take the Inner as the axis of the object world is to risk a kind of solipsism. Emerson recognizes this danger in "Experience," for when he writes that he cannot feel his son's death, his refusal to express shame or embarrassment about this lack displays not only the privative depths of his loss but also his detachment from his audience. The solipsist has no one to be embarrassed in front of, but a subject surprised by the outside world has every reason to blush. In this way, "The Outer—from the Inner" describes the recoil of a not entirely knowable reality, though its post-romanticism remains a negative one, offering no alternative to the Cartesian doubts that slight the surprising presence of nature.

Similar claims can be made about other Dickinson poems written prior to 1866, including "The Brain—is wider than the Sky," "Heaven is so far of the Mind" (1862; F413), "I never saw a Moor" (1864; F800), "Soto! Explore thyself!" (1864; F814), and "Perception of an Object costs" (1865; F1103). Given the sheer quantity and valences of Dickinson's poems, it is probably impossible to prove that her imagination generally moves from negative post-romantic critiques toward a more positive empirical skepticism. Yet it may matter that 13.8 percent of Dickinson's pre-1866 poems begin with some variant of the first-person singular, after which the percentage drops to a mere 5.3 percent.[23] Higginson would surely resent such measures, and numbers obviously can tell us only so much about Dickinson's art. But Dickinson herself increasingly faced the problem of inferring general laws from multitudinous experiences, suggesting that her interests in romantic subjectivity give way to a more empirical outlook.

Comparing "To hear an Oriole sing" (1862; F402) with "Experiment to me" (1865; F1081) can help to trace the difference. Like the first three stanzas of "The Outer—from the Inner," "To hear an Oriole sing" flirts with romantic doubt: the singing one hears may neither correlate with an external "Bird" nor bridge inter-subjective gaps among the "Crowd." A reader can tire of such skeptical possibilities when the poem repeats that the "Ear" "Attireth" what it "hear[s]." And when "The Skeptic" arrives to inform the naïve positivist that the "Tune" is not in the "Tree" but "In Thee!,'" we might feel, as in most philosophical dialogues, that the conclusion has been overdetermined for some time. Unless the lesson of the romantic Skeptic ironically disproves itself, for—dramatically speaking—the Skeptic appears in the object world to announce that the object world does not exist: *Listen to me! You cannot trust what you're hearing!* From a Cavellian perspective, solipsism feels counter-intuitive because it is a false position. Or to paraphrase "Experience," "To hear an Oriole sing" treats romantic skeptics as if they were real—perhaps they are. Whatever the case, the poem dwells on paradoxes of romantic subjectivity without offering alternative ways of knowing what are really in the trees around us.

"Experiment to me" sketches a more positive approach without recurring to naïve positivism. The first line of the poem begins with familiar romantic skepticism, worrying whether things in a "Tree" are actually real or mere "Figure[s]." But whereas "To hear an Oriole sing" ends with a subtle, provisional acknowledgment of the Outer, "Experiment to me" assumes through most of its course the existence of other objects, which are not propositions to be weighed but, rather, constitute the ground of the poem itself. We move quickly, even impatiently, past Cartesian doubt, for if nuts at the start may be only Figures, the speaker shares with other "Squirrels" a common desire for "meat." Uncertainty certainly exists—"every one" of the nuts "Equally Plausibly" has a "Kernel" of truth—but rather than bandy untestable theses with an untestable Skeptic, the poem describes a more practical method involving repeated experiments and probabilistic thinking within a community of inquirers. Under the real imperatives of hunger, the best way to get meat is to crack a nut and move on to the next plausible one. Good advice for squirrels, empiricists, and readers embarrassed by the riches of over 1,700 Dickinson poems.

A poem from 1878 can stand as a final example of how one might find in Dickinson's work an unevenly increasing resistance to romantic skepticism:

> Whoever disenchants
> A single Human soul
> By failure or irreverence
> Is guilty of the whole—
>
> As guileless as a Bird
> As graphic as a Star
> Till the suggestion sinister
> Things are not what they are— (F1475)

"[S]oul," "guilty," and the sin in "sinister" can insist on the poem's Christian bearing, though the final tautology indicates that any interpretation is susceptible to its own initial beliefs. The explicitness of the poem's self-supporting logic might turn us from biblical to more philosophical falls. The opening, implicit praise of enchantment potentially sets the poem against positivism, and if the last word of the poem were "seem," readers might trace a familiar descent into romantic uncertainty. But to suffer the suggestion that "Things are not what they are" is not nobly to bear an epistemological doubt that tragically unsettles relations between Outer and Inner: it is simply to be wrong. Real truth is simply what it is, the poem concludes, making counterintuitive romantic skepticism, not positivist realism, that which disenchants. In this reading, premised as it is on a post-romantic, realist suppression of seeming, romantics with their urge for synthesis are "guilty of the whole," and the "failure or irreverence" applies to idealists insufficiently convinced of things as they are. The epistemology of "Whoever Disenchants" is as tautological as Scottish realism insofar as untestable skeptical arguments leave us no choice but to take our perceptions as self-evident. The ending of the poem can even paraphrase *Walden—Talk of romantic subjectivity! ye disenchant the earth*—inviting readers to ask how better to appreciate the actual wonders of this world. As if echoing Thoreau again, Dickinson wrote to her sister-in-law Susan Gilbert Dickinson sometime around 1870, "Oh Matchless Earth—We underrate the chance to dwell in Thee."[24]

CHANCES FOR HEAVEN

From Kant's shocking sublime and more genial free play of the imagination, to the vaunting estrangement of Novalis and the Schlegels, to Fichte and Schelling's unconscious productions, to Schiller and Goethe's falls into knowledge, to the affective epiphanies of Coleridge and Wordsworth that show nature to be suddenly alien or intimate, romanticism stages surprising encounters between subjects and the object world, oftentimes— as happens in "Experience"—disrupting causal chains. Romantics famously depart from positivist epistemologies and mechanistic logic, and yet the philosophical approaches of transatlantic romanticism, so invested in subject-object relations, are not much interested in chance as a subject of inquiry, except to valorize its counter-Enlightenment energies and recommend an openness to aleatory experience, even while envisioning totalizing designs in which chance is only nominal. With the exception of De Quincey and (by some taxonomies) Austen, the management of chance is not particularly inspiring for most British romantics, who—as Catherine Gallagher and Mary Poovey argue—share affinities with emerging probabilistic sciences but still tend to resist probabilistic thinking and the spread of quantification.[25] Dickinson is hardly a booster of probabilism, but compared to romantics across the Atlantic and others closer to Concord, she more seriously engages the logic of chance, especially as it relates to tensions between science and faith. Like Melville, Dickinson dramatizes the threat chance poses to Christianity, even as she suspends her judgment regarding the possibilities of absolute chance.

Like most educated Americans of her day, Dickinson had ample opportunity to engage the probabilistic revolution in theoretical terms. Women across the nineteenth century were generally considered intellectually unsuited for the abstract rigors of mathematics, and the calculation of chances in political economy, gaming, and business remained male-coded pursuits. That said, Benjamin Franklin, Benjamin Rush, and Noah Webster advocated basic arithmetical education for American women, and Emma Willard and Catherine Beecher in the early 1820s began teaching female students higher branches of mathematics, though they justified their efforts on the conventional grounds that mathematics strengthened the character and minds of young women destined to be teachers and mothers, not scientists. If a 1799 article joked about establishing a girls' school for whist that would instruct young women in the doctrine of chances, by mid-century Caroline Herschel, Maria Agnesi, and Maria Mitchell were recognized for their mathematical accomplishments. By the 1870s, even conservative magazines praised the life of the mathematician and astronomer Mary Somerville, who (as articles repeatedly pointed out) mastered Laplace's *Philosophical Essay on Probabilities* on her own.[26]

There is no evidence that Dickinson studied probability theory in any formal sense, though some of her poems employ mathematical concepts, and she was steeped in the empirical methods of Scottish Common Sense and Baconian science.[27] Among writers who explore chance and probability, Dickinson at various points in her life read or had immediate access to Hume, Franklin, De Quincey, Dickens, Thoreau, Ruskin, and George Eliot, while among the magazines to which her family subscribed, *Harper's*, *Scribner's*, and *The Atlantic* discussed the contributions of Quetelet, Darwin, Francis Galton, and probabilistic science in general. These magazines referred to the doctrine of chances in regard to miracles, telepathy, Confederate vessels running the Union blockade, and the authorship of plays attributed to Shakespeare. Dickinson would have been especially interested in commentaries on aesthetics and chance: how the history of art attests to the creative power of accidents; how romantic views of inspiration "substituted chance for law in the poetic art"; and how novels should follow "the law of chances" (a logic frequently invoked in *Atlantic* reviews). Also in *The Atlantic*, an 1863 critique of Buckle objected to both the chanciness and the determinism of the law of large numbers, while "The Impossibility of Chance" (1868) denied both chance and free will by appealing to the iron-linked causal chains of associationist psychology and natural theology. A generation after Poe, Thoreau, Douglass, and Melville, the probabilistic revolution had become more visible, though by no means entirely accepted.[28]

An untitled *Scribner's* piece from 1872 indicates how deeply probabilistic thinking was altering nineteenth-century life. Offering a self-consciously old-fashioned perspective, a speaker recalls the joys of surprising summer showers while lamenting modern weather forecasting and its "Law of Periodicity." Weather prediction in the mid-nineteenth century had quickly become a sophisticated quantitative science, spurred by frequentist methods, telegraph networks, and extended data collecting efforts by Britain's Meteorological Office (founded in 1854), the Smithsonian Institute (which coordinated weather observations in America beginning in 1849), and Matthew Fontaine Maury (who in the mid-1850s extended his oceanographic studies to land-based meteorology). Hawthorne's "A Visit to the Clerk of the Weather" (1836) and Melville's "Lightning-Rod Man" exploit the differences between mythic and probabilistic views of weather (the former tale provoking an 1859 article titled "Statistics of Science" to complain about Hawthorne's frivolity; the later commencing with a celebration of unpredictability: "What grand irregular thunder"). Less ironic than Hawthorne and Melville, but sharing their doubts about the science of forecasting, the author of the *Scribner's* piece pejoratively compares modern meteorology to canned vegetables, steamboats, safety pins, parlor skates, and Huxley's protoplasm. Nonetheless, he concludes, "Maybe to somebody—far off—the summer rain is dearer because Old Probabilities, in that formal scientific way of his, said that it was coming." "Old Probabilities" may seek to mythologize the increasing quantification of the weather, though it also shows how familiar the management of chance had become in some quarters by 1872. The author's thoughts on the reaction of someone "far off" suggests how probabilistic methods and the technologies they entail sped the rise of mass culture and imagined communities. Yet just as advances in weather forecasting actually exposed the aleatory limits of science to many nineteenth-century observers, the *Scribner's* article recognizes the potential wonders of probabilistic expectation, even while equating the new sciences of chance with modern disenchantment.[29]

Scholars have not regarded chance as a crucial concept or word for Dickinson, though it appears over twenty times in her verse, including a poem from 1875 that indicates her acquaintance with Old Probabilities:

> Luck is not chance—
> It's Toil—
> Fortune's expensive smile
> Is earned—
> The Father of the Mine
> Is that old fashioned Coin
> We spurned— (F1360)

The careful distinctions of this poem initially deny and then finally intimate the untamable power of chance. As in most nineteenth-century accounts of probability theory (and confident ads for modern-day investment services), "chance" is first presented as nominal when "Luck" is associated with "Toil," emphasizing how hard work coupled with experience put aleatory uncertainty under human control. Like articles from Dickinson's day defending financial speculation, "earned" vindicates under the labor theory of value those who profit from the management of chance. Quickly though, "Father" potentially cuts short any rational overreaching by gesturing toward a deeper causation. It is a seeming moment of Christian reassurance: behind chance, luck, and even human toil resides an omnipotent designer. Elsewhere, Dickinson more clearly exposes the teleological inclinations of such claims, as suggested in an earlier poem that ends, "To what delicious Accident/Does finest Glory fit!" (1873; F1285)—a potentially subversive point about providential overdetermination also available in "Luck is not chance." That the "old fashioned" Father of "Luck is not chance" is "spurned" by acquisitive moderns might suggest that Dickinson anticipates Weber's essay on the Protestant ethic. And when Father is equated with "Coin," we might move further toward cultural criticism ("In God We Trust" was first put on American specie during the Civil War) or semiotic heterodoxy (God as signifier, an economy governing other Dickinson poems). Yet given the first line of "Luck is not chance," it is difficult not to attribute to Coin some aleatory force that undermines the poem's opening axiom that chance simply does not exist. If coins invoke the causal indeterminacies of skepticism (as in Emerson's "Montaigne" and Montaigne's famous medallion inscribed with "What do I know?"), then what is speciously spurned at the end of Dickinson's poem is a robust version of chance—one that probabilistic toil cannot master, and one more appropriately associated with a feminine, pre-Christian "Fortune" than with a masculine, law-giving Father.

"Luck is not chance" is not one of Dickinson's best poems. It does not move beyond philosophical sophistication toward the affective comportments such sophistication might require, and its most interesting formal gambit is the juxtaposition of its first two fragmented lines on chance with the more unified fifth line occasioned by "Father," ironic though such unity may be. The poem does present Dickinson's signature challenge by balancing seemingly irreconcilable readings, in this case pitting the possibilities of chance against not only Christian cosmology but also romantic recuperations of such (if indeed "The Father of the Mine" echoes "The Child is Father of the Man" in Wordsworth's paean to continual surprise under the argument from design). The modernity of British romanticism need not preclude what Wordsworth in his poem calls "natural piety," but unlike "My heart leaps up when I behold" (1807), "Luck is not chance" is not much interested in romantic subjectivity, nor does it pay unambiguous tribute to natural theology.[30] Godly order and absolute chance are neither confirmed nor denied by Dickinson's linking of Father and Coin, even as the poem conspicuously conflates two tropes that represent increasingly antagonistic worldviews.

We know that frictions between faith and science drive Dickinson's imagination. For most critics, Dickinson tries with varying degrees of success to reconcile the two under the argument from design, though Nina Baym has recently made the more aggressive argument that Dickinson's "Scientific Skepticism" rejects conventional syntheses of theism and science. Roger Lundin argues more provisionally that, especially after Darwin and the Civil War, Dickinson began questioning the argument from design, a claim supported by many Dickinson poems that simultaneously announce and challenge God's plan in tonal registers that run from glee and reverence to irony, pleading, and anger (a gamut brilliantly traversed in her early poem, "Bring me the sunset in a cup"

[1860; F140]). Lundin rightfully regards Dickinson's poems on natural theology as experimental and diverse, but neither his brief mention of chance nor Baym's welcome attention to differences between inference and proof addresses the centrality of chance in Dickinson's meditations on science and God.[31]

In addition to Dickinson's reading in canonical literature and print culture, Edward Hitchcock no doubt shaped her approach to chance and probability. Unlike many defenders of natural theology, Hitchcock was neither a minister with a smattering of science nor a scientist hoping to justify his or her work. He left his post as a Congregational minister to study chemistry with the prestigious Benjamin Silliman before becoming president of Amherst College, where his views governed Dickinson's curricula at Amherst Academy and Mount Holyoke Female Seminary, including readings from Butler's *Analogy*, Paley's *Natural Theology*, and Archibald Alexander's *The Evidences of Christianity* (1831). As suggested by a Dickinson poem that remembers him as "The Scientist of Faith" (1872; F1261), Hitchcock championed God's rational government, going so far as to call Ecclesiastes' quote on time and chance an example of "blank atheism." More poetically, Hitchcock gave generic praise to the astronomer who finds order in the stars:

> Where others see a spark, he sees a sun;
> Where wild confusion, he sweet harmony,
> And where all seems by chance, he sees a God—
> A God how great, how mighty, and how good!

This poem is thoroughly conventional in content and form, but as forthrightly as Hitchcock denied absolute chance, he remained an empirical, probabilistic thinker who acknowledged the fallibility of science.[32]

Hitchcock's probabilism tempered his religious orthodoxy, as shown in his 1855 introduction to Whewell's *The Plurality of Worlds* (1854), a controversial book that weighed the chances of extraterrestrial life by estimating the number of planets and stars, as well as the distances between them. Whewell framed his analysis by asking whether inhabitable worlds were "probable or improbable," ultimately arguing that it is likely to the point of moral certainty that extraterrestrial life does not exist. Hitchcock shared both Whewell's probabilistic outlook and his enthusiasm for the argument from design, but his introduction maintains that one cannot rule out the extraordinary chance that other inhabitable planets might exist. This, despite the fact that a plurality of worlds was often taken to embarrass Christian cosmology: Why does Genesis not mention multiple worlds? Did God send saviors to them, too? Will extraterrestrial and earthly souls mingle in the afterlife? Are extraterrestrials also made in the image of God? As practiced by Hitchcock, however, probabilistic thinking encouraged religious wonder, including the off chance that angels live in outer space, of which Hitchcock asked hopefully, "[Is] there not a probability?" Hitchcock's theism is thoroughly teleological, but his introduction to *The Plurality of Worlds* verges toward empirical skepticism insofar as his methods are inductive, fallibilist, and self-consciously open to outré probabilities, even angels of the odd, so much so that one might wonder if anything can be morally certain.[33]

Like Hitchcock, Dickinson recognizes the infinite possibilities of probabilism, though she more daringly faces not just the bounds of human knowledge but also the potential of an absolute chance beyond the reach of science. "'Arcturus' is his other name" (1859, F117) seems a standard romantic critique of empiricism, though the tone is more winsome and the depictions of natural science more nuanced than what romantic texts typically achieve. The poem begins with officious empiricists disenchanting nature, recalling Carlyle's complaint in *Sartor Resartus* (1834) that "Science" intends to "destroy Wonder" and set "Mensuration and Numeration" in its stead.[34] When the poem calls "'Heaven'" a "'Zenith'" to be "mapped, and charted, too!" it may be chiding Hitchcockian efforts to locate angels astronomically; and when Dickinson turns to magnetic drift ("if the 'poles' should frisk about"), she identifies the random playfulness of supposedly fixed laws. Dickinson further questions scientific prediction in "Sunset at Night—is natural" (1862, F427):

> Eclipses be—predicted—
> And Science bows them in—
> But do One face us suddenly—
> Jehovah's Watch—is wrong—

Turning Paley's watchmaker analogy against natural theology, and perhaps recalling Hume's claim that future sunrises are mere probabilities, Dickinson notes that natural laws can always be undone by sudden anomalies. She repeats this point in "Meeting by Accident" (1882; F1578), a poem that sets chance against "design" and "Destiny" by describing an extraordinary "error" that only happens once a "Century," so infrequently that such meetings cannot be predicted by frequentist methods. All three of these poems have elements of embarrassed surprise: in "'Arcturus,'" the soul entering an ever-changing heaven finds herself unfashionably dressed; in "Eclipses," the unexpected eclipse is a faux pas that violates science's bowing protocols; and "Meeting by Accident" suggests the unpredictable trials of courtship as in Austen, Eliot, and Henry James. Beyond such embarrassment lurks Dickinson's resentment—disappointment with an inconstant heaven, chagrin at God's fallibility, bitterness that life's pleasant accidents are so niggardly rare.

For Butler, Paley, Hitchcock, and seemingly every explicator of the argument from design (including Dickinson's beloved Charles Wadsworth), chance is simply not a living option, natural observations are overdetermined, and appropriate feelings toward God's order fall somewhere within the relatively narrow bounds of resignation and reverence, satisfaction and wonder. Dickinson transgresses such limits in accusatory poems such as "To interrupt His Yellow Plan" (1863; F622). Here a mandarin God oversees the universe on the grand scale of "Astronomy," while humans below are subjected to "The Caprices of the Atmosphere," which sounds like weather until "Snow" becomes "Balls" and then "Bomb[s]," instruments of sudden death that Old Probabilities cannot entirely predict and that remain brutally hard for a Christian to justify in the midst of the Civil War. While theorists of chance asserted providential plans in which order reigns across large numbers, Dickinson insists on the painful, shabby experience of living through an inscrutable plot.

Dickinson's struggles with theodicy and providence are legion and can lead her speakers from abject acceptance to spiteful belief to the very graveside of God. Dickinson may have even read or heard recited Jean Paul Richter's "Speech of Christ" (1845), translated in 1847 by Carlyle (whose portrait hung in Dickinson's bedroom). Richter describes a nightmare about God's death and the grief of an orphaned Jesus:

> [Christ] lifted up his eyes to the Nothingness and to the empty Immensity, and said, 'Frozen, dumb Nothingness! cold, eternal Necessity! insane Chance! knew ye what is beneath you? When will ye destroy the building and me? Chance! knowest thou thyself when with hurricanes thou wilt march through the snow-storm of stars and extinguish one sun after the other?

Critics have speculated about affinities between Dickinson and Richter's text, though even at moments of her highest infidelity, Dickinson never reaches such rhetorical hysteria.³⁵ She certainly condemns God's fumbling management, be He burglar, banker, or father, and she laments a deity whose hand is amputated or whose person is nowhere to be found, leaving seekers behind in an existential crisis as bleak and flattened as a disc of snow. Chance can be what takes God's place, and the nineteenth century can call it atheism. Thomas Hardy, like Ahab, can even go so far as to prefer the known evils of a malevolent God to the uncertain happenstances of "Crass Casualty" and "dicing Time."³⁶

But if the possibilities of chance are nearly unbearable for some Christians, they can also be for Dickinson wonderful, as in the "Miscellaneous Enterprise" and "purposeless" sporting of a Butterfly that, as far as the speaker can tell, enchants "Without Design" (1863, F610). Reiterating the phrase, "Four Trees—opon a solitary Acre" (1863; F778) conveys the minimalist, solemn majesty of a world "Without Design." And chance also offers open-ended hope, as when Dickinson wrote in an 1882 fragment note to her sister-in-law Susan, "A fresh Morning of Life with it's [sic] impregnable chances." Dickinson often associates chance with danger (variants to three of her poems interchange "chance" and "risk"), but like Douglass, she sometimes uses chance as a synonym for opportunity.³⁷ "Impossibility, like Wine" (1865; F939) points to chance's range of meaning by associating "Chance's faintest tincture" with both "Enchantment" and "Doom." Which is to say that, for Dickinson, the possibilities of chance do not necessarily lead toward a privative nightmare of post-Christian modernity. As in "Luck is not chance," aleatory experience severely complicates Christian cosmology, but while Dickinson dismisses easy arguments from design, her serious considerations of chance do not foreclose the potential of providence. When describing the antinomian playfulness of a jay in "No Brigadier throughout the Year" (1883; F1596), Dickinson's manuscripts include three alternatives to the line, "His Future—a Dispute": "His Chances a Redoubt," "His Doctrines a Redoubt"; and "His Dogmas a Redoubt." Who knows what aural preferences Dickinson weighed, but her equanimity toward Chance, Doctrine, and Dogma suggests an extraordinary suspension of judgment, an open-mindedness about the impregnability of doubt and the need to doubt again.

As with natural theology, eschatology for Dickinson and her culture represented a point of potential conflict between faith and the sciences of chance, especially in light of Matthew's warnings that the gate is strait, the way is narrow, and many are called but few chosen. An anxious soul on the verge of exhausting self-scrutiny might well wonder in an age of rising probabilism, *So exactly how many, and how few?* That some ministers argued against approaching salvation as a quantitative concern indicates that at least some Christians of the time were tempted to estimate their estates in this way. The urge to calculate upon one's salvation is evident as early as the Middle Ages, when pietistic practices such as prayers, penances, and indulgences were assigned values according to strict formulas.[38] If the medieval urge to quantify eschatology sought certainty (x years of purgatory for y sins minus z years for mitigating behavior), and if numerology remained on the margins of Christian discourse, an impulse in the nineteenth century was more strictly probabilistic.

The New Light minister Nathanael Emmons wrote in 1795 that it is impossible to estimate one's predestined state "according to the *doctrine of chances*," for while "we know the proportion between the number of blanks and prizes in a lottery," we do not know the number of the saved and the damned. Similarly, the "Caviler" in an 1818 dialogue responded to a pious interlocutor: "How great are the chances that you are not in the number of the elect! How many thousands are passed by! How few are chosen! How much more probable is it that you are among the thousands than among the few!" The predictable rejoinder was to rely on God's mercy, for hope cannot be justified by "a mathematical calculation of the chances," a point repeated in an 1844 article that proscribed Christians from imposing "the doctrine of chances on the great question of their eternal salvation." At a time when opponents of utilitarian ethics condemned Franklinian and Pecksniffian moral calculations, religious leaders recommended unconditional faith over probabilistic eschatology, though the urge to determine the odds of redemption remained in serious and satirical forms.[39]

It may not matter how many angels can dance on the head of a pin, but whether one has a place at the heavenly table or not was for many a pressing question. Thomas Browne, a Dickinson favorite, discussed the number of saved and damned in *Religio Medici*, advising his readers to contemplate God's glory instead of weighing their chances for heaven. William Gahan's frequently reprinted sermon, "On the Small Number of the Elect" (1799), also drew on scholastic traditions when arguing that there are more beings in heaven than in hell if one counts angels and the choir, though restricting the question to human souls, hell has more occupants, even after excluding non-Christians and non-baptized infants. More numerically, an 1872 article insisted that the Second Coming would be spiritual, not temporal, if only because the earth did not have enough room for the raising and judging of all the dead:

> I have said that the idea of Christ's temporal reign upon the earth is opposed to probability. I have somewhere met with the calculation that during the 6,000 years of the earth's existence there have been so many people on its surface [later given as 36,627,843,273,074,256] as to have made the whole of it a world of graves—each containing 128 people.[40]

Such reckoning upon the Final Reckoning is hardly representative of nineteenth-century Christian discourse, but it does indicate how the probabilistic revolution took eschatological forms. That such forms seem strange to many modern readers suggests how more hopeful the nineteenth century was of buttressing faith with scientific method.

Dickinson herself never explicitly numbered the meek members of the resurrection, but her religious imagination did dwell on what she called "the chances for Heaven."[41]

Evidence appears throughout her career with varying degrees of earnestness. "Soul, Wilt thou toss again?" (1859; F89) compares the final judgment to a game of "hazard" and a "Raffle" in which "Hundreds have lost indeed,/But tens have won an all," as Pascal's wager pushes predestination, moral law, and even God Himself to the margins. Another early poem, "You're right—'the way *is* narrow'" (1861; F249), sounds like teenage sarcasm ("'difficult the Gate'—/And 'few there be'—Correct again") before translating Matthew's nagging admonitions into the probabilistic language of finance. "I gave Myself to Him" (1862; F426) more seriously labors under the "Mutual—Risk" occasioned by Jesus's sacrifice, while "A Pit—but Heaven over it" (1863; F508) calls the fear of damnation "the Prop/that holds my chances up." When "Not probable—The barest Chance" (1863; F678) imagines perishing on the verge of heaven, the poor odds of salvation threaten to reduce the struggling believer to trembling despondence. Sermons on Matthew could insist that calculation does not dispel and actually exacerbates fears of the final judgment. Surely it is theologically more correct and emotionally safer to bracket probabilistic thinking—to reason that in Heaven "Some new Equation" will be given (1862; F403), to wait "Till Algebra is easier—/Or simpler proved—above" (1863; F516), and to trust one's singular poetic intuitions over the quantitative logic invited by Matthew, a point suggested in "I reckon—When I count at all" (1863; F533). As "Somehow myself survived the Night" (1871; F1209) puts it, a Christian "Without the Formula" for salvation still remains "A Candidate for Morning Chance."

And still it can be devilishly hard to disregard one's chances for heaven, to attend solely to one's soul and not the large number of others that are called and may or may not be chosen, especially if the number of the elect is fixed and relatively small. Even for fiercely individualistic Protestants such as Dickinson, the rise of probabilism, including Malthusian notions of scarcity, might incline one to think about salvation in the mass and therefore worry that one's soul might "perish from the chance's list" (1865; F927). This seems the case in "A Solemn thing within the Soul" (1862; F467), a terrific poem that begins with solitary self-reflection as the soul "feel[s] itself get ripe." However, comparison and judgment intrude upon Christian improvement when the poem invokes the surrounding "Orchard": other fruits are no doubt "farther up"; the "Maker" has multiple "Ladders" on multiple trees; "You hear a Being—drop—" as an overripe soul plummets into oblivion. The poem assures us it is "wonderful—to feel the sun," but the Maker is "cool of eye, and critical of Work"—perhaps a Calvinist defense of grace, though also a jab at Matthew's astringent eschatology in which bad trees are known by bad fruits, and only a few of many fruits are chosen. One can imagine Dickinson thinking during the revivals that swept her school and town: *All of you are going to heaven, and I can come too? Really? I thought the way was narrower than that. . . .*

As much as it resists probabilistic anxiety by trying to focus on a single pilgrim's progress, "A Solemn thing within the Soul" cannot fully reclaim its opening self-possession. The poem ends:

> But solemnest—to know
> Your chance in Harvest moves
> A little nearer—Every sun
> The single—to some lives.

What is most solemn is no longer the ripening feeling of the soul; it is the knowing that one's potential salvation advances under what can be taken to be two competing logics of chance. The first concerns the soul's preparation and suggests how some Calvinist views of redemption cohere with probabilistic degrees of belief as experienced by the subject. The watchful Christian can infer her election from incremental advances of faith, all the while acknowledging that nothing is guaranteed, for the Maker is the ultimate decider, even if His picking can feel to humans like chance. Knowing that one's chances are improving can bring some measure of succor, and yet as the poem moves toward a degree of reassurance, its paratactic end reasserts a second, less comforting aleatory logic, which cannot repress the knowledge that many lives are at stake, that some souls have better chances than others, and that—as Augustine and Calvin saw it—the number of the elect is fixed. As if to emphasize judgment over mercy, the potential eye-rhyme of "moves" and "loves" is slanted toward a more Matthew-like "lives." By some modern standards of justice, an inflexible number of the elect can feel outrageous: we ought to be graded on the quality of our work, not according to the mass logic of a curve. More maddeningly, the all-important Harvesting of souls should have nothing to do with chance. For Dickinson, however, links between Father and Coin cannot be definitively severed. One might feel the gradual ripening of the soul and even the singular interest of God's son, but salvation must always come as a surprise. To think otherwise is to insist on God's predictability by subordinating Him to more powerful laws.

The gradual but unguaranteed advance on heaven in "A Solemn thing within the Soul" is also dramatized in the crawling of "I know that He exists," the climbing of "I gained it so" (1863; F639), and the weary, groping, calculative pilgrimage of "Not probable—The barest Chance." The unfulfilled endings of all these poems suggest that, while Dickinson understands the Puritan doctrine of preparation and more general theologies of works, she still believes in the primary force of surprising moments of grace. As her speakers anticipate their unpredictable determinations, Dickinson focuses less on God's dispensations and more on the experience of living with the knowledge that one can only guess at His probable providence, if such designs even exist. Following the habits of Puritan forbearers who scrutinized experience for eschatological signs while denying the sureties of prediction, Dickinson's expectant, recurring poise takes diverse affective forms. What is different is the stark way Dickinson acknowledges how being suspended under predestination can feel like chance. In an 1884 letter (or poem), Dickinson wrote to Susan:

> Morning might come by Accident—Sister—
> Night comes by Event—
> To believe the final line of the Card would foreclose Faith—
> Faith is *Doubt*.[42]

Twain chose humor over accuracy when he wrote, "Faith is believing what you know ain't so."[43] For Dickinson, rebirth might come by Accident, and probabilism is one way to approach such uncertainty, though no amount of calculation can—or should—preempt the spirit's potential surprise. Much mid-nineteenth-century literature describes the painstaking efforts demanded by the doctrine of chances. Dickinson shows how difficult it is not to think about salvation in such disenchanted terms.

Whether Dickinson's religious heritage encourages an empirical outlook is open to debate. Puritan hermeneutics may make some American writings distinctively attentive to the natural world, and Dickinson's New Englandly way of seeing no doubt owes something to the Mind that Jonathan Edwards so dauntingly represents. That said, the Ramist logic of Puritan theology is too deductive for Baconian science, while Edwards's youthful essay about flying spiders has probably borne as much evidentiary weight as a brief (and often fallacious) exercise should. More significant is Edwards's immersion in Locke, which suggests that Dickinson's empiricism is not solely beholden to theological or New World perspectives, for her skepticism, even when spiritually inflected, can be taken as a philosophy of science applied to everyday experience. While Unitarians and some latter-day Puritans sang of the "steps to heaven" in "Nearer, My God, to Thee" (1841), Dickinson writes in "What mystery pervades a well!" (1877; F1433): "But nature is a stranger yet; . . . /[T]hose who know her, know her less,/The nearer her they get." Though she never pursues naturalist researches in the formal manner of Thoreau, Dickinson is a seeker of natural law who understands that the asymptotic incrementalism of empiricism simultaneously conditions probabilistic expectations and feelings of surprise under chance.

Dickinson describes empiricism as unavoidably fraught in her deceptively simple poem, "I stepped from Plank to Plank" (1865; F926). The speaker takes a "slow and cautious way," not knowing which step will be the "final inch," concluding, "This gave me that precarious Gait/Some call Experience." Most nineteenth-century philosophers of science preferred to think of their methods as more stable and elegant, and they often invoked Bacon in *Novum Organum*:

> There are and can be but two ways of investigating and discovering Truth. The one leaps from the senses and particulars to the most general axioms. . . . The other raises axioms from the senses and particulars, by ascending steadily, step by step, so that at last the most general may be reached; and this way is the true one.

In an era when Lamark, Lyell, and Darwin showed nature itself to advance incrementally, John Herschel advocated empiricism's "slow and measured steps from the known to the unknown," perpetuating a methodical image of scientific method that many commentators equated with inevitable progress. Indicating the teleological assumptions and disciplinary formation of the sciences, an 1855 article from *The American Journal of Science and Arts* envisioned a pyramid of books rising from specialized to general studies so that, "step by step, the ascent will be to that universal monograph, which shall draw within its compass all the high generalities of that great epic cosmos in which science will attain its far off final consummation." Ideologically and rhetorically analogous to discourses of manifest destiny, scientific hubris of the nineteenth century shows that the mad scientists of the era's fiction may not be such monstrous caricatures after all.[44]

Less dramatically, philosophers of science in the nineteenth century resisted triumphal empiricism in at least two ways. The first was most vigorously asserted by Whewell, who co-opted Bacon's famous metaphor when lodging the Kantian objection that deductions actually drive supposedly empirical inferences. "Deduction descends steadily and methodically, step by step," Whewell wrote. Whereas, "Induction mounts by a leap which is out of the reach of method. She bounds to the top of the stair at once." For Whewell, inductions gather facts so as to support convictions already determined in the mind, a possibility that Dickinson dialectically considers in "Experience is the Angled Road" (1865; F899). The poem begins with a Baconian defense of the trials and errors of induction: "Experience" may be unavoidably "Angled," but it is still "Preferred against the Mind," which (contra Whewell and the beginning of "The Outer—from the Inner") only "Presum[es]" to "lead." The poem then takes up a "Quite Opposite" position by noting that "Man" is compelled to "choose Himself/His Preappointed Pain," not unlike Whewell's claim that a priori forms pre-appoint the meaning of experience. Freedom versus fate is obviously at issue, and especially unnerving is that Dickenson opts for "Pain" over a straight rhyming "plan," not only making her prosody precariously angled and distancing herself from cheerful arguments from design, but also leaving the philosophical conflict between Bacon and Whewell unreconciled. On the one hand, pain is an experienced sensation returning us to the poem's opening point that empirical progress necessarily includes missteps. On the other hand, as Elaine Scarry and some nineteenth-century defenders of vivisection argued, pain can be said to have no external referent and thus to occur in the mind. By setting empirical induction and a priori deduction in suspended juxtaposition, "Experience is the Angled Road" demonstrates if nothing else "How complicate/The Discipline of Man." As science came to think of itself as a discipline, some philosophers sought synergist compromises between Bacon and Whewell, induction and deduction. In his influential 1830 book, *Preliminary Discourse on the Study of Natural History*, John Herschel argued that science requires both logical approaches so that the "path by which we rise to knowledge [is] made smooth and beaten in its lower steps." Insisting more forcefully on the pain of trials and errors, and poetically enacting the disorientation caused by competing logics, "Experience is the Angled Road" shows that there is no smooth or straight path to truth.[45]

A second way to rein in triumphal empiricism is to remember Hume, who powerfully combined empiricism and skepticism under an inching epistemological method. "[T]o advance by timorous and sure steps," Hume wrote, "to review frequently our conclusions . . . by these means we shall make both a slow and short progress." Alexander Bain took up a similarly modest position when discussing "the hazard of Induction" in his *Logic* (1870). For Bain, we can confidently trace links between past and present, but the "*leap into the future*" involves inferential "steps" that he calls "perilous" and "precarious."[46] "I stepped from Plank to Plank" and "Experience is the Angled Road" also question empirical methods by destabilizing logical connections between experience and knowledge understood as prediction. If the tragedy of each poem is that the possibilities of surprise bring mainly trepidation and pain, the irony is that experience, a supposedly prudent approach to truth, teaches that no amount of experience can master chance. Recognizing the skeptical potential of empiricism and the threat of chance lurking within probabilism, Herschel and other philosophers of science emphasized the moral certainty of their methods. Dickinson, however, remains unconvinced. In "Nature and God—I Neither Knew" (1864; F803), she refers to the limited vision of "Herschel" (even if it is John's astronomer father, William), and in "Experiment escorts us last"

(1870; F1181), she concludes that nature "Will not allow an Axiom," no matter the length of one's study. Nature's vastness and our inability to infer absolute truths appear again in "The Frost was never seen" (1870; F1190), a poem in which even vigilant observers of nature must admit, "Unproved is much we know." For Dickinson, the small steps of experience lead only to partial and provisional knowledge. They advance neither in a straight line nor toward a guaranteed end, nor—to think in terms of logic and aesthetics—do they move with confident grace.

The uneasy gaits of Dickinson's speakers can indicate embarrassment, fear, and pain, though other poems more variously explore how it feels to walk under the possibilities of chance. "A Bird, came down the Walk" (1862; F359) is usually taken to address subject/object dualism from a romantic perspective, though perception is not at issue so much as a natural superabundance that remains beyond human comprehension.[47] The poem marks the limits of empiricism by dramatizing the unpredictability of naturalist observation—subverting the natural theology of Tennyson's *In Memoriam* (1850) (Tennyson writes, "not a worm is cloven in vain"), going further than Higginson's 1863 essay "The Life of Birds" (which follows Darwin in denying that humans can know the consciousness of animals), and rejecting the recuperations of Mary Treat's "Our Familiar Birds" (an 1877 *Harper's* article that renders birds knowable by predicting their behavior). "A Bird, came down the Walk" anticipates Higginson and Treat by combining first-person narration and scientific method as Dickinson describes the timorous steps, careful hopping, and cautious observations of bird watching.[48] The slow, short progress of speaker and bird sets up the poem's wild conclusion in which the bird suddenly flies and then seemingly swims away in astonishingly mixed metaphors. Like Thoreau's game with the loon of *Walden*, "A Bird, came down the Walk" shows how incremental methods premise aleatory surprise. If Tennyson finds belief in what we cannot prove, Dickinson the skeptical watcher of nature experiences a less settled sense of wonder.

Written earlier though voiced through a more mature speaker, "These are the days when Birds come back" (1859; F122) suggests that even jaded observers of nature remain subject to surprise and that even the absence of surprise can enliven its possibilities. The unlikely heat of an Indian summer nearly fools the poem's experienced speaker, who—having some knowledge of Old Probabilities—concedes, "Almost thy plausibility/Induces my belief." Recognizing the plausibility of extraordinary events but resisting their epistemological and emotional force, the inductive speaker is intent on restraining surprise, meteorological and ultimately spiritual. Yet her obduracy cannot help but register the stirring rareness of the "old—old sophistries of June," for the swelling, pleading lyricism that ends the poem indicates that even well-worn hearts can be surprised by their desire for a surprise that cannot be utterly foresworn. The feeling is more profound than that of Charlie Brown trying to kick the football from Lucy's hold, but the lesson is analogous: hope springs eternal, even for losers and lost souls heading toward darker days.

An obverse example of the entanglements of surprise and repetitious experience is "Apparently with no surprise" (1884; F1668), a poem that destabilizes the argument from design by turning to theodicy and epistemology. An innocent flower is apparently unsurprised when beheaded by a sudden frost, while above "The Sun proceeds unmoved/To measure off another Day/For an Approving God." The flower knows too little to be surprised (clearly it is not a perennial), while the experience of a bored, mensurative

All-Knowing makes Him too knowledgeable to be emotionally moved. To be susceptible to surprise is to have partial, imperfect knowledge—to comprehend patterns just enough to register anomalies, to walk step-by-step, plank-by-plank between flowers and God. Emerson in *Nature* is ashamed by such empirical plodding; it is "as if a banished king should buy his territories inch by inch, instead of vaulting at once into his throne."[49] By contrast, Dickinson's poems about paupers who find themselves kings show that epiphanies, attractive as they are, can be disorienting to the point of self-loss. Extra-rational leaps are fine inventions for those celebrating Archimedes, Galileo, and Newton, but empirical discipline is more prudent in an emergency, even if it cannot eliminate and, in fact, subtends surprise.[50]

This is not to say that Dickinson renders surprise explicable, for if she theorizes its conditioning by repetitious experience, the moment itself proves elusive. "Tell all the truth but tell it slant" (1872; F1263) is about the incremental and thus inadequate relating of "The Truth's superb surprise." The poem describes the dangers of revealing totalized truth, ending with a warning foreshadowed throughout: such truth is "Too bright"; it is like "Lightning"; it can "blind." Instead of Dickinson's usual dialectical reversals and metaphorical eclecticism, here there is a careful accretion of meaning, fitting for a poem whose announced moral is, "The Truth must dazzle gradually." For a poem taken to justify Dickinson's obliqueness, "Tell all the truth but tell it slant" is a remarkably legible performance in that the rhymes are not slanted, the syntax is unbroken, and the logic is more or less linear. "Circuit" may contain a shock, and some gendered irony may lurk in the line, "Or every man be blind."[51] But such readings ultimately suggest how unrepresentative the poem is, for we seldom have to work so hard to make Dickinson complicated. Unless this seemingly conventional poem, which comes well after Dickinson's early phase of traditional versification, actually demonstrates through its unsurprising unsuperbness that we can never prepare for the truly surprising.

That surprise cannot be known beforehand makes tautological sense, though Dickinson more provocatively suggests in another poem that it cannot be known even in retrospect:

> He fumbles at your Soul
> As Players at the Keys—
> Before they drop full Music on—
> He stuns you by Degrees—
>
> Prepares your brittle nature
> For the ethereal Blow
> By fainter Hammers—further heard—
> Then nearer—Then so—slow—
>
> Your Breath has time to straighten—
> Your Brain to bubble cool—
> Deals One—imperial Thunderbolt—
> That scalps your naked soul—
>
> When Winds hold Forests in their Paws—
> The Universe—is still—(1862; F477)

This poem can sound like a more eloquent version of "Tell all the truth but tell it slant" with the perspective switched from that of the teller to the receiver of truth. A more significant difference is that for all the patient accretion of meaning, the incremental stunning by degrees actually increases the final surprise of the poem. If we can, as Walter Benjamin suggests, erect a kind of "shock defense" by trying to locate surprising incidents in time, such preparedness in Dickinson's poem only increases suspense.[52] Though a power "Prepares" our brittle selves, and we hear the "Hammers" approaching, and time itself seems to slow with the portending moment of truth—and though Dickinson spends two lines in the third stanza to give us time to straighten and cool, to literally steel ourselves—the "Thunderbolt" interrupts stanzaic organization and puts all defenses to rout, abandoning the poem's musical and metallurgical metaphors for language that outrages sense. Whitman may surprise us by getting naked and plunging his tongue to our bare-stripped hearts, but "scalps your naked soul" is too extreme for transcendental oneness—slanting the poem's rhyme scheme, violating its tropes, and scrambling dualisms of body and spirit. Emerson in "The Poet" calls on the imagination "to flow, and not to freeze." Dickinson goes further by showing how flowing can slow and finally straighten cool, and how this is not a symptom of creative stagnation but a prelude for something shockingly new.

The truncated stanza that ends "He fumbles at your Soul" delivers this kind of shock. When surprised, bodies go numb and minds go blank (even sometimes for Dickinson, visa versa). Despite its patient incremental efforts to track the transition into transport, the poem does not or cannot describe it in detail immediately after the fact. The last two lines of the poem are alien—eerily whispery, a static tingling after a bolt—juxtaposing a formal feeling of pause and stillness with winds and paws that move through time and space. "He fumbles at your Soul" is set in lyric time as surprise escapes consciousness and language; it is a kind of uncountable experience that empiricism and induction can frame but never know.[53] George Herbert's "Sin" (1633) with its bibliomanic "millions of surprises" may lurk in the background of the poem, but Dickinson withholds the didactic conclusions of Herbert, "Tell all the truth but tell it slant," and Edwards's "Faithful Narrative of the Surprising Work of God" (1738). Nor are there romantic assurances of anything like an impending resolution. Nor does Dickinson, so often a taxonomist of the emotions, associate the poem's shock with a dominant mood of embarrassment, pain, terror, pleasure, or enchantment. Stripped of any other affect that might color the experience, "He fumbles at your Soul" is Dickinson's closest approach to surprise.

Eight years after beginning their correspondence and on the eve of their first meeting, Dickinson wrote to Higginson at his Amherst hotel, "The incredible never surprises us because it is incredible." This cryptic note may aspire to a world-weariness—a fallibilist disowning of all capacities for prediction, and a defensiveness that seeks to forestall surprise by maturely expecting the unexpected. One year earlier, Higginson adopted a similar posture in the preface to his novel *Malbone* (1869): "One learns, in growing older, that no fiction can be so strange nor appear so improbable as would the simple truth."[54] Poe's emotionally disengaged ratiocinative tales push this logic to an extreme where everything is incredible and nothing surprises, though for Dickinson, who cared deeply about Higginson's visit, improbabilities do not lead to a flattening of affect. The incredible is not surprising because surprise depends on the violation of credible expectations based in experience. Nineteenth-century philosophers of science theoretically recognized that chance escapes empirical prediction, though intellectual and professional aspirations led most to emphasize their epistemological competence over their probabilistic uncertainty. Unwilling to bracket the difficulties of inferring predictions from experience, Dickinson observes and enacts feelings of chance, which is to say that she credibly details a lived life of surprise.

HAVING AN EXPERIENCE

After sending a total of six poems to Higginson in 1862 and receiving his comments (which are not extant), Dickinson replied, "You think my gait 'spasmodic'—I am in danger—Sir."[55] The spasmodic school of poetry, a movement in Britain in the 1850s and '60s, was associated with "sudden transitions," "shocks of spiritual electricity," and the "power to startle and surprise"—phrases that Gerald Massey in a definitive 1858 essay applied to the spasmodics in general and Dickinson's revered Brownings in particular.[56] Beginning with the publication of Dickinson's *Poems* (1890), readers have celebrated and sometimes regretted her similarly tonic effects. Higginson wrote of her verse in 1890, "It absolutely startles one," while other early reviewers noted its "galvanic shocks," tendency to "startle and surprise," and "surprising, sudden, and irregular turns."[57] Whether or not Higginson and Dickinson had the spasmodics in mind in their 1862 correspondence, Dickinson's response is unapologetic: a precarious gait is appropriate under risky conditions, sir. In accordance with her empirical skepticism and concomitant openness to chance, Dickinson's poetics enact experiences of surprise—with rhyme schemes that almost play it straight, uneven prosodic steps and leaps, orderly architectures that crumble on the verge of completion, and an oeuvre that establishes familiar habits to the point of predictability until suddenly some new poem—or an old one, for that matter—violates the expectations of even seasoned Dickinson readers. Moving toward pragmatist concepts of discrete experiences that render provisional unity, this final section seeks an aesthetic description of Dickinson's ongoing but differentiated surprises.

At an elemental level, Dickinson evokes feelings of chance foot by foot, line by line, and stanza by stanza. The shocks of her off rhymes come not only from conceptual disjunctions ("Pain" instead of "plan," "lives" instead of "loves") but also from their aural incongruities: centuries of verse and hymns, along with Dickinson's regularized stanzas, prepare readers for rhymes that are not forthcoming, even as anticipated words remain palpable in their absence. Cristanne Miller has detailed the "expectant anxiety" generated by Dickinson's techniques, including her "patterned use, and patterned disruption, of communal forms." Dickinson's formal ruptures have been associated with aesthetic iconoclasm, post-structural semiotics, and psychological and historical traumas, though empirical skepticism explains in a very different way the indeterminacies of her irregular prosody—indeterminacies that are less about Wittgensteinian duck-rabbit games and more about the expected but unpredictable surprise of a round of duck-duck-goose. The later game creates suspense and surprise through temporal sequencing, not ambiguous representation, thereby exploiting the aleatory interplay of repetition, probability, prediction, and anomaly.[58]

Modern scholars of stochastic grammar and probabilistic linguistics have demonstrated that language usage entails the conscious and unconscious management of chance. We are constantly anticipating the next word in a sequence, whether we base expectations on grammatical rules (a transitive verb should be paired with a direct object) or experience (when someone says, "Wuthering," a literary critic is prepared to hear "Heights"). Semantics is also a probabilistic operation. For instance, we take the *buzzing* in *Mary likes buzzing bees* to be an adjective modifying *bees* (as opposed to an action performed by *Mary*), not because of any formal grammatical logic but because it is the most likely meaning. Nineteenth-century linguists lacked the probabilistic sophistication of their modern heirs, but Champollion, Babbage, and Henry Layard used frequentist methods in their cryptologist work, an approach deployed by Poe in "The Gold-Bug" and discussed by the probability theorist George Boole in *An Investigation in the Laws of Thought* (1854). A pedagogical article from 1844 noted the precariousness of probabilistic linguistics, complaining that beginning readers are like gamblers who rely on the doctrine of chances only to find that vowels in English are not governed by "the law of periodicity" but are, rather, "as lawless as chaos."[59] Dickinson's poetry is hardly chaotic, but—like the sudden turns of spasmodic verse and the misdirecting syntax of such texts as "Benito Cereno" and "The Beast in the Jungle" (1903)—it exploits the fallibility of probabilistic reading when unlikely constructions ambush comprehension, forcing readers to advance more warily. This may be why advanced students reciting Dickinson often sound like less accomplished language users. It is also why they sometimes unintentionally reenact Higginson's editorial sins by straightening Dickinson's rhymes and forcing her meters into more conventional, more predictable patterns.

Nothing is like encountering a Dickinson poem, even if one has encountered it before. For Susan Howe, "[Dickinson's] writing is infinitely open.... To this day I can be utterly surprised by something new I find in it, *or* I can be comforted by familiar beauties there" (emphasis added).[60] It is a truism that literature pleases in both ways, though Dickinson's entanglement of repetition and surprise can replace Howe's "or" with an "and." In my experience, no amount of notes, secondary criticism, or professional and personal investment can keep a once familiar Dickinson poem from suddenly transforming into something strange. The experience can be embarrassing in the classroom and debilitating at a keyboard, though Dickinson's surprises are of course also wonderful, even for devotees who, paradoxically, have learned to expect to be surprised by her work.

In what I take to be a meta-critical anticipation of responses to her own work, Dickinson explores how it feels to be experienced under conditions of surprise, to know that one never precisely knows what is coming next:

> Wonder—is not precisely knowing
> And not precisely knowing not—
> A beautiful but bleak condition
> He has not lived who has not felt—
>
> Suspense—is his maturer Sister—
> Whether Adult Delight is Pain
> Or of itself a new misgiving—
> This is the Gnat that mangles men—

Philip Fisher, in *Wonder, the Rainbow, and the Aesthetics of Rare Experience* (1998), does not discuss Dickinson or chance, though many of his insights apply. Fisher argues that of all the narrative arts, lyric poetry best inspires wonder (an aspect of surprise), particularly when it violates grammar and syntax so that "expectation itself ceases to work and the experience of wonder can take over." Like Dickinson, Fisher attends to the decline of wonder through the "domestication of experience," though less apposite is his claim that what follows surprise is a pleasurable sense of wholeness, as in one of Fisher's favorite examples, Wordsworth's "My heart leaps up when I behold." In "Wonder—is not precisely knowing," the "bleak" beauty of Dickinson's "Wonder" is starker, while her "Suspense" is epistemologically and emotionally more fraught than the post-wondering state of Wordsworth. (For instance, Wordsworth's use of "leaps" instead of "leapt" suggests the predictability of his heart's always leaping).[61] As a mature feeling of expecting the unexpected, Dickinson's Suspense does not end skepticism but leads to "new misgiving[s]." She may link Wonder to masculine, romantic exultation while feminizing the wiser comportment of Suspense, though she also suggests that Suspense is a general human condition, that to be "mangled" by the anticipation of surprise is to be neither a flower nor a god but a man.

The painful open-endedness of Dickinson's surprise can sound like some versions of the romantic sublime, except that it is firmly grounded in temporal, incremental sequencing (as opposed to the psycho-metaphysical dynamics governing subject-object relations). If for Dickinson the actual moment of surprise cannot be reclaimed, the moments that frame it can be. "Wonder—is not precisely knowing" describes the conditions preceding surprise, as does "I know Suspense—it steps so terse" (1873; F1283), which associates ongoing uncertainty with precarious gaits. As suggested by "These tested Our Horizon" (1865; F934), suspenseful expectations cannot escape chance by mastering it through empirical methods. The speaker writes of birds in unpredictable flight:

> Our Retrospection of Them
> A fixed Delight,
> But Our Anticipation
> A Dice—a Doubt—

If "Retrospection" in this poem domesticates wonder without destroying delight, here and elsewhere Dickinson is primarily concerned with the feelings of chance that follow surprise and remain stubbornly resistant to closure. "'It is finished' can never be said of us," Dickinson wrote in 1878, a line that can also refer to poems that leave readers with ongoing doubt.[62] When "I felt a Funeral, in my Brain" (1862; F340) ends "And Finished knowing—then—," Dickinson imagines that even death may not terminate anticipatory anxiety. The "Or More—" that concludes "One need not be a Chamber—to be Haunted" makes a related point insofar as the suspense of impending surprise has no end under dicey conditions.

When other nineteenth-century American poets confront the possibilities of skepticism, they generally reclaim a more settled order, even if it is ultimately tragic. Bryant's natural theology, Whittier's reliable hearths, and Longfellow's predictable duties all mitigate threats of uncertainty, while knowledge for Lydia Sigourney, Frances Sargent Osgood, and Sarah Piatt can be awful, not so much in its provisionality as in its absolute irrevocability. In Poe's most skeptical poem, the terrors of a haunted chamber end not with "More—" but with "nevermore!" And though Whitman remains garrulously open-ended, he ends *Song of Myself* with a period in 1856, teasing his readers with a coming totality under the auspices of his subsuming self. As we have seen, Emerson is relatively open to surprise as an aesthetic practice under conditions of chance. "Experience" even praises the mangling of men: "Life is a series of surprises, and would not be worth taking or keeping if it were not. . . . We thrive by casualties. Our chief experiences have been casual." The etymology of "casualty" includes the Latin word for "chance," and *Webster's American Dictionary of the English Language* (1828) defines "casual" as "coming by chance" and "without design." (It even uses for its sample sentence, "Atheists assert that the existence of things is casual"). Dickinson's poems powerfully acknowledge the casual cruelties of experience, but she remains less willing than Emerson and her poetic contemporaries to re-inscribe surprise within a providential order in which chance is only nominal.

Freedom from teleology and its aesthetic counterpart, formal unity, expands the possibilities of surprise; contingency, unpredictability, and open-endedness emerge as language loosens itself from conventional totalities. Yet there is something enervating, even self-annihilating, about unbounded chance and perpetual wonder. As Frost notes in his famous comment on tennis nets, and as Aurora Leigh learns in Italy, true wonder is subtended by measures of constraint, for the only thing less compelling than an utterly predictable text is one in which anything and everything is likely enough to happen. For all her openness to experimentation and chance, Dickinson's formal surprises depend on the framework of her disciplined prosody, while her shocking conceptual and imaginative leaps require some initial, mundane steps. Most difficult to explain is the seeming paradox that while Dickinson's poems so often stop with intimations of "More," they simultaneously constitute singular experiences that bring satisfying feelings of closure. As Fisher argues, and as Bain asserted in 1874 with his "law of Novelty," surprise is what distinguishes discernible, singular moments from the horizon of everyday experience.[63] Influenced by Bain and attending to both the infinite possibilities and the probabilistic limits of chance, pragmatism is especially helpful in describing the unending but discrete experiences that Dickinson evokes and theorizes. To borrow a formulation from "The Brain—is wider than the Sky," pragmatists take surprise to differentiate meaningful syllables from the ongoing flux of experience's sound.

From Susan Manning's work on Dickinson's transitions, to New's focus on her "episodic knowledge" of nature, to Jed Deppman's interest in Rorty's ethic of conversation as a model for Dickinson's dialectical thought, literary scholars have begun to interpret Dickinson from pragmatist perspectives.[64] Among other things, early pragmatists were empirical skeptics who sought to tame chance while at the same time acknowledging the power of undomesticated surprise. Peirce wrote of inductive knowledge, "[I]t is liable at any moment to be utterly shattered by a single experience," and he equated scientific progress with a kind of embarrassment: "[A]ll knowledge begins by the discovery that there has been an erroneous expectation." Like Dickinson, Frost, and Henry James, Peirce once compared the impending and fleeting feeling of truth to encountering a door: it is "the sense of something opposing one's Effort, something preventing one from opening a door slightly ajar; which is known in its individuality by the actual shock, the Surprising element, in any Experience." Experience is obviously crucial for pragmatism, though as Rorty's suspicion of the term suggests, pragmatists are wary of treating experience as an all-encompassing concept, which is why Peirce emphasizes how a "single experience" is marked off by its surprising "individuality." For Peirce, empiricism requires that experience be rendered in analyzable units, even if analysis remains forever incomplete.[65]

Though generally associated with the endless flux and "big blooming buzzing confusion" of lived life, William James also argues that experiences are discretely known, even as they encroach upon each other in constant interconnection. Just as Emerson's "Experience" starts on a stair and not a ramp, experience for James is not a smooth stream of consciousness, that memorable and easily misunderstood metaphor from *Principles of Psychology* (1890). Experience is made up of pools and currents, resting places and sudden movements, more helpfully figured in James's *Psychology* as a bird alternately perching and flying. Critics working in the tradition of Poirier have used James's thinking on transitions to explicate poetic and epistemological lubricity. Yet for James leaps in consciousness, as ecstatic as they are, depend on identifiable perches—temporarily stable experiential states between which transitions occur and from which they can be registered. James's radical empiricism may be best known for rejecting philosophies that take consciousness and experience to be "chopped up," but it also resists the romantic "integration of all things" into an undifferentiated oneness. As with Dickinson and Peirce, surprise for James depends on discrete experiential moments, for it occurs within temporal sequences in which our predictions prove insufficient. James typically sees such moments as productive, as when he trades the "orderliness" of a utopian lake resort for the "chances" and "precipitousness" that make life more significant. And yet for all his ringing phrases, motivational talks, and rugged celebrations of risk, James vindicates a claim from Stanley Fish: "Pragmatism is the philosophy not of grand ambitions but of little steps."[66]

Never one to be accused of letting eloquence get the best of him, Dewey provides a more disciplined account of what it means to have a singular aesthetic experience. Dewey's *Art as Experience* (1934) rejects romantic visions of oneness so as to ground aesthetics in material, everyday life, and the book's best-known chapter, "Having an Experience," begins with James's stream of consciousness and concludes with James's metaphor of the itinerant bird.[67] Under the aegis of radical empiricism—"Experience occurs continuously" but is like "a flight of stairs"—Dewey argues that art distinguishes moments of "unity" from the "humdrum" continuities of life. In keeping with his broader worldview that "precarious probability" *almost* allows one to "escape from the perils of uncertainty," Dewey's aesthetic is one of managed chance. He claims that art is neither "a matter of caprice nor yet of routine," or as he puts it in *Experience and Nature* (1925), art is "spontaneous, unexpected, fresh, unpredictable" but also an "alternative to luck."[68] Dewey's emphasis on unity should not be mistaken for New Critical formalism, for he conjoins the making and reception of art insofar as observers cannot help but imagine the contexts and processes that go into aesthetic creation.

As a result, artist and observer are unified by the same singular experience of surprise, a claim that for Dewey and other pragmatists includes the act of writing itself. James writes: "[A]ll sorts of novelties and surprises lie in wait. These words I write even now surprise me." Dewey argues, "All discourse, oral or written . . . says things that surprise the one that says them." As Steven Meyer has shown, Gertrude Stein built a pragmatist aesthetic around surprising acts of unconscious composition, and Frost completes the circuit in "The Figure a Poem Makes" (1939): "No surprise for the writer, no surprise for the reader." As appreciative as James and Dewey are of romanticism's championing of intuition and circumscription of positivism, they formulate artistic surprise under the logic of a radical, skeptical empiricism that relinquishes dreams of metaphysical oneness and settles instead for temporary moments of unity.[69]

For Dickinson, such thinking constitutes a meta-poetic theory. In one of the first negative reviews of her verse, *The Literary World* in 1890 speculated that Dickinson's voice was "strange even to her own ears."[70] Perhaps it was, but as pragmatism attests, literature entails a surprising strangeness for readers and writers alike, not simply in first instances of comprehension or composition but also over the long run. The many variants of Dickinson's manuscripts suggest that her poems continued to surprise her well after they were written, as if the unified experience of some earlier draft proved to be a temporary perch. As critics make more palpable Dickinson's physical environs and the materiality of her manuscripts, it seems increasingly clear that walls, drawers, vistas, voices, and boots of lead potentially refer to scenes of writing and revision in which Dickinson is surprised by her own words.[71] "The Outer—from the Inner" can end with an embarrassed star-poet looking down upon the suddenly revealed secrets of her own lake-manuscript. "He fumbles at your Soul" can be about a poet astonished by her own rising powers. "It struck me—every Day" (1863; F636), a poem Thoreau might have admired, describes how the diurnal writing of poetry entails both repetition and surprise. "A word dropped careless on a page" (1872; F1268) links the writing of poems with chance.

In a letter from 1853, Dickinson commented on an article in *The Springfield Republican*: "Who writes those funny accidents, where railroads meet each other unexpectedly, and gentleman in factories get their heads cut off quite informally?"[72] In Dickinson's culture, extraordinary incursions of chance were paradoxically becoming an everyday experience; and for Dickinson, the feeling of poetry and the feeling of accidents both involve losing one's head. In a tantalizingly brief reading of "Experience is the Angled Road," Howe sets Dickinson within the "cultural landscape" of pragmatism and joins other scholars in taking Dickinson's poems as reflections on the process of writing. Howe finds in "Experience is the Angled Road" an "openness to the order which chance can create," an intuition that applies to other Dickinson poems and informs crucial aspects of her thought—from her resistance to romanticism and struggles with faith, to her critiques of science and affinities with pragmatism, to her sense of herself as a poet walking precariously between toil and chance, suspense and wonder, repetition and surprise.[73]

Small steps and provisional revisions do not end for Dickinson in epic culmination. Like the partially collated observations of Thoreau's unfinished "Kalendar," Dickinson's fascicles and loose manuscripts show that some achievements are precisely the sum of their parts, including (as radical empiricists insist) the contingent relations between them. Dickinson's superabundance of short poems practically demand an intertextual approach implied but not overdetermined by her unfinished efforts to organize her life's work. Whitman's constant recompilations also ask us to ask what it is between his poems, though his aggregative, epic, book making desires can temporarily overcome his love of particularity and open-endedness. Dickinson seems more consistently skeptical of unified order and teleological closure, even as her poems achieve the fleeting feeling of singular experience. There is no representative Dickinson text, no *Song of Myself* or *Leaves of Grass*. She left instead a wooden chest with over 1700 poems—some stitched together, some laying loose, many containing variances, all obliging critics to proceed poem by poem and to encounter her achievements incrementally and precariously.

It may be tempting to find in Dickinson's openness to chance a lesson intended by a more mature sister who recommends embracing the unexpected, scalding though it may be. Dickinson, however, is wary of adopting didactic, prophetic, or therapeutic tones. "The Brain—is wider than the Sky" notwithstanding, her writings do not lend themselves to motivational slogans, and her project is not to instruct herself or her reader on how most productively to encounter the possibilities of chance. Except, perhaps, when Dickinson's repeated reflections on our susceptibility to chance suggest that one ought not to resist surprise, which cannot be chosen for or against. There may even be some modest wisdom in Dickinson's expectant poise:

> The Riddle we can guess
> We speedily despise—
> Not anything is stale so long
> As Yesterday's surprise—(1870; F1180)

A more confident epistemology might substitute "solve" for "guess," but the real trick of the poem is that "long" replaces what should more logically be "quickly" or "fast." "[L]ong" insists that old surprises abide in domesticated forms. Their legacy is not disenchanted certitude but, rather, the sudden and slow progress of experience with its stable, stale knowledge that can never predict tomorrow's leaps of partial discovery.

Some of Dickinson's biographers may need to be excused for leveraging largely undocumented dramas in her life, but literary critics are more surely justified in honoring the richly demonstrated inducements of her verse. The image of an outwardly placid but inwardly extravagant Dickinson is sharpened by romantic ideals of authorship, nineteenth-century gender constructions, and a host of Dickinson poems that boast operatically of wild nights and volcanic passions. Yet one can still imagine a life of constant writing and even dulling repetitions—draft after draft, poem after poem, year after year, with (as far as we know) virtually no feedback and relatively little variation in content, voice, and form. When selecting a second batch of poems to send to Higginson in 1862, Dickinson worried that "they look alike, and numb" and "might not differ" from earlier examples—a feeling that even an admirer of Dickinson might share when selecting poems for a survey course, trying to place a vaguely remembered line, or dallying with Dickinson's numerous poems beyond the point of critical stamina.[74] Dickinson's reticence about her personal life is not the only obstacle to construing a narrative for a career that remains remarkably consistent. This is hardly to diminish Dickinson's achievement but is instead to suggest that the entanglement of repetition and surprise extends to her artistic self-consciousness and critical reception. Dickinson might well deserve a section in the literary history of boredom, and she certainly anticipates a lesson of MFA programs and earnest dissertation advisors—keep on writing step by step, bird by bird, chapter by chapter until inspiration and knowledge surprises you. It is easy enough to generalize about the virtues of patient work. What distinguishes Dickinson is her rendering of repetitious experience punctuated by moments of chance. To be a poet and theorist of surprise is to be a precarious observer of the quotidian and to notice carefully the modern conditions under which chance strikes us every day.

Lost Causes and the Civil War

I should have liked to see you, before you became improbable. War feels to me an oblique place. . . .
I found you were gone, by accident, as I find Systems are, or Seasons of the year, and obtain no
cause—but suppose it a treason of Progress—that dissolves as it goes.
—Dickinson to Higginson, February 1863, after Higginson took command of the First South
Carolina Volunteers, a regiment of ex-slaves

Surprise quiz—identify the source of the following passage:

> There is no human affair which stands so constantly and so generally in close connection
> with War. . . . [F]rom the outset there is a play of possibilities and probabilities,
> good and bad luck, which . . . makes War of all branches of human activity the most like
> a gambling game. . . . War is the province of chance.

A. Thucydides, *History of the Peloponnesian War* (fifth century,BC)
B. Niccoló Machiavelli, *The Prince* (1532)
C. Carl Von Clausewitz, *On War* (1832)
D. Ulysses S. Grant, *Personal Memoirs* (1885)

The correct answer is "C," though Clausewitz's sentiments are to some degree shared by
Thucydides, Machiavelli, and Grant, all of whom believe that the proverbial chances of
war can be controlled but never vanquished. Best known for coining the phrase "the fog
of war" and describing war as "politics by other means," Clausewitz regarded war as a
probabilistic undertaking requiring not only the doctrine of chances but also experience-
based intuitions and estimations that at times surpass the limits of calculative reason.

Clausewitz was seldom read in antebellum America; military theorists under the
influence of Napoleonic strategy preferred the more technical, geometrical, epistemologically untroubled work of the Swiss-born Antoine-Henri Jomini and the New Yorker
Henry Wager Halleck. Against Clausewitz, Halleck wrote in his popular textbook

Elements of Military Art and Science (1846): "War is not, as some seem to suppose, a mere game of chance. Its principles constitute one of the most intricate of modern sciences; and the general who understands the art of rightly applying its rules, and possesses the means of carrying out its precepts, may be morally certain of success." Under the logic and language of moral certainty, Halleck held that military reason can rule chance, though his mediocre performance as a Union field-general during the Civil War exposed his overcommitment to abstract theory (and helps explain his partially satirical nickname, "Old Brains").[1] Following Halleck, antebellum military science on the whole was insufficiently attentive to chance, as was the overall lead up to the Civil War itself, as suggested by pervasive providential rhetoric in both the North and South. That each side expected the conflict to be resolved quickly in its favor and became frustrated by the war's unpredictable course indicates a widespread failure to account for the aleatory possibilities of war.

That some postbellum observers came to recognize this failure is part of the story of chance's rise in America, a narrative that can include battlefield recollections (from Grant, Holmes Jr., William Tecumseh Sherman, and George Cary Eggleston), poetic treatments of the war (from Dickinson, Whitman, and Melville), fictional representations of the conflict (by Twain, Stephen Crane, and Ambrose Beirce), and commentaries that inaugurated the backformation of an antebellum period naïve in the ways of chance. Dismissing Hawthorne's supposedly "old fashioned" providentialism, Henry James wrote that the Civil War "mark[ed] an era in the history of the American mind," forcing God's ostensibly destined people to confront "a world in which everything happens."[2] Howells, in *A World of Chance* (1893), caricatures American transcendentalists as blithely innocent of chance, while Twain, in *Pudd'nhead Wilson* (1894) and "Fenimore Cooper's Literary Offenses" (1895), describes antebellum Americans as lacking probabilistic sense. As powerful a spokesperson as there is for postbellum America's fall into modernity, Henry Adams saw the Civil War as an unbridgeable gap separating him from his ancestry and initiating him into a universe of chance, a primal scene reenacted across postbellum literature and continued in scholarship today.[3]

In some ways, this dominant narrative is right—the Civil War did indeed make more visible the possibilities of chance in U.S. thought and culture—though at least two counternarratives qualify such claims. The first, which has largely concerned this book, is that the rise of chance was well under way before the Civil War. The complexity, chaos, and violence of the conflict put increasing pressure on providential accounts of the war, but "the chances of war" was a common phrase and outlook in the antebellum period and long before.[4] In the lead-up to the conflict and during its course, many commentators figured the possibilities of war in terms of fortune, risk, luck, gambling, unpredictable weather, and unknowable causation, while an 1861 article in *The Southern Literary Messenger* a mere two months after the first Battle of Bull Run suggested how established probabilistic concepts helped condition understandings of the war.

Titled "Reflections on the Present Crisis," the piece invoked the new sciences of chance in order to predict Confederate victory:

> It is said, the free-will of man, nay, even his most capricious passions neutralize each other, when large numbers of men are considered. The logic of statistics proves that 'the

greater the number of individuals, the more completely does the will of each, as well as individual peculiarities, moral or physical, disappear'. . . . Although the movements of the aggregate are made up of the actions of separate atoms, yet these actions, viewed individually, do not seem to evolve the law. . . . When we read such evidences from the science of statistics as these,—that from certain annual records it has been educed, that the same number of marriages, both congruous and incongruous—the same annual recurrence of the fixed wedding day—the same number of crimes—of the same description—the same regularity in the sentences passed on criminals—take place: that forgetfulness as well as free-will is under constant laws; the number of undirected letters put into the post-office in London and Paris is very nearly the same, year after year respectively—a firmer faith is induced in the dogma, that the actions of men and the revolutions and convulsions of the social and political spheres are overruled, are controlled by . . . Providence.[5]

Alluding to Laplace's dead letters, Poisson's large numbers, Quetelet's statistics, Maxwell's law of gasses, and quoting Mary Somerville's *Physical Geography* (1849), "Reflections on the Present Crisis" attempts to tame the chances of war under a scientific logic made compatible with, but not equivalent to, conventional views of providence. The re-inscription of chance within God's grand design proved more difficult as unprecedented causalities mounted, but as we have seen, some antebellum authors did not require the Civil War to confront the radical possibilities of chance, whose challenge to teleological order preceded the firing on Fort Sumter.

A second counter-narrative that helps shrink the gap between antebellum and postbellum approaches to chance involves the enduring explanatory power of Christianity, and here a final literary example suggests how providentialism could retrospectively manage the chances of the Civil War to the point of denying chance entirely. Elizabeth Stuart Phelps was well aware of the probabilistic revolution. *The Silent Partner* (1871) explores the nexus of statistics, chance, and Mills's political philosophy; her short story, "Jack" (1887), appeals to the "law of chances" in its ruminations on accidents and social ills. Phelps discusses scientific advances, including Darwinism, in many of her works; and she engages such commentators on chance as Howells, George Eliot, and Oliver Wendell Holmes Sr.[6] At the same time, Phelps was a not undutiful granddaughter of the orthodox Calvinist Moses Stuart, and her wildly popular novel *The Gates Ajar* (1868) curtails the aleatory threat of the Civil War in creative but ultimately conservative ways.

The Gates Ajar is, among other things, a book about chance and mourning. The narrator Mary Cabot loses her brother Roy in the Civil War and is thrown into religious skepticism, until Aunt Winifred arrives to reassure Mary with a spiritualist view of heaven. Like Emerson's "Experience," *The Gates Ajar* elides its immediate object of mourning, for the main casualty in the novel is not so much Roy as Mary's faith in a providence unmenaced by chance. The novel opens with Mary angry at her Calvinist neighbors: "They tell me that it should not have been such a shock. 'Your brother had been in the army so long that you should have been prepared for anything. Everybody knows by what a hair a soldier's life is always hanging.'" In Mary's Edwardsian community, to be "prepared for anything" is not to regard chance in the manner of an empirical skeptic who expects the unexpected but, rather, to accept without philosophical and emotional scruple the unknowable determinations of God. Mary finds some fleeting relief in Cowper's "God Works in a Mysterious Way," but in her servant's words, she cannot stop herself from "rebellin' agin Providence."[7] The dramatic question of *The Gates Ajar* is whether Mary will recover from her fall into chance, and the intellectual issue for Phelps and her wartorn culture is on what grounds such a recovery might occur.

In Phelps's novel, the specter of chance arrives with Roy's random death and comes to take eschatological form. Mary worries if she will "stand any chance" of joining Roy in heaven, and she yearns for "a future probable or possible, which makes the very incompleteness of life sweet, because of the symmetry which is waiting somewhere." Mary hopes that in heaven somehow it will be even, some new equation given, but—less open than Dickinson to chance—she and Phelps more determinedly seek an end to probabilistic uncertainty. One calculating neighbor ill advisedly tells Mary to be "resigned in an arithmetical manner," and her coldly logical minister tries to help her by noting that it is "probable" that she and Roy will know each other in heaven. Thankfully, Aunt Winifred is more sympathetic, for when Mary cries that her reunion with Roy "is probable, only *probable*," Winifred answers: "My child, do not be troubled about that. It is not probable, it is sure." Lest Winifred be mistaken for an antinomian fanatic, she concedes that her "belief must rest on analogy and conjecture," and yet she offers reassurance with a providential re-inscription of chance: "I can lay it [my surety] down as one of those probabilities for which Butler would say, 'the presumption amounts nearly to a certainty.'"[8] Practically speaking (and as with Henry Wager Halleck), moral certainty eliminates the relevance of chance, and when combined with Winifred's sentimental spiritualism, it slowly leads Mary back to providence.

The Gates Ajar instructed over 200,000 nineteenth-century readers how to encounter the debilitating chances of war, and the novel goes further by suggesting how tragic chances on the home front might similarly be overcome. When Winifred reveals at the end of the book that she has terminal breast cancer, Mary asks, "There is no chance?" To which Winifred answers, "No chance."[9] What should be a stinging announcement of death becomes a victory for a mourner and victim who have learned to vanquish chance under the logic of moral certainty: God's plan is not probable; it is sure. *The Gates Ajar* in this way is both more radical and more conservative than sometimes described, even by Phelps herself.[10] Phelps subordinates the dry arguments of Calvinism to spiritualism, sympathy, and embodiment, yet she relies on Joseph Butler's venerable logic to recuperate Christian faith. Phelps also simultaneously challenges and follows patterns of Civil War mourning.[11] The meaning of Roy's death has little to do with the political causes and sacrificial narratives so often invoked on behalf of fallen soldiers, most powerfully by Lincoln at Gettysburg, and yet Phelps's embrace of moral certainty conforms to an American providential faith that no amount of trauma or intimations of chance can seem to shake in the nineteenth-century and beyond.

This book was written during a period of U.S. history governed by the denial and underestimation of chance. Whether driven by providential worldviews, teleological visions of the end of history, or overdetermined, slam-dunk interpretations of inconclusive evidence, America's first war of the twenty-first century proceeded under the banner of infallibility, not the more modest sense that holy and Enlightenment missions will likely never be finished, at least in this world. In financial domains, quantitative experts on risk abetted by a widespread faith in unregulated markets and rational actors failed to pay proper respects to the unpredictable power of chance. Something similar might be said of professionals charged with preventing oil spills, shielding cities from floods, and protecting nuclear plants from natural disasters. As a polity, we seem incapable of acting on the moral certainty that global climate change is both real and human caused. These are oversimplifications to be sure, but it is telling how even new millennial managers of chance failed to sufficiently acknowledge its possibilities. Maybe we will someday discover the gene or synaptic pathway that impels humans toward false senses of certainty and uncertainty, and perhaps more accurate political and economic models will come to better predict policy outcomes. But even if the lost causes that shape our world are found, a segment of American history begun two centuries ago suggests that the unending claims of chance will continue to take their toll and invoke our wonder. The probabilistic revolution remains unfinished, and calls for more educational emphasis on the quantitative sciences will not achieve modernity anytime soon. If writers of the nineteenth century lacked some tools for handling chance, they continue to teach what it means and how it feels to live everyday with the imperatives of uncertainty.

NOTES

INTRODUCTION
1. Thomas Day and James Murdock, *Brief Memoirs of the Class of 1797* (New Haven: B. L. Hamlen, 1848), 26; "Ellington, July 30," *Middlesex Gazette* (August 17, 1804).
2. Edgar Allan Poe, *Poetry and Tales* (New York: Library of America, 1984), 554. Herman Melville, *Moby-Dick*, in *Redburn, White-Jacket, Moby-Dick* (New York: Library of America, 1983), 1021.
3. Ian Hacking, *The Emergence of Probability* (Cambridge: Cambridge University Press, 1975); Barbara Shapiro, *Probability and Certainty in Seventeenth-Century England: A Study of the Relationships between Natural Science, Religion, History, Law, and Literature* (Princeton: Princeton University Press, 1983); Mary Poovey, *A History of the Modern Fact* (Chicago: University of Chicago Press, 1998).
4. Ian Hacking, *The Taming of Chance* (New York: Cambridge University Press, 1990); Lorraine Daston, *Classical Probability in the Enlightenment* (Princeton: Princeton University Press, 1988); Theodore Porter, *The Rise of Statistical Thinking, 1820–1900* (Princeton: Princeton University Press, 1986); Stephen M. Stigler, *The History of Statistics: The Measurement of Uncertainty before 1900* (Cambridge: Harvard University Press, 1986). See also Daniel R. Headrick, *When Information Came of Age: Technologies of Knowledge in the Age of Reason and Revolution* (Oxford: Oxford University Press, 2000). For a history of the subject written in the nineteenth century, see Isaac Todhunter, *A History of the Mathematical Theory of Probability* (1865; rpt. London: Macmillan, 1949).
5. *The Empire of Chance: How Probability Changed Science and Everyday Life*, eds. Gerd Gigerenzer et al. (Cambridge: Cambridge University Press, 1989); *The Probabilistic Revolution, Volume 1*, eds. Lorenz Krüger, Lorraine Daston, and Michael Heidelberger (Cambridge: MIT Press, 1990). Charles Peirce, *The Essential Peirce: Selected Philosophical Writings*, 2 vols, eds. Nathan Houser, Christian Kloesel, et al. (Bloomington: Indiana University Press, 1992, 1998), 1:358.
6. Pierre Laplace, *A Philosophical Essay on Probabilities*, trans. Frederick Truscott and Frederick Emory (New York: Dover, 1951), 1. Peirce, *The Essential Peirce*, 1:149.
7. Jackson Lears, *Something for Nothing: Luck in America* (New York: Penguin, 2003). See also Oz Frankel, *States of Inquiry: Social Investigations and Print Culture in Nineteenth-Century Britain and the United States* (Baltimore: Johns Hopkins University Press, 2006); Ronald Zboray, *A Fictive People: Antebellum Economic Development and the American Reading Public* (New York: Oxford University Press, 1993), 122–135; Patricia Cline Cohen, *A Calculating People: The Spread of Numeracy in Early America* (Chicago: University of Chicago Press, 1982); Anne Fabian, *Card Sharps, Dream Books, and Bucket Shops: Gambling in Nineteenth-Century America* (Ithaca: Cornell University Press, 1990); Margo Anderson, *The American Census: A Social History* (New Haven: Yale University Press, 1988).

8. Frances Trollope, *Domestic Manners of the Americans* (1832; London: Richard Bentley, 1839), 96. Alexis de Tocqueville, *Democracy in America*, ed. Richard D. Heffner (New York: Penguin, 1956), 215; "Life Insurance at the South," *The Commercial Review* (May 1847). [No title], *The Morning Chronicle* (July 8, 1851).

9. "Death of Adams and Jefferson," *Richmond Enquirer* (June 17, 1831); "The Presidential Succession," *Harper's Monthly* (January 20, 1883).

10. Frank Norris, *McTeague* (New York: Penguin, 1964), 103.

11. For technical overviews, see Lawrence Sklar, *Physics and Chance: Philosophical Issues in the Foundations of Statistical Mechanics* (New York: Cambridge University Press, 1993); and Alfred Mele, *Free Will and Luck* (Oxford: Oxford University Press, 2006). For moral luck, see the competing views in Nicholas Rescher's *Luck: The Brilliant Randomness of Everyday Life* (New York: Farrar, Straus and Giroux, 1995), and Bernard Williams, *Moral Luck: Philosophical Papers, 1973–1980* (New York: Cambridge University Press, 1981), as well as Thomas Nagel's, "Moral Luck," *Moral Questions* (Cambridge: Cambridge University Press, 1979), 24–38. I have also learned much from Steven Wandler's dissertation, "Moral Luck and American Fiction: Identity, Aesthetics, History," Boston University, 2009.

12. For figurations of chance, see Rescher, *Luck*, 8–12; H. R. Patch, *The Goddess Fortuna in Medieval Literature* (Cambridge: Harvard University Press, 1927); Ian Baucom, *Specters of the Atlantic: Finance Capital, Slavery, and the Philosophy of History* (Durham: Duke University Press, 2005), 80–82; and Susan Mizruchi, "Risk Theory and the Contemporary American Novel," *American Literary History* 22:1 (Spring 2010), 109–135.

13. *Probabilistic Linguistics*, eds. Rens Bod, Jennifer Hay, and Stefanie Jannedy (Cambridge: MIT Press, 2003) ("language"); Joy J. Geng and Marlene Behrmann, "Spatial Probability as an Attentional Cue in Visual Search," *Perception and Psychophysics* 67:7 (2005), 1252–1268 ("visual data"); Fei Xu and Vashti Garcia, "Intuitive Statistics by 8-Month-Old Infants," *Proceedings of the National Academy of Sciences* 105:13 (April 2008), 5012–5015 ("infants"); Paul Glimcher, Michael Dorris, and Hannah Bayer, "Physiological Utility Theory and the Neuroeconomics of Choice," *Games and Economic Behavior* 52 (August 2005), 213–256 ("monkeys").

14. Ulrich Beck, *Risk Society: Towards a New Modernity*, trans. Mark Ritter (London: Sage Publications, 1992).

15. Lorraine Daston, "Life, Chance and Life Chances," *Daedalus* 137:1 (Winter 2008), 6.

16. Poe, *Poetry and Tales*, 421, 507.

17. Douglas Lane Patey, *Probability and Literary Form: Philosophic Theory and Literary Practice in the Augustan Age* (Cambridge: Cambridge University Press, 1984); Ross Hamilton, *Accident: A Philosophical and Literary History* (Chicago: University of Chicago Press, 2007); Michael Witmore, *Culture of Accidents: Unexpected Knowledges in Early Modern England* (Stanford: Stanford University Press, 2001); Thomas Kavanagh, *Enlightenment and the Shadows of Chance: The Novel and the Culture of Gambling in Eighteenth-Century France* (Baltimore: Johns Hopkins University Press, 1993); and Leland Monk, *Standard Deviations: Chance and the Modern British Novel* (Stanford: Stanford University Press, 1993). See also Martha Nussbaum, *The Fragility of Goodness: Luck and Ethics in Greek Tragedy and Philosophy*, 2nd ed. (New York: Cambridge University Press, 2001); and Gillian Beer, "The Reader's Wager: Lots, Sorts, and Futures," in *Open Fields: Science and Cultural Encounter* (Oxford: Clarendon Press, 1996), 273–294. For postmodernism, see for instance, N. Katherine Hayles, *Chaos Bound: Orderly Disorder in Contemporary Literature and Science* (Ithaca: Cornell University Press, 1990).

18. Walter Benn Michaels, *The Gold Standard and the Logic of Naturalism: American Literature at the Turn of the Century* (Berkeley: University of California Press, 1987), esp. 215–244; Wai Chee Dimock, *Residues of Justice: Literature, Law, Philosophy* (Berkeley: University of California Press, 1996), 96–139; Brook Thomas, *American Literary Realism and the Failed*

Promise of Contract (Berkeley: University of California Press, 1997), 122–155; Susan Mizruchi, *The Science of Sacrifice: American Literature and Modern Social Theory* (Princeton: Princeton University Press, 1998); Nan Goodman, *Shifting the Blame: Literature, Law, and the Theory of Accidents in Nineteenth-Century America* (Princeton: Princeton University Press, 1998); Eric Wertheimer, *Underwriting: The Poetics of Insurance in America, 1722–1872* (Stanford: Stanford University Press, 2006); Jason Puskar, *Accident Society: Fiction, Collectivity, and the Production of Chance* (Stanford: Stanford University Press, 2012). I was fortunate to read Puskar's manuscript after completing a draft of my own.

19. Andrew Delbanco, *The Death of Satan: How Americans Have Lost the Sense of Evil* (New York: Farrar, Straus and Giroux, 1995), esp. 143; Louis Menand, *The Metaphysical Club* (New York: Farrar, Straus and Giroux, 2001), 177–200; James Dawes, *The Language of War: Literature and Culture in the U.S. from the Civil War through World War II* (Cambridge: Harvard University Press, 2002), 26–69. Lears, *Something for Nothing.*

20. Samuel Johnson writes that the "conjectural critick" is always subject to the "chance of errour," for even the best interpretation is "but one reading of many probable" (*Preface to Shakespeare* [1765], in *Rasselas, Poems, and Selected Prose,* ed. Bertrand H. Bronson [New York: Holt, Rinehart and Winston, 1952], 304). Modern literary criticism implicitly follows Johnson's example in the general agreement that no single reading of a text is indisputability the true one. William Empson names probability as one type of literary-critical ambiguity (and links it to quantum physics) in *7 Types of Ambiguity* (1930; New York: New Directions, 1966), 5, 81. Even objectivist critics such as E. D. Hirsch Jr. see interpretive arguments as probabilistic ("Objective Interpretation," *PMLA* 75 [1960], 463–479).

21. John Tyndall, "The Belfast Address," *Literature and Science in the Nineteenth Century: An Anthology,* ed. Laura Otis (Oxford: Oxford University Press, 2002), 3.

22. For the rising power of experience as an analytic concept in modern Western thought, see Martin Jay, *Songs of Experience: Modern American and European Variations on a Universal Theme* (Berkeley: University of California Press, 2005). For helpful overviews of romantic science, see Jennifer J. Baker, "Natural Science and the Romanticisms," *ESQ: A Journal of the American Renaissance* 53:4 (Winter 2007), 387–412; Richard Holmes, *The Age of Wonder: How the Romantic Generation Discovered the Beauty and Terror of Science* (New York: Pantheon Books, 2008); and Laura Dassow Walls's books on Emerson, Thoreau, and Von Humboldt. George Levine, *Dying to Know: Scientific Epistemology and Narrative in Victorian England* (Chicago: University of Chicago Press, 2002), 278.

23. Eric Wilson, *Romantic Turbulence: Chaos, Ecology, and American Space* (New York: St. Martin's Press, 2000). See also Ira Livingston, *Arrow of Chaos: Romanticism and Postmodernity* (Minneapolis: University of Minnesota Press, 1997), esp. 6–9; and Angus Fletcher, *A New Theory for American Poetry: Democracy, the Environment, and the Future of Imagination* (Cambridge: Harvard University Press, 2004), 190–208, 225–245.

24. Gillian Beer, *Darwin's Plots: Evolutionary Narrative in Darwin, George Eliot, and Nineteenth-Century Fiction,* 3rd ed. (1983; Cambridge: Cambridge University Press, 2009), esp. 29–32. See also Levine, *Dying to Know,* 220–243. Though he remains focused on the influence of British romantics on American authors, Lee Rust Brown suggests how different uses of science can help differentiate British and American romanticism (*The Emerson Museum: Practical Romanticism and the Pursuit of the Whole* [Cambridge: Harvard University Press, 1997], 89). For a brief discussion of British romanticism and induction that suggests some emerging dynamics between literature and the new sciences of chance, see Poovey, *A History of the Modern Fact,* 325–328.

25. Richard Rorty, *Contingency, Irony, and Solidarity* (New York: Cambridge University Press, 1989); Menand, *The Metaphysical Club*; Joan Richardson, *A Natural History of Pragmatism: The Fact of Feeling from Jonathan Edwards to Gertrude Stein* (Cambridge: Cambridge University Press, 2007); Robert Brandom, "When Philosophy Paints Its Blue on Gray:

Irony and the Pragmatist Enlightenment," *boundary* 2 29 (Spring 2002), 1–28; Richard Poirier, *Poetry and Pragmatism* (Cambridge: Harvard University Press, 1992).

26. William James, "What Pragmatism Means" (1907), *Writings*, 2 vols. (New York: Library of America, 1987), 2:509.

27. Ralph Waldo Emerson, "The Poet" (1844), *Essays and Lectures* (New York: Library of America, 1983), 448.

28. William James, "The One and the Many" (1907), *Writings* 2:548.

CHAPTER 1

1. D. H. Lawrence, *Studies in Classic American Literature* (1923; New York: Viking, 1961), 65. T. S. Eliot, "From Poe to Valéry" (1948), *To Criticize the Critic and Other Writings* (Lincoln, Neb.: University of Nebraska Press, 1992), 41.

2. Edgar Allan Poe, *Poetry and Tales* (New York: Library of America, 1984), 38. Further references to this edition will be cited parenthetically as *PT*.

3. For Schiller and an extended reading of "Sonnet—To Science," see John Limon, *The Place of Fiction in the Time of Science: A Disciplinary History of American Writing* (New York: Cambridge University Press, 1990), 70–80.

4. Peter Dear, *Discipline and Experience: The Mathematical Way in the Scientific Revolution* (Chicago: University of Chicago Press, 1995), 245.

5. Edgar Allan Poe, *Essays and Reviews* (New York: Library of America, 1984), 8, 1243. Subsequent references to this edition will be cited parenthetically as *ER*.

6. *The Poe Log: A Documentary Life of Edgar Allan Poe, 1809–1849*, eds. Dwight Thomas and David K. Jackson (Boston: G.K. Hall, 1987), 719. Poe to George Isbell, February 29, 1848, *The Letters of Edgar Allan Poe*, 2 vols., ed. John Ward Ostrom (Cambridge: Harvard University Press, 1948), 2:363. For a slightly different version of this complaint, see *Eureka* (*PT* 1266).

7. John Irwin, *The Mystery to a Solution: Poe, Borges, and the Analytic Detective Story* (Baltimore: Johns Hopkins University Press, 1994), esp. 318–397. See also Lawrence Frank, *Victorian Detective Fiction and the Nature of Evidence: The Scientific Investigations of Poe, Dickens, and Doyle* (New York: Palgrave Macmillan, 2003), 29–43.

8. Jorge Luis Borges, *Borges: A Reader*, eds. Emir Rodriquez Monegal and Alastair Reid (New York: E.P. Dutton, 1981), 147.

9. Poe to Charles Fenno Hoffman, September 20, 1848, *The Letters of Edgar Allan Poe*, 2:380; *PT* 508. See also *The Scarlet Letter* (1850), another narrative of detection, which accords Chillingworth and Dimmesdale only nominally intuitive powers (Nathaniel Hawthorne, *The Scarlet Letter* [New York: Library of America, 1990], 116).

10. Poe to Philip P. Cooke, August 9, 1846, *The Letters of Edgar Allan Poe*, 2:328.

11. For Poe, Barnum, and hoaxes, see Jonathan Elmer, *Reading at the Social Limit: Affect, Mass Culture, and Edgar Allan Poe* (Stanford: Stanford University Press, 1995), 182–192. Broader accounts of Barnum's appeal to willfully and thus only partially duped audiences include James W. Cook, *The Arts of Deception: Playing with Fraud in the Age of Barnum* (Cambridge: Harvard University Press, 2001).

12. David Van Leer, "Detecting Truth: The World of the Dupin Tales," *New Essays on Poe's Major Tales*, ed. Kenneth Silverman (New York: Cambridge University Press, 1993), 65–92; Loisa Nygaard, "Winning the Game: Inductive Reasoning in Poe's 'The Murders in the Rue Morgue,'" *Studies in Romanticism* 33:2 (Summer 1994), 223–254.

13. Mary Poovey, *A History of the Modern Fact* (Chicago: University of Chicago Press, 1998).

14. Barbara Shapiro, *Probability and Certainty in Seventeenth-Century England: A Study of the Relationships between Natural Science, Religion, History, Law, and Literature* (Princeton: Princeton University Press, 1983), 5 (see also 56–70). Richard Whately, *Elements of Logic* (1826; London: Lumley, 1848), 257–258. William Whewell, *The Philosophy of the*

Inductive Sciences, 2 vols. (London: John W. Parker, 1840), 1:54. More generally, see L. Jonathan Cohen, *Knowledge and Language: Selected Essays of L. Jonathan Cohen*, ed. James Logue (Dordrecht: Kluwer, 2002), 245–259; and Theodore Bozeman, *Protestants in an Age of Science: The Baconian Ideal and Antebellum American Religious Thought* (Chapel Hill: University of North Carolina Press, 1977), 64–71. For the problem of induction as a continuing challenge in the twentieth century, see Nelson Goodman, *Fact, Fiction, and Forecast* (Cambridge: Harvard University Press, 1955), 63–86; and Karl Popper, *Conjectures and Refutations* (New York: Harper and Row, 1968).

15. Poe to George Isbell, February 29, 1848, *The Letters of Edgar Allan Poe*, 2:363.

16. William Whewell, *The Philosophy of the Inductive Sciences*, 2 vols. (London: John W. Parker, 1840), 1:24. John F. W. Herschel, *Preliminary Discourse on the Study of Natural Philosophy* (London: Longman, Brown, Green, and Longmans, 1851), 196–197; John Stuart Mill, *A System of Logic: Ratiocinative and Inductive*, 2 vols. (London: Longmans, Green, Reader, and Dyer, 1875), 2:87–94. See also Herschel's review of Whewell in the *Quarterly Review* (June 1841). For an overview of the state of logic in antebellum America, see a detailed, generally supportive review of Mill's *System of Logic* in *The United States Magazine and Democratic Review* (November 1844), reprinted in *The North American Review* (October 1845), as well as a more hostile review in *The Christian Examiner* (May 1846), which charged Mill with denying transcendental truths by relying too heavily on induction and probability.

17. Cohen, *Knowledge and Language*, 155–174. For an excellent discussion of Peirce and guessing with reference to Poe, see Jason Puskar, *Accident Society: Fiction, Collectivity, and the Production of Chance* (Stanford: Stanford University Press, 2012).

18. Martin Jay, *Songs of Experience: Modern American and European Variations on a Universal Theme* (Berkeley: University of California Press, 2005), 47.

19. Poe's "Thou Art the Man" (1844) also seems to allude to *The Ninth Bridgewater Treatise*, in which Babbage discusses how "*dead bodies*" will "confront the murderer" as if to say, "*Thou art the man*" (Charles Babbage, *The Ninth Bridgewater Treatise* [London: John Murray, 1838], 118–119). For Poe and Babbage, see Terence Whalen, *Edgar Allan Poe and the Masses: The Political Economy of Literature in Antebellum America* (Princeton: Princeton University Press, 1999), 249–273.

20. "The Gambler," *Times and Hartford Advertiser* (September 16, 1823); "Causes and Effects," *City Gazette and Commercial Daily Advertiser* (August 15, 1822); "First Epistle of S. S. Southworth to the Editor of the R.I. Republican," *Rhode-Island Republican* (July 2, 1834).

21. John Tillotson, "The Wisdom of Being Religious," in *The Works of the Most Reverend Dr. John Tillotson, Vol. I* (Edinburgh: Hamilton et al., 1748), 23.

22. For compatibility between probability theory and the argument from design, see Ian Hacking, *The Emergence of Probability* (Cambridge: Cambridge University Press, 1975), 166–175. A prototypical example of the effort to align probability theory with Christianity is De Moivre's 1717 disclaimer: "*[A]ltho' Chance produces Irregularities . . . those Irregularities will bear no proportion to the recurrency of that Order which naturally results from ORIGINAL DESIGN*" (Abraham De Moivre, *The Doctrine of Chances: Or, A Method of Calculating the Probabilities of Events in Play*, 3rd ed. [1717; London: A. Millar, 1756], 251).

23. "Gossip with Readers and Correspondents," *The Knickerbocker, or New York Monthly Magazine* (December 1850).

24. Pierre Laplace, *A Philosophical Essay on Probabilities*, trans. Frederick Truscott and Frederick Emory (New York: Dover, 1951), 196. John Stuart Mill, *A System of Logic: Ratiocinative and Inductive*, 2 vols. (London: Longmans, Green, Reader, and Dyer, 1875), 1:288. De Morgan quoted in Theodore Porter, *The Rise of Statistical Thinking, 1820–1900*

(Princeton: Princeton University Press, 1986), 75. Antonio Damasio, *Descartes' Error: Emotion, Reason, and the Human Brain* (New York: Putnam, 1994).

25. Lorraine Daston, *Classical Probability in the Enlightenment* (Princeton: Princeton University Press, 1988), 58–111.

26. Paul Glimcher, Michael Dorris, and Hannah Bayer, "Physiological Utility Theory and the Neuroeconomics of Choice," *Games and Economic Behavior* 52 (August 2005), 213–256; Justin Halberda and Lisa Feigenson, "Individual Differences in Nonverbal Number Acuity Predict Math Achievement," *Nature* 455 (2008), 665–668. Jonah Lehrer, *Proust Was a Neuroscientist* (New York: Houghton Mifflin, 2007). For a historically grounded account of romantic literature as a precursor to modern neuroscience (focusing on early psychology, not mathematics or probability), see Alan D. Richardson, *British Romanticism and the Science of the Mind* (Cambridge: Cambridge University Press, 2001).

27. Shawn Rosenheim, "Detective Fiction, Psychoanalysis, and the Analytic Sublime," *The American Face of Edgar Allan Poe*, eds. Shawn Rosenheim and Stephen Rachman (Baltimore: Johns Hopkins University Press, 1995), 160–161. Briefly, Cuvier in the text cited by Dupin actually emphasizes the gentle nature of orangutans and downplays their similarity to humans. Nicholas Rescher, *Luck: The Brilliant Randomness of Everyday Life* (New York: Farrar, Straus and Giroux, 1995), 8 ("Horace").

28. A counter-example is "Instinct vs. Reason—A Black Cat" (1840) in which Poe claims that "the boundary between instinct and reason is of a very shadowy nature" and ultimately attributes intuition to God ("the divine mind itself acting *immediately* upon its creatures") (*PT* 372, 370).

29. Porter, *The Rise of Statistical Thinking*. See also Patricia Cline Cohen, *A Calculating People: The Spread of Numeracy in Early America* (Chicago: University of Chicago Press, 1982); Stephen M. Stigler, *The History of Statistics: The Measurement of Uncertainty before 1900* (Cambridge: Harvard University Press, 1986); and Mary Poovey, "Figures of Arithmetic, Figures of Speech: the Discourse of Statistics in the 1830s," in *Questions of Evidence: Proof, Practice, and Persuasion across the Disciplines*, eds. James Chandler, Arnold Davidson, and Harry Harootunian (Chicago: University of Chicago Press, 1991), 401–421. For the penetration of statistical thinking and the construction of mass society in twentieth-century America, see Sarah Elizabeth Igo, *The Averaged American: Surveys, Citizens, and the Making of a Mass Public* (Cambridge: Harvard University Press, 2007).

30. "The Science of Statistics," *The Commercial Review* (March 1847). Percy Shelley, *A Defence of Poetry* (1821; 1840), in *Shelley's Poetry and Prose*, eds. Donald Reiman and Neil Fraistat (New York: Norton, 2002), 530.

31. Ralph Waldo Emerson, *Representative Men* (1850), in *Essays and Lectures* (New York: Library of America, 1983), 670. See also Emerson's "Manners" (1844).

32. Barbara Packer, "Emerson and the Terrible Tabulations of the French," *The Transient and Permanent: The Transcendentalist Movement and Its Contexts*, eds. Charles Capper and Conrad Edick Wright (Boston: Massachusetts Historical Society, 1999), 148–167. For Emerson and statistics, see also Eric Wertheimer, *Underwriting: The Poetics of Insurance in America, 1722–1872* (Stanford: Stanford University Press, 2006), 133–134. Walt Whitman, *Leaves of Grass and Other Writings*, ed. Michael Moon (New York: Johns Hopkins University Press, 2002), 362, 616, 622, 623. For *Leaves of Grass* and the taming of chance from the perspective of *naturphilosophie* and hermeneutics (but not quantitative science), see Eric Wilson, *Romantic Turbulence: Chaos, Ecology, and American Space* (New York: St. Martin's Press, 2000), 118–140; and Kerry Larson, *Imagining Equality in Nineteenth-Century American Literature* (Cambridge: Cambridge University Press, 2008), 97–106.

33. Leer, "Detecting Truth"; Mark Seltzer, "The Crime System," *Critical Inquiry* 30 (Spring 2004), 557–583; Leon Chai, *The Romantic Foundations of the American Renaissance* (Ithaca: Cornell University Press, 1987), 116–120.

34. See also Poe's "Chapter of Suggestions" (1845): "The theory of chance, or . . . the Calculus of Probabilities, has this remarkable peculiarity, that its truth in general is in direct proportion with its fallacy in particular" (*ER* 1292).

35. Adolphe Quetelet, *A Treatise on Man and the Development of His Faculties*, trans., ed. Solomon Diamond (1842; Gainesville, Fla.: Scholars' Facsimiles and Reprints, 1969), 5, 7. This is the first English translation of Quetelet's 1835 book.

36. Quetelet responds to Charles Dupin in *A Treatise on Man* (85). For Charles Dupin, see Daston, *Classical Probability*, 365–366; and Porter, *The Rise of Statistical Thinking*, 82–84. Irwin's account of Poe and Charles Dupin is convincing, though it focuses on politics, not probability theory (*Mystery to a Solution*, 340–356).

37. Thomas Dunn English, "Hints to Authors: On the Germanesque," *John Donkey* (June 3, 1848).

38. James Beattie, *Elements of Moral Science*, 2 vols. (Edinburgh: Cadell and Creech, 1793), 2:595; Michael McKeon, *The Origins of the English Novel, 1600–1740* (Baltimore: Johns Hopkins University Press, 1987), 53–64. Patey, *Probability and Literary Form*, esp. 127, 155–166. For a compatible argument of how probabilism shaped novels in eighteenth-century France, see Kavanagh, *Enlightenment and the Shadows of Chance*.

39. Lord Kames (Henry Home), *Elements of Criticism* (New York: Huntington and Savage, 1847), 418. For Kames in America, see Theo Davis, *Formalism, Experience, and the Making of American Literature in the Nineteenth Century* (New York: Cambridge University Press, 2007), 32–44. For antebellum reviewers, see Nina Baym, *Novels, Readers, and Reviewers: Responses to Fiction in Antebellum America* (Ithaca: Cornell University Press, 1984), 78–80.

40. "National and Historical Novels," *Court and Lady's Magazine, Monthly Critic, and Museum* (June 1837).

41. "Victor Hugo and the French Drama," *The Gentleman's Magazine* (November 1837).

42. Michael Witmore, *Culture of Accidents: Unexpected Knowledges in Early Modern England* (Stanford: Stanford University Press, 2001), 111–129; Francis Bacon, *The New Organon*, eds. Lisa Jardine and Michael Silverthorne (Cambridge: Cambridge University Press, 2000), 148. See also McKeon, *Origins of the English Novel*, esp. 71.

43. Quetelet, *A Treatise on Man*, v.

44. Review of *The Narrative of Arthur Gordon Pym*, rpt. in *Edgar Allan Poe: The Critical Heritage*, ed. I. M. Walker (London: Routledge and Kegan Paul, 1986), 96. For other prefaces that assert the plausibility of the implausible, see Melville's *Mardi* (1849) and Caroline Kirkland's *A New Home: Who'll Follow?* (1839), a book that Poe praised for its "*truth* and novelty" (*ER* 1181).

45. "Statistics of French Periodical Literature," *The Gentleman's Magazine* (February 1839).

46. For the "chancy, complex, and chaotic" world of antebellum print culture, see Ronald Zboray, *A Fictive People: Antebellum Economic Development and the American Reading Public* (New York: Oxford University Press, 1993), 18. For Poe and print culture, see Whalen, *Edgar Allan Poe and the Masses*; Meredith McGill, *American Literature and the Culture of Reprinting, 1834–1854* (Philadelphia: University of Pennsylvania Press, 2003), 141–217; and Leon Jackson, *The Business of Letters: Authorial Economies in Antebellum America* (Stanford: Stanford University Press, 2008).

47. Quetelet, *A Treatise on Man*, 6, x.

48. "Nature and History of Vital Statistics," *New York Journal of Medicine and Collateral Sciences* (November 1844). Guns and pistols were the most popular murder weapons.

49. Kathleen Woodward, *Statistical Panic: Cultural Politics and Poetics of the Emotions* (Durham: Duke University Press, 2009), 215. See also an 1874 article that complains about people frightened by reported accidents: "Every published instance of injury by lightning keeps dozens of them at their windows. . . . They enter railway cars and steamers with a mental calculation of the doctrine of chances as to their emerging alive; they sit down to

torturing dinners with thoughts of supposititious trichinae" ("Editor's Table," *Appleton's Journal* [July 18, 1874]).

50. References to the study of dead letters include: Laplace, *A Philosophical Essay on Probabilities*, 61; "Essay Philosophique sur les Probabilités," *Edinburgh Review* 23 (September 1814), 320–340; Whewell, *The Philosophy of the Inductive Sciences*, 2:553; *The Popular Encyclopedia, Vol. VII* (Glasgow: Blackie and Son, 1841), 542; M. A. Quetelet, *Letters on the Theory of Probabilities*, trans. Olinthus Downes (London: Charles and Edwin Layton, 1846), 150; and J. R. McCulloch, *The Principles of Political Economy* (4th ed.; Edinburgh: Adam and Charles Black, 1849), 251. Similar studies with similar results were performed in London and Washington, D.C., though after Poe and Melville's stories ("The Theory of Chances," *Flag of Our Union* [November 11, 1854], reprinted from the *Boston Journal*). De Moivre, *The Doctrine of Chances*, v.

51. Van Leer, "Detecting Truth," 88; Seltzer, "The Crime System," 559–563. See also Seltzer's "Statistical Persons," *Diacritics* 17 (1987), 82–98. For abortion and the real Rogers's case, see Laura Saltz, "'(Horrible to Relate!)': Recovering the Body of Marie Roget," *The American Face of Edgar Allan Poe*, 237–267.

52. For Weber and Durkheim, see Susan Mizruchi, *The Science of Sacrifice: American Literature and Modern Social Theory* (Princeton: Princeton University Press, 1998), 8–12. As if predicting Whitman, Tocqueville wrote in 1840, "As all the citizens who compose a democratic community are nearly equal and alike, the poet cannot dwell upon any one of them; but the nation itself invites the exercise of his powers. The general similitude of individuals, which renders any one of them taken separately as an improper subject of poetry, allows poets to include them all in the same imagery, and to take a general survey of the people itself" (*Democracy in America*, 181).

53. Quetelet, *A Treatise on Man*, 7.

54. Georg Simmel, "The Metropolis and Mental Life" (1903), *The Sociology of Georg Simmel*, trans. and ed. Kurt H. Wolff (Glencoe, Ill.: The Free Press, 1950), 410.

55. William Wordsworth, *The Prelude*, in *William Wordsworth*, ed. Stephen Gill (Oxford: Oxford University Press, 1984), 483–486. Quetelet, "Researches on the Propensity for Crime at Various Ages" (1831), translated and quoted in Daniel R. Headrick, *When Information Came of Age: Technologies of Knowledge in the Age of Reason and Revolution* (Oxford: Oxford University Press, 2000), 83. Referring to Quetelet's averages, Peirce praises "the great utility which such fictions sometimes have in science" (Charles Peirce, *The Essential Peirce: Selected Philosophical Writings*, 2 vols, eds. Nathan Houser, Christian Kloesel, et al [Bloomington: Indiana University Press, 1992–1998], 1:144).

56. Wilkie Collins, *My Miscellanies* (New York: Harper and Brothers, 1899), 128.

57. Robert Montgomery, *The Omnipresence of the Deity: A Poem* (London: Simpkin and Marshall, 1834).

58. For Buster Keaton and accidents, see Ross Hamilton, *Accident: A Philosophical and Literary History* (Chicago: University of Chicago Press, 2007), 281–286; Witmore, *Culture of Accidents*.

59. "Mutual Life Insurance," *Merchant's Magazine and Commercial Review, Vol. 16* (New York: Freeman Hunt, 1847), 153.

60. For "The Angel of the Odd" as an attack on Dunn English, see J. Gerald Kennedy, "'A Mania for Composition': Poe's Annus Mirabilis and the Violence of Nation-Building," *American Literary History* 17:1 (2005), 30n14.

61. Aristotle, *Poetics*, trans. Malcolm Heath (New York: Penguin, 1996), 41, 45. For deep literary histories that begin with Aristotle on chance but emphasize the *Metaphysics*, see Witmore, *Culture of Accidents*; and Hamilton, *Accident*. Etienne Dumont, *A Treatise on Judicial Evidence*, trans. Jeremy Bentham (London: Baldwin, Cradock, and Joy, 1825), 282; Peirce, *The Essential Peirce*, 1:198. John Venn, *The Logic of Chance* (London: Macmillan and Co., 1876), xxvi, 448–449.

62. For Balzac and Dickens's extraordinary realism, see Donald Fanger, *Dostoevsky and Romantic Realism: A Study of Dostoevsky in Relation to Balzac, Dickens, and Gogol* (Evanston: Northwestern University Press, 1998), 91–94. Bucket says in *Bleak House*, "I don't suppose there's a move on the board that would surprise *me* ... any possible move whatever ... being a probable move according to my experience" (Charles Dickens, *Bleak House* [New York: Penguin, 1971], 782). Wilkie Collins, *Basil* (1852; New York: Harper and Brothers, 1874), v. Nathaniel Hawthorne, *The Blithedale Romance*, eds. Seymour Gross and Rosalie Murphy (New York: Norton, 1978), 2 (see also his preface to *The House of the Seven Gables* [1851], which grants romances a "certain latitude" from the "probable and ordinary course of man's experience"). Henry James, *The Art of the Novel: Critical Prefaces*, ed. Richard Blackmur (New York: Scribner, 1962), 84. Joseph Conrad, *Lord Jim* (Mineola, New York: Dover, 1999), 55. Paul Auster, *The New York Trilogy* (New York: Penguin, 1990), 3.

63. See, for instance, *The Purloined Poe: Lacan, Derrida, and Psychoanalytic Reading*, eds. John P. Muller and William J. Richardson (Baltimore: Johns Hopkins University Press, 1988); Barbara Johnson, *The Critical Difference: Essays in the Contemporary Rhetoric of Reading* (Baltimore: Johns Hopkins University Press, 1980), 110–146; Joseph Riddel, *Purloined Letters: Originality and Repetition in American Literature*, ed. Mark Bauerlein (Baton Rouge: Louisiana State University Press, 1995), 140–148.

64. Johnson, *The Critical Difference*, 110–146.

65. "The Philosophy of Chance," *The Magnolia* (December 1842).

66. Tocqueville, *Democracy in America*, 18. Jackson Lears, *Something for Nothing: Luck in America* (New York: Penguin, 2003).

67. Arthur Conan Doyle, *The Complete Sherlock Holmes* (New York: Doubleday, 1927), 901.

68. For a materialist discussion of "The Purloined Letter" as simultaneously a (post)modern and an antebellum text, see John Carlos Rowe, "Poe, Antebellum Slavery, and Modern Criticism," in *Poe's Pym: Critical Explorations*, ed. Richard Kopley (Durham: Duke University Press, 1992), 122–126.

69. "The Chess Game," *The Baltimore Monument: A Weekly Journal, Devoted to Polite Literature, Science, and the Fine Arts* (October 15, 1836). "Are Games of Contrivance Injurious?" *American Annals of Education* (July 1838). "Chess," *The Family Magazine; or, Monthly Abstract of General Knowledge* (1837), 379. For an account linking chess to indeterminacy, see Sacvan Bercovitch, "Games of Chess: A Model of Literary and Cultural Studies," *Centuries' Ends, Narrative Means*, ed. Robert Newman (Stanford: Stanford University Press, 1996), 15–57.

70. Charles Lamb, *Essays of Elia* (Menston, England: The Scolar Press, 1969), 83. William Chatto, *Facts and Speculations on the Origin and History of Playing Cards* (London: John Russell Smith, 1838), 17. "The Science of Chess," *Godey's Lady's Book* (April 1844); William Burton, "The Three Breakfasts," *The Lady's Book* (November 1844). Burton may also satirize Poe's logical rhetoric in "Descent into the Maelstrom" (1841), which refers to "Sexagesima" (*PT* 436). For Hume on his deathbed, see *Hume's Reception in Early America*, ed. Mark G. Spencer (Bristol: Thoemmes Press, 2002), esp. 187.

71. "A Catechism of Whist," *Blackwood's Edinburgh Magazine* (November 1835). For handbooks, see the often reissued works of Edmond Hoyle, T. Matthews, and Major A. (a pseudonym). Jonathan Harrington Green, *An Exposure of the Arts and Miseries of Gambling* (Philadelphia: G.B. Zieber, 1847), 189. William Pole, "Games at Cards Played by Machinery," *New York Times* (January 30, 1876). William Pole, *The Philosophy of Whist: An Essay on the Scientific and Intellectual Aspects of the Modern Game* (London: Thos. de la Rue and Co., 1884), 3–4. William Pole, *The Evolution of Whist* (London: Longmans, Green, 1894), 97. For gaming in the postbellum period in general, see Michael Orienda, *Sporting with the Gods: The Rhetoric of Play and Game in American Culture* (New York: Cambridge University Press, 1991), 161–191.

72. Laplace, *A Philosophical Essay on Probabilities*, 3. Quetelet quoted in Porter, *The Rise of Statistical Thinking*, 105.

73. By reading Poe's mistake as unintentional, I side with William Wimsatt against Leon Chai (see Chai, *The Romantic Foundations of the American Renaissance*, 120).

74. Walter Benjamin, "On Some Motifs in Baudelaire" (1939), *Illuminations*, ed. Hannah Arendt, trans. Harry Zohn (1955; New York: Harcourt, Brace, and World, 1968), 176–180; Stéphane Mallarmé, "A Throw of the Dice" (1897), *Collected Poems*, trans. Henry Weinfield (Berkeley: University of California Press, 1994), 78–80. The title of Mallarmé's poem is sometimes translated as, "A Throw of the Dice Will Never Abolish Chance."

75. Samuel Johnson, *The Rambler: In Three Volumes* (London: G. Walker, 1820), 3:242. George Eliot, *Daniel Deronda* (New York: Barnes and Noble Classics, 2005), 12, 14. By creating a calculating heroine who remains vulnerable to the enchantments of chance, Eliot—like Poe—proleptically vindicates the improbabilities of her least plausible novel. Joan Dayan, *Fables of Mind* (New York: Oxford, 1987), 14.

76. Ian Hacking, *The Taming of Chance* (New York: Cambridge University Press, 1990), 200–201. For a helpful summary of Peirce's views of chance, see Andrew Reynolds, *Peirce's Scientific Metaphysics: The Philosophy of Chance, Law, and Evolution* (Nashville, Tenn.: Vanderbilt University Press, 2002), 142–175.

77. Nancy Harrowitz, "The Body of the Detective Model: Charles S. Peirce and Edgar Allan Poe," *The Sign of Three: Dupin, Holmes, Peirce*, eds. Umberto Eco and Thomas Sebeok (Bloomington: Indiana University Press, 1983), 179–197. Harrowitz also discusses Peirce's knowledge of Poe (195), as does Joseph Brent in *Charles Sanders Peirce: A Life: Revised and Enlarged Edition* (Bloomington: Indiana University Press, 1993), 22. See also Paul Grimstad, "C. Auguste Dupin and Charles S. Peirce: An Abductive Affinity," *The Edgar Allan Poe Review* 6:2 (2005), 22–30.

78. Peirce, *The Essential Peirce*, 15, 44, 216, 10–11, 348. Peirce on logic needing aesthetics quoted in Brent, *Charles Sanders Peirce*, 53. For Peirce's crime solving and relations to Poe, see Puskar, *Accident Society*.

79. See, for instance, Peirce's "The Fixation of Belief" (1877).

80. Riddel, *Purloined Letters*, 143. Rosenheim, "Detective Fiction and Psychoanalysis," 155. Irwin, *The Mystery to a Solution*, 11; Cavell, "Being Odd, Getting Even," *The American Face of Edgar Allan Poe*, 3–36. Cavell's most explicit reference to "The Purloined Letter" is his title, but by departing from Lacan and Derrida, he conjures the critical history of the story. For Hegel, see *The Phenomenology of Spirit* (1807), section 79. Here I generally follow D. A. Miller's critique of deconstructive accounts of *Bleak House*: it is not that post-structural readings of "The Purloined Letter" are untrue; rather, they are too abstract (*The Novel and the Police* [Berkeley: University of California Press, 1988], 99).

81. William James, *Writings*, 2 vols. (New York: Library of America, 1987), 2:508.

82. Richard Rorty, "Philosophy as a Kind of Writing: An Essay on Derrida," *Consequences of Pragmatism: Essays, 1972–1980* (Minneapolis: University of Minnesota Press, 1982), 90–109.

83. James, *Writings*, 2:522; 2:779; 2:579.

84. J. Hillis Miller, "English Romanticism, American Romanticism: What's the Difference?" in *Transatlantic Literary Studies: A Reader*, eds. Susan Manning and Andrew Taylor (Baltimore: Johns Hopkins University Press, 2007), esp. 90–91; Lorenzo Fabbri, *The Domestication of Derrida: Rorty, Pragmatism and Deconstruction*, trans. Daniele Manni, eds. Vuslat Demirkoparan and Ari Lee Laskin (New York: Continuum, 2008).

85. Richard Poirier, *Poetry and Pragmatism* (Cambridge: Harvard University Press, 1992), 186.

86. Peirce, *The Essential Peirce*, 1:358. For the influence of De Morgan, whom Peirce met in 1870, see Brent, *Charles Sanders Peirce: A Life*, 79–80. James, *Writings*, 2:859–860.

87. Louis Menand, *The Metaphysical Club* (New York: Farrar, Straus and Giroux, 2001); Joan Richardson, *A Natural History of Pragmatism: The Fact of Feeling from Jonathan Edwards to Gertrude Stein* (Cambridge: Cambridge University Press, 2007).

88. James, *Writings*, 2:1177. For intersubjectivity and radical empiricism, see Robert Chodat, *Worldly Acts and Sentient Things: The Persistence of Agency from Stein to DeLillo* (Ithaca: Cornell University Press, 2008), 61–62.

89. John Keats, "Lamia," *The Poetical Works of John Keats*, ed. H. Buxton Forman (New York: Thomas Y. Crowell, 1895), 221, 238, 240.

90. Bacon, *The New Organon*, 69. Note that a vulture is sometimes substituted for an eagle in nineteenth-century accounts of Prometheus.

91. "Edgar Allan Poe," *Scribner's Monthly* (May 1880).

CHAPTER 2

1. Nathaniel Hawthorne, *The English Notebooks*, in Herman Melville, *Journals*, eds. Howard C. Horsford and Lynn Horth, vol. 15 of *The Writings of Herman Melville* (Chicago: Northwestern University Press and the Newberry Library, 1989), 628–629.

2. Herman Melville, *Journals*, 9, 4. For Melville's early relation to romantic philosophy, see Robert Milder, *Exiled Royalties: Melville and the Life We Imagine* (Oxford: Oxford University Press, 2006), 27–49.

3. Unless otherwise indicated, information on Melville's library, borrowing, and reading comes from Merton Sealts Jr., *Melville's Reading: Revised and Enlarged Edition* (Columbia: University of South Carolina Press, 1988). For the revival of skepticism in the Early Modern period, see Richard Popkin, *The History of Scepticism from Savonarola to Bayle*, 3rd ed. (Oxford: Oxford University Press, 2003).

4. Melville, *Journals*, 628; William James, *Writings*, 2 vols. (New York: Library of America, 1987), 2:537.

5. Herman Melville, *Moby-Dick*, in *Redburn, White-Jacket, Moby-Dick* (New York: Library of America, 1983), 795. Subsequent references to this text cited parenthetically.

6. Seneca, *Seneca's Morals by Way of Abstract*, trans. Roger L'Estrange (Philadelphia: Grigg and Elliot, 1834), 119. Melville owned an edition of this translation, which he almost certainly read prior to 1849. For Melville's learning in classical philosophy, see Merton M. Sealts Jr., *Pursuing Melville: 1940–1980* (Madison: University of Wisconsin Press, 1982), 23–30, 250–336. Seneca's call for cheerful submission to providence is also ironically echoed in the final line of Melville's "Lee in the Capitol" (1866). For the stoics and providence, see Genevieve Lloyd, *Providence Lost* (Cambridge: Harvard University Press, 2008), 90–128.

7. In the nineteenth century, "providence" had stronger Christian connotations than the more secular "fate," though the two terms were often used synonymously and were generally taken to be compatible. See, for instance, John Kitto, *The Cyclopedia of Biblical Literature, Vol. II* (1845; New York: American Book Exchange, 1881), 797. Influential discussions of the compatibility of fate and providence appear in Chrysippus (see Lloyd, *Providence Lost*, 91) and Boethius, *The Consolation of Philosophy*, trans. Philip Ridpath (c.524; London: C. Dilly, 1785), 167.

8. Thomas Browne, *Religio Medici*, in *The Works of Sir Thomas Browne, Volume I*, ed. Charles Sayle (1643; London: Grant Richards, 1904), 27–28.

9. Michel de Montaigne, *The Complete Essays*, trans. and ed. M. A. Screech (New York: Penguin, 1987), 614, 202, 1017, 379, 550. For Montaigne's advice on drinking, see Emerson's "Montaigne" (1850), *Essays and Lectures* (New York: Library of America, 1983), 692. Melville celebrates punch-driven philosophizing in his letters to Hawthorne.

10. Michael Colacurcio, "'Excessive and Organic Ill': Melville, Evil, and the Question of Politics," *Religion and Literature* 34:3 (Autumn 2002), 1–26.

11. On the contrast between the providentialism of the Stoics and the probabilism of Carneades and later skeptics, see Bury's introduction to Sextus Empiricus, *Outlines of Pyrrhonism*, trans. R. G. Bury (Cambridge: Harvard University Press, 1933), xxxiv-xxxvi.
Seneca, *Seneca's Morals*, 339. Diogenes Laertius, *Lives of Eminent Philosophers*, 2 vols.,
trans. R. D. Hicks (Cambridge: Harvard University Press, 1991), 511. Melville owned an
1853 copy of *Lives*, though he probably had earlier access to this canonical work. Sextus
Empiricus, *Outlines of Pyrrhonism*, 339, 343. For Aristotle, accident, and whiteness, see
Ross Hamilton, *Accident: A Philosophical and Literary History* (Chicago: University of Chi-
cago Press, 2007), 11–16. Mark S. Lussier discusses chance and Coleridge's "Rime" in
Romantic Dynamics: The Poetics of Physicality (New York: St. Martin's Press, 2000), 80–81.

12. Francis Newman, *Lectures on Logic, or On the Science of Evidence Generally Embracing Both
Demonstrative and Probable Reasonings with the Doctrine of Causation* (Oxford: J. H. Park,
1838), 131–132. John Calvin, *Institutes of the Christian Religion*, 2 vols., trans. John Allen
(Philadelphia: Presbyterian Board, 1921), 1:192. John Milton, *A Treatise on Christian
Doctrine*, trans. Charles R. Sumner (Cambridge: Charles Knight, 1825), 203. For Milton's
views on fate and free will in *Paradise Lost* and *de doctrina Christiana*, see Stephen M.
Fallon, "'Elect above the rest': Theology and Self-Representation in Milton," *Milton and
Heresy*, eds. Stephen B. Dobranski and John Peter Rumrich (New York: Cambridge Uni-
versity Press, 1998), 93–116. For Puritanism and chance, see Margo Todd, "Providence,
Chance, and the New Science in Early Stuart Cambridge," *Historical Journal* 29:2 (June
1986), 697–711. Wai Chee Dimock, *Residues of Justice: Literature, Law, Philosophy* (Berkeley: University of California Press, 1996), 128–135; Michael Witmore, *Culture of Accidents: Unexpected Knowledges in Early Modern England* (Stanford: Stanford University
Press, 2001), 17–61; and Hamilton, *Accidents*, 30–41 all discuss Christian denials of
chance stretching back to Augustine.

13. Jonathan Edwards, *A Careful and Strict Inquiry into the Modern Prevailing Notions of that
Freedom of the Will* (New York: Leavitt and Allen, 1857), 15, 82. For Watts's etiological
views in general and denial of chance in particular, see *Essay on the Freedom of the Will in
God and in Creatures* (1732), in *The Works of the Rev. Isaac Watts*, Vol. IV (Leeds: Edward
Bains, 1813), 489. For "soft determinism" and Edwards's legacy in antebellum America,
see Allen C. Guelzo, *Edwards on the Will: A Century of American Theological Debate* (Mid-
dletown: Wesleyan University Press, 1989), esp. 7–8.

14. Jackson Lears, *Something for Nothing: Luck in America* (New York: Penguin, 2003), 140.
Sacvan Bercovitch, *The American Jeremiad* (Madison: University of Wisconsin Press,
1978); and *The Rites of Assent: Transformations in the Symbolic Construction of America*
(New York: Routledge, 1993).

15. Charles Grandison Finney, "Atheism," *Skeleton of a Course of Theological Lectures, Vol. I*
(Oberlin, Ohio: James Steele, 1840), 33; Lyman Beecher, "The Being of a God," *Political
Atheism and Kindred Subjects* (Boston: John P. Jewett, 1852), 22. Theodore Parker, "Cud-
worth's Intellectual System" (1840), *Saint Bernard and Other Papers*, ed. Charles Wendte
(Boston: American Unitarian Association, 1911), 74. John Wesley, "On the Education of
Children" (1811), *The Works of the Reverend John Wesley, Volume II*, ed. John Emory (New
York: Mason and Lane, 1840), 311. Orville Dewey, *Discourses on Human Nature, Human
Life, and the Nature of Religion* (1847; New York: Charles S. Francis, 1868), 215. For an
overview of atheism in nineteenth-century America, see James Turner, *Without God,
Without Creed: The Origins of Unbelief in America* (Baltimore: Johns Hopkins University
Press, 1985).

16. Anthony Collins, *A Philosophical Inquiry Concerning Human Liberty* (London: Progressive
Publishing, 1890), 72. Anthony Ashley Cooper, *Characteristicks of Men, Manners, Opinions, Times* (London: 1714), 277. Thomas Reid, *Essays on the Powers of the Human Mind*
(1822; London: Thomas Tegg, 1827), 326.

17. "Desirableness of God's Providence," *New York Evangelist* (August 7, 1851); John Cumming, "The Christian Religion or No Religion," *Pulpit Eloquence of the Nineteenth Century*, ed. Henry Fish (1857; New York: Dodd, Mead, and Co., 1871), 693–694.

18. Colin Jager, *The Book of God: Secularization and Design in the Romantic Era* (Philadelphia: University of Pennsylvania Press, 2007).

19. For the seventeenth-century roots of moral certainty, see Barbara Shapiro, *Probability and Certainty in Seventeenth-Century England: A Study of the Relationships between Natural Science, Religion, History, Law, and Literature* (Princeton: Princeton University Press, 1983), 94–101.

20. For the probable improbabilities of miracles, see for instance Mark Hopkins, *Lectures on the Evidences of Christianity* (Boston: T.R. Marvin, 1846), 343. Martin Farquhar Tupper, *Probabilities: An Aid to Faith* (London: Thomas Hatchard, 1854), 46, 27, 93–95. Melville owned a copy of Tupper's verse and alludes to him in *Clarel* (1876). See also Hershel Parker, *Herman Melville: A Biography*, 2 vols. (Baltimore: Johns Hopkins University Press, 1996, 2002), 1:829, 2:40, 2:810.

21. "The Existence of the Deity," *The United States Magazine and Democratic Review*, ed. Thomas Prentice Kettell, vol. 21 (New York: 1847), 102, 103, 110-111, 258 (the article ran in two installments in August and September). Melville borrowed an unidentified volume of *The United States Magazine and Democratic Review* from Evert Duyckinck in 1850 and seems to have been a regular reader of the magazine (to which Hawthorne contributed short stories in the late 1830s and early 1840s). For how modern notions of intelligent design have roots in the eighteenth and nineteenth centuries, see Jager, *Book of God*, 216–217.

22. Religious readings of *Moby-Dick* typically focus on the mystery of iniquity: Lawrance Thompson, *Melville's Quarrel with God* (Princeton: Princeton University Press, 1952); T. Walter Herbert, *Moby-Dick and Calvinism: A World Dismantled* (New Brunswick: Rutgers University Press, 1977); and William Braswell, *Melville's Religious Thought: An Essay in Interpretation* (New York: Octagon Books, 1977), 57–73.

23. Montaigne, *Essays*, 607.

24. Exceptions are Eric Wilson, who briefly mentions "The Mat-Maker" chapter in *Romantic Turbulence: Chaos, Ecology, and American Space* (New York: St. Martin's Press, 2000), 87–88, and Eric Wertheimer, who discusses the logic of insurance in "The Lightning-Rod Man" (*Underwriting: The Poetics of Insurance in America, 1722–1872* [Stanford: Stanford University Press, 2006], 98–117). Though my interests here are different, I generally agree with both that Melville recognizes an unmasterable power in chance. Two interesting if indirect commentaries on *Moby-Dick*, etiology, and chance are Hart Crane's "At Melville's Tomb" (1926) and Kurt Vonnegut's *Cat's Cradle* (1963).

25. Like *Moby-Dick*, Conrad also conflates chance, sea life, and non-Christian beliefs in his novel *Chance* (1914) when Marlowe ends the book with a sly disclaimer, "Hang it all, for all my belief in Chance I am not exactly a pagan" (*Chance: A Tale in Two Parts* [London: Methuen and Co., 1914], 406).

26. For an overview of tidology and specific discussions of Whewell, see Michael Reidy, *Tides of History: Ocean Science and Her Majesty's Navy* (Chicago: University of Chicago Press, 2008). For maritime insurance and the doctrine of chances, see J. R. McCullough, *The Principles of Political Economy*, 4th ed. (1830; Edinburgh: Adam and Charles Black, 1849), 249–256; and Mary Ruwell, *Eighteenth-Century Capitalism: The Formation of American Marine Insurance Companies* (New York: Garland, 1993). Henry David Thoreau, *Walden and Other Writings*, ed. William Howarth (New York: Modern Library, 1981), 18.

27. Charles Wilkes, *Narrative of the United States Exploring Expedition*, 5 vols. (New York: Putnam, 1856), 1:368, 5:486.

28. *In Memoriam: Matthew Fontaine Maury* (Cambridge: University of Cambridge, 1873), 8. For general information on Maury, see Chester Hearn, *Tracks in the Sea: Matthew*

Fontaine Maury and the Mapping of the Oceans (New York: International Marine/ McGraw-Hill, 2002).

29. Matthew Fontaine Maury, *Explanation and Sailing Directions to Accompany the Wind and Current Charts* (Washington, D.C.: C. Alexander, 1853), 41, 42, 90, 301, 302, 292, 344.

30. Leland Monk, *Standard Deviations: Chance and the Modern British Novel* (Stanford: Stanford University Press, 1993), 5, 23–24. See also the entry on "Chaos" in Pierre Bayle, *An Historical and Critical Dictionary, Vol. I* (London: Hunt and Clarke, 1826), 320–340.

31. See, for instance, William Spanos, *The Errant Art of Moby-Dick: The Canon, the Cold War, and the Struggle for American Studies* (Durham: Duke University Press, 1995).

32. Dennis C. Marnon and Steven Olsen-Smith, "Melville's Marginalia in *The Works of Sir William D'Avenant,*" *Leviathan* 6:1 (March 2004), 83.

33. Diogenes Laertius, *Lives of Eminent Philosophers*, 2:659. Cicero, *De Officiis*, trans. George Gardiner (London: Methuen, 1899), 39, 55–56, 7.

34. For instance, Thompson discusses etiology in "The Mat-Maker" without referring to chance (*Melville's Quarrel with God*, 197), while Herbert only mentions "The Mat-Maker" in passing (*Moby-Dick and Calvinism*, 167).

35. Bernard Williams, *Shame and Necessity* (1993; Berkeley: University of California Press, 2008).

36. *Moby-Dick* mentions Bowditch's *The Practical Navigator* (1802), the so-called seaman's bible (1255).

37. Walter E. Bezanson emphasizes this line in his description of *Moby-Dick's* movement from chaos and chance toward order in "*Moby-Dick: Work of Art,*" rpt. in *Moby-Dick*, eds. Hershel Parker and Harrison Hayford, 2nd ed. (New York: Norton, 2002), 641–657.

38. For Melville and religious doubt with emphasis on the higher criticism, see Ilana Pardes, *Melville's Bibles* (Berkeley: University of California Press, 2008), 46–72; Susan Mizruchi, *The Science of Sacrifice: American Literature and Modern Social Theory* (Princeton: Princeton University Press, 1998), 95–109; Elisa New, "Bible Leaves! Bible Leaves!," *Poetics Today* 19:2 (1988), 281–303; Lawrence Buell, *New England Literary Culture: From Revolution Through Renaissance* (Cambridge: Cambridge University Press, 1986), 178–185. Herman Melville, *Redburn* in *Redburn, White-Jacket, Moby-Dick*, 317. There is no evidence that Melville read Hume firsthand.

39. David Hume, *Dialogues Concerning Natural Religion and Other Writings* (Cambridge: Cambridge University Press, 2007), 20–21. David Hume, *Enquiry Concerning Human Understanding*, in *Essays and Treatises on Several Subjects, Vol. II* (Edinburgh: T. Caddell, 1793), 80, 87. For *Moby-Dick*, Butler, and Paley (but not Hume), see James Duban, *Melville's Major Fiction: Politics, Theology, and Imagination* (Dekalb, Ill.: Northern Illinois University Press, 1983), 117–123. Duban argues that Melville invokes the miracles controversy to debunk "providential historiography" (123).

40. Hume, *Enquiry Concerning Human Understanding*, 88.

41. For general examples of such readings in the last fifty years, see Milton Stern, *The Fine Hammered Steel of Herman Melville* (Urbana: University of Illinois Press, 1957), 243; Paul Brodtkorb, *Ishmael's White World: A Phenomenological Reading of Moby Dick* (New Haven: Yale University Press, 1965), 128–129; John Seelye, *Melville: The Ironic Diagram* (Evanston: Northwestern University Press, 1970), 64; and Spanos, *The Errant Art of Moby-Dick*.

42. Before attending to connections between Captain Ahab, Jonah, and Job, Thompson dismisses King Ahab rather quickly: "Obviously, then, it is not difficult to use either one of these Ahabs, for Christian purposes, as a horrible object lesson which teaches us that while virtue and obedience are rewarded, wicked defiance is neither expedient nor profitable because it brings down retribution" (*Melville's Quarrel with God*, 152–153). See also Herbert, *Moby-Dick and Calvinism*, 118–119, 143. Buell points out that the biblical Ahab is by no means a stable figure (*New England Literary Culture*, 185). Others have discussed

the rich political associations of Ahab in the antebellum period; see especially Michael Paul Rogin, *Subversive Genealogy: The Politics and Art of Herman Melville* (Berkeley: University of California Press, 1985), 106–148; and Pardes, *Melville's Bibles*, 98–122.

43. Eric Auerbach, *Mimesis: The Representation of Reality in Western Culture* (1953; Princeton: Princeton University Press, 2003), 28, 44, 49.

44. George Robert Gleig, *The History of the Bible, Vol. II* (New York: Harper and Brothers, 1835), 42. William Sherlock, *A Discourse Concerning the Divine Providence* (Pittsburgh: J.L. Read, 1851), 45. Matthew Henry, *The Comprehensive Commentary on the Holy Bible: Ruth—Psalm LXIII*, ed. William Jenks (Brattleboro: Fessenden and Co., 1836), 286. James Hildyard, *Sermons Chiefly Practical* (London: John Parker, 1845), 156. G. W. Mylne, *What is Chance?: A Dialogue* (London: Wertheim and Macintosh, 1849), 19–20. John Dick, *Lectures on Theology, Vol. I* (New York: M.W. Dodd, 1850), 429.

45. Kitto, *Cyclopedia*, 574–575; Stephen Charnock, *Discourses upon the Existence and Attributes of God, Vol. I* (1682; New York: Robert Carter, 1856), 439. Pardes discusses Kitto in *Melville's Bibles*, 47–49. For another possible source of compatibilism for Melville, see Benjamin Franklin's "On the Providence of God" (1730) and "Letter from Theophilus, Relating to the Divine Prescience" (1741), both of which were available in the antebellum period. Turner provides a helpful overview of total versus particularist versions of providence (*Without God, Without Creed*, 35–40). The etiology of *Paradise Lost* is, of course, immensely complicated; for an incisive account, see Steven Knapp, *Literary Interest: The Limits of Anti-Formalism* (Cambridge: Harvard University Press, 1993), 5–29.

46. *Melville and Milton: An Edition and Analysis of Melville's Annotations on Milton*, ed. Robin Grey (Pittsburgh: Duquesne University Press, 2004), 51. For broader context, see Kevin Van Anglen, *The New England Milton: Literary Reception and Cultural Authority in the Early Republic* (University Park, Pa.: Pennsylvania State University Press, 1993).

47. Newman, *Lectures on Logic*, 132.

48. Quetelet, *Treatise on Man*, x; John F. W. Herschel, *Preliminary Discourse on the Study of Natural Philosophy* (London: Longman, Brown, Green, and Longmans, 1851), 217–218, and "On the Estimation of Skill in Target-Shooting," *Familiar Lectures on Scientific Subjects* (London: A Strahan, 1866); for Poisson, see Daston, *Classical Probability*, 284; James Clerk Maxwell, *Theory of Heat* (1871), in *Literature and Science in the Nineteenth Century: An Anthology*, ed. Laura Otis (Oxford: Oxford University Press, 2002), 72; for Eliot, see the archery contests in *Daniel Deronda* (the tragedy of the story is, in part, that one only gets one shot at marriage). Thomas Huxley, "Criticisms on *The Origin of Species*" (1864), in Charles Darwin, *On the Origin of Species*, ed. Joseph Carroll (Toronto: Broadview Press, 2003), 622; James, *Writings*, 2:409.

49. Herman Melville, *White-Jacket*, in *Redburn, White-Jacket, Moby-Dick*, 417.

50. F. O. Matthiessen registers his mild disappointment in *American Renaissance: Art and Expression in the Age of Emerson and Whitman* (New York: Oxford University Press, 1941), 456. Edward Said is among those who misremember Ahab being bound to the whale. For this and other misprisions, see Takayuki Tatsumi, "Literary History on the Road: Transatlantic Crossings and Transpacific Crossovers," *PMLA* 119:1 (January 2004), 92–102; and John Bryant, "Rewriting *Moby-Dick*: Politics, Textual Identity, and the Revision Narrative," *PMLA* 125:4 (October 2010), 1043–1060.

51. Witmore, *Culture of Accidents*, 61.

52. For humor and non-teleology in Melville, see John Bryant, *Melville and Repose: The Rhetoric of Humor in the American Renaissance* (New York: Oxford University Press, 1993), 186–208; and Wertheimer, *Underwriting*, 98–117.

53. Michael Colacurcio, *Godly Letters: The Literature of the American Puritans* (Notre Dame: University of Notre Dame Press, 2006), 275–303.

54. Alfred Mele, *Free Will and Luck* (New York: Oxford University Press, 2006); John Searle, *Freedom and Neurobiology: Reflections on Free Will, Language, and Political Power* (New York: Columbia University Press, 2007), 37–78.

55. Patey, *Probability and Literary Form*, 73; Kitto, *Cyclopedia*, 575.

56. Geoffrey Sanborn, *The Sign of the Cannibal: Melville and the Making of a Postcolonial Reader* (Durham: Duke University Press, 1998), 167.

57. Tillotson, "The Wisdom of Being Religious," 379. Ironically, Tillotson echoes Montaigne, whose question may not be as rhetorical: "[I]f atoms do, by chance, happen to combine themselves into so many shapes, why have they never combined together to form a house or a slipper? By the same token, why do we not believe that if innumerable letters of the Greek alphabet were poured all over the market-place they would eventually happen to form the text of the *Iliad*?" (*Essays*, 612).

58. "Physical Science, in Its Relation to Natural and Revealed Religion," *Southern Quarterly Messenger* (April, 1851).

59. Benjamin Franklin, *Autobiography*, eds. J. A. Leo Lemay and P. M. Zall (New York: Norton, 1986), 8.

60. Nathaniel Hawthorne, *Tales and Sketches* (New York: Library of America, 1982), 434. As Arthur Riss has pointed out to me, a similar ambiguity ends *The House of the Seven Gables* when a bystander comments on Hepzibah Pyncheon's new wealth: "If you choose to call it luck, it is all very well; but if we are to take it as the will of Providence, why, I can't exactly fathom it!" (Nathaniel Hawthorne, *The House of the Seven Gables* [New York: Dover, 1999], 223–224). Sacvan Bercovitch, *The Office of the Scarlet Letter* (Baltimore: Johns Hopkins University Press, 1991), xi.

61. *Melville and Milton*, 173.

CHAPTER 3

1. Hershel Parker, *Herman Melville: A Biography*, 2 vols. (Baltimore: Johns Hopkins University Press, 1996, 2002), 1:883.

2. Herman Melville, *Pierre* in *Pierre, Israel Potter, The Piazza Tales, The Confidence-Man, Uncollected Prose, Billy Budd, Sailor* (New York: Library of America, 1984), 107, 165–167. Subsequent citations to this text appear parenthetically.

3. Oliver Wendell Holmes Jr., *The Essential Holmes: Selections from the Letters, Speeches, Judicial Opinions, and Other Writings*, ed. Richard A. Posner (Chicago: University of Chicago Press, 1997), 183. Samuel Otter, *Melville's Anatomies* (Berkeley: University of California Press, 1999), 238.

4. Wai Chee Dimock, *Residues of Justice: Literature, Law, Philosophy* (Berkeley: University of California Press, 1996), 137. Jonathan Edwards, *A Careful and Strict Inquiry into the Modern Prevailing Notions of that Freedom of the Will* (New York: Leavitt and Allen, 1857), 59.

5. Bercovitch, *Rites of Assent*, 250–251; Myra Jehlen, *American Incarnation: The Individual, the Nation, and the Continent* (Cambridge: Harvard University Press, 1986), 202; John Carlos Rowe, *At Emerson's Tomb: The Politics of Classic American Literature* (New York: Columbia University Press, 1997), 64. See also Emory Elliott, "Art, Religion, and the Problem of Authority in *Pierre*," *Ideology and Classic American Literature*, eds. Sacvan Bercovitch and Myra Jehlen (Cambridge: Cambridge University Press, 1986), 337–351; Wai Chee Dimock, *Empire for Liberty: Melville and the Poetics of Individualism* (Princeton: Princeton University Press, 1989), 140–175; and Brian Higgins and Hershel Parker, *Reading Melville's* Pierre; or, The Ambiguities (Baton Rouge: Louisiana State University Press, 2006), esp. 102.

6. Aristotle, *Physics*, trans. Robin Waterfield (Oxford: Oxford University Press, 1996), 42–45.

7. For *Pierre* and sexual taboo, see Richard Brodhead, *Hawthorne, Melville, and the Novel* (Chicago: University of Chicago Press, 1976), 163–193; Jehlen, *American Incarnation*,

185–201; Peter Creech, *Closet Writing/Gay Reading: The Case of Melville's Pierre* (Chicago: University of Chicago Press, 1993). Robert S. Levine discusses race and *Pierre* in *Dislocating the Race and Nation: Episodes in Nineteenth-Century American Literary Nationalism* (Chapel Hill: University of North Carolina Press, 2008), 147–162.

8. Aristotle, *Poetics*, trans. Malcolm Heath (New York: Penguin, 1996), 13–14, 17. For chance in the *Poetics* (and translations of key lines), see Dorothea Frede, "Necessity, Chance, and 'What Happens for the Most Part,'" *Essays on Aristotle's* Poetics, ed. Amélie Oksenberg Rorty (Princeton: Princeton University Press, 1992), 197–219. Archibald Alison, *Essays on the Nature and Principles of Taste, Vol. I* (1790; Edinburgh: Archibald Constable and Company, 1815), 60, 105. For Alison in America, see Theo Davis, *Formalism, Experience, and the Making of American Literature in the Nineteenth Century* (New York: Cambridge University Press, 2007), 32–44.

9. For *Pierre's* resistance to sentimental traditions, see Nina Baym, "Melville's Quarrel with Fiction," *PMLA* 34 (1979), 909–923; and Gillian Brown, *Domestic Individualism: Imagining Self in Nineteenth-Century America* (Berkeley: University of California Press, 1990), 135–169. Otter places *Pierre* both within and outside of sentimental conventions (*Melville's Anatomies*, 208–254). See also Priscilla Wald's discussion of *Pierre's* violation of readers' expectations ("Hearing Narrative Voices in Melville's *Pierre,*" *boundary 2* 17:1 [Spring 1990], 100–132).

10. Higgins and Parker, *Reading Melville's* Pierre, 150–151.

11. *The Letters of Herman Melville*, eds. Merrell R. Davis and William H. Gilman (New Haven: Yale University Press, 1960), 150. For a discussion that takes Melville's letter at its word, see Charlene Avallone, "Calculations for Popularity: Melville's *Pierre* and *Holden's Dollar Magazine,*" *Nineteenth-Century Literature* 43 (1988), 82–110. Views of Melville's complicated but generally hostile relationship to the economics of antebellum print culture include William Charvat, *The Profession of Authorship in America*, ed. Matthew J. Bruccoli (1966; New York: Columbia University Press, 1992), 262–283; Michael T. Gilmore, *American Romanticism and the Marketplace* (Chicago: University of Chicago Press, 1985), 52–70, 113–145; and Stephen Railton, *Authorship and Audience: Literary Performance in the American Renaissance* (Princeton: Princeton University Press, 1991), 152–189. For *Pierre* and literary professionalism, see John Evelev, *Tolerable Entertainment: Herman Melville and Professionalism in Antebellum New York* (Amherst: University of Massachusetts Press, 2006), 147–179.

12. [no title], *Russell's Magazine* (June 1859).

13. Samuel Johnson, *Preface to Shakespeare* (1765), *Rasselas, Poems, and Selected Prose,* ed. Bertrand H. Bronson (New York: Holt, Rinehart and Winston, 1952), 325.

14. William James, *Writings*, 2 vols. (New York: Library of America, 1987), 2:860. Scholars occasionally compare Melville and pragmatism, sometimes in the name of "naturalism" and particularly with *Billy Budd*, which came late enough to be influenced—at least in theory—by classical pragmatism. See, for instance, Thomas Hove, "Naturalist Psychology in *Billy Budd,*" *Leviathan* 5:2 (October 2003), 51–65; and Andrew Delbanco, *Melville: His World and Work* (New York: Knopf, 2005), 311. William Potter associates *Clarel* (1876) with Jamesian religious pluralism in *Melville's Clarel and the Intersympathy of Creeds* (Kent, Ohio: Kent State University Press, 2004), xx. Deleuze also hints at Melville's affinities with pragmatism in *Essays: Critical and Clinical,* trans. Daniel Smith and Michael Greco (Minneapolis: University of Minnesota Press, 1997), 86–87. See also, Maurice S. Lee, "Melville, Douglass, the Civil War, Pragmatism," *Frederick Douglass and Herman Melville: Essays in Relation*, eds. Robert Levine and Samuel Otter (Chapel Hill: University of North Carolina Press, 2008), 396–415.

15. Quoted in Robert D. Richardson, *William James: In the Maelstrom of American Modernism* (Boston: Houghton Mifflin, 2006), 443.

16. James, *Writings*, 1:449; 2:548.

17. All quotes from "The Will to Believe" are from James, *Writings*, 1:457–479.

18. James, *Writings*, 2:152, 1:609, 2:1097.

19. James, *Writings*, 1:476. For James's most explicit approach to the question of free will versus determinism, see his tellingly short discussion in "Some Metaphysical Problems" (*Writings*, 2:537–540).

20. Herman Melville, *Israel Potter*, in *Pierre, Israel Potter, The Piazza Tales, The Confidence-Man, Uncollected Prose, Billy Budd, Sailor*, 555.

21. For pragmatism as attuned to tragedy, see Sidney Hook's classic defense, "Pragmatism and the Tragic Sense of Life" (1960). Unconvinced views include Cornel West, *The American Evasion of Philosophy* (Madison: University of Wisconsin Press, 1989), 114–124; and Roger Lundin, *From Nature to Experience: The American Search for Cultural Authority* (New York: Rowman and Littlefield, 2005).

22. Lord Byron, *Don Juan*, in *The Major Works*, ed. Jerome J. McGann (Oxford: Oxford University Press, 1986), 683.

23. Nicholas Rescher provides an excellent historical account of Buridan's ass in *Scholastic Meditations* (Washington, D. C.: Catholic University of America Press, 2005), 1–48. For De Quincey, see *Literary Reminiscences, from The Autobiography of an Opium Eater, Vol. I* (Boston: Ticknor, Reed, and Fields, 1851), 141.

24. Edwards, *Freedom of the Will*, 37, 57.

25. Charles Dickens, 1850 preface to *Martin Chuzzelwit* (Oxford: Oxford University Press, 1982), 717.

26. The most searching accounts of agency in "Bartleby" include Allan Moore Emery, "The Alternatives of Melville's 'Bartleby,'" *Nineteenth-Century Fiction* 31:2 (September 1976), 170–187; and Branka Arsic, *Passive Constitutions, or 7 1/2 Times Bartleby* (Stanford: Stanford University Press, 2007), 12–32.

27. Edwards, *Freedom of the Will*, 37. For Gataker, see Rescher, *Scholastic Meditations*, 24–25; and Todd, "Providence, Chance, and the New Science in Early Stuart Cambridge." Montaigne, *Essays*, 692. Pierre Bayle, *An Historical and Critical Dictionary, Vol. III* (London: Hunt and Clarke, 1826), 269. Caleb Pitt, *An Essay on the Philosophy of Christianity, Vol. 1* (London: William Booth, 1824): 302–303.

28. Dan McCall, *The Silence of Bartleby* (Ithaca: Cornell University Press, 1989), esp. x, 144.

29. Colacurcio, "Excessive and Organic Ill," 8.

30. Deleuze, *Essays*, 68–90; Jacques Derrida, *Resistances of Psychoanalysis*, trans. Peggy Kamuf, Pascale-Anne Brault, and Michael Naas (Stanford: Stanford University Press, 1998), 24; Giorgio Agamben, *Potentialities: Collected Essays in Philosophy*, trans. Daniel Heller-Roazen (Stanford: Stanford University Press, 1999), 243–274.

31. For the lawyer of "Bartleby" as a modern capitalist under conditions of risk, see David Anthony, *Paper Money Men: Commerce, Manhood, and the Sensational Public Sphere in Antebellum America* (Columbus: Ohio State University Press, 2009), 183–186.

32. [no title], *The Baltimore Gazette* (September 18, 1834). For a representative defense of financial speculation, see "Stock Markets," *The United States Magazine and Democratic Review* (September 1850).

33. Franklin to Priestley, September 19, 1772, *Benjamin Franklin: Writings* (New York: Library of America, 1987), 878. For risk management in the eighteenth century, see Jennifer Baker, *Securing the Commonwealth: Debt, Speculation, and Writing in the Making of Early America* (Baltimore: Johns Hopkins University Press, 2005), 148–150, 158–162. For Edwards's rejection of the calculative adjudication of moral dilemmas, see Sharon Cameron, *Impersonality: Seven Essays* (Chicago: University of Chicago Press, 2007), 38–40.

34. Sextus Empiricus, *Outlines of Pyrrhonism*, trans. R. G. Bury (Cambridge: Harvard University Press, 1933), 7, 9, 19; Bayle, *An Historical and Critical Dictionary*, 54.

35. For more on "Bartleby" and dead letters within a probabilistic framework, see Elizabeth Duquette's "The Office of *The Dead Letter*," an essay I was fortunate to see in manuscript form.

36. "Divine Providence," *Christian Observer* (May 1, 1856), quoting James McCosh, *The Method of Divine Government, Physical and Moral* (New York: Carter, 1851), 206.

37. McCall, *The Silence of Bartleby*, 133; Milton Stern, "Towards 'Bartleby the Scrivener,'" *The Stoic Strain in American Literature: Essays in Honor of Marston LaFrance*, ed. Duane J. MacMillan (Toronto: University of Toronto Press, 1979), 35.

38. Charles Dickens, *Hard Times*, ed. Kate Flint (New York: Penguin, 1995), 284. Elizabeth Barrett Browning, *Aurora Leigh and other Poems*, eds. John Robert Glorney Bolton and Julia Bolton Holloway (New York: Penguin, 1995), 41; Herman Melville, "The Paradise of Bachelors and the Tartarus of Maids," *Pierre, Israel Potter, The Piazza Tales, The Confidence-Man, Uncollected Prose, Billy Budd, Sailor*, 1257. Catherine Gallagher, *The Body Economic: Life, Death, and Sensation in Political Economy and the Victorian Novel* (Princeton: Princeton University Press, 2006), esp. 82 ("over-determined fictions"). Statistical Society of Bristol quoted in Daniel R. Headrick, *When Information Came of Age: Technologies of Knowledge in the Age of Reason and Revolution* (Oxford: Oxford University Press, 2000), 85 ("duties to the poor"); Jane Thrailkill, *Affecting Fictions: Mind, Body, and Emotion in American Literary Realism* (Cambridge: Harvard University Press, 2007), 54–83. For dismal sociology in general, see Mary Poovey, "Figures of Arithmetic, Figures of Speech: the Discourse of Statistics in the 1830s," in *Questions of Evidence: Proof, Practice, and Persuasion across the Disciplines*, eds. James Chandler, Arnold Davidson, and Harry Harootunian (Chicago: University of Chicago Press, 1991), 401–421. For the inverse relationship between moral impetus and large numbers, see Paul Slovic, "The More Who Die, the Less We Care," *The Irrational Economist: Making Decisions in a Dangerous World*, eds. Erwann Michel-Kerjan and Paul Slovic (New York: PublicAffairs, 2010), 30–40.

39. For Melville's critique of charity, see Susan Ryan, *The Grammar of Good Intentions: Race and the Antebellum Culture of Benevolence* (Ithaca: Cornell University Press, 2005), 60–76.

40. Melville, *Pierre, Israel Potter, The Piazza Tales, The Confidence-Man, Uncollected Prose, Billy Budd, Sailor*, 1203. Newspapers in the mid-nineteenth century frequently applied the doctrine of chances to steamship and railroad accidents.

41. Shaw, Melville's father-in-law, sentenced John Webster to death for the murder of George Parker. Webster's attorney argued that murder must be by "purpose, or design, and in contradistinction from accident or mischance," and he ended his defense with probabilistic reasoning: "[W]hat is reasonable doubt? . . . It is not a mere probability, arising from the doctrine of chances, that it is more likely to be so than otherwise." To convict, he argued, a jury must have "a reasonable, moral certainty" ("The Webster Case—Charge of Chief Justice Shaw," *The Western Law Review* [July 1850]). For *Billy Budd* and the Webster case, see Tom Quirk, *Nothing Abstract: Investigations in the American Literary Imagination* (Columbia: University of Missouri Press, 2001), 81–96. Herman Melville, *Billy Budd* in *Pierre, Israel Potter, The Piazza Tales, The Confidence-Man, Uncollected Prose, Billy Budd, Sailor*, 1386, 1434.

CHAPTER 4

1. Thomas Jefferson, *Notes on the State of Virginia*, in *Writings* (New York: Library of America, 1984), 289, 187.

2. See, for instance, Lindon Barrett, "Presence of Mind: Detection and Racialization in 'The Murders in the Rue Morgue,'" and Elise Lemire, "'The Murders in the Rue Morgue': Amalgamation Discourses and the Race Riots of 1838 in Poe's Philadelphia," both in *Romancing the Shadow: Poe and Race*, eds. J. Gerald Kennedy and Liliane Weissberg (New York: Oxford University Press, 2001), 157–176, 177–204.

3. For a good overview of the rise of scientific racism up to and including the antebellum period, see Ezra Tawil, *The Making of Racial Sentiment: Slavery and the Birth of the Frontier* (New York: Cambridge University Press, 2006), 26–68.

4. James Albert Ukawsaw Gronniosaw, *A Narrative of the Most Remarkable Particulars in the Life of James Albert Ukawsaw Gronniosaw, an African Prince* (1770), in *Pioneers of the Black Atlantic: Five Slave Narratives from the Enlightenment, 1772–1815*, eds. Henry Louis Gates Jr. and William L. Andrews (Washington, D.C.: Counterpoint, 1998), 33.

5. For Christianity as inhibiting African-American political consciousness, see for instance Eugene Genovese, *Roll, Jordan, Roll: The World the Slaves Made* (New York: Pantheon, 1974), 280–285. Recent revisionist work includes Cedrick May, *Evangelism and Resistance in the Black Atlantic, 1760–1835* (Athens: University of Georgia Press, 2008); Yolanda Pierce, *Hell Without Fires: Slavery, Christianity, and the Antebellum Spiritual Narrative* (Gainesville: University Press of Florida, 2005); John Ernest, *Liberation Historiography: African American Writers and the Challenge of History, 1794–1861* (Chapel Hill: University of North Carolina Press, 2004); Joanna Brooks, *American Lazarus: Religion and the Rise of African-American and Native American Literatures* (New York: Oxford University Press, 2003); and Eddie Glaude Jr., *Exodus!: Religion, Race, and Nation in Early Nineteenth-Century Black America* (Chicago: University of Chicago Press, 2000). An especially good discussion of providentialism and abolitionism appears in John Salliant, *Black Puritan, Black Republican: The Life and Thought of Lemuel Haynes, 1753–1833* (Oxford: Oxford University Press, 2003), 83–116. For a strong exception to the providentialist tradition in slave narratives, see Venture Smith's largely secular narrative.

6. This is less true of historians interested in the market revolution during the demise of slavery in the United States. See *The Antislavery Debate: Capitalism and Abolitionism as a Problem in Historical Interpretation*, ed. Thomas Bender (Berkeley: University of California Press, 1992).

7. Alexander Crummell, "The English Language in Liberia" (1861), in *Pamphlets of Protest: An Anthology of Early African-American Protest Literature, 1790–1860*, eds. Richard Newman, Patrick Rael, Philip Lapsansky (New York: Routledge, 2001), 298.

8. John Patrick Daly, *When Slavery Was Called Freedom: Evangelicalism, Proslavery, and the Causes of the Civil War* (Lexington: University Press of Kentucky, 2002). On the matter of slavery, Jefferson was content to "await with patience the workings of an overrulling [*sic*] providence" (Thomas Jefferson, *Writings*, ed. Merrill Peterson [New York: Viking, 1984], 592). Hawthorne similarly deferred to an "inscrutable Providence" in "Chiefly about War-Matters" (*Atlantic Monthly* [July 1862], 50). See also Lincoln's "Proclamation for Thanksgiving" (1863), and Melville's "Supplement" to *Battle-Pieces* (1866). For the anti-abolitionism of Edwardsean providentialism in the antebellum period, see Kenneth Minkema and Harry Stout, "The Edwardsean Tradition and Antislavery Debate, 1740–1865," *The Journal of American History* 92:1 (June 2005), 47–74. For institutional anti-abolitionism among Northern churches, see John McKivigan, *The War against Proslavery Religion: Abolitionism and the Northern Churches, 1830–1865* (Ithaca: Cornell University Press, 1984).

9. Robert Alexander Young, "Ethiopian Manifesto" (1829), *Pamphlets of Protest*, 88. William Hayden, *Narrative of William Hayden* (Cincinnati: Hayden, 1846), 38. Martin Delany, *Blake, or The Huts of America* (Boston: Beacon Press, 1970), 21. Glaude, *Exodus!* Frederick Douglass, *The Frederick Douglass Papers; Series One: Speeches, Debates, and Interviews: Volumes 1–5*, ed. John Blassingame (New York: Yale University Press, 1979–1985), 4:5. Subsequent references to Blassingame's volumes will be cited parenthetically by volume number and page.

10. Henry Brown, *The Narrative of Henry "Box" Brown* (1851), in *Black Men in Chains: Narratives of Escaped Slaves*, ed. Charles H. Nichols (New York: Lawrence Hill, 1972), 186. John

Thompson, *Life of John Thompson, A Fugitive Slave* (1856), in *Black Men in Chains*, 230. Moses Roper, *A Narrative of the Adventures and Escape of Moses Roper* (1837), in *North Carolina Slave Narratives: The Lives of Moses Roper, Lunsford Lane, Moses Grandy, and Thomas H. Jones*, ed. William L. Andrews (Chapel Hill: University of North Carolina Press, 2003), 73. William and Ellen Craft, *Running a Thousand Miles for Freedom* (1860), in *Slave Narratives* (New York: Library of America, 2000), 734. For reactions to Dewey, see Hershel Parker, *Herman Melville: A Biography, Volume 2, 1851–1891* (Baltimore: Johns Hopkins University Press, 2002), 65–67, 456–457; Charles Capper, *Margaret Fuller: An American Romantic Life, The Private Years* (New York: Oxford University Press, 1992), 312–313; Samuel Ringgold Ward, *Autobiography of a Fugitive Negro* (London: John Snow, 1855), 110. For a deep history of abolitionism and theodicy, see Salliant, *Black Puritan, Black Republican*.

11. Charles Buck, *A Theological Dictionary*, 2 vols. (Philadelphia: W.W. Woodward, 1807), 1:51, 2:472, 2:840. Lydia Maria Child, *An Appeal in Favor of that Class of Americans Called Africans* (New York: J.S. Taylor, 1836), 29. Note, too, that Eugene Genovese has argued that fatalism can be a useful survival strategy under extreme forms of oppression (*Roll, Jordan, Roll*, 637–647).

12. Bernard Williams, *Shame and Necessity* (1993; Berkeley: University of California Press, 2008),.103–129. For slavery, economics, and migrations, see Ira Berlin, *Generations of Captivity* (Cambridge: Harvard University Press, 2003), 159–244; and Steven Deyle, *Carry Me Back: The Domestic Slave Trade in American Life* (Oxford: Oxford University Press, 2005), statistics quoted from 4. William Wells Brown, *The Black Man: His Antecedents, His Genius, and His Achievements*, 4th ed. (Boston: Robert Walcutt, 1868), 22; Josiah Henson, *Father Henson's Story of His Own Life* (Boston: John P. Jewett, 1858), 60.

13. John Ernest, "Representing Chaos: William Craft's *Running a Thousand Miles to Freedom*," *PMLA* 121:2 (2006), 469–483. For what Buell calls the "normalizing impulse" in early American self-construction, see Sacvan Bercovitch, *The Puritan Origins of the American Self* (New Haven: Yale University Press, 1975); Mitchell Breitwieser, *Cotton Mather and Benjamin Franklin: The Price of Representative Personality* (New York: Cambridge University Press, 1984); James Olney, "'I was Born': Slave Narratives, Their Status as Autobiography and as Literature," *The Slave's Narrative*, eds. Charles T. Davis and Henry Louis Gates Jr. (New York: Oxford University Press, 1985), 148–175; and Lawrence Buell, "Autobiography in the American Renaissance," *American Autobiography: Retrospect and Prospect*, ed. Paul John Eakin (Madison: University of Wisconsin Press, 1991), 52. Paul Gilroy, *The Black Atlantic: Modernity and Double Consciousness* (Cambridge: Harvard University Press, 1992), 221.

14. Solomon Northup, *Twelve Years a Slave*, eds. Sue Eakin and Joseph Logsdon (Baton Rouge: Louisiana State University Press, 1968), 98.

15. Nan Goodman, *Shifting the Blame: Literature, Law, and the Theory of Accidents in Nineteenth-Century America* (Princeton: Princeton University Press, 1998), 35–64.

16. Walt Whitman, *Leaves of Grass and Other Writings*, ed. Michael Moon (New York: Johns Hopkins University Press, 2002), 630.

17. Northrup, *Twelve Years a Slave*, 99.

18. Patricia Cline Cohen, *A Calculating People: The Spread of Numeracy in Early America* (Chicago: University of Chicago Press, 1982), esp. 149.

19. Jefferson, *Notes*, 266; Benjamin Peirce quoted in Joseph Brent, *Charles Sanders Peirce: A Life: Revised and Enlarged Edition* (Bloomington: Indiana University Press, 1993), 34. Walter Benn Michaels, *The Gold Standard and the Logic of Naturalism: American Literature at the Turn of the Century* (Berkeley: University of California Press, 1987), 103–136; Ian Baucom, *Specters of the Atlantic: Finance Capital, Slavery, and the Philosophy of History* (Durham: Duke University Press, 2005), 80–112. William Harper, "Memoir on Slavery"

(1837), *The Ideology of Slavery: Proslavery Thought in the Antebellum South, 1830–1860*, ed. Drew Gilpin Faust (Baton Rouge: Louisiana State University Press, 1981), 110; J. H. Van Evrie, *Negroes and Negro 'Slavery': The First an Inferior Race; The Latter its Normal Condition* (New York: Van Evrie, Horton, 1863), 119; Samuel Cartwright, *Slavery in the Light of Ethnology,* in *Cotton is King,* ed. E. N. Elliott (Augusta, Georgia: Pritchard, Abbott, and Looms, 1860), 694. Thomas Dew, "Review of the Debate in the Virginia Legislature" (1831–1832), rpt. in *The Ideology of Slavery,* 64.

20. George Fitzhugh, *Cannibals All! Or, Slaves without Masters* (Richmond: A. Morris, 1857), 238, 72, 294; George Fitzhugh, *Sociology for the South; or The Failure of Free Society* (Richmond: A. Morris, 1854), 265. Harriet Beecher Stowe, *Uncle Tom's Cabin* (New York: Penguin, 1981), 290, 109. For general beliefs in the improvidence of slaves, see Genovese, *Roll, Jordan, Roll,* 295–308.

21. Stewart quoted in John Ernest, *Liberation Historiography,* 71. "Prejudice Against Color in the Light of History," *The Colored American* (March 18, 1837); H. Gregoire, "Extracts from *An Enquiry Concerning the Intellectual and Moral Faculties and Literature of Negroes,*" *Freedom's Journal* (November 14, 1828); "A Colored Navigator," *The Colored American* (October 27, 1838); "The Intellect of Negroes," *The Colored American* (May 13, 1837). "Reminiscences, etc.," *The National Era* (June 10, 1847).

22. Henry Bibb, *The Narrative of the Life and Adventures* (1849), in *Slave Narratives,* 461, 471, 515, 533. Harriet Jacobs, *Incidents in the Life of a Slave Girl,* ed. Jean Fagan Yellin (1861; Cambridge: Harvard University Press, 1987), 54, 128. Stowe, *Uncle Tom's Cabin,* 70.

23. Frederick Douglass, *My Bondage and My Freedom,* in *Autobiographies* (New York: Library of America, 1994), 307, 340. Subsequent references to this volume will be cited parenthetically by page number only. "Box" Brown, *The Narrative,* 194–195; Crafts, *Running a Thousand Miles,* 684 (the Crafts are probably drawing from E. D. E. N. Southworth's *The Hidden Hand* [1859], which misquotes Shakespeare in the same way and probably draws on the Crafts in its own depiction of cross-dressing); John Brown, *Slave Life in Georgia,* ed. Louis Alexis Chamerovzow (London: Brown, 1854), 90–91.

24. Stowe, *Uncle Tom's Cabin,* 472.

25. Olaudah Equiano, *The Interesting Narrative of the Life of Olaudah Equiano* (1789), in *Slave Narratives,* 59.

26. Houston A. Baker Jr., *Blues, Ideology, and Afro-American Literature* (Chicago: University of Chicago Press, 1984), esp. 43.

27. Bibb, *The Narrative of the Life and Adventures,* 460.

28. James W. C. Pennington, *The Fugitive Blacksmith,* 2nd ed. (London: Charles Gilpin, 1849), 13.

29. James Franklin, *The Science of Conjecture: Evidence and Probability before Pascal* (Baltimore: Johns Hopkins University Press, 2001).

30. For legal debates about higher law, see Gregg Crane, *Race, Citizenship, and Law in American Literature* (New York: Cambridge University Press, 2002); and Deak Nabers, *Victory of Law: The Fourteenth Amendment, the Civil War, and American Literature* (Baltimore: Johns Hopkins University Press, 2006). For Southern thinkers, see Eugene Genovese, *The Mind of the Master Class: History and Faith in the Southern Slaveholders' Worldview* (New York: Cambridge University Press, 2005), 613–635.

31. Charles Sumner, "Argument," *The North Star* (February 22, 1850); Henry David Thoreau, *Journal, Volume 3,* eds. Robert Sattelmeyer, Mark R. Patterson, and William Rossi (Princeton: Princeton University Press, 1991), 234. "Spirit of the Press in Regard to the Cincinnati Convention," *Frederick Douglass's Paper* (May 13, 1852). Fitzhugh, *Sociology for the South,* 183. "Reformers," *The National Era* (September 3, 1857).

32. "The Philosophy of Human Nature," *The Provincial Freeman* (August 12, 1854). "Prejudice Against Color," *The North Star* (May 5, 1848). [William Wilson], "From Our Brooklyn

Correspondent," *Frederick Douglass's Paper* (February 5, 1852). "Origin of the Races," *The Provincial Freeman* (May 16, 1857). "Mode of Effort," *The Colored American* (June 5, 1841). "Prospectus," *The Liberator* (June 18, 1847). For the shift in slave narratives from abstract reasoning to facts, see Philip Gould, "The Rise, Development, and Circulation of the Slave Narrative," *The Cambridge Companion to the African American Slave Narrative*, ed. Audrey A. Fisch (New York: Cambridge University Press, 2007), 19. For Obama as a pragmatist, see James Kloppenberg, *Reading Obama: Dreams, Hopes, and the American Political Tradition* (Princeton: Princeton University Press, 2010).

33. Douglass, *Life and Writings*, 2:161. Douglass, *Life and Writings*, 2:460; Frederick Douglass, *Selected Speeches and Writings*, ed. Philip S. Foner, abridged and adapted by Yuval Taylor (Chicago: Lawrence Hill Books, 1999), 218. For Douglass and manumission, see his letter to Henry C. Wright, December 22, 1846 in *The Frederick Douglass Papers: Correspondence, Volume 1: 1842–1852*, ed. John R. McKivigan (New Haven: Yale University Press, 2009), 183–190.

34. John Stauffer, *The Black Hearts of Men: Radical Abolitionists and the Transformation of Race* (Cambridge: Harvard University Press, 2002); and *The Works of James McCune Smith: Black Intellectual and Abolitionist*, ed. John Stauffer (Oxford: Oxford University Press, 2006).

35. J. M. Smith to R. Hamilton, August 1864 in *Black Abolitionist Papers, Volume V, The United States, 1859–1865*, ed. C Peter Ripley (Chapel Hill: The University of North Carolina Press, 1992), 299. See also Stauffer, *The Black Hearts of Men*, 11, 124.

36. Ralph Ellison, "An American Dilemma: A Review," *Shadow and Act* (1964; New York: Vintage, 1995), 304–305. Susan Mizruchi, *The Science of Sacrifice: American Literature and Modern Social Theory* (Princeton: Princeton University Press, 1998); Oz Frankel, *States of Inquiry: Social Investigations and Print Culture in Nineteenth-Century Britain and the United States* (Baltimore: Johns Hopkins University Press, 2006), 204–233. Samuel Otter, *Philadelphia Stories: America's Literature of Race and Freedom* (Oxford: Oxford University Press, 2010), 202–209. For the controversy over the 1840 census, see Cohen, *A Calculating People*, 175–204. Before realizing the inaccuracy of the census data, Jarvis initially accepted the racist argument that high rates of insanity in free blacks were due to the "liabilities and dangers of active self-direction" for which they were ill suited (quoted in Cohen, *A Calculating People*, 192). For the political origins of statistics, see Mary Poovey, "Figures of Arithmetic, Figures of Speech: the Discourse of Statistics in the 1830s," in *Questions of Evidence: Proof, Practice, and Persuasion across the Disciplines*, eds. James Chandler, Arnold Davidson, and Harry Harootunian (Chicago: University of Chicago Press, 1991), 401–421; and Daniel R. Headrick, *When Information Came of Age: Technologies of Knowledge in the Age of Reason and Revolution* (Oxford: Oxford University Press, 2000), 72–95.

37. "Freedom and Slavery for Afric-Americans," *The Works of James McCune Smith*, 62. For excellent notes on this piece, see also *The Black Abolitionist Papers, Volume III: The United States, 1830–1846*, ed. C. Peter Ripley (Chapel Hill: University of North Carolina Press, 1991), 430–441. James McCune Smith, "The Influence of Climate on Longevity with Special Reference to Life Insurance," *The Merchants' Magazine and Commercial Review* (April 1846); and James McCune Smith, "Lay Puffery of Homeopathy: Letter from Dr. James McC. Smith," *The Annalist* 2:18 (June 15, 1848). Smith's statistical work was also reported in *Frederick Douglass's Paper* (July 15, 1853, and May 19, 1854). For pro-slavery statistical works, see Josiah Nott and George Gliddon, "Vital Statistics of Negroes and Mulattos" (1844); Hinton Helper, *The Impending Crisis of the South* (1857); and Thorton Stringfellow, *Scriptural and Statistical Views in Favor of Slavery* (Richmond: J. W. Randolph, 1856).

38. *Douglass's Monthly, Vol. 1–3*, 20. James McCune Smith, "Civilization: Its Dependence on Physical Circumstances," *The Works of James McCune Smith*, 251. Note, too, that Quetelet during the Civil War argued against polygenesist views of race (Theodore Porter, *The Rise of*

Statistical Thinking, 1820–1900 [Princeton: Princeton University Press, 1986], 108). McCune Smith also refers to Quetelet as "the highest authority in vital statistics" in "Heads of the Colored People—No. X: The Schoolmaster (Continued)," *The Works of James McCune Smith*, 231. For resistance to the new sciences of chance in black intellectual circles, see Robert Gordon, "In the Constitution of Man there Exists a Religious Element: Theology is the Only Science that Meets It," *The Anglo-African Magazine* (August 1859), 280.

39. M. Luke Bresky, "'Latitudes and Longitudes of Our Condition': The Nationality of Emerson's Representatives," *ESQ* 48:4 (Winter 2002), 211–245.

40. Note that multiple versions of this speech exist and that some phrases have been quoted from the version Douglass gave to the Carlyle Indian Industrial School in 1870 (*The Frederick Douglas Papers*, Library of Congress, Folder 1; http://memory.loc.gov/cgi-bin/ampage).

41. Quetelet, *Treatise on Man*, x.

42. Robert S. Levine, *Martin Delany, Frederick Douglass, and the Politics of Representative Identity* (Chapel Hill: University of North Carolina Press, 1997).

43. Frederick Douglass, "The Prospect of the Future" (August, 1860), *Douglass's Monthly*, Vol. 1–3, 306.

44. Widespread providential views are traced in Nicholas Guyatt, *Providence and the Invention of the United States, 1607–1876* (New York: Cambridge University Press, 2007); and Mark A. Noll, *The Civil War as a Theological Crisis* (Chapel Hill: University of North Carolina Press, 2006), 75–94. David Blight, *Frederick Douglass's Civil War: Keeping Faith in Jubilee* (Baton Rouge: Louisiana State University Press, 1989). See also Maurice O. Wallace, "Violence, Manhood, and War in Douglass," *The Cambridge Companion to Frederick Douglass*, ed. Maurice Lee (New York: Cambridge University Press, 2009), 73–88.

45. Douglass, *Selected Speeches and Writings*, 554.

46. J. Stanley, "A Tribute to a Fallen Black Soldier" (1863), *Lift Every Voice: African American Oratory, 1787–1900*, eds. Philip S. Foner and Robert J. Branham (Tuscaloosa: University of Alabama Press, 1998), 410.

47. Charles Mills, *Blackness Visible: Essays on Philosophy and Race* (Ithaca: Cornell University Press, 1998), 167–200; Bernard Boxill, "Radical Implications of Locke's Moral Theory: The Views of Frederick Douglass," *Subjugation and Bondage: Critical Essays on Slavery and Social Philosophy*, ed. Tommy L. Lott (New York: Rowman and Littlefield, 1998), 29–48; Peter C. Myers, *Frederick Douglass: Race and Rebirth of American Liberalism* (Lawrence: University Press of Kansas, 2008); Russ Castronovo, *Necro Citizenship: Death, Eroticism, and the Public Sphere in the Nineteenth-Century United States* (Durham: Duke University Press, 2001), 50–61; Arthur Riss, *Race, Slavery, and Liberalism in Nineteenth-Century American Literature* (New York: Cambridge University Press, 2006), 164–185.

48. For Douglass's hybrid style, see Paul Giles, "Douglass's Black Atlantic: Britain, Europe, Egypt," in *The Cambridge Companion to Frederick Douglas*, 132–145; and Ivy Wilson, *Specters of Democracy: Blackness and the Aesthetics of Politics in the Antebellum U.S.* (Oxford: Oxford University Press, 2011), 28–36. For Douglass and poetry, see William Gleason, "Volcanoes and Meteors: Douglass, Melville, and the Poetics of Insurrection," *Frederick Douglass and Herman Melville: Essays in Relation*, eds. Robert Levine and Samuel Otter (Chapel Hill: University of North Carolina Press, 2008), 110–133.

49. Booker T. Washington, *Frederick Douglass* (Philadelphia: George Jacobs, 1906), 351; Benjamin Brawley, *The Negro Genius* (1937; Cheshire, Conn.: Biblo and Tannen, 1966), 57; Clarence Thomas, *Grutter v. Bollinger* (2003). For highly selective, politically conservative accounts of Douglass, see The Frederick Douglass Institute and Douglass's enshrinement in the "Conservative Hall of Fame" on the Web site Boycottliberalism.com.

50. For nonessential racial identity, see Walter Benn Michaels, *Our America: Nativism, Modernism, and Pluralism* (Durham: Duke University Press, 1995) ("do"); and Glaude, Jr., *Exodus!* ("suffer").

51. Leslie Butler, *Critical Americans: Victorian Intellectuals and Transatlantic Liberal Reform* (Chapel Hill: University of North Carolina Press, 2007). See also Murney Gerlach, *British Liberalism and the United States: Political and Social Thought in the Late Victorian Age* (New York: Palsgrave, 2001).

52. John Stuart Mill, *Autobiography* (1873; New York: Penguin, 1989), 172. John Stuart Mill, *On Liberty*, ed. Edward Alexander (London: Broadview, 1999), 109. James McCune Smith, "On the Fourteenth Query of Thomas Jefferson's Notes on Virginia," *The Works of James McCune Smith*, 280–281. Wilhelm Von Humboldt, *The Limits of State Action*, ed. J. W. Burrow (Indianapolis: Liberty Fund, 1993), 32. Smith, "Civilization," 261. For a classic account of the ideology of racial purity in mid-nineteenth-century America, see Reginald Horsman, *Race and Manifest Destiny: The Origins of American Racial Anglo-Saxonism* (Cambridge: Harvard University Press, 1981). For a white supremacist rejection of Mill's *On Liberty*, see Albert Taylor Bledsoe, "What is Liberty?" *Southern Review* 5 (1869), 249–274. For the link between Mills's abolitionism and his inductive philosophy, see Richard Reeves, *John Stuart Mill: Victorian Firebrand* (London: Atlantic Books, 2007), 342.

53. Henry Buckle, *History of Civilization in England, Volume I* (New York: Appleton, 1858), 16, 8–9, 24. Henry Buckle, "Mill on Liberty" (1863), *Essays* (New York: Appleton, 1863), 106.

54. For Lincoln and equal chances, see Scott Sandage, *Born Losers: A History of Failure in America* (Cambridge: Harvard University Press, 2005), 189–225.

55. Charles Mills, *The Racial Contract* (Ithaca: Cornell University Press, 1997). Comparisons between the chance-based utilitarian strand of Douglass's political philosophy and John Rawls's *Theory of Justice* (1971) are too complicated to argue at length here, though it may be worth mentioning that, while Rawls is certainly interested in taming chance, which he refers to as "natural chance" and more generally as "risk," he criticizes utilitarianism for failing "to take seriously the plurality and distinctness of individuals" insofar as utilitarianism tends to extend the principles of choice for a single individual to that of an entire society (John Rawls, *Theory of Justice: Revised Edition* [Cambridge: Harvard University Press, 1999], 11, 26). Douglass does not fall so readily into this error, though despite his emphasis on diversity and his recognition of the *rhetorical* failings of absolutist claims, he remains vulnerable to Rawls's critique, if only because of his abiding sense that beneath cultural and even biological differences humans share a single universalized nature.

56. Susan Mizruchi, "Becoming Multicultural," *American Literary History* 15:1 (Spring 2003), 39. See also Mizruchi's *The Rise of Multicultural America: Economy and Print Culture, 1865-1915* (Chapel Hill: University of North Carolina Press, 2008).

57. For brief references to Douglass as pragmatic, see Giles Gunn, *Beyond Solidarity*, xii–xiii; Blight, *Douglass's Civil War*, esp. 155–165; Martin, *The Mind of Frederick Douglass*, 33; and Levine, *Martin Delany, Frederick Douglass, and the Politics of Representative Identity*, 5. For Douglass's relationship to philosophy, see Maurice Lee, *Slavery, Philosophy, and American Literature, 1830–1860* (New York: Cambridge University Press, 2005), 93–132.

58. George M. Fredrickson, *The Inner Civil War: Northern Intellectuals and the Crisis of the Union with a New Preface* (New York: Harper and Row, 1965); Cornel West, *The American Evasion of Philosophy* (Madison: University of Wisconsin Press, 1989); Louis Menand, *The Metaphysical Club* (New York: Farrar, Straus and Giroux, 2001).

59. Oliver Wendell Holmes Jr. to Morris Cohen, February 5, 1919, in Oliver Wendell Holmes Jr., *The Essential Holmes: Selections from the Letters, Speeches, Judicial Opinions, and Other Writings*, ed. Richard A. Posner (Chicago: University of Chicago Press, 1997), 110. Subsequent references to this volume cited parenthetically as *EH*.

60. Menand, *The Metaphysical Club*, 3–69.

61. Oliver Wendell Holmes Sr., *The Autocrat of the Breakfast Table* (1858; New York: Airmont, 1968), 57.

62. Oliver Wendell Holmes, *The Collected Works of Justice Holmes,* 5 vols., ed. Sheldon M. Novick (Chicago: University of Chicago Press, 1995), 3:497; *EH* 77; *EH* 97.

63. Oliver Wendell Holmes Jr., *Touched with Fire: Civil War Letters and Diary of Oliver Wendell Holmes Jr., 1861–1864,* ed. Mark De Wolfe Howe (Cambridge: Harvard University Press, 1947), 28.

64. David Blight, *Race and Reunion: The Civil War in American Memory* (Cambridge: Belknap Press of Harvard University Press, 2001).

65. Holmes, *Touched with Fire,* 79.

66. Goodman, *Shifting the Blame,* 98–107.

67. Douglass, "Our Free Colored Population" (August 1859), *Douglass's Monthly, Vol. 1–3,* 125; Douglass, "Self-Made Men" (1870; Carlyle School version), 16.

68. Sandra Day O'Connor's majority opinion in *Grutter v. Bollinger* (2003) affirms the value of "widely diverse people, cultures, ideas, and viewpoints" but also holds that in the context of higher education "race-conscious admissions policies must be limited in time." What such limits should be is unclear.

69. Charles Peirce, *The Essential Peirce: Selected Philosophical Writings,* 2 vols, eds. Nathan Houser, Christian Kloesel, et al. (Bloomington: Indiana University Press, 1992-1998), 1:29. Ross Posnock, *Color and Culture: Black Writers and the Making of the Modern Intellectual* (Cambridge: Harvard University Press, 1998). W. James to B. T. Washington, March 28, 1909, *The Correspondence of William James,* eds. Ignas Skrupskelis and Elizabeth Berkeley (Charlottesville: University of Virginia Press, 1992), 12:192. Fredrickson, *The Inner Civil War,* 229–236; Menand, *The Metaphysical Club,* 147–148.

70. Stanley Fish, "Truth and Toilets: Pragmatism and the Practices of Life," *The Revival of Pragmatism: New Essays on Social Thought, Law, and Culture,* ed. Morris Dickstein (Durham: Duke University Press, 1998), 418–433. Toni Morrison, *Playing in the Dark: Whiteness and the Literary Imagination* (New York: Vintage, 1992); Cornel West, "Afterword: A Conversation between Cornel West and Bill E. Lawson," *Pragmatism and the Problem of Race,* eds. Bill E. Lawson and Donald F. Koch (Bloomington: Indiana University Press, 2004), 225–230. James Kloppenberg, *Uncertain Victory: Social Democracy and Progressivism in European and American Thought, 1870–1920* (Oxford: Oxford University Press, 1988).

71. Michaels, *Our America,* esp. 64. See also Werner Sollors, "A Critique of Pure Pluralism," *Reconstructing American Literary History,* ed. Sacvan Bercovich (Cambridge: Harvard University Press, 1986), 250–279. West, *The Evasion of American Philosophy,* 147; West, "Afterword," 229; Eddie Glaude Jr., *In a Shade of Blue: Pragmatism and the Politics of Black America* (Chicago: University of Chicago Press, 2007); *Pragmatism and the Problem of Race,* eds. Lawson and Koch.

72. Anna Julia Cooper, *A Voice from the South* (Oxford: Oxford University Press, 1990), 186, 151. For Cooper's insights into the limits of logic, including superficial statistical thinking, see her review of Howells's *An Imperative Duty* (1892), as well as Todd Vogel's *ReWriting White: Race, Class, and Cultural Capital in Nineteenth-Century America* (New Brunswick: Rutgers University Press, 2004), 85–102. Pauline Hopkins, *Contending Forces: A Romance Illustrative of Negro Life North and South* (Oxford: Oxford University Press, 1988), 300, 295. For women, calculation, and foresight in the early republic, see Jennifer Baker, *Securing the Commonwealth: Debt, Speculation, and Writing in the Making of Early America* (Baltimore: Johns Hopkins University Press, 2005), 137–156. See also Nina Baym, *American Women of Letters and the Nineteenth-Century Sciences: Styles of Affiliation* (New Brunswick: Rutgers University Press, 2002).

73. Helen H. Jun, "Black Orientalism: Nineteenth-Century Narratives of Race and U.S. Citizenship," *American Quarterly* 58:4 (2006), 1047–1066.

74. Alain Locke, "The New Negro," *The New Negro,* ed. Alain Locke (New York: Touchstone, 1992), 3.

75. W. E. B. Du Bois, "The Conservation of Races" (1897), *Writings* (New York: Library of America, 1986), 817. W. E. B. Du Bois, "The Black Man Brings His Gifts," *Harlem, Mecca of the New Negro*, ed. Alain Locke (rpt; Baltimore: Black Classic Press, 1980), 655. Mizruchi, *The Science of Sacrifice*, 269–366. W. E. B. Du Bois, *The Philadelphia Negro: A Social Study* (New York: Benjamin Bloom, 1899), iv–v. W. E. B. Du Bois, *The Souls of Black Folk* (1903), in *Writings*, 431. For anti-racist anti-abstraction, see Elizabeth Duquette, "Embodying Community, Disembodying Race: Josiah Royce on 'Race Questions and Prejudices,'" *American Literary History* 16:1 (Spring 2004), 29–57.

76. W. E. B. Du Bois, "My Evolving Program for Negro Freedom," *What the Negro Wants*, ed. Rayford Logan (Chapel Hill: University of North Carolina Press, 1944), 57–58. Posnock, *Color and Culture*, 114–121. See also Maria Farland, "W. E. B. Du Bois, Anthropometric Science, and the Limits of Racial Uplift," *American Quarterly* 58:4 (December 2006), 1017–1045. Kenneth Warren, *So Black and Blue: Ralph Ellison and the Occasion of Criticism* (Chicago: University of Chicago Press, 2003), 50. For another literary work that takes up the complicated relationship between race, statistics, probability, and hereditary science, see Howells's *An Imperative Duty*.

CHAPTER 5

1. For myths of scientific revelation, see John Waller, *Fabulous Science: Fact and Fiction in the History of Scientific Discovery* (Oxford: Oxford University Press, 2002). An extreme case for discontinuous scientific progress is Paul Feyerabend, *Against Method* (London: New Left Books, 1975). For scientific discipline, patience, and gradualism in nineteenth-century science and literature, see George Levine, *Dying to Know: Scientific Epistemology and Narrative in Victorian England* (Chicago: University of Chicago Press, 2002).

2. Henry David Thoreau, *Journal*, vols. 1–6, 8, gen. eds. John Broderick and Robert Sattelmeyer (Princeton: Princeton University Press, 1981–2002), 4:71. Subsequent references to this series made parenthetically in the text with Arabic numerals indicating volume number. References to *The Writings of Henry David Thoreau: Journal*, vols. 1–14, eds. Bradford Torrey and Francis H. Allen (New York: AMS Press, 1968) will appear parenthetically in the text with Roman numerals indicating volume number.

3. See, for instance, Nina Baym, "Thoreau's View of Science," *Journal of the History of Ideas* 26 (1965), 221–234 ("waning power"); Richard Poirier, *A World Elsewhere: The Place of Style in American Literature* (New York: Oxford University Press, 1966), 83–89 ("imaginative powers"); Stanley Cavell, *The Senses of Walden* (New York: Viking Press, 1972) ("less enamored with idealism"); Lawrence Buell, *The Environmental Imagination: Thoreau, Nature Writing, and the Formation of American Culture* (Cambridge: Belknap Press of Harvard University Press, 1995) ("ecocriticsm").

4. Alfred I. Tauber, *Henry David Thoreau and the Moral Agency of Knowing* (Berkeley: University of California Press, 2001), 131 ("delicate equilibrium"); Robert D. Richardson, "Introduction," *Faith in a Seed: The Dispersion of Seeds and Other Late Natural History Writings* (Washington, D.C.: Island Press, 1993), 6 ("inextricable); William Rossi, "Historical Introduction" to Thoreau's *Journal*, 3:496 ("higher empiricism"); Michael Berger, *Thoreau's Late Career and The Dispersion of Seeds* (Rochester, N.Y.: Camden, 2000), 78 ("higher empiricism"); Laura Dassow Walls, *Seeing New Worlds: Henry David Thoreau and Nineteenth-Century Natural Science* (Madison: University of Wisconsin Press, 1995), 4 ("empirical holism"); Buell, *Environmental Imagination*, 24 ("synthesis"); David Robinson, *Natural Life: Thoreau's Worldly Transcendentalism* (Ithaca: Cornell University Press, 2004), 177 ("synthesis").

5. See, for instance, Buell, *The Environmental Imagination*, 117; Tauber, *Thoreau and the Moral Agency of Knowing*, 105–113; Berger, *Thoreau's Late Career*, 20n16; Robinson, *Natural Life*, 201.

6. Theodore Porter, *The Rise of Statistical Thinking, 1820–1900* (Princeton: Princeton University Press, 1986); Jonathan Crary, *Techniques of the Observer: On Vision and Modernity in the Nineteenth Century* (Cambridge: MIT Press, 1992), esp. 17n21.

7. Ralph Waldo Emerson, "Thoreau" (1862), *Transcendentalism: A Reader*, ed. Joel Myerson (Oxford: Oxford University Press, 2000), 655; Ralph Waldo Emerson, *Essays and Lectures* (New York: Library of America, 1983), 487, 208.

8. As reported in Thoreau's journal, Emerson told Thoreau of one reader's response to *Walden*: "[He] relished it merely as a capital satire and joke, and even thought that the survey and map of the pond were not real, but a caricature of the Coast Surveys" (VII:103).

9. Henry David Thoreau, *Walden*, in *Walden and Other Writings*, ed. William Howarth (New York: The Modern Library, 1981), 83. Subsequent reference to this work cited parenthetically in the text.

10. David Hume, *A Treatise of Human Nature*, eds. David Fate Norton and Mary J. Norton (Oxford: Oxford University Press, 2000), 59.

11. Thomas Reid, *Inquiry into the Human Mind on Principles of Common Sense* (London: T. Cadell, 1785), 124, 98–99.

12. Terence Martin, *The Instructed Vision: Scottish Common Sense Philosophy and the Origins of American Fiction* (Bloomington: Indiana University Press, 1961), 33–34. For a corrective to Martin, see Davis, *Formalism, Experience, and the Making of American Literature*. Note, too, that Thoreau owned John Abercrombie's *Inquiry Concerning the Intellectual Powers* (1830), a book derived from Reid that asserts (contra Hume) the epistemological sufficiency of impressions.

13. Montaigne, *Essays*, 766. Montaigne also writes in *An Apology for Raymond Sebond*: "We register the appearance of objects; to judge them we need an instrument of judgement; to test the veracity of that instrument we need practical proof; to test that proof we need an instrument. We are going round in circles. . . . We ourselves, our faculty of judgement and all moral things are flowing and rolling ceaselessly" (*Essays*, 679–680).

14. Cavell, *The Senses of Walden*, 12.

15. Charles Peirce, *The Essential Peirce: Selected Philosophical Writings*, 2 vols, eds. Nathan Houser, Christian Kloesel, et al. (Bloomington: Indiana University Press, 1992–1998), 2:70.

16. Emerson, *Essays and Lectures*, 60.

17. James Beattie, *An Essay on the Nature and Immutability of Truth* (London: Dilly, 1772), 482.

18. Immanuel Kant, *Prolegomena to Any Future Metaphysics That Will Be Able to Come Forward as Science*, ed. Gary Hatfield (New York: Cambridge University Press, 2004), 9, 119.

19. Cavell, *The Senses of Walden*, 64.

20. Henry David Thoreau, *The Maine Woods*, ed. Joseph J. Moldenhauer (Princeton: Princeton University Press, 1972), 71.

21. Stanley Cavell, *Conditions Handsome and Unhandsome: The Constitution of Emersonian Perfectionism* (Chicago: University of Chicago Press, 1990), 33, 38.

22. For Thoreau's linguistic theory, see Michael West, *Transcendental Wordplay: America's Romantic Punsters and the Search for the Language of Nature* (Athens: Ohio State University Press, 2000), 183–218.

23. Buell, *The Environmental Imagination*, 96.

24. Henry David Thoreau, *Early Essays and Miscellanies*, eds. Joseph Moldenhauer and Edwin Moser (Princeton: Princeton University Press, 1975), 103.

25. William Rossi, "Poetry and Progress: Thoreau, Lyell, and the Geological Principles of *A Week*," *American Literature* 66:2 (1994), 275–300. For erosion, see *Cape Cod*, in *Walden and Other Writings*, 469. For Thoreau and the *point d'appui*, see Walter Benn Michaels, "*Walden's* False Bottoms," *Glyph* 1 (1977), 132–149.

26. J. A. Bennett, *The Divided Circle: A History of Instruments for Astronomy, Navigation, and Surveying* (Oxford: Phaidon, Christie's, 1987), 143–208. See also Andro Linklater, *Measuring America: How an Untamed Wilderness Shaped the United States and Fulfilled the Promise of Democracy* (New York: Walker, 2002).

27. Rick Van Noy, *Surveying the Interior: Literary Cartographers and the Sense of Place* (Reno: University of Nevada Press, 2003), 8. Unfortunately I have not been able to consult Patrick Chura's *Thoreau the Land Surveyor* (Gainesville: University Press of Florida, 2010).

28. Emerson, "Thoreau," 655.

29. Charles Davies, *Elements of Surveying and Navigation* (New York: A. S. Barnes, 1846), 79; John Gummere, *A Treatise of Surveying Containing the Theory and Practice* (Philadelphia: Thomas, Cowperthwait, 1846), 254.

30. Emerson, *Essays and Lectures*, 32; Kant, *Prolegomena*, 9.

31. Augustus de Morgan, *An Essay on Probabilities and on Their Application to Life Contingencies and Insurance Offices* (London: Longman, Orme, Brown et al., 1838), 18–22. Quetelet, *Letters on the Theory of Probabilities*, 38.

32. A. D. Bache, *Smithsonian Contributions to Knowledge* (Washington D.C.: Smithsonian, 1863), 72. See also F. R. Hassler, "Survey of the Coast," *Army and Navy Chronicle* (January 14, 1836), and a review of John Millington's *Elements of Civil Engineering*, in *New York Review* (July 1839). Gillespie wrote: "When a number of separate observations of an angle have been made, the mean or average of them . . . is taken as the true reading. . . . [P]robable error is equal to the square root of the sum of the squares of the errors . . . divided by the number of observations. . . . These rules are proved by the 'Theory of Probabilities'" (*A Treatise on Land-Surveying* [New York: Appleton, 1851], 252). See also Gummere, *A Treatise on Surveying*, 106.

33. Quoted in Van Noy, *Surveying the Interior*, 70.

34. Henry David Thoreau, "Walking," *Wild Apples and Other Natural History Essays*, ed. William Rossi (Athens: University of Georgia Press, 2002), 64.

35. "The Pond in Winter" generally praises Gilpin, whom Thoreau engaged at length in a journal entry from 1854. Thoreau agrees with Gilpin's emphasis on the "roughness" of nature's beauty, though he objects that Gilpin "does not go beneath the surface," for by locating the pleasure of the picturesque in the "'*sensations of the mind*,'" Gilpin slights the natural world (VII:53–59). For connections between the irregularity of the picturesque and chaos theory, see Tom Stoppard's *Arcadia* (1993), a work that recognizes some roots of modern chance in nineteenth-century literature.

36. See, for instance, David Hume, *An Enquiry Concerning Human Understanding*, ed. Thom Beauchamp (Oxford: Clarendon Press, 2000), 113.

37. See, for instance, Cavell, *The Senses of Walden*, 100–101; and Tauber, *Thoreau and the Moral Agency of Knowing*, 104–138.

38. For literature and financial speculation in the nineteenth century, see (most influentially) Walter Benn Michaels, *The Gold Standard and the Logic of Naturalism: American Literature at the turn of the Century* (Berkeley: University of California Press, 1987); and (more recently) Anthony, *Paper Money Men*.

39. "The Routine of English Country Sports," *Spirit of the Times* (January 23, 1841). [no title], *North American Review* (October 1842). "Science of the Rod," *Spirit of the Times* (September 8, 1849); [no title], *Littell's Living Age* (April 1, 1848).

40. "Letter from the Sporting Grounds," *Spirit of the Times* (September 2, 1848). See also "A Scientific Sportsman," *Spirit of the Times* (March 10, 1849); and "Angling in the United States," *Spirit of the Times* (March 2, 1850).

41. James Wilson, *The Rod and the Gun* (Edinburgh: Adam and Charles Black, 1844), 6, 12. Humphrey Davy, *Salmonia, or Days of Fly-Fishing* (London: Smith, Elder and Co. Cornhill, 1840), 127. William Chatto, *The Angler's Souvenir* (New York: Frederick Warne, 1886), 304.

42. For Thoreau and the Irish, see William Gleason, *The Leisure Ethic: Work and Play in American Literature, 1840–1940* (Stanford: Stanford University Press, 1999), 44–56. See also Dana Nelson, "Thoreau, Manhood, and Race: Quiet Desperation versus Representative Isolation," *A Historical Guide to Henry David Thoreau*, ed. William E. Cain (Oxford: Oxford University Press, 2000), 61–94.

43. Note, too, that angling in the mid-nineteenth century was becoming a marker of class requiring appropriate dress and etiquette, a gentrification of the sport that Thoreau predictably disliked. See Colleen J. Sheehy, "American Angling: The Rise of Urbanism and the Romance of the Rod and Reel," *Hard at Play: Leisure in America, 1840–1940*, ed. Kathryn Grover (Amherst: University of Massachusetts Press, 1992), 77–92; and Robert Sattelmeyer, "'The True Industry for Poets': Fishing with Thoreau," *ESQ* 33:4 (1987), 189–201.

44. Emerson, "Thoreau," 668; William Ellery Channing, *Thoreau: The Poet-Naturalist* (Boston: Roberts Brothers, 1873), 317, 202.

45. Walls, *Seeing New Worlds*. See also Laura Dassow Walls, *The Passage to Cosmos: Alexander von Humboldt and the Shaping of America* (Chicago: University of Chicago Press, 2009).

46. Walls, *Seeing New Worlds*, 224. See also Robinson, *Natural Life*, 195; and Sharon Cameron on the cultivated "randomness" of Thoreau's journals (*Writing Nature: Henry Thoreau's Journal* [Oxford: Oxford University Press, 1985], 5). For Thoreau's naturalism within a broad context of early American phenology, see Leo Stoller, "A Note on Thoreau's Place in the History of Phenology," *Isis* 47 (1956), 172–181.

47. Walls, *Seeing New Worlds*; Tauber, *Thoreau and the Moral Agency of Knowing*, 104–139.

48. William Paley, *Natural Theology*, in *The Works of William Paley*, 5 vols. (London: Rivington, 1825), 5:44; Robert Chambers, *Vestiges of the Natural History of Creation* (London: George Routledge, 1887), 61. Paley also writes in *Natural Theology*: "There must be *chance* in the midst of design: by which we mean, that events which are not designed, necessarily arise from the pursuit of events which are designed" (5:357).

49. *The Empire of Chance: How Probability Changed Science and Everyday Life*, eds. Gerd Gigerenzer et al. (Cambridge: Cambridge University Press, 1989), 123–162.

50. Chambers, *Vestiges*, 244.

51. Gillian Beer, *Darwin's Plots: Evolutionary Narrative in Darwin, George Eliot, and Nineteenth-Century Fiction*, 3rd ed. (1983; Cambridge: Cambridge University Press, 2009), 29–32; Joan Richardson, *A Natural History of Pragmatism: The Fact of Feeling from Jonathan Edwards to Gertrude Stein* (Cambridge: Cambridge University Press, 2007), 82. Janet Browne, "Darwin's Botanical Arithmetic and the 'Principle of Divergence,'" *Journal of the History of Biology* 13:1 (1980), 53–89. Daniel Dennett, *Darwin's Dangerous Idea: Evolution and the Meanings of Life* (New York: Simon and Schuster, 1995). Gigerenzer et al., *The Empire of Chance*, 66–67.

52. Charles Darwin, *On the Origin of Species by Means of Natural Selection*, ed. Joseph Carroll (Ontario: Broadview Press, 2003), 102. "Interesting Scientific Theory," *Boston Investigator* (February 15, 1860). For the reception of Darwinism in America, see Ronald Numbers, *Darwinism Comes to America* (Cambridge: Harvard University Press, 1998).

53. Darwin to Asa Gray, May 22, 1860, *The Life and Letters of Charles Darwin*, ed. Francis Darwin, 3 vols. (London: John Murray, 1888), 2:312.

54. Herschel quoted in a letter from Darwin to Charles Lyell, December 12, 1859, *The Life and Letters of Charles Darwin*, 2:240. Thomas Henry Huxley, "On the Reception of the 'Origin of Species,'" *The Life and Letters of Charles Darwin*, 199.

55. Darwin to Joseph Hooker, July 12, 1870, *On the Origin of Species*, 494. For Darwin's deathbed quote, see Colin Jager, *The Book of God: Secularization and Design in the Romantic Era* (Philadelphia: University of Pennsylvania Press, 2007). 125.

56. Darwin, *On the Origin of Species*, 392.

57. Beers, *Darwin's Plots*, esp. 23–70.

58. Thoreau, *Cape Cod*, 467.

59. H. Daniel Peck, *Thoreau's Morning Work: Memory and Perception in A Week on the Concord and Merrimack Rivers, the "Journal," and Walden* (New Haven: Yale University Press, 1994), 75.

60. Emerson, "Thoreau," 668. Cavell, *Senses of Walden*, esp. 59; Wai Chee Dimock, *Through Other Continents: American Literature across Deep Time* (Princeton: Princeton University Press, 2006), 7–22. Tyndall quoted in Levine, *Dying to Know*, 4.

61. As Lee Rust Brown has argued, such disarticulated description can reflect the collecting impetus of the natural historian (*The Emerson Museum*, 73).

62. Henry David Thoreau, *Wild Fruits*, ed. Bradley P. Dean (New York: Norton, 2000), 63.

63. Ibid., 125.

64. Buell, *Environmental Imagination*, 113.

65. The last few pages of Thoreau's final journal contain lots of unidentified additions and divisions that show him calculating averages of unidentified phenomena, as if he used the pages as a scratch pad. These rough calculations are not included in published versions.

66. Charles Darwin, *Autobiography* (1876), in Darwin, *On the Origin of Species*, 443.

67. Ruskin quoted in M. M. Mahood, *The Poet as Botanist* (Cambridge: Cambridge University Press, 2008), 149. For critics emphasizing affinities between Thoreau and Ruskin, see Robert D. Richardson Jr., *Henry Thoreau: A Life of the Mind* (Berkeley: University of California Press, 1986), 358–362; and Buell, *The Environmental Imagination*, 90–91. More equivocal views include Peck, *Thoreau's Morning Work*, 81, 110. For Turner as anticipating thermodynamic laws of chance, see Michel Serres, *Hermes: Literature, Science, Philosophy*, eds. Josué V. Harari and David F. Bell (Baltimore: Johns Hopkins University Press, 1982), 54–64.

68. John Ruskin, *Modern Painters, Vol. I* (New York: Merrill, 1873), xlv, xxix, xxvii, xviii.

69. John Ruskin, *Modern Painters, Vol. II* (New York: Merrill, 1873), 35–36; Ruskin, *Modern Painters, Vol. I*, 65, 55.

70. Henry David Thoreau, *Faith in a Seed: The Dispersion of Seeds and Other Late Natural History Writings*, ed. Bradley Dean (Washington, D.C.: Island Press, 1993), 130, 61.

71. Henry David Thoreau, "The Succession of Forest Trees," *Wild Apples*, 93–94.

72. Ibid., 98.

73. Ibid., 108. Thoreau, *Wild Fruits*, 147, 270–271.

74. Emerson, "Thoreau," 666.

75. Peter Allan Dale, *In Pursuit of Scientific Culture: Science, Art, and Society in the Victorian Age* (Madison: University of Wisconsin Press, 1989); Levine, *Dying to Know*.

76. Beer, *Darwin's Plots*, 18, 49.

77. Thoreau, *The Maine Woods*, 69–71.

78. John Burroughs, *The Last Harvest* (Boston: Houghton Mifflin, 1922), 147, 151. C. G. Willis, B. Ruhfel, R. B. Primack, A. J. Miller-Rushing, and C. C. Davis, "Phylogenetic patterns of species loss in Thoreau's woods are driven by climate change," *Proceedings of the National Academy of Sciences* 105:44 (November 2008), 17029–17033. See also Berger, *Thoreau's Late Career*, 48–75.

79. Many thanks to the Morgan Library Special Collections for making Thoreau's tables available.

80. For other early Americans "disposed to delight in numbers," see Patricia Cline Cohen, *A Calculating People: The Spread of Numeracy in Early America* (Chicago: University of Chicago Press, 1982), 17.

81. Burroughs, *The Last Harvest*, 113. Alan Hodder, *Thoreau's Ecstatic Witness* (New Haven: Yale University Press, 2001), 250–300 ("spiritual"); Tauber, *Thoreau and the Moral Agency of Knowing* ("humanist"); Buell, *Environmental Imagination* ("ecocritical").

82. Emerson, *Essays and Lectures*, 202, 275, 282, 694. For a compatible account of Fuller embracing the fallibility of deep time, see Dimock, *Through Other Continents*, 64–66.

83. Alexander Pope, *Essay on Criticism* (1711), *The Major Works*, ed. Pat Rogers (Oxford: Oxford University Press, 2006), 29. Richardson, *Thoreau: A Life of the Mind*, 93–96. Fuller quoted in Charles Capper, *Margaret Fuller: An American Romantic Life, The Public Years* (Oxford: Oxford University Press, 2007), 16–17.

84. Emerson, *Essays and Lectures*, 100. Of course, it may be a cracked binding and not simple coincidence that Thoreau blindly turned to an essay he clearly knew well.

85. For Cavell's resistance to pragmatism, see "What's the Use of Calling Emerson a Pragmatist," *The Revival of Pragmatism: New Essays on Social Thought, Law, and Culture*, ed. Morris Dickstein (Durham: Duke University Press, 1998), 72–80. Garrett Stewart discusses Cavell's legacy (and lack thereof) in American romantic literary criticism: "The Avoidance of Stanley Cavell," *Contending with Stanley Cavell*, ed. Russell Goodman (Oxford: Oxford University Press, 2005), 140–156. For Cavell's resistance to scientific positivism (and his linking of it with pragmatism as represented by Dewey), see *Conditions Handsome and Unhandsome*, 13–16.

86. *The Correspondence of William James*, 1:9, 1:6–7, 8:332.

87. William James, *Writings*, 2 vols. (New York: Library of America, 1987), 2:778, 2:1160–1161, 2:536, 2:511.

88. Andrew Reynolds, *Peirce's Scientific Metaphysics: The Philosophy of Chance, Law, and Evolution* (Nashville, Tenn.: Vanderbilt University Press, 2002), 3–7; Hilary Putnam, "Pragmatism and Realism," *The Revival of Pragmatism*, 37–53, esp. 45–46.

89. Peirce, *Essential Peirce*, 1:304–305.

90. James, *Writings*, 1:465.

91. Charles Peirce, *The Collected Papers of Charles Peirce*, eds. Charles Hartshorne and Paul Weiss (Cambridge: Belknap Press of Harvard University Press, 1960–1966), 5:589.

92. Susan Howe, *Pierce-Arrow* (New York: New Directions, 1999), 119.

93. Richardson, *A Natural History of Pragmatism*, esp. 62–136; Elisa New, *The Line's Eye: Poetic Experience, American Sight* (Cambridge: Harvard University Press, 1998).

94. Peirce, *The Essential Peirce*, 1:313. Peirce quoted in Howe, *Pierce-Arrow*, 116.

CHAPTER 6

1. William Whewell, *The Philosophy of the Inductive Sciences*, 2 vols. (London: John W. Parker, 1840), 2: 242–243; Edward O. Wilson, *Consilience* (New York: Knopf, 1998), 8. Thomas Wentworth Higginson, *Atlantic Essays* (Boston: James Osgood, 1871), 28. Thomas Wentworth Higginson, *Book and Heart: Essays on Literature and Life* (New York: Harper and Bros., 1897), 33.

2. Levertov quoted in introductory materials to *Titanic Operas*, ed. Martha Nell Smith (http://www.emilydickinson.org/titanic/levertov.html). For Dickinson's quote, see T. W. Higginson to M. E. Higginson, August 17, 1870, in *The Letters of Emily Dickinson*, 3 vols., eds. Thomas H. Johnson and Theodora Ward (Cambridge: Belknap Press of Harvard University Press, 1958), 2:474.

3. Philip Fisher, *Wonder, the Rainbow, and the Aesthetics of Rare Experiences* (Cambridge: Harvard University Press, 1998), 1. Christopher R. Miller, "Jane Austen's Aesthetics and Ethics of Surprise," *Narrative* 13:3 (October 2005), 254; and "Wordsworth's Anatomies of Surprise," *Studies in Romanticism* 46:4 (Winter 2007), 409–431. For romanticism and aleatory concepts, see also Eric Wilson, *Romantic Turbulence: Chaos, Ecology, and American Space* (New York: St. Martin's Press, 2000); Ira Livingston, *Arrow of Chaos: Romanticism and Postmodernity* (Minneapolis: University of Minnesota Press, 1997); and Karl Heinz Bohrer, trans. Ruth Crowley, *Suddenness: On the Moment of Aesthetic Appearance* (New York: Columbia University Press, 1994).

4. Emily Dickinson, *The Poems of Emily Dickinson: Reading Edition*, ed. R. W. Franklin (Cambridge: Harvard University Press, 1998), #1347 (1874). All quotations, dates,

and numbers (prefixed with an *F*) relating to Dickinson's poems are taken from this volume.

5. See, for instance, Robert Weisbuch, *Emily Dickinson's Poetry* (Chicago: University of Chicago Press, 1975), 12–19; Joanne Diehl, *Dickinson and the Romantic Imagination* (Princeton: Princeton University Press, 1981); Suzanne Juhasz, *The Undiscovered Continent: Emily Dickinson and the Space of the Mind* (Bloomington: Indiana University Press, 1983); Cristanne Miller, *Emily Dickinson: A Poet's Grammar* (Cambridge: Harvard University Press, 1987), esp. 149–153; and Gary Stonum, *The Dickinson Sublime* (Madison: University of Wisconsin Press, 1990). Virginia Jackson, *Dickinson's Misery: A Theory of Lyric Reading* (Princeton: Princeton University Press, 2005), 6.

6. See, for instance, Christopher Benfey, *Emily Dickinson and the Problem of Others* (Amherst: University of Massachusetts Press, 1984); Margaret Dickie, *Lyric Contingencies: Emily Dickinson and Wallace Stevens* (Philadelphia: University of Pennsylvania Press, 1991); Sharon Cameron, *Lyric Time: Dickinson and the Limits of Genre* (Baltimore: Johns Hopkins University Press, 1979) and *Choosing Not to Choose: Dickinson's Fascicles* (Chicago: University of Chicago Press, 1992); Susan Manning, "How Conscious Could Consciousness Grow?: Emily Dickinson and William James," *Soft Canons: American Women Writers and Masculine Tradition*, ed. Karen Kilcup (Iowa City: University of Iowa Press, 1999), 306–331; and Anne-Lise François, *Open Secrets: The Literature of Uncounted Experience* (Stanford: Stanford University Press, 2008), esp. 197–217.

7. Elisa New, *The Line's Eye: Poetic Experience, American Sight* (Cambridge: Harvard University Press, 1998), 9.

8. For Dickinson's reading, see Jack Capps, *Emily Dickinson's Reading, 1836–1886* (Cambridge: Harvard University Press, 1966); Richard Sewall, *The Life of Emily Dickinson, Volume Two* (New York: Farrar, Straus and Giroux, 1974), 668–705; and Jed Deppman, *Trying to Think with Emily Dickinson* (Amherst: University of Massachusetts Press, 2008), 75–108.

9. For representative readings of poem F450 that emphasize subject-object dualism, see Inder Nath Kher, *The Landscape of Absence: Emily Dickinson's Poetry* (New Haven: Yale University Press, 1974), 40; and Josef Raab, "The Metapoetic Element in Dickinson," *The Emily Dickinson Handbook*, eds. Gudren Grabher, Roland Hagenbuchle, and Cristanne Miller (Amherst: University of Massachusetts Press, 1999), 286–287.

10. Ralph Waldo Emerson, *Essays and Lectures* (New York: Library of America, 1983), 32.

11. Emerson, *Essays and Lectures*, 483, 484, 491. For Emerson and chance, see Eric Wertheimer, *Underwriting: The Poetics of Insurance in America, 1722–1872* (Stanford: Stanford University Press, 2006), 118–140.

12. For Dickinson as a philosopher of moods, see Benfey, *Emily Dickinson and the Problem of Others*. For differences between Emerson and Dickinson, see Mary Loeffelholz, "'Question of Monuments': Emerson, Dickinson, and American Renaissance Portraiture," *Modern Language Quarterly* 59:4 (December 1998), 445–469; New, *The Line's Eye*; and Lawrence Buell, "Emersonian Anti-Mentoring: From Thoreau to Dickinson and Beyond," *Michigan Quarterly Review* 41:3 (Fall 2002), 347–360.

13. David Hume, *An Enquiry Concerning Human Understanding*, ed. Thom Beauchamp (Oxford: Clarendon Press, 2000), 114.

14. Christopher Ricks, *Keats and Embarrassment* (Oxford: Clarendon Press, 1974), 42. Note that Keat's quite libidinous "Oh, blush not so!" (1883) was not published until Dickinson neared the end of her life. Friedrich Schiller, *On the Naïve and Sentimental in Literature*, trans. Helen Watanabe-O'Kelly (Manchester: Carcanet New Press, 1981), 25.

15. For a fuller discussion of Dickinson and unconscious production, see Maurice S. Lee, "Dickinson's Superb Surprise," *Raritan* 28:1 (Summer 2008), 45–67.

16. Silvan Solomon Tomkins, *Exploring Affect: The Selected Writings of Silvan S. Tompkins*, ed. E. Virginia Demos (Cambridge: Cambridge University Press, 1995), 68–70, 247–251;

Jerome Kagan, *Surprise, Uncertainty, and Mental Structures* (Cambridge: Harvard University Press, 2002).

17. Thomas Burgess, *The Physiology or Mechanism of Blushing* (London: John Churchill, 1839), 180, 11. "The Blush," *The Lady's Book, Vol. I* (Philadelphia: L.A. Godey, 1830), 208. Charles Darwin, *The Expression of the Emotions in Man and Animals* (New York: D. Appleton, 1913), 336. For blushing and science, see also Geoffrey Sanborn, "Mother's Milk: Frances Harper and the Circulation of Blood," *ELH* 72:3 (Fall 2005), 691–715. Note that Ricks makes a similar move by reading Keats through Burgess and Darwin, though Keats, who died in 1821, seems to me more enlisted than invested in the science of blushing (*Keats and Embarrassment*, esp. 50–68).

18. Miller, "Jane Austen's Aesthetics and Ethics of Surprise," 255; Richard Whatley, "Northanger Abbey and Persuasion," *Quarterly Review* 24 (January 1821). See also David Southward, "Jane Austen and the Riches of Embarrassment," *Studies in English Literature, 1500-1900* 36 (Autumn 1996), 763–784. For Austen's engagement with probabilistic thought, see Peter Knox-Shaw, *Jane Austen and the Enlightenment* (Cambridge: Cambridge University Press, 2004), 114–118.

19. There is no evidence that Dickinson read Austen, though her wide reading in popular novels and the strong affinities between *Northanger Abbey* and poem F407 suggest at least some familiarity.

20. Henry James, *Confidence* (1880; New York: Grosset and Dunlap, 1962), 23; Henry James, *The Bostonians* (1886; New York: Signet Classic, 1980), 228; Jane Austen, *Pride and Prejudice* (New York: Dover, 1995), 168.

21. Allen Tate, *Reactionary Essays on Poetry and Ideas* (New York: Scribner's, 1936), 13. Robert Lowell, for instance, wrote in 1930 that Dickinson was "unanalytical" and discovered truths "subconsciously" (quoted in *Emily Dickinson: Critical Assessments, Vol. II*, ed. Graham Clarke [East Sussex: Helm, 2002], 348).

22. Marjorie Perloff, "Emily Dickinson and the Theory Canon," SUNY Buffalo Electronic Poetry Center (http://epc.buffalo.edu/authors/perloff/art-cles/dickinson.html); Jed Deppman, *Trying to Think with Emily Dickinson* (Amherst: University of Massachusetts Press, 2008). See also the forthcoming collection on Dickinson and Philosophy, eds. Marianne Noble, Jed Deppman, and Gary Stonum.

23. Based on Franklin's dates and index of first lines, 155 of Dickinson's 1,120 pre-1866 poems begin with "I," "I'd," "I'm," "I'll," "I've," Me," "My," or "Myself," compared to 30 of 565 poems written during or after 1866. Of the undated poems, almost all of which come from the later career, only 5 of 103 begin in the first-person singular (4.8%). Alfred Habegger suggests a similar trajectory (*My Wars Are Laid Away in Books: The Life of Emily Dickinson* [New York: Modern Library, 2002], 498–499).

24. Dickinson to S. G. Dickinson, 1870, *The Letters of Emily Dickinson*, 2:478.

25. Catherine Gallagher, *The Body Economic: Life, Death, and Sensation in Political Economy and the Victorian Novel* (Princeton: Princeton University Press, 2006), 7–34; Mary Poovey, "Figures of Arithmetic, Figures of Speech: the Discourse of Statistics in the 1830s," in *Questions of Evidence: Proof, Practice, and Persuasion across the Disciplines*, eds. James Chandler, Arnold Davidson, and Harry Harootunian (Chicago: University of Chicago Press, 1991), 401–421. De Quincey's work in political economy no doubt alerted him to the probabilistic revolution, and his essay "Conversation" (1847) notes how wagering "rose suddenly into a philosophical rank, when successively, Huyghens [sic], the Bernoullis, and De Moivre, were led . . . to throw the light of a high mathematical analysis upon the whole doctrine of Chances" (*Letters to a Young Man and Other Papers* [Boston: Ticknor, Reed, and Fields, 1854], 131–132). That said, in De Quincey's 1823 translations of "The Fatal Marksman" and "The Dice," supernatural and (by my lights) romanticized causal forces win out over more rationalist accounts of chance.

26. Kim Tolley, *The Science Education of American Girls: A Historical Perspective* (New York: Routledge Falmer, 2003), 75–94. "Proposal to Erect a School for Whist for Young Ladies," *The Sporting Magazine* (April 1799). For Somerville, see for instance, Ingleby Scott, "Caroline Herschel, Sophie Germain, and Mrs. Somerville," *Littell's Living Age* (November 10, 1860); [no title], *Southern Review* (April 1874); "An Extraordinary Character," *Methodist Quarterly Review* (July 1876); and "Mary Somerville," *Dickinson's Theological Quarterly* (January 1877).

27. Seo-Young Jennie Chu, "Dickinson and Mathematics," *The Emily Dickinson Journal* 15.1 (2006), 35–55; Deppman, *Trying to Think*, 53–57, 76–79; Richard E. Brantley, *Experience and Faith: The Late-Romantic Imagination of Emily Dickinson* (New York: Palgrave Macmillan, 2004).

28. Charles Collins, "The Value of Accident," *The Atlantic* (February 1870); "Diversions of the Echo Club," *The Atlantic* (July 1872), 82; George Parsons Lathrop, "Combination Novels," *The Atlantic* (December 1884), 803.

29. [no title], *Scribner's Monthly* (July 1872), 364–365. C. D. Wilder, "Statistics of Science," *Prairie Farmer* (April 7, 1859); Herman Melville, "The Lightning-Rod Man," in *Pierre, Israel Potter, The Piazza Tales, The Confidence-Man, Uncollected Prose, Billy Budd, Sailor* (New York: Library of America, 1984), 756. Katharine Anderson, *Predicting the Weather: Victorians and the Science of Meteorology* (Chicago: University of Chicago Press, 2005), 131–170.

30. William Wordsworth, "My heart leaps up when I behold," *William Wordsworth*, ed. Stephen Gill (Oxford: Oxford University Press, 1984), 246. For Wordsworth and design, see Colin Jager, *The Book of God: Secularization and Design in the Romantic Era* (Philadelphia: University of Pennsylvania Press, 2007), 158–200.

31. For Dickinson as reconciler, see Sewall, *The Life of Emily Dickinson*, 342–357; and Brantley, *Experience and Faith*. Nina Baym, *American Women of Letters and the Nineteenth-Century Sciences: Styles of Affiliation* (New Brunswick: Rutgers University Press, 2002), 133–151. Roger Lundin, *Emily Dickinson and the Art of Belief* (Grand Rapids, Mich.: William B. Eerdmans, 1998). See also Patrick Keane, *Emily Dickinson's Approving God: Divine Design and the Problem of Suffering* (Columbia: University of Missouri Press, 2008).

32. Edward Hitchcock, *Religious Lectures on Peculiar Phenomena in the Four Seasons* (Amherst: J.S. and C. Adams, 1850), 66. Edward Hitchcock, *Reminiscences of Amherst College: Historical, Scientific, Biographical and Autobiographical* (Northampton: Bridgman and Childs, 1863), 285.

33. William Whewell, *Plurality of Worlds, with an introduction by Edward Hitchcock* (Boston: Gould and Lincoln, 1855), viii, xvi. For a broader intellectual context, see Michael Crowe, *The Extraterrestrial Life Debate, 1750–1900: The Idea of a Plurality of Worlds from Kant to Lowell* (New York: Cambridge University Press, 1986), 316–354. See also Poe's angelic dialogues for outer-space angels.

34. Thomas Carlyle, *Sartor Resartus: The Life and Opinions of Herr Teufelsdröckh* (New York: Odyssey Press, 1937), 68.

35. Jean Paul Richter, *Flower, Fruit, and Thorn Pieces: Or, The Married Life, Death, and Wedding of the Advocate of the Poor, Firmian Stanislaus Siebenkäs*, trans. Edward Henry Noel (Boston: James Munroe, 1845), 338. For Dickinson and Richter, see Lundin, *Emily Dickinson and the Art of Belief*, 240–241; and Brantley, *Experience and Faith*, 142.

36. Thomas Hardy, "Hap" (1866), *Selected Poems of Thomas Hardy*, ed. John Crowe Ransom (New York: Collier Books, 1960), 1. For theodicy in Dickinson, see for instance James McIntosh, *Nimble Believing: Dickinson and the Unknown* (Ann Arbor: University of Michigan Press, 2004); and Keane, *Emily Dickinson's Approving God*.

37. Dickinson to S. G. Dickinson, c. 1882, *The Letters of Emily Dickinson*, 3:733. Dickinson also uses the phrase "impregnable chances" in 1882 letters to Thomas Niles and Otis Lord

(3:725, 3:727). The three poems that interchange "chance" and "risk" are "'Morning'—means 'Milking'—to the Farmer—" (1861; F191), "My first well Day—since many ill—" (1862; F288), and "Soul, take thy risk" (1867; F1136).

38. Thomas Lentes, "Counting Piety in the Middle Ages," *Ordering Medieval Society: Perspectives on Intellectual and Practical Modes of Shaping Social Relations*, ed. Bernhard Jussen, trans. Pamela Selwyn (Philadelphia: University of Pennsylvania Press, 2001), 55–91.

39. Nathanael Emmons, *A Candid Reply to the Reverend Doctor Hemmenway's Remarks* (Worcester, Mass.: Leonard Worcester, 1795), 62–63. T. Southwood Smith, "Illustration of the Divine Government," *The Eclectic Review, July–December* (London: Josiah Conder, 1818), 551–552; "The Great Stake: Probation Turned into a Game," *New York Observer and Chronicle* (January 6, 1844).

40. "Is Christ's Reign Upon Earth to be a Spiritual or a Temporal One—or Both?," *The British Controversialist, and Literary Magazine* (London: Houston and Sons, 1872), 188.

41. Dickinson to recipient unknown, about 1861, *The Letters of Emily Dickinson*, 2:375 (the second "Master" letter).

42. Dickinson to S. G. Dickinson, 1884, *The Letters of Emily Dickinson*, 3:830. For Dickinson and Puritanism, see Colacurcio, *Doctrine and Difference*, 241–248.

43. Mark Twain, *Following the Equator* (1897), in *The Portable Mark Twain*, ed. Bernard De Voto (New York: Penguin, 1979), 563.

44. Francis Bacon, *Novum Organum*, trans. G. W. Kitchin (Oxford: University Press, 1855), 14. John Herschel, *A Treatise on Astronomy* (Philadelphia: Carey, Lea, and Blanchard, 1835), 9. E. B. Hunt, "On an Index of Papers on Subjects of Mathematical and Physical Science," *The American Journal of Science and Arts* (New York: G.P. Putnam, 1855), 343.

45. Whewell, *The Philosophy of the Inductive Sciences*, 2:257. Elaine Scarry, *The Body in Pain: The Making and Unmaking of the World* (New York: Oxford University Press, 1985). For vivisection, see for instance James Paget, *Vivisection: Its Pains and Its Uses* (1881). John F. W. Herschel, *Preliminary Discourse on the Study of Natural Philosophy* (London: Longman, Brown, Green, and Longmans, 1851), 175.

46. Hume, *An Enquiry Concerning Human Understanding*, 113. Alexander Bain, *Logic: Deductive and Inductive*, 2 vols. (London: Longmans, Green, Reader, and Dyer), 2:2, 1:272–273.

47. See, for instance, Virginia Jackson, "Poetry and Experience," *Raritan* 20:2 (Fall 2000), 130–132; New, *The Line's Eye*, 165–167.

48. Alfred Tennyson, *In Memoriam*, in *The Major Victorian Poets: Tennyson, Browning, Arnold*, ed. William E. Buckler (Boston: Houghton Mifflin, 1973), 85. For Treat, see Tina Gianquitto, *Good Observers of Nature: American Women and the Scientific Study of the Natural World, 1820–1885* (Athens: University of Georgia Press, 2007), 136–176.

49. Emerson, *Essays and Lectures*, 46.

50. For the myth of scientific epiphany, see John Waller's aptly titled *Leaps in the Dark* (Oxford: Oxford University Press, 2004).

51. Stonum, *The Dickinson Sublime*, 64.

52. Walter Benjamin, "On Some Motifs in Baudelaire" (1939), *Illuminations*, ed. Hannah Arendt, trans. Harry Zohn (1955; New York: Harcourt, Brace, and World, 1968), 163.

53. Cameron, *Lyric Time*; François, *Open Secrets*. In this regard, Miller may not go far enough when writing that surprise "can only be represented through indirection and retrospection" ("Jane Austen's Aesthetics and Ethics of Surprise," 255).

54. Dickinson to T. W. Higginson, August 16, 1870, *Selected Letters*, 207. Thomas Wentworth Higginson, *Malbone: An Oldport Romance* (Boston: Fields, Osgood, and Co., 1869), 2.

55. Dickinson to T. W. Higginson, June 7, 1862, *The Letters of Emily Dickinson*, 2:409.

56. Gerald Massey, "Poetry—The Spasmodists," *North British Review* (February 1858).

57. *Emily Dickinson's Reception in the 1890s: A Documentary History*, ed. Willis J. Buckingham (Pittsburgh: University of Pittsburgh Press, 1989), 85, 127, 113.

58. Miller, *Emily Dickinson: A Poet's Grammar*, 29. See also Cristanne Miller, "Dickinson's Structured Rhythms," *A Companion to Emily Dickinson*, eds. Martha Nell Smith and Mary Loeffelholz (London: Wiley-Blackwell, 2008), 391–414.

59. For probabilistic linguistics, including the buzzing bees example (20–24), see *Probabilistic Linguistics*. "Seventh Annual Report of the Secretary of the Board of Education," *The Common School Journal* (April 15, 1844). Though Dickinson challenges clear distinctions between schematic (experience-based) and semantic (language-based) categories, see also Kagan's *Surprise, Uncertainty, and Mental Structures* for discussions of linguistics and surprise.

60. Susan Howe, *The Birth-Mark: Unsettling the Wilderness in American Literary History* (Hanover: Wesleyan University Press, 1993), 155.

61. Fisher, *Wonder, the Rainbow, and the Aesthetics of Rare Experiences*, 23, 121. Dickinson also serves as a counter example to Tony Tanner's thesis that American literature presents a willfully naïve sense of wonder (*The Reign of Wonder: Naivety and Reality in American Literature* [Cambridge: Cambridge University Press, 1965]).

62. Dickinson to J. G. Holland, June 1878, *The Letters of Emily Dickinson*, 2: 613.

63. Fisher, *Wonder, the Rainbow, and the Aesthetics of Rare Experiences*, 20; Alexander Bain, *Mind and Body: The Theories of Their Relation* (New York: Appleton, 1874), 51.

64. Manning, "How Conscious Could Consciousness Grow?"; New, *The Line's Eye*, 164; Deppman, *Trying to Think with Emily Dickinson*, 21–48.

65. Charles Peirce, *The Collected Papers of Charles Peirce*, eds. Charles Hartshorne and Paul Weiss (Cambridge: Belknap Press of Harvard University Press, 1960–1966), 2:479; 7:111–112; Charles Peirce, *The Essential Peirce: Selected Philosophical Writings*, 2 vols, eds. Nathan Houser, Christian Kloesel, et al (Bloomington: Indiana University Press, 1992, 1998), 2:88, 2:483. For doors ajar, see Dickinson's "I cannot live with You" (1863; F706), James's "The Jolly Corner" (1908), and Frost's "The Door in the Dark" (1928). Richard Rorty, *Philosophy and the Mirror of Nature* (1979; Princeton: Princeton University Press, 2009), 149–151. See also George Santayana: "The word experience is like a shrapnel shell, and bursts into a thousand meanings" (*Character and Opinion in the United States, with Reminiscences of William James and Josiah Royce and Academic Life in America* [New York: Scribner's, 1921], 71).

66. William James, *Writings*, 2 vols. (New York: Library of America, 1987), 2:1008. James, *Writings* 2:778. James, *Writings* 1: 863–864. Stanley Fish, "Truth and Toilets: Pragmatism and the Practices of Life," *The Revival of Pragmatism: New Essays on Social Thought, Law, and Culture*, ed. Morris Dickstein (Durham: Duke University Press, 1998), 433.

67. Richard Shusterman links Dewey's aesthetics to everyday experience and the body (*Pragmatist Aesthetics: Living Beauty, Rethinking Art* [Oxford: Blackwell, 1992]); John Lysaker discusses Dewey's aesthetics as dialectical materialism ("Binding the Beautiful: Art as Criticism in Adorno and Dewey," *Journal of Speculative Philosophy* 12 [1998]: 233–244). For Dewey as presaging reader response, see Winfried Fluck, "Pragmatism and Aesthetic Experience," in *Pragmatism and Literary Studies*, ed. Winfried Fluck (Tübingen: Gunter Narr Verlag, 1999), 227–242.

68. John Dewey, *Art as Experience*, (1934; New York: Penguin, 2005), 36, 37, 42, 51. John Dewey, *The Quest for Certainty* (1929), in *The Later Works, 1925–1953: Vol. 4, 1929*, ed. Jo Ann Boydston (Carbondale: Southern Illinois University, 1984), 6. John Dewey, *Experience and Nature* (New York: Dover, 1958), 359, 372.

69. James, *Writings* 2:1091. Dewey, *Experience and Nature*, 194. Steven Meyer, *Irresistible Dictation: Gertrude Stein and the Correlations of Writing and Science* (Stanford: Stanford University Press, 2001). Robert Frost, "The Figure a Poem Makes," *Complete Poems of Robert Frost* (New York: Holt, Rinehart and Winston, 1964), vi. For pragmatism and romanticism, see Russell Goodman, *American Philosophy and the Romantic Tradition* (New York: Cambridge University Press, 1990).

70. Quoted in *Emily Dickinson's Reception in the 1890s*, 48.

71. See, for instance, Diane Fuss, *The Sense of an Interior: Four Writers and the Rooms that Shaped Them* (New York: Routledge, 2004), 23–70; Cameron, *Choosing not to Choose*; and Jackson, *Dickinson's Misery*.

72. Dickinson to Dr. and Mrs. J. G. Holland, autumn 1853, *The Letters of Emily Dickinson*, 1:264.

73. Susan Howe, "Experience is the Angled Road," *The Emily Dickinson Journal* 15:2 (2006), 34–37.

74. Dickinson to T. W. Higginson, April 25, 1862, *The Letters of Emily Dickinson*, 2:261.

CODA

1. Henry Wager Halleck, *Elements of Military Art and Science* (New York: Appleton, 1846), 145. For military science in nineteenth-century America, see Christopher Bassford, *Clausewitz in English: The Reception of Clausewitz in Britain and America, 1815–1945* (New York: Oxford University Press, 1994), esp. 50–56. See also John Keegan, *The American Civil War: A Military History* (New York: Random House, 2009), 96–97.

2. Henry James, *Hawthorne* (1879; New York: Harper and Brothers, 1901), 166, 139–40.

3. For modern scholarship, see note #19 to the "Introduction."

4. Using Google Book's Ngram function, the frequency of "the chances of war" in the nineteenth century peaks in the mid-1840s.

5. "Reflections on the Present Crisis," *Southern Literary Messenger* (October 1861)

6. Elizabeth Stuart Phelps, "Jack," *Century Illustrated Magazine* (June 1887). For Phelps's general interest in science, see Lisa Long, *Rehabilitating Bodies: Health, History, and the American Civil War* (Philadelphia: University of Pennsylvania Press, 2004), 58–83.

7. Elizabeth Stuart Phelps, *The Gates Ajar*, in *Three Spiritualist Novels* (Urbana: University of Illinois Press, 2000), 3, 21, 5.

8. Ibid., 57, 9, 41, 43, 50.

9. Ibid., 129.

10. Phelps discusses how *The Gates Ajar* was accused of blasphemy in *Chapters from a Life* (Boston: Houghton Mifflin, 1896), 119.

11. See, for instance, Drew Gilpin Faust, *This Republic of Suffering: Death and the American Civil War* (New York: Random House, 2008), esp. 9–11, 186–187.

INDEX

Grimstad, Paul, 41
Griswold, Rufus, 17
Gronniosaw, James Albert Ukawsaw, 91, 93
Grutter v. Bollinger, 216n68
guessing, 21
Gulliver's Travels (Swift), 23

Hacking, Ian
  on absolute chance, 40–41
  on taming of chance, 5
Halleck, Henry Wager, 185–86
Hamilton, Ross, 10
Hamlet (Shakespeare), 74, 78
Hard Times (Dickens), 13, 33, 86–87
Hardy, Thomas, 168
Harrowitz, Nancy, 41
Hawthorne, Nathaniel, 48–49, 70, 81, 88, 164
Heart of Darkness (Conrad), 57
"He fumbles at your Soul" (Dickinson), 175–76, 182
Henry, Matthew, *Comprehensive Commentary on the Holy Bible*, 65
Henson, Josiah, 93
Herbert, George, "Sin," 176
Herschel, John
  on empiricism, 172
  Preliminary Discourse on the Study of Natural Philosophy, 20–21, 173
Higginson, Thomas Wentworth
  Dickinson and, 154–55, 176, 177, 183, 185
  "Literature and Art," 155
  "A World Outside Science," 155
Hildyard, James, "The Judgments of God Upon the Wicked," 65
"His Cheek is his Biographer" (Dickinson), 160
History of Civilization in England (Buckle), 111, 112
History of the Bible (Gleig), 65
History of the Mathematical Theory of Probability (Todhunter), 22
Hitchcock, Edward, 166
Holly, James, 96
Holmes, Oliver Wendell, Jr.
  Melville and, 72–73, 87
  race and, 15, 114–16
Hopkins, Pauline, 117
Howe, Susan, 152, 178

Howells, William Dean, 11
  The Rise of Silas Lapham, 85
  A World of Chance, 77, 186
Hume, David
  on miracles, 63
  skepticism and, 123–24, 173
  Treatise of Human Nature, 124

"I felt a Funeral, in my Brain" (Dickinson), 179
"I know Suspense—it steps so terse" (Dickinson), 179
"Impossibility, like Wine" (Dickinson), 168
Incidents in the Life of a Slave Girl (Jacobs), 96
induction
  Melville and, 57, 59–60
  science and, 20–21
  Whewell and, 20, 57, 155, 173
Institutes of the Christian Religion (Calvin), 53
intelligent design, 8, 55. *See also* argument from design
intuition, 19, 21, 23–25, 37, 41
"I reason, Earth is short" (Dickinson), 140
Irving, Washington, 135
Irwin, John, 19
Israel Potter (Melville), 80
"I stepped from Plank to Plank" (Dickinson), 172, 173
"It struck me—every Day" (Dickinson), 182

"Jack" (Phelps), 187
Jackson, Virginia, 156
Jacobs, Harriet, *Incidents in the Life of a Slave Girl*, 96
James, Henry, 11, 186
James, William
  on pragmatism, 42–43, 79–80, 151
  "Pragmatism's Concept of Truth," 43
  Principles of Psychology, 181
  quote by, 16
  on race, 116
  on skepticism, 14
  "Will to Believe," 79–80, 81, 152
Jarvis, Edward, 103
Jay, Martin, 22
Jefferson, Thomas
  Notes on the State of Virginia, 89–90, 95
  on probability theory, 3

Printed in the USA/Agawam, MA
November 27, 2012

570664.019